WHEN ALL THE HEROES ARE GONE, WHO WILL FILL THEIR SHOES?

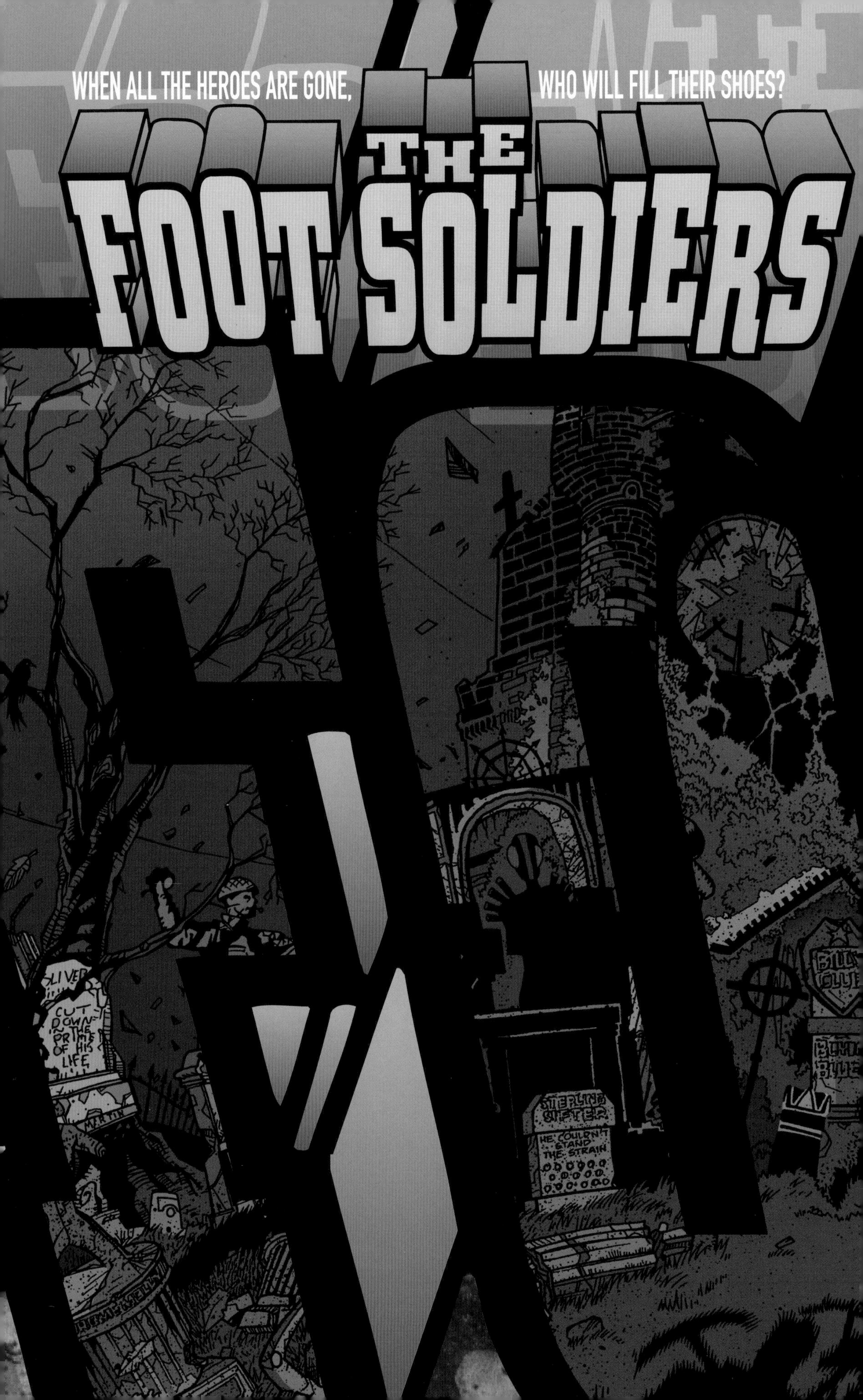

WHEN ALL THE HEROES ARE GONE,
WHO WILL FILL THEIR SHOES?
THE FOOT SOLDIERS
CUT DOWN IN THE PRIME OF HIS LIFE
HE COULDN'T STAND THE STRAIN

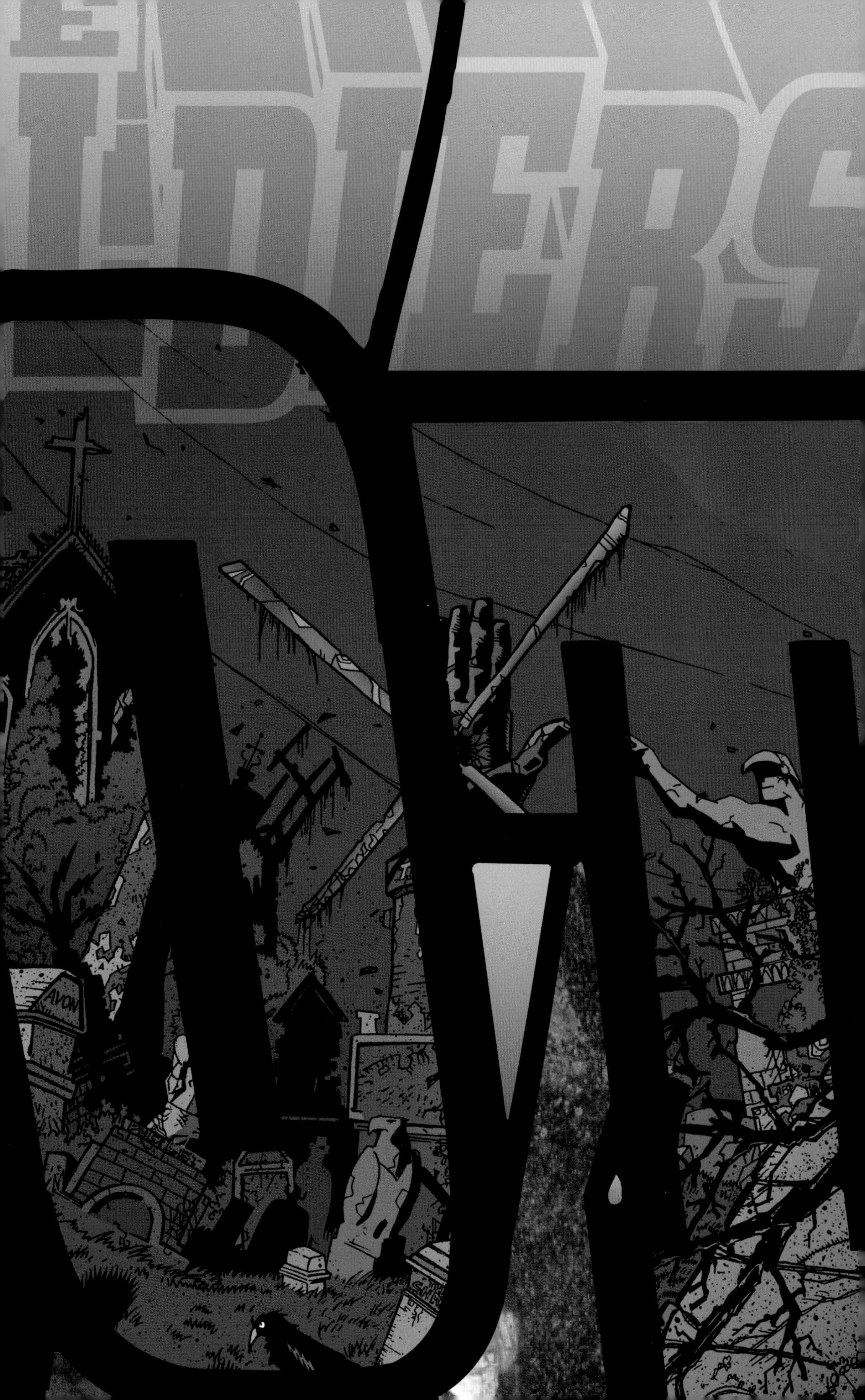
AVON

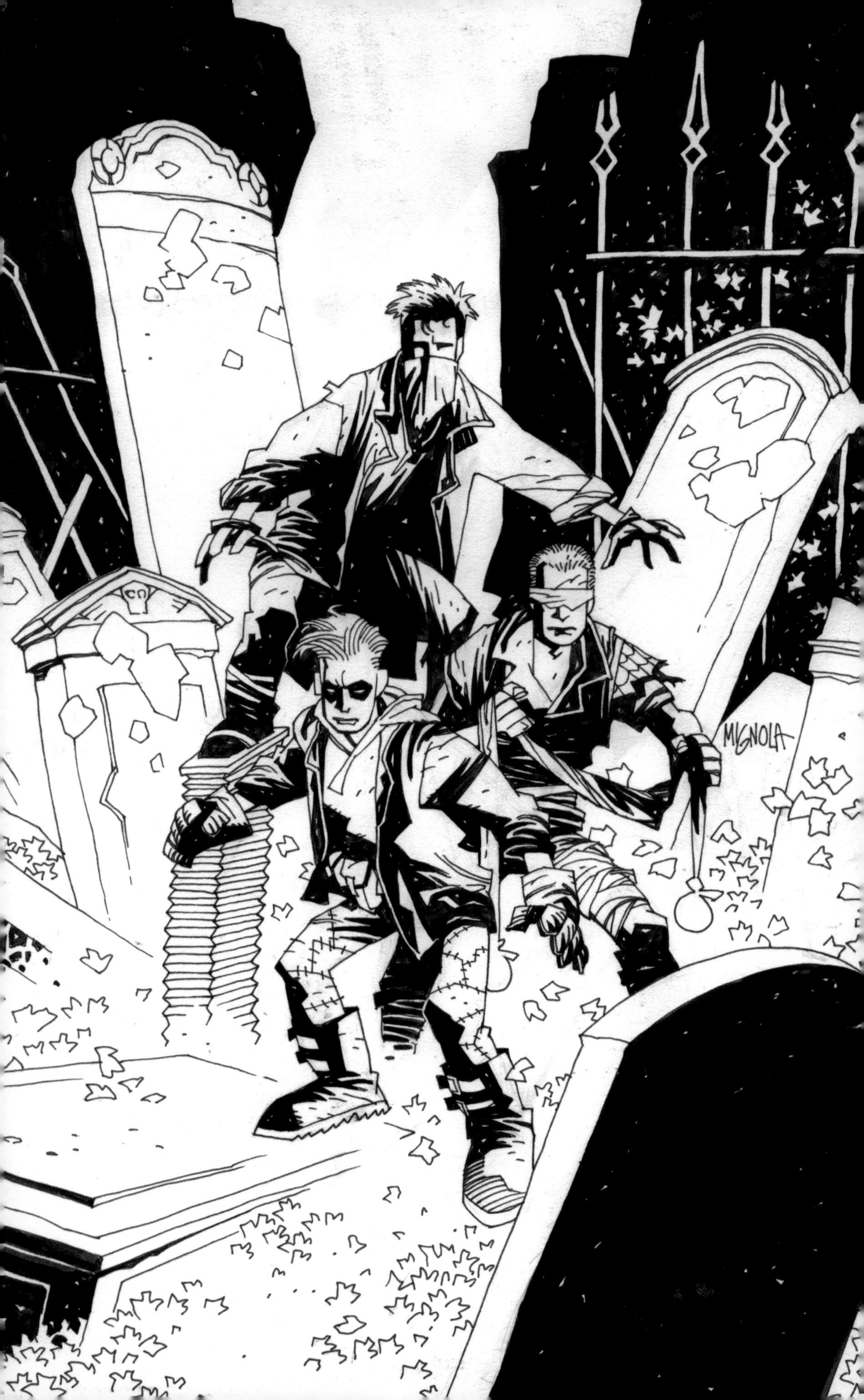
MIGNOLA

The blood
of the heroes
is seed

(with apologies to
TERTULLIAN,
2nd Century B.C.)

THE FOOT SOLDIERS

VOLUME ONE: FIRST STEPS

WRITER & CREATOR Jim Krueger

PENCILER Mike Oeming

INKER Jason Martin

COLORIST Jeff Balke & Zach Brunner

LETTERING Sean Konot

COVER ARTISTS
JOHN K SNYDER III, MIKE MIGNOLA, ALEX ROSS
WALT SIMONSON, TIM SALE, STEVE YEOWELL, ZACH BRUNNER
& MATTHEW DOW SMITH

ROUNDABOUT SHORTCUT
Pencils by Neil Vokes -- Inks by Mike Oeming

FOOT SOLDIERS LOGO DESIGNER Todd Klein

COLLECTION DESIGN Dave Lanphear

Special thanks to
Rick Van Velsor, Chris Carroll, Mel Sanchez, James Desimone,
Amy Meyer Hodman, Vito Incorvaia, James Brennan and Jeff Simons –
my first Foot Soldiers for this project.

Representation for Jim Krueger:
Josh Schechter / josh@hyphenla.com / (310) 202-2000.

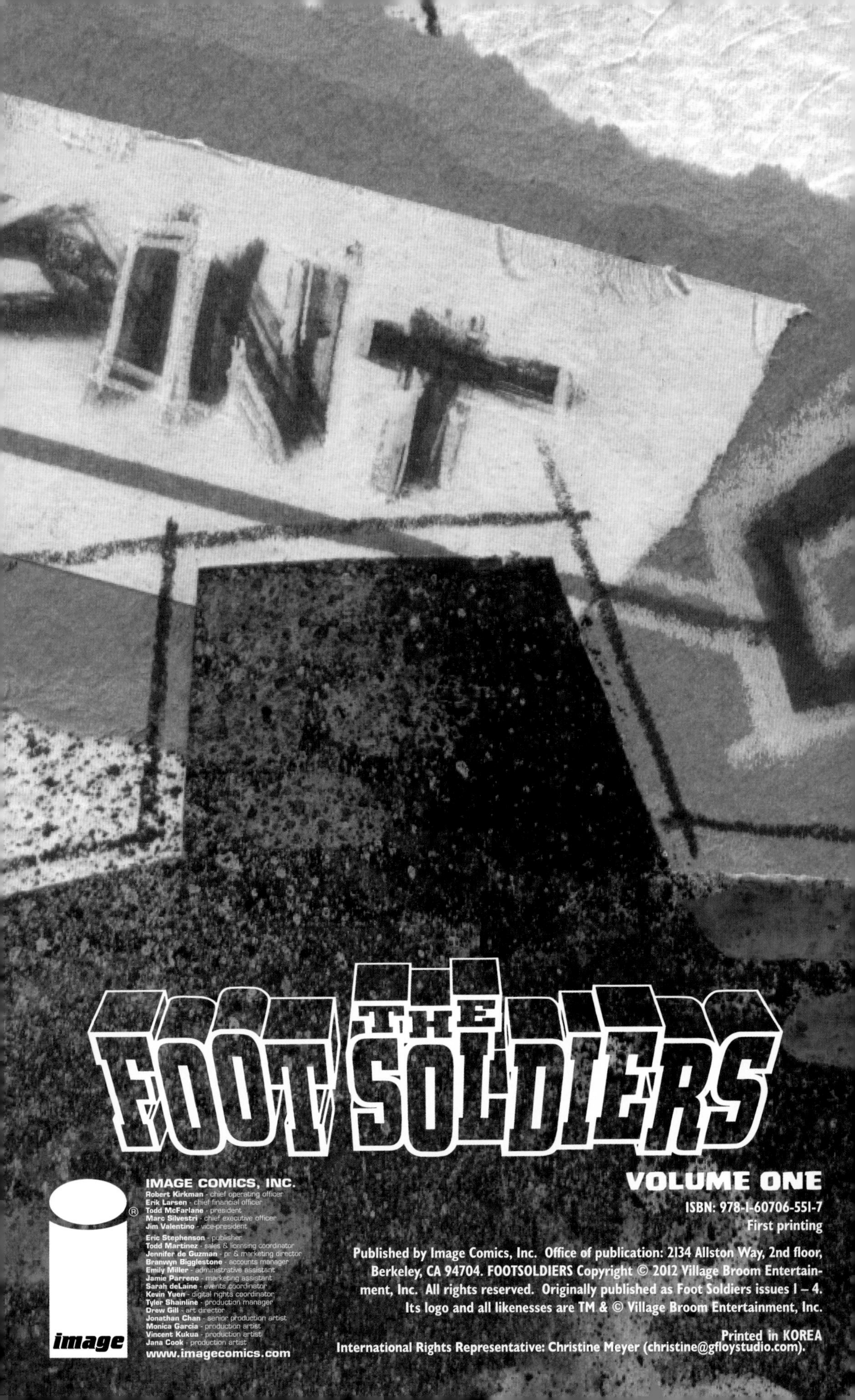

THE FOOT SOLDIERS

VOLUME ONE

ISBN: 978-1-60706-551-7
First printing

Published by Image Comics, Inc. Office of publication: 2134 Allston Way, 2nd floor, Berkeley, CA 94704. Originally published as Foot Soldiers issues 1 – 4.

Printed in KOREA
International Rights Representative: Christine Meyer (christine@gfloystudio.com).

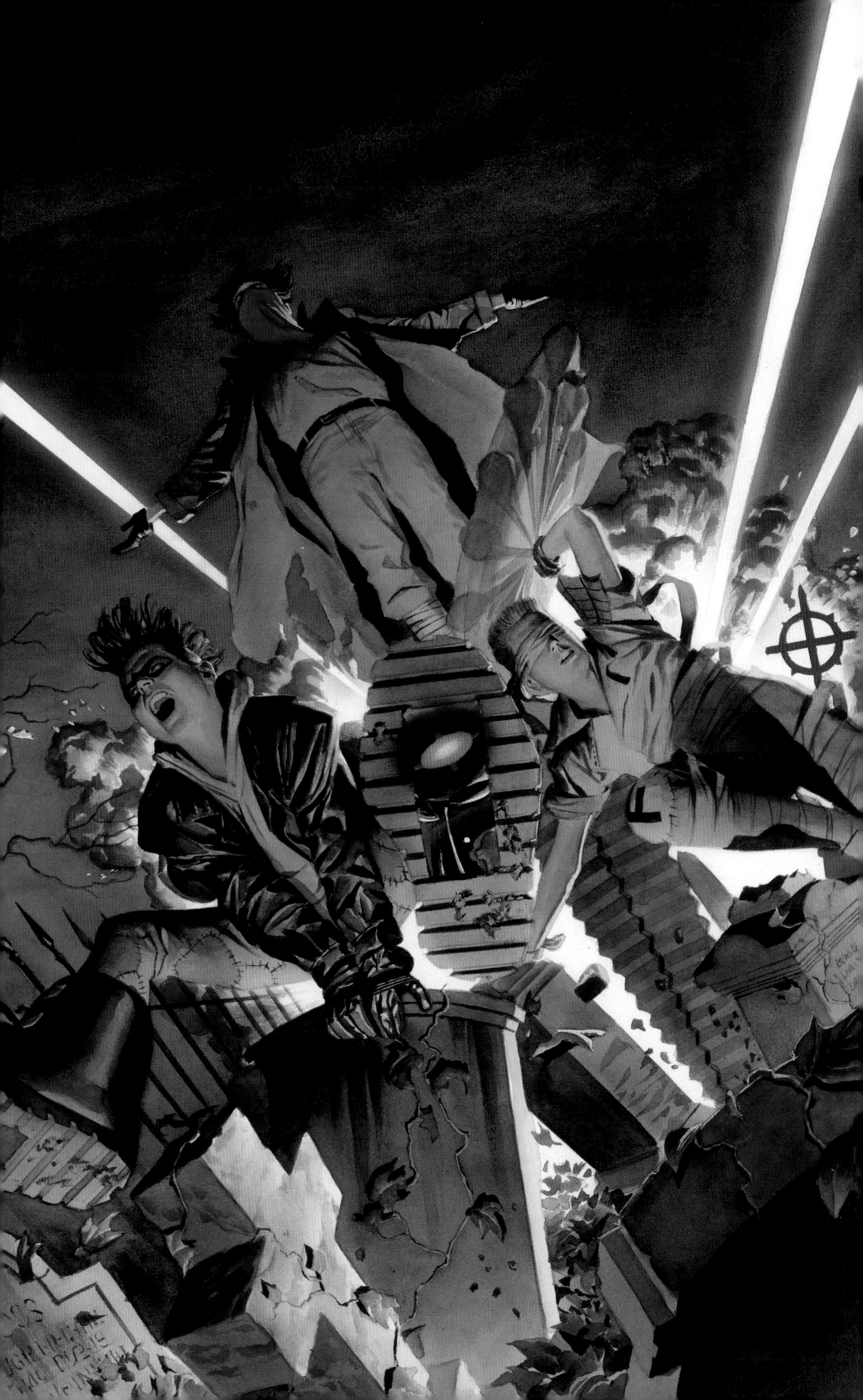

FiRST STEPS
CHAPTER ONE

"I don't get it," Johnny exclaimed.
"Why do we have to wear masks?"
The old man smiled. "There is no
room for personal glory in this, boy.
No room for self in what you are about
to do. For it to be good, it must be
done in secret."

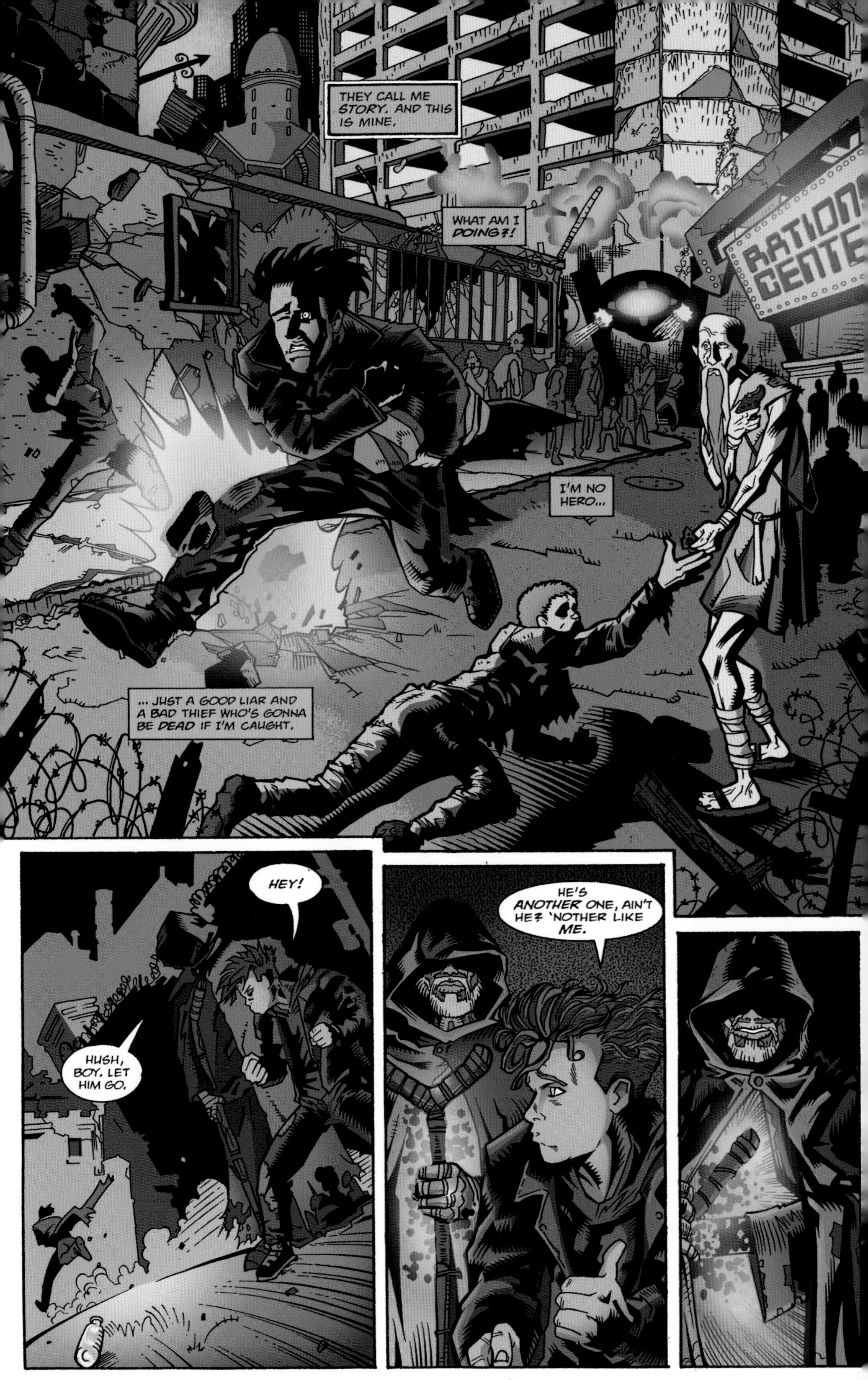
THEY CALL ME STORY. AND THIS IS MINE.
WHAT AM I DOING?!
RATION CENTE
I'M NO HERO...
... JUST A GOOD LIAR AND A BAD THIEF WHO'S GONNA BE DEAD IF I'M CAUGHT.
HEY!
HUSH, BOY. LET HIM GO.
HE'S ANOTHER ONE, AIN'T HE? 'NOTHER LIKE ME.

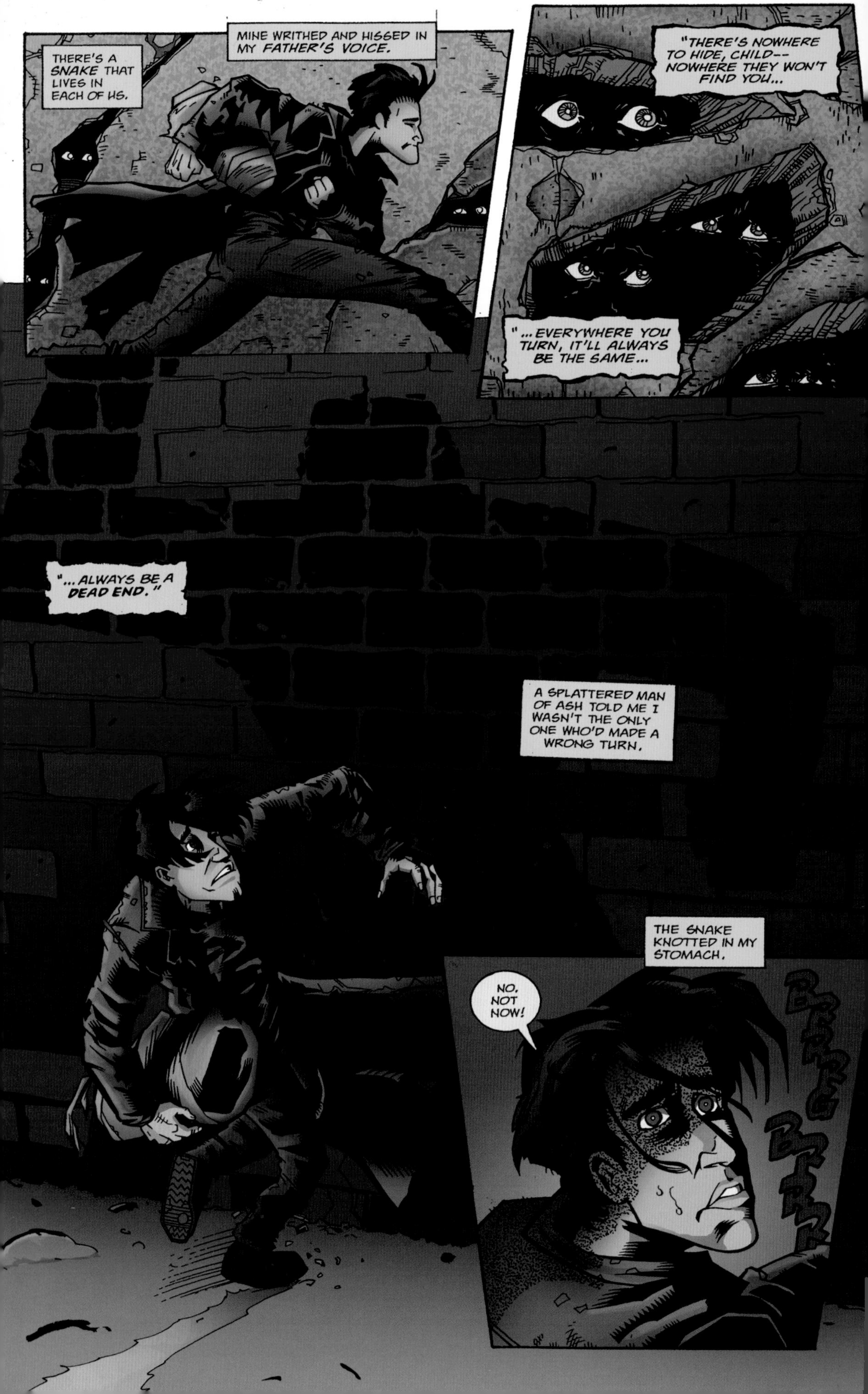
THERE'S A SNAKE THAT LIVES IN EACH OF US.
MINE WRITHED AND HISSED IN MY FATHER'S VOICE.
"THERE'S NOWHERE TO HIDE, CHILD-- NOWHERE THEY WON'T FIND YOU...
"...EVERYWHERE YOU TURN, IT'LL ALWAYS BE THE SAME...
"...ALWAYS BE A DEAD END."
A SPLATTERED MAN OF ASH TOLD ME I WASN'T THE ONLY ONE WHO'D MADE A WRONG TURN.
THE SNAKE KNOTTED IN MY STOMACH.
NO, NOT NOW!

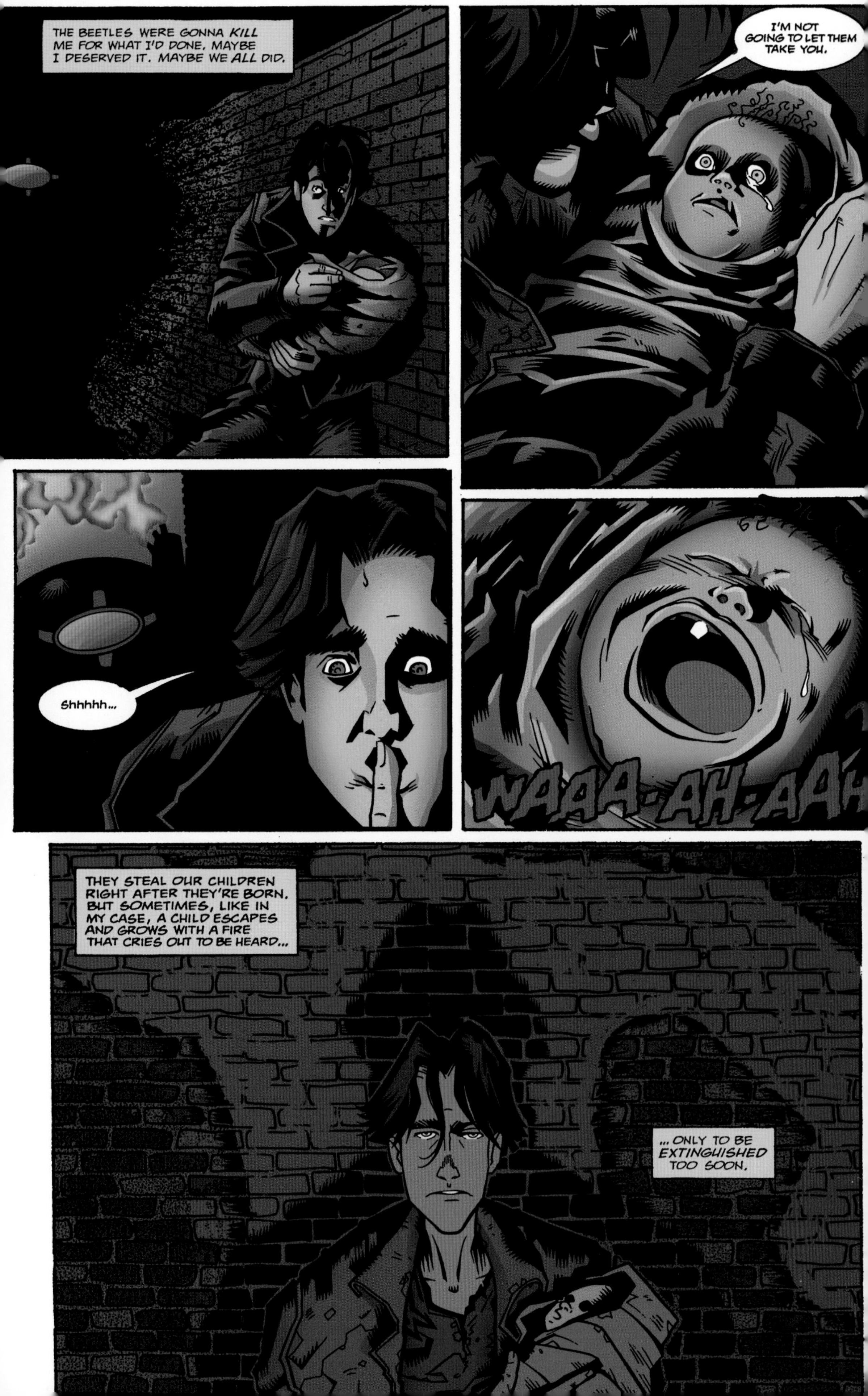
THE BEETLES WERE GONNA KILL ME FOR WHAT I'D DONE. MAYBE I DESERVED IT. MAYBE WE ALL DID.
I'M NOT GOING TO LET THEM TAKE YOU.
Shhhhh...
WAAA-AH-AAH
THEY STEAL OUR CHILDREN RIGHT AFTER THEY'RE BORN. BUT SOMETIMES, LIKE IN MY CASE, A CHILD ESCAPES AND GROWS WITH A FIRE THAT CRIES OUT TO BE HEARD...
...ONLY TO BE EXTINGUISHED TOO SOON.

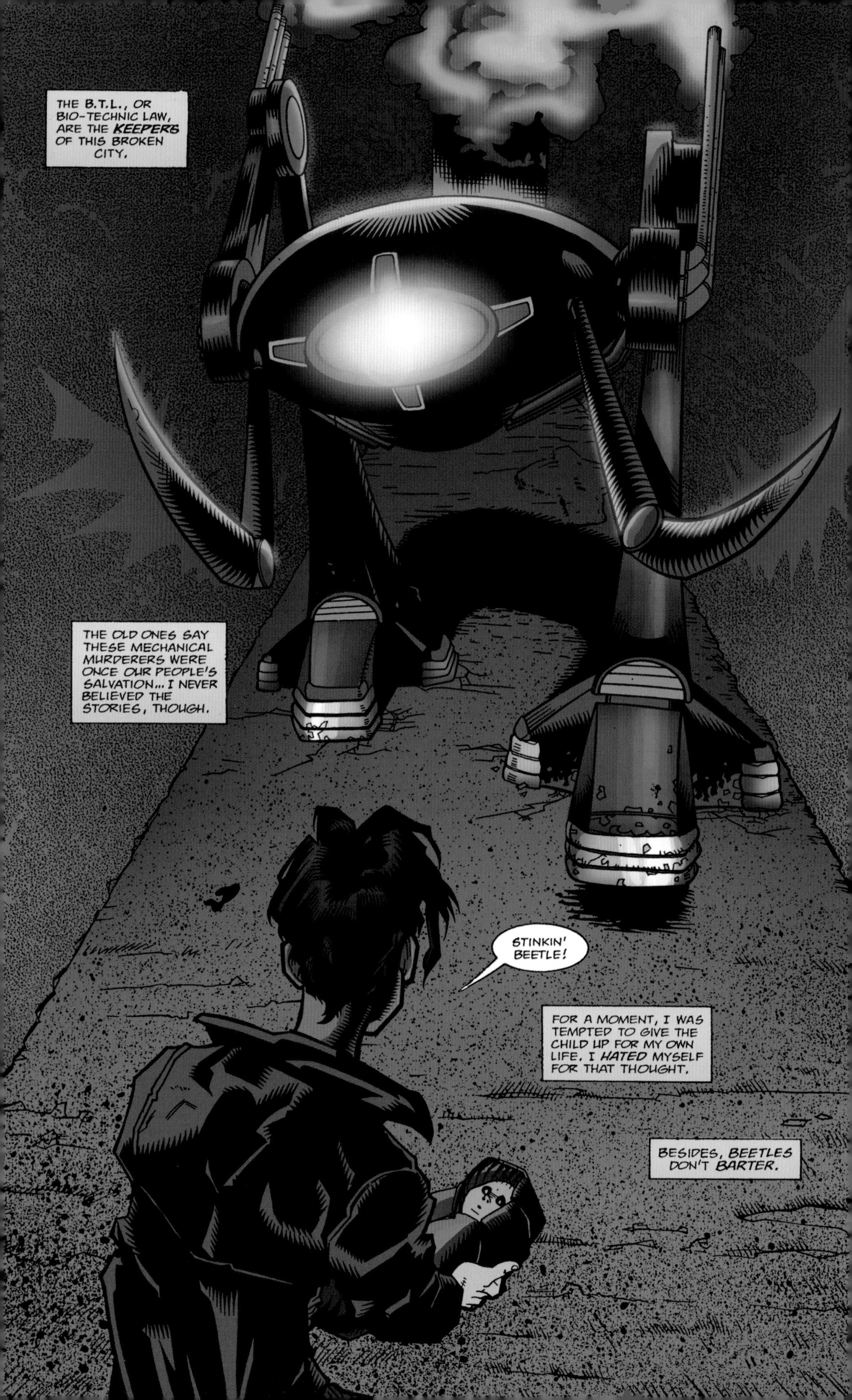
THE B.T.L., OR BIO-TECHNIC LAW, ARE THE KEEPERS OF THIS BROKEN CITY.
THE OLD ONES SAY THESE MECHANICAL MURDERERS WERE ONCE OUR PEOPLE'S SALVATION... I NEVER BELIEVED THE STORIES, THOUGH.
STINKIN' BEETLE!
FOR A MOMENT, I WAS TEMPTED TO GIVE THE CHILD UP FOR MY OWN LIFE. I HATED MYSELF FOR THAT THOUGHT.
BESIDES, BEETLES DON'T BARTER.

I'M DEAD.

WH-WHY DIDN'T YOU FRY ME?

SOMETHING I COULDN'T SEE PULLED THE BABY FROM MY ARMS. THE BEETLE OPENED SLIGHTLY, AND STRANGE HANDS CLUTCHED AT THE CHILD.

I REALIZED THEN, THE *BABY* I WAS TRYING TO SAVE WAS THE ONLY THING KEEPING ME *ALIVE.*

BUT INSTEAD OF ASHING ME LIKE THE GUY ON THE WALL, THE BEETLE STOOD THERE, MOTIONLESS.

?

AND IN DOING NOTHING, IT DID THE IMPOSSIBLE. *IT LET ME GO.*

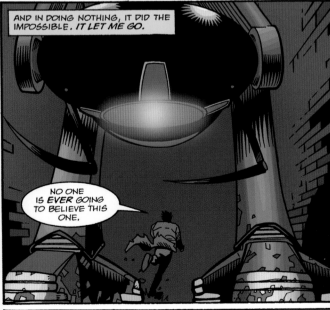

NO ONE IS *EVER* GOING TO BELIEVE THIS ONE.

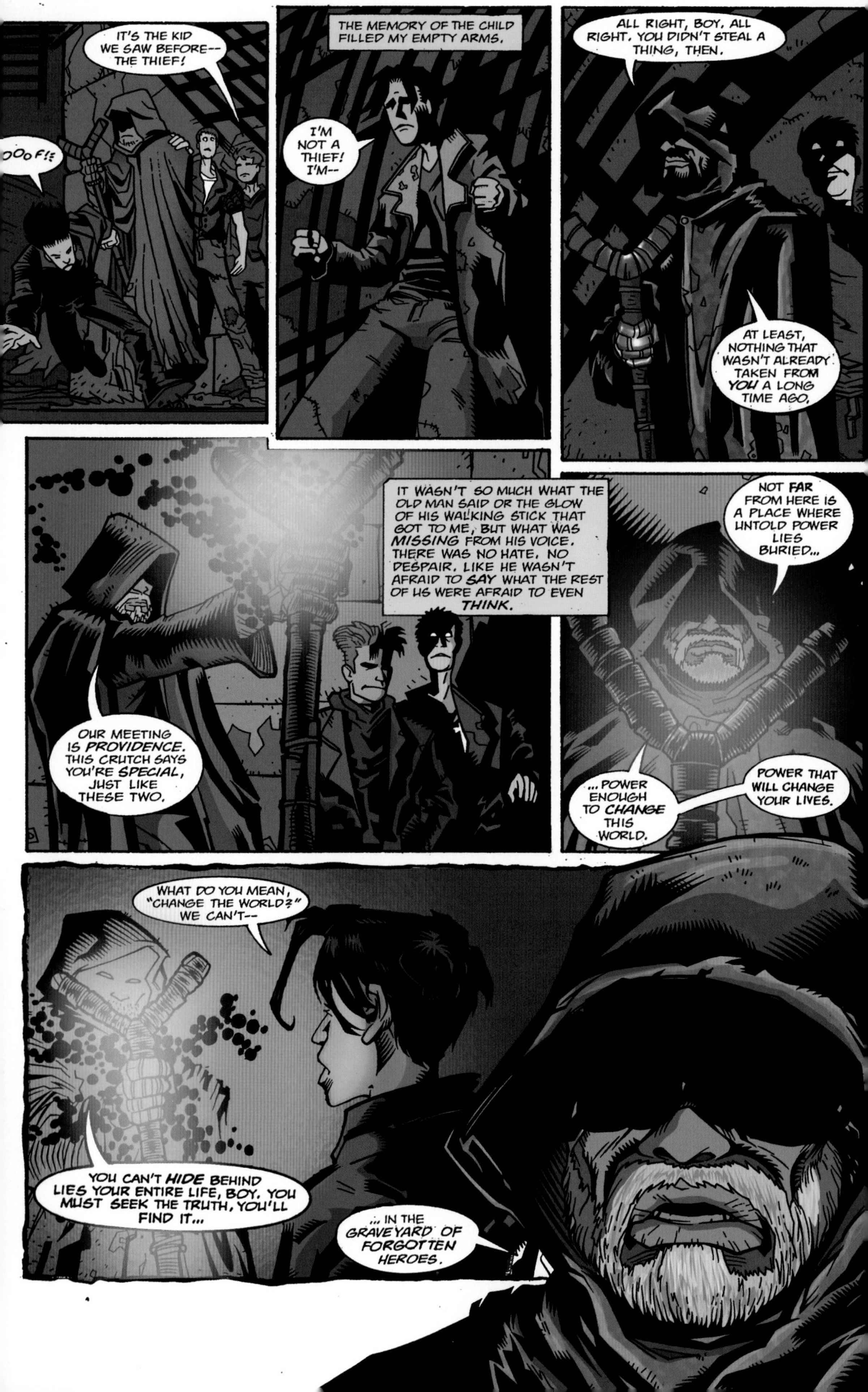
IT'S THE KID WE SAW BEFORE-- THE THIEF!
OOOF!!
THE MEMORY OF THE CHILD FILLED MY EMPTY ARMS.
I'M NOT A THIEF! I'M--
ALL RIGHT, BOY, ALL RIGHT. YOU DIDN'T STEAL A THING, THEN.
AT LEAST, NOTHING THAT WASN'T ALREADY TAKEN FROM YOU A LONG TIME AGO.
IT WASN'T SO MUCH WHAT THE OLD MAN SAID OR THE GLOW OF HIS WALKING STICK THAT GOT TO ME, BUT WHAT WAS MISSING FROM HIS VOICE. THERE WAS NO HATE. NO DESPAIR. LIKE HE WASN'T AFRAID TO SAY WHAT THE REST OF US WERE AFRAID TO EVEN THINK.
OUR MEETING IS PROVIDENCE. THIS CRUTCH SAYS YOU'RE SPECIAL, JUST LIKE THESE TWO.
NOT FAR FROM HERE IS A PLACE WHERE UNTOLD POWER LIES BURIED...
...POWER ENOUGH TO CHANGE THIS WORLD.
POWER THAT WILL CHANGE YOUR LIVES.
WHAT DO YOU MEAN, "CHANGE THE WORLD?" WE CAN'T--
YOU CAN'T HIDE BEHIND LIES YOUR ENTIRE LIFE, BOY. YOU MUST SEEK THE TRUTH. YOU'LL FIND IT...
... IN THE GRAVEYARD OF FORGOTTEN HEROES.

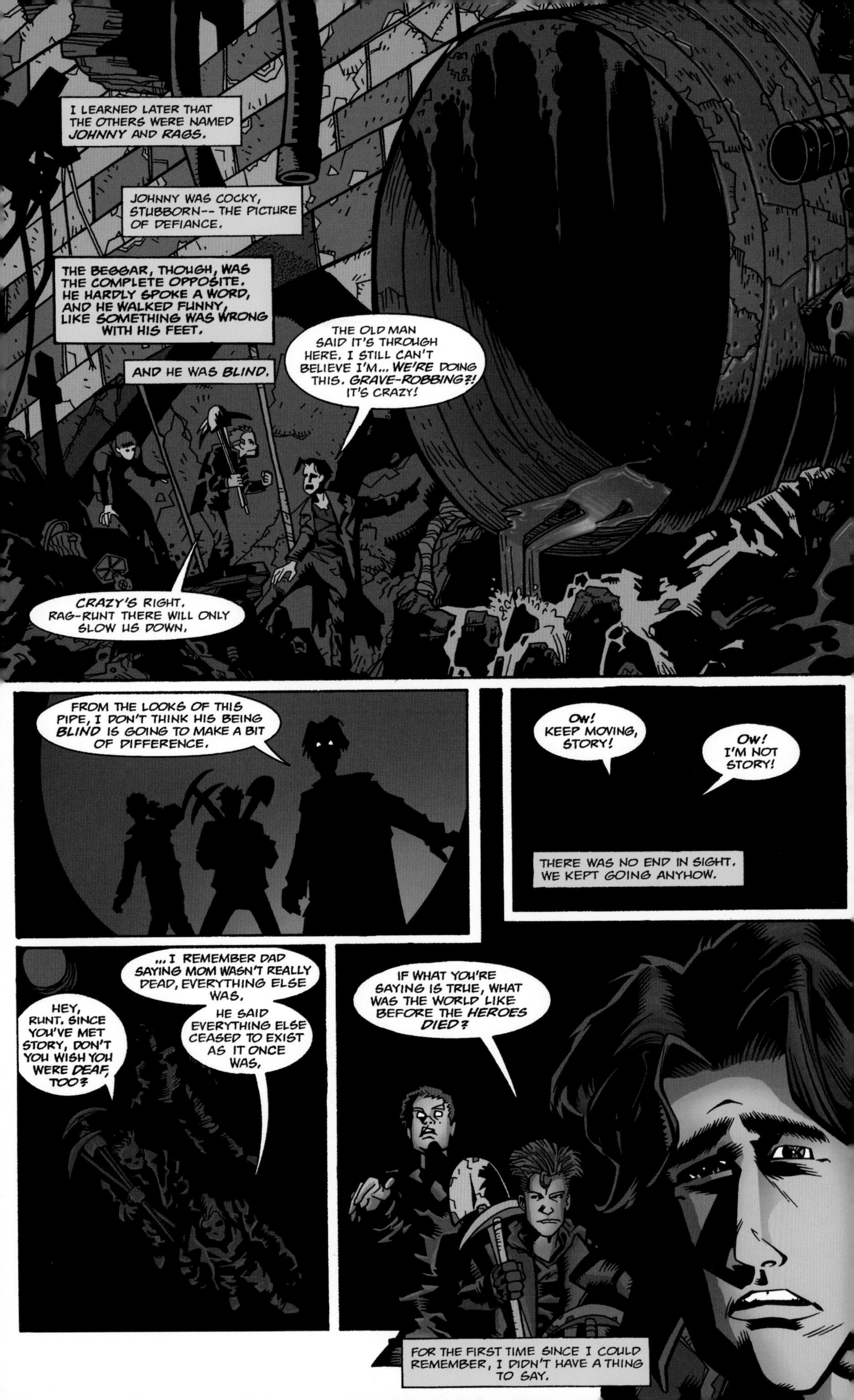
I LEARNED LATER THAT THE OTHERS WERE NAMED *JOHNNY* AND *RAGS*.
JOHNNY WAS COCKY, STUBBORN-- THE PICTURE OF DEFIANCE.
THE BEGGAR, THOUGH, WAS THE COMPLETE *OPPOSITE*. HE HARDLY SPOKE A WORD, AND HE WALKED FUNNY, LIKE SOMETHING WAS WRONG WITH HIS FEET.
AND HE WAS *BLIND*.
THE OLD MAN SAID IT'S THROUGH HERE. I STILL CAN'T BELIEVE I'M... *WE'RE* DOING THIS. *GRAVE-ROBBING?!* IT'S CRAZY!
CRAZY'S RIGHT. RAG-RUNT THERE WILL ONLY SLOW US DOWN.
FROM THE LOOKS OF THIS PIPE, I DON'T THINK HIS BEING *BLIND* IS GOING TO MAKE A BIT OF DIFFERENCE.
OW! KEEP MOVING, STORY!
OW! I'M NOT STORY!
THERE WAS NO END IN SIGHT. WE KEPT GOING ANYHOW.
HEY, RUNT. SINCE YOU'VE MET STORY, DON'T YOU WISH YOU WERE *DEAF*, TOO?
...I REMEMBER DAD SAYING MOM WASN'T REALLY DEAD, EVERYTHING ELSE WAS.
HE SAID EVERYTHING ELSE CEASED TO EXIST AS IT ONCE WAS.
IF WHAT YOU'RE SAYING IS TRUE, WHAT WAS THE WORLD LIKE BEFORE THE *HEROES DIED?*
FOR THE FIRST TIME SINCE I COULD REMEMBER, I DIDN'T HAVE A THING TO SAY.

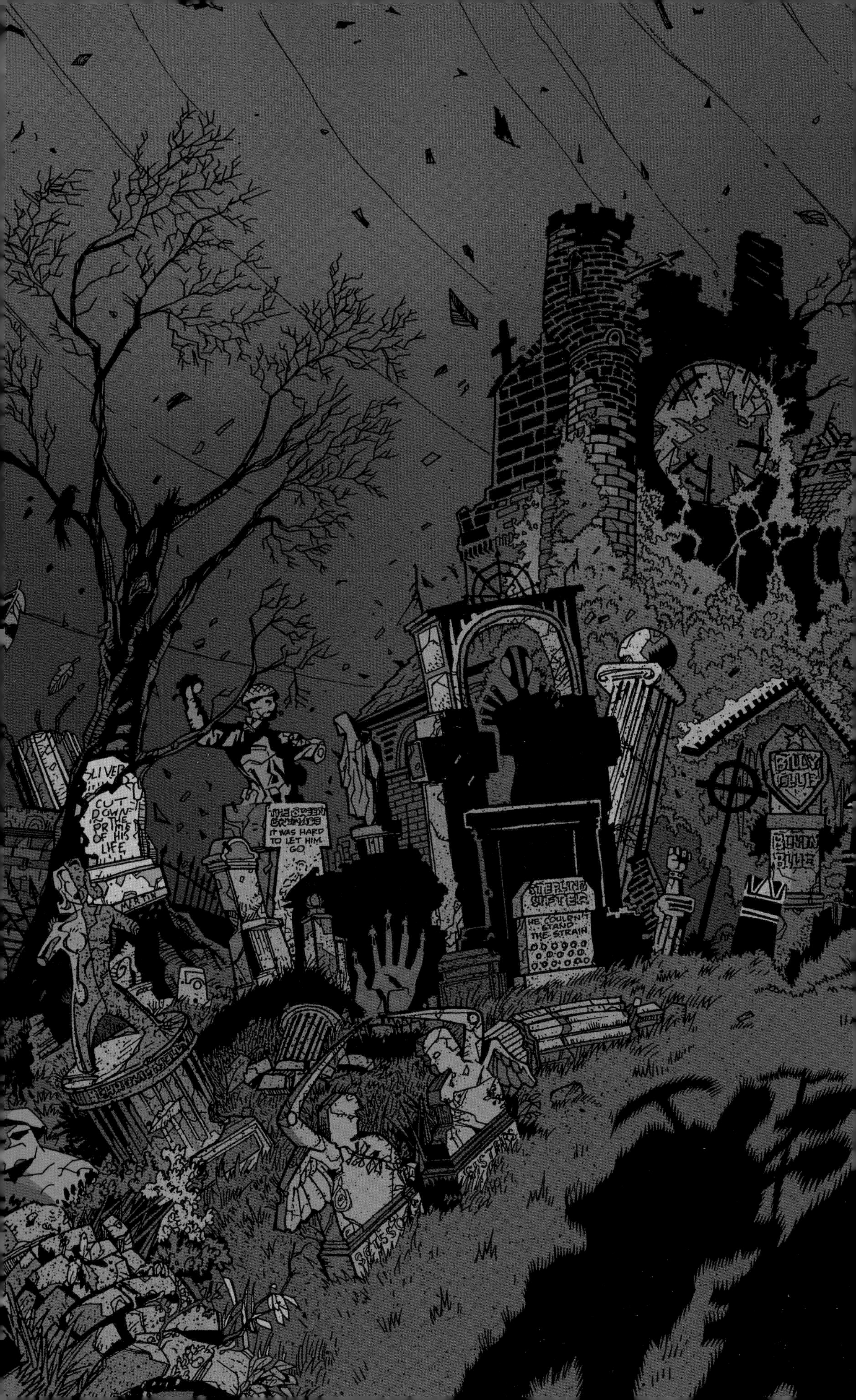
CUT DOWN IN THE PRIME OF HIS LIFE
IT WAS HARD TO LET HIM GO
HE COULDN'T STAND THE STRAIN
BILLY CLUB

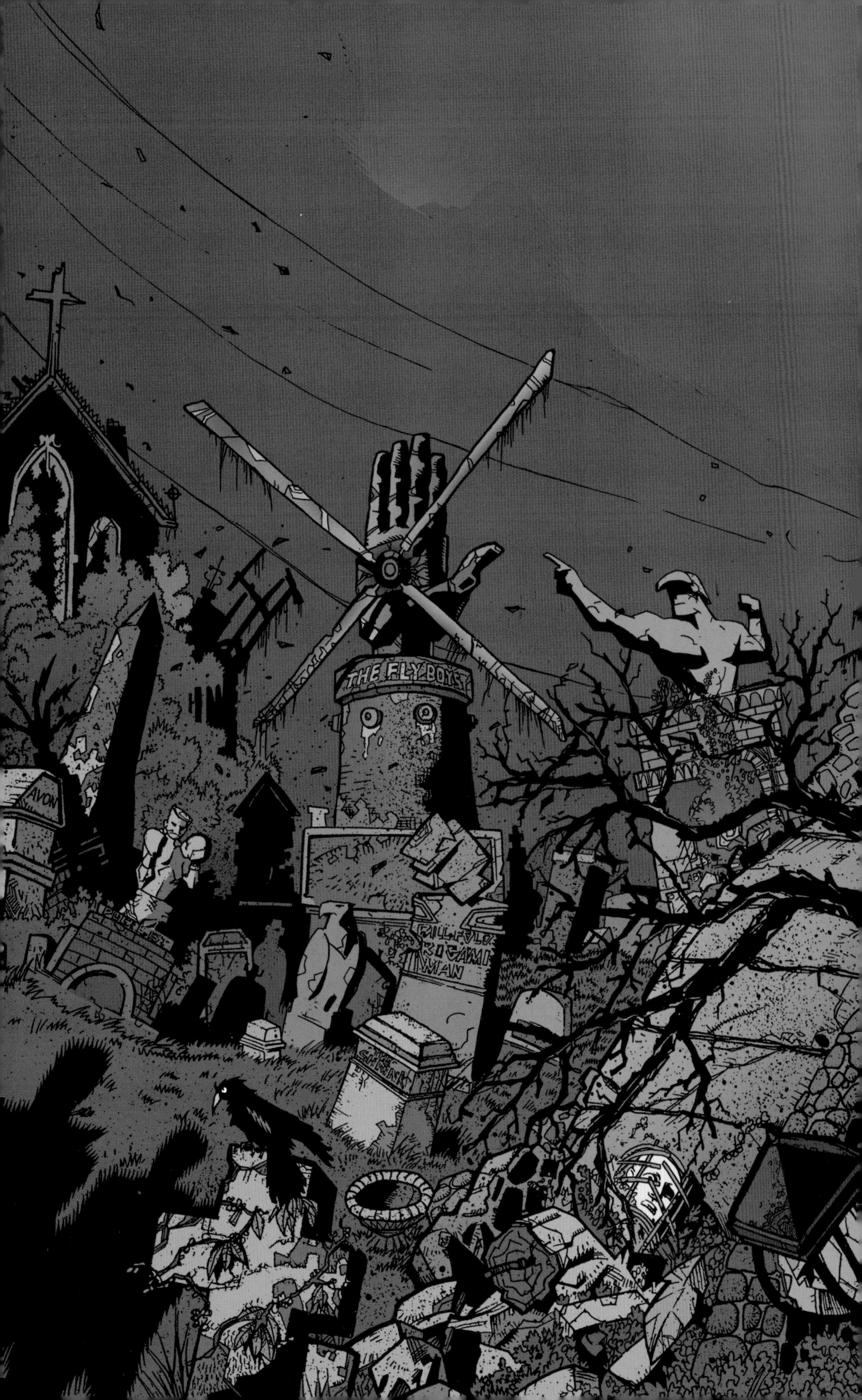
THE FLY BOYS
AVON
MAN

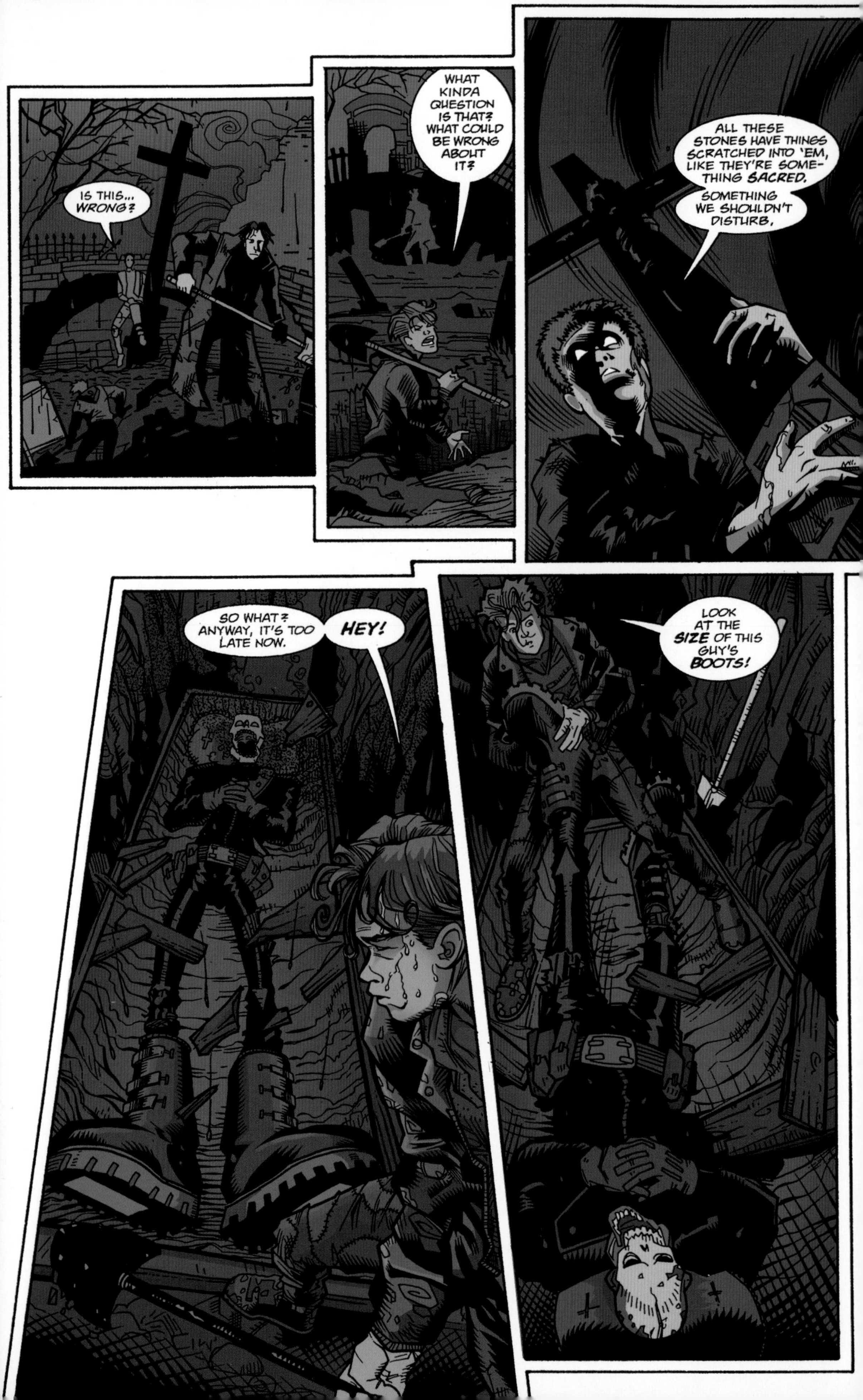
IS THIS... WRONG?
WHAT KINDA QUESTION IS THAT? WHAT COULD BE WRONG ABOUT IT?
ALL THESE STONES HAVE THINGS SCRATCHED INTO 'EM, LIKE THEY'RE SOME- THING SACRED.
SOMETHING WE SHOULDN'T DISTURB.
SO WHAT? ANYWAY, IT'S TOO LATE NOW.
HEY!
LOOK AT THE SIZE OF THIS GUY'S BOOTS!

Huh. WONDER WHY THE SOLES ARE MIRRORED?!

WOULD YOU QUIT LOOKING AT ME, RAG-RUNT?! GIVES ME THE CREEPS.

JERK, HE KNOWS I COULDN'T LOOK AT HIM EVEN IF I WANTED TO.

WHAT DID THE OLD MAN SEE IN ME THAT NO ONE ELSE CAN? AREN'T I WORTH AS MUCH AS JOHNNY OR STORY...

...EVEN IF NOTHING IS ALL WE'RE WORTH?

WHAT I WOULDN'T GIVE TO SHOW THEM.

WHUP!

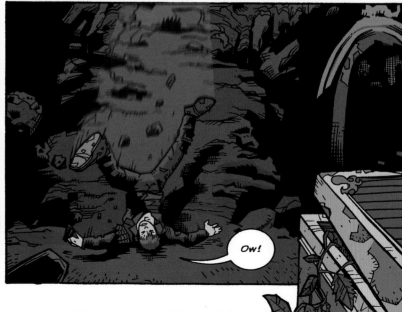

Ow!

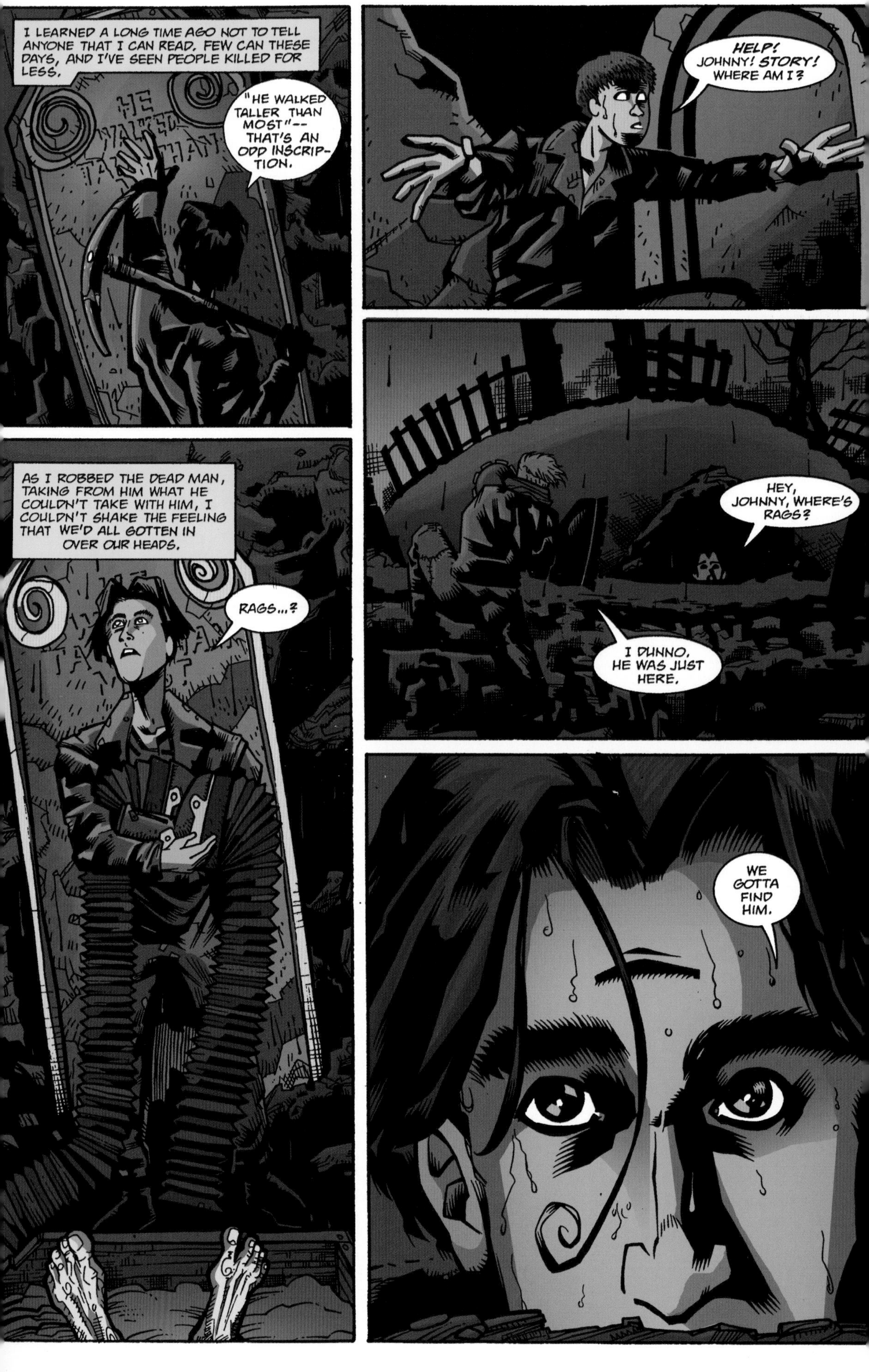
I LEARNED A LONG TIME AGO NOT TO TELL ANYONE THAT I CAN READ. FEW CAN THESE DAYS, AND I'VE SEEN PEOPLE KILLED FOR LESS.
"HE WALKED TALLER THAN MOST"-- THAT'S AN ODD INSCRIPTION.
HELP! JOHNNY! STORY! WHERE AM I?
AS I ROBBED THE DEAD MAN, TAKING FROM HIM WHAT HE COULDN'T TAKE WITH HIM, I COULDN'T SHAKE THE FEELING THAT WE'D ALL GOTTEN IN OVER OUR HEADS.
RAGS...?
HEY, JOHNNY, WHERE'S RAGS?
I DUNNO, HE WAS JUST HERE.
WE GOTTA FIND HIM.

LOOK-- HE MUSTA FELL DOWN THERE, IT'D SERVE HIM RIGHT IF WE JUST *LEFT!*

WE CAN'T DO THAT, JOHNNY.

WHY'D YOU RUN OFF, YA LITTLE *CRIPPLE?*

I DIDN'T--

LEAVE HIM ALONE. LET'S TAKE A LOOK AROUND.

ANYTHING WRONG?

HERE IS MR. LION, THE DECEIVER

HE MUST NEVER WAKE AGAIN

Uh...? NO... COURSE NOT.

HERE IS MR. LION, THE DECEIVER

WE PRIED ON ANCIENT HINGES AND TORE AT RUST-CAKED LOCKS.

URGH!

AND FINALLY, AS OUR MUSCLES BEGAN TO GIVE OUT, CENTURY-OLD SEALS SNAPPED AND CRUMBLED TO DUST.

I *CUT* MYSELF.

WHAT'S A LITTLE BLOOD? CHECK *THIS* OUT!

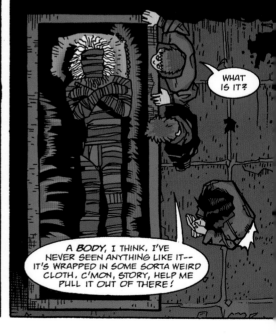

WHAT IS IT?

A *BODY*, I THINK. I'VE NEVER SEEN ANYTHING LIKE IT-- IT'S WRAPPED IN SOME SORTA WEIRD CLOTH. C'MON, STORY, HELP ME PULL IT OUT OF THERE!

HEY, MY CUT'S *DISAPPEARING!* I CAN'T EVEN FEEL IT ANYMORE.

IT'S... IT'S COMING *BACK* AGAIN... WHEN I PULL MY HAND AWAY FROM THE RAGS!?!

IF THEY COULD *HEAL* MY CUT, WHAT WOULD THEY DO TO SOMEONE WHO'S --

--BLIND?

HERE, TRY THIS, RUNT.

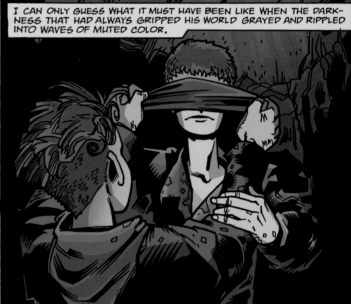

I CAN ONLY GUESS WHAT IT MUST HAVE BEEN LIKE WHEN THE DARKNESS THAT HAD ALWAYS GRIPPED HIS WORLD GRAYED AND RIPPLED INTO WAVES OF MUTED COLOR.

WHAT'S HAPPENING, RAGS?

I CAN *SEE!*

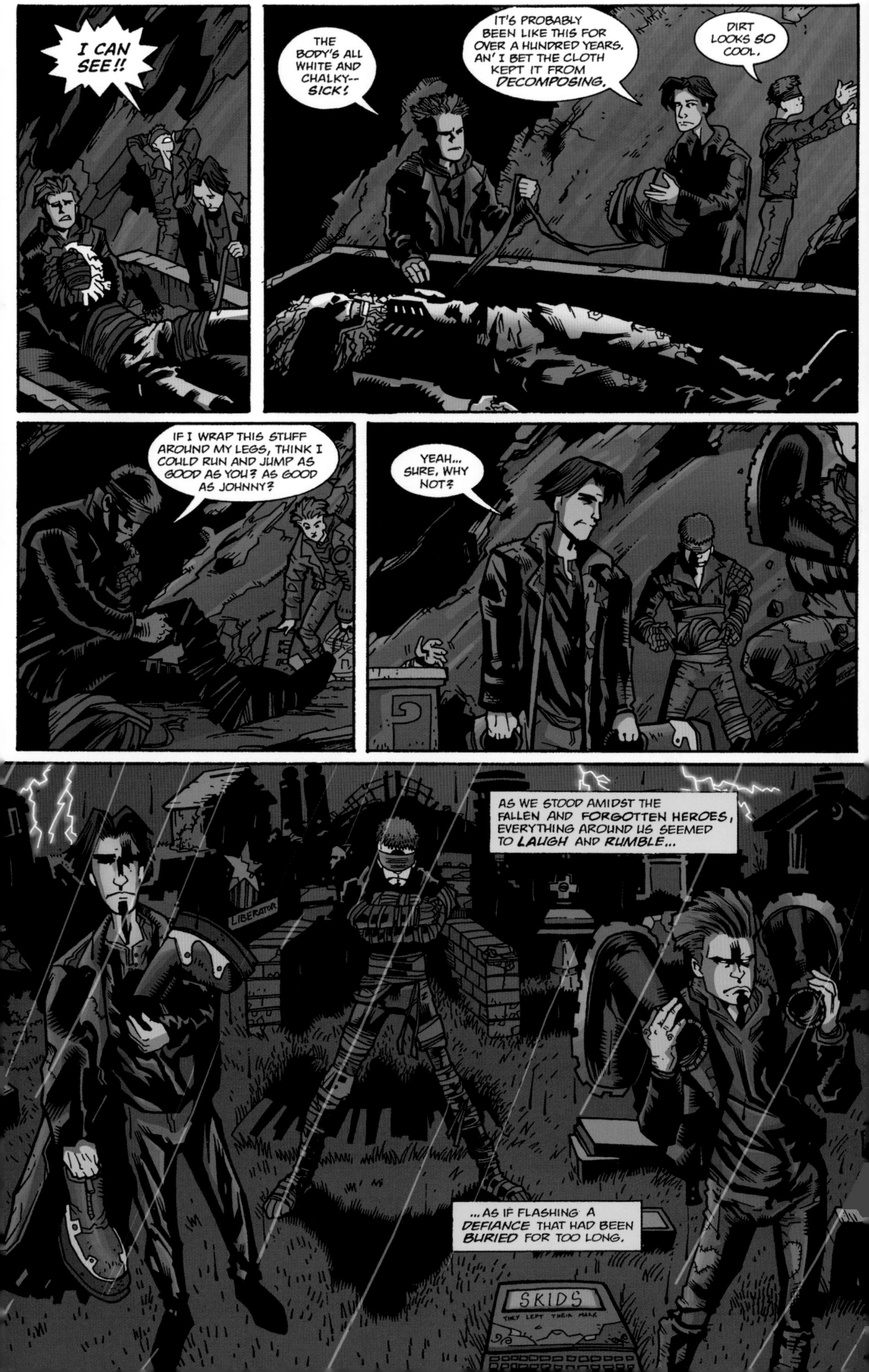

I CAN SEE!!
THE BODY'S ALL WHITE AND CHALKY-- SICK!
IT'S PROBABLY BEEN LIKE THIS FOR OVER A HUNDRED YEARS. AN' I BET THE CLOTH KEPT IT FROM DECOMPOSING.
DIRT LOOKS SO COOL.
IF I WRAP THIS STUFF AROUND MY LEGS, THINK I COULD RUN AND JUMP AS GOOD AS YOU? AS GOOD AS JOHNNY?
YEAH... SURE, WHY NOT?
AS WE STOOD AMIDST THE FALLEN AND FORGOTTEN HEROES, EVERYTHING AROUND US SEEMED TO LAUGH AND RUMBLE...
LIBERATOR
...AS IF FLASHING A DEFIANCE THAT HAD BEEN BURIED FOR TOO LONG.
SKIDS
THEY LEFT THEIR MARK

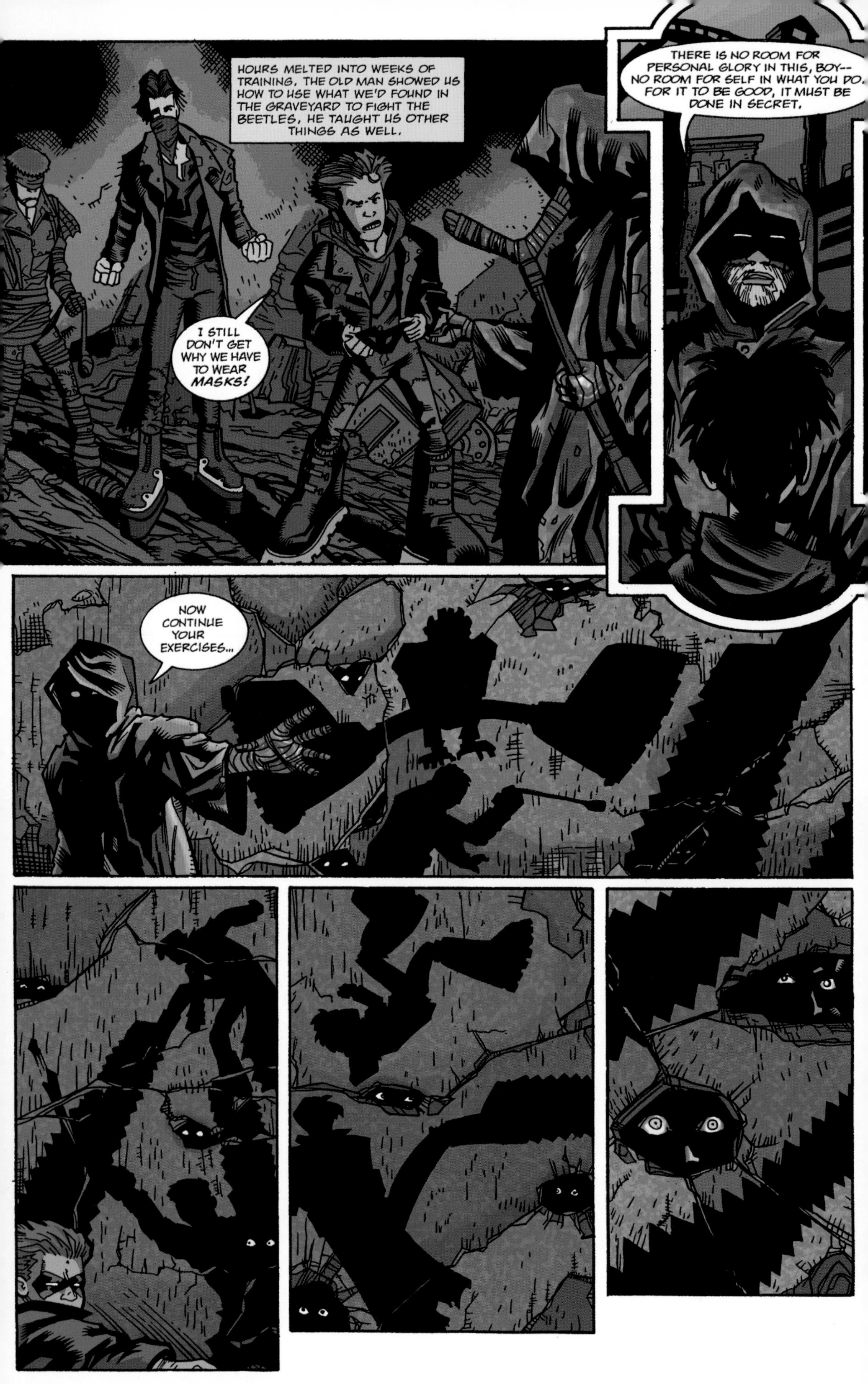
HOURS MELTED INTO WEEKS OF TRAINING. THE OLD MAN SHOWED US HOW TO USE WHAT WE'D FOUND IN THE GRAVEYARD TO FIGHT THE BEETLES. HE TAUGHT US OTHER THINGS AS WELL.
I STILL DON'T GET WHY WE HAVE TO WEAR MASKS!
THERE IS NO ROOM FOR PERSONAL GLORY IN THIS, BOY-- NO ROOM FOR SELF IN WHAT YOU DO. FOR IT TO BE GOOD, IT MUST BE DONE IN SECRET.
NOW CONTINUE YOUR EXERCISES...

WE'RE READY-- I KNOW WE ARE. I CAN'T WAIT TO STOMP SOME BEETLE *BUTT*.

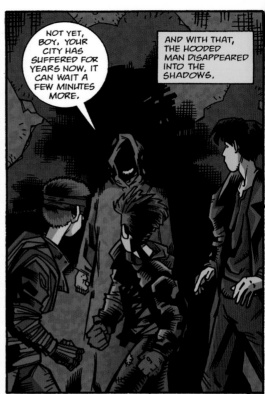

NOT YET, BOY, YOUR CITY HAS SUFFERED FOR YEARS NOW. IT CAN WAIT A FEW MINUTES MORE.

AND WITH THAT, THE HOODED MAN DISAPPEARED INTO THE SHADOWS.

I'M TIRED OF THIS.

IF THE BEETLES KILL ANYBODY NOW, IT'LL BE ON *OUR* HANDS...

...'CAUSE WE COULDA *STOPPED* IT!

IT'S *NOT TIME* YET, JOHNNY!

THE OLD MAN SAID TO *WAIT*.

NO.

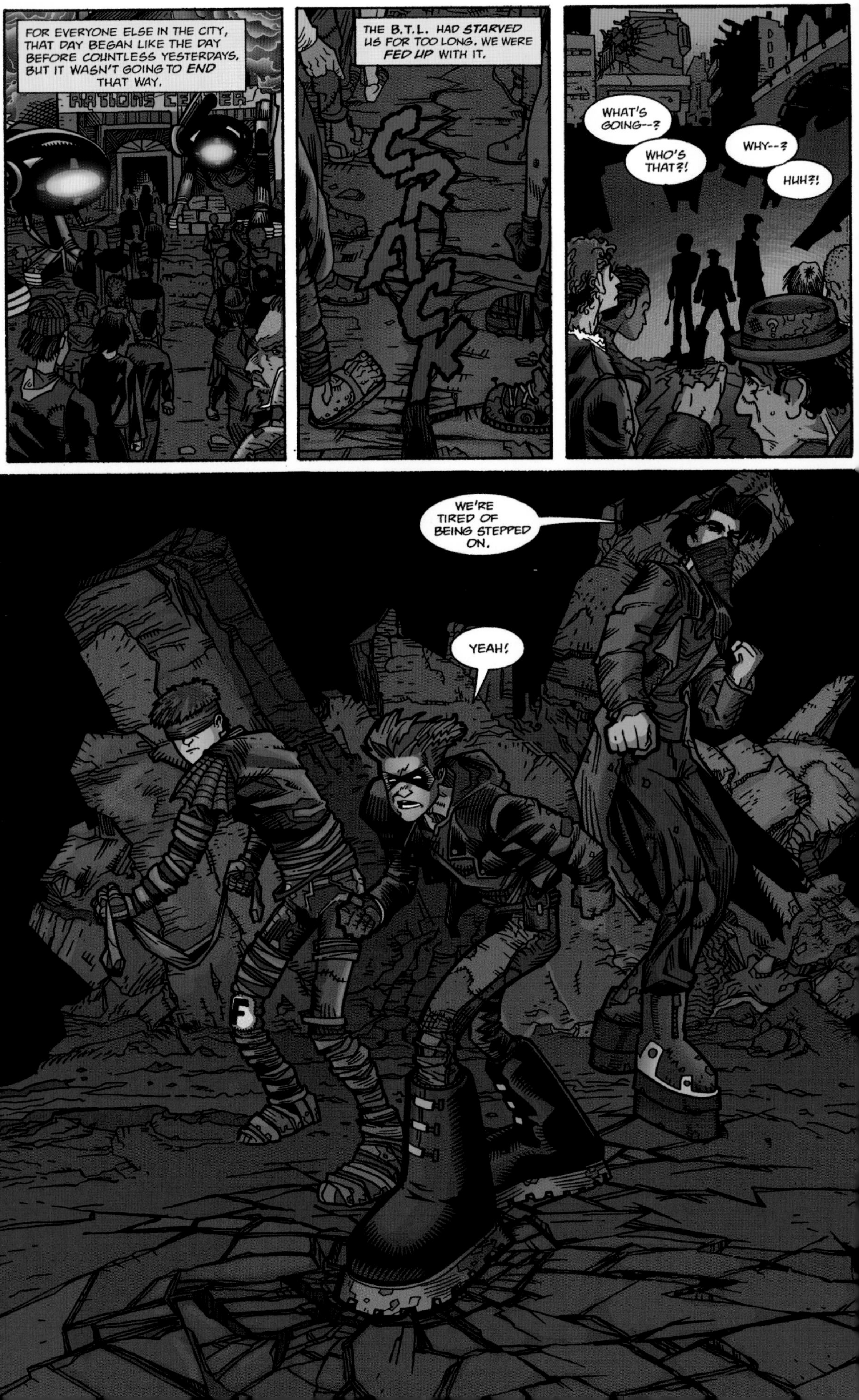
FOR EVERYONE ELSE IN THE CITY, THAT DAY BEGAN LIKE THE DAY BEFORE COUNTLESS YESTERDAYS, BUT IT WASN'T GOING TO END THAT WAY.
RATIONS CENTER
THE B.T.L. HAD STARVED US FOR TOO LONG. WE WERE FED UP WITH IT.
CRACK
WHAT'S GOING--?
WHO'S THAT?!
WHY--?
HUH?!
WE'RE TIRED OF BEING STEPPED ON.
YEAH!

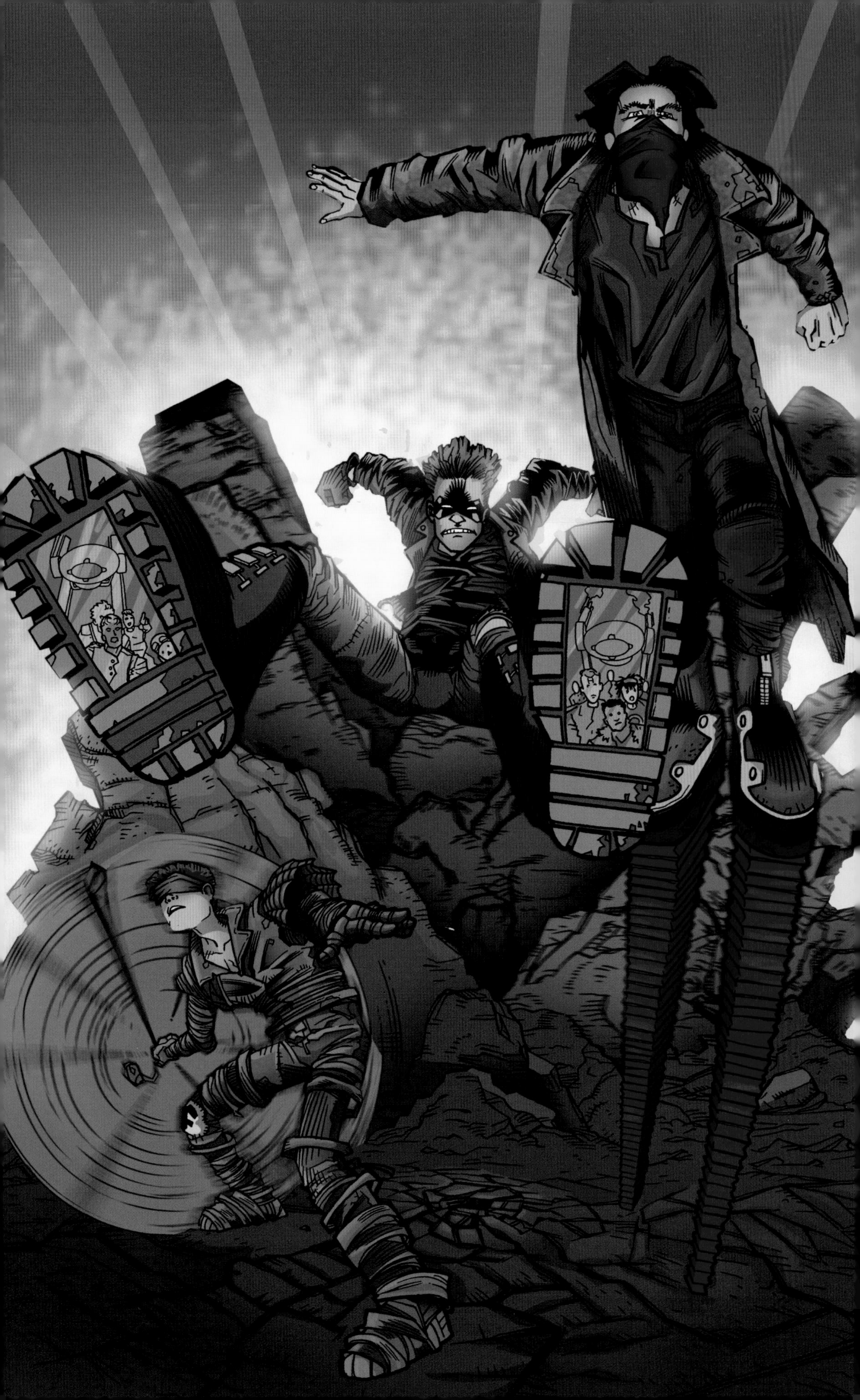

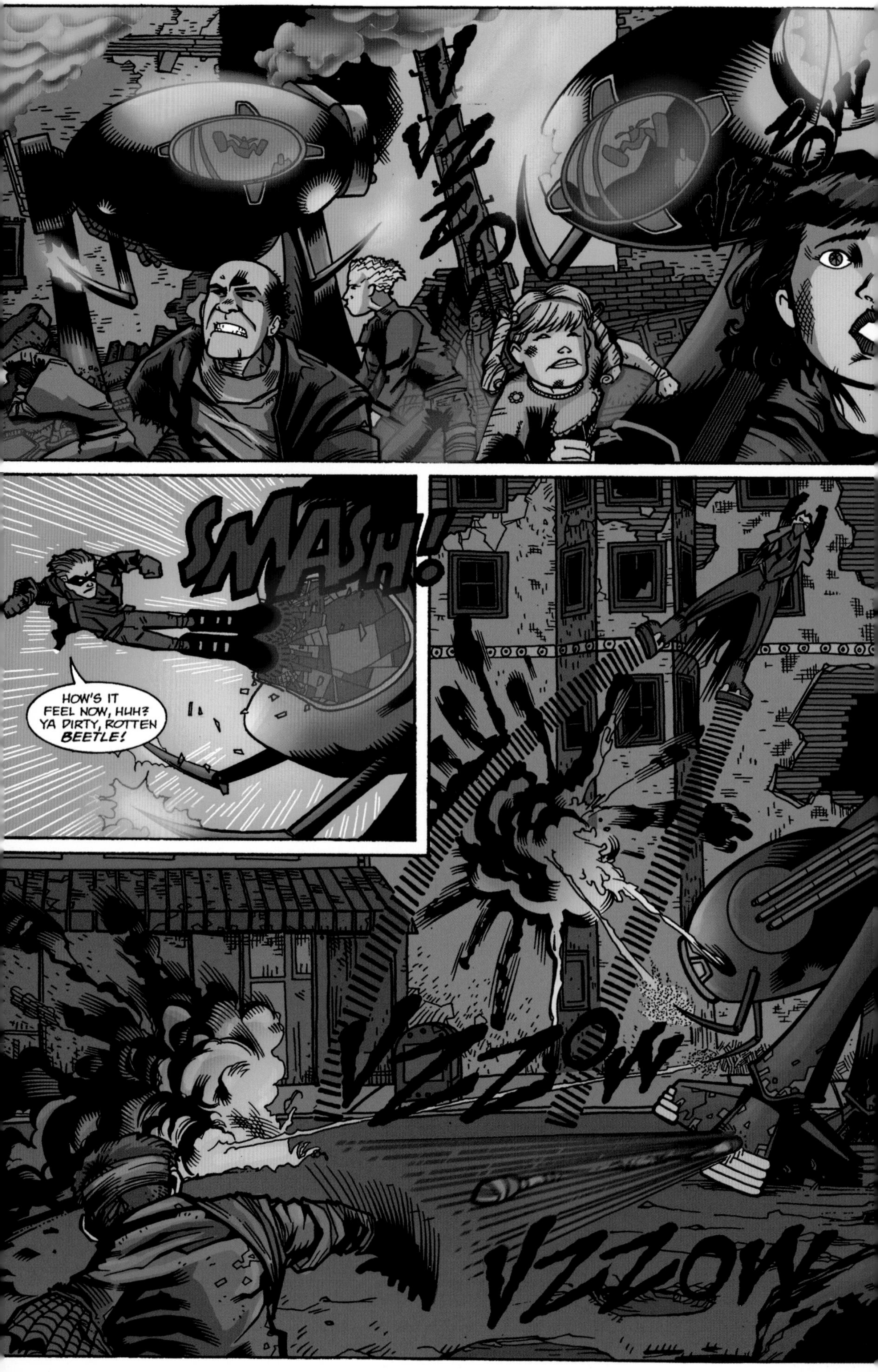
VVZZZOWW
VZZOW
SMASH!
HOW'S IT FEEL NOW, HUH? YA DIRTY, ROTTEN *BEETLE!*
VZZOW
VZZOW

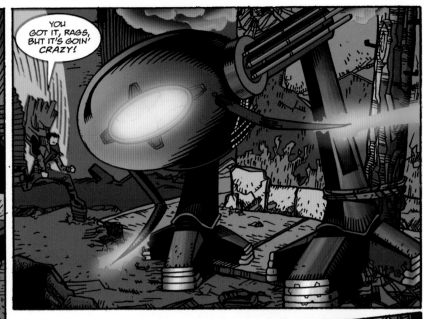

FA-WAP!

YOU GOT IT, RAGS, BUT IT'S GOIN' CRAZY!

I'LL STOP IT!

SPLANGG!

KRRRACK

YEEE-HA!

KICK! KICK! KICK! KICK!

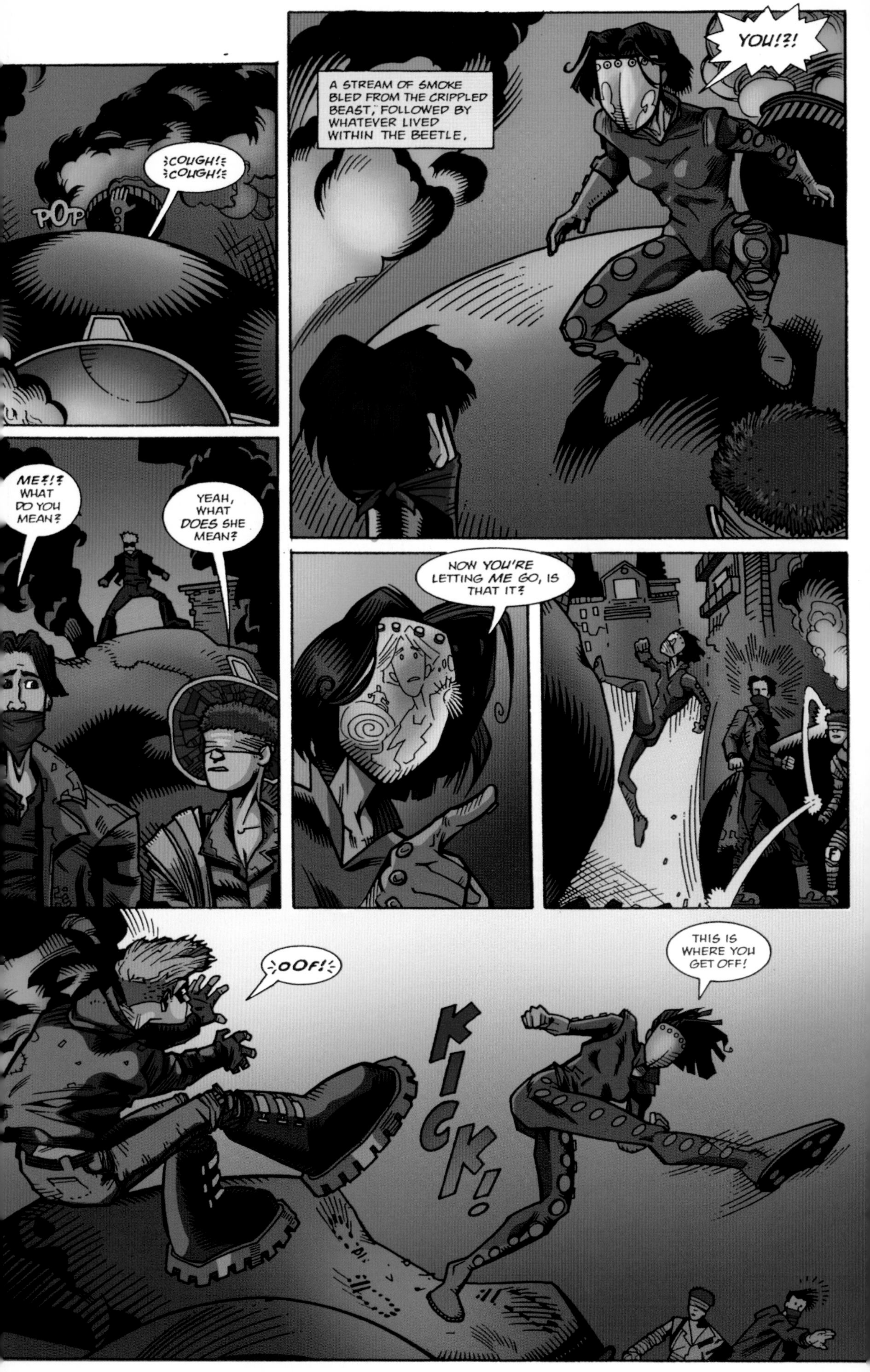

POP
COUGH! COUGH!
A STREAM OF SMOKE BLED FROM THE CRIPPLED BEAST, FOLLOWED BY WHATEVER LIVED WITHIN THE BEETLE.
YOU!?!
ME?!? WHAT DO YOU MEAN?
YEAH, WHAT DOES SHE MEAN?
NOW YOU'RE LETTING ME GO, IS THAT IT?
OOF!
THIS IS WHERE YOU GET OFF!
KICK!

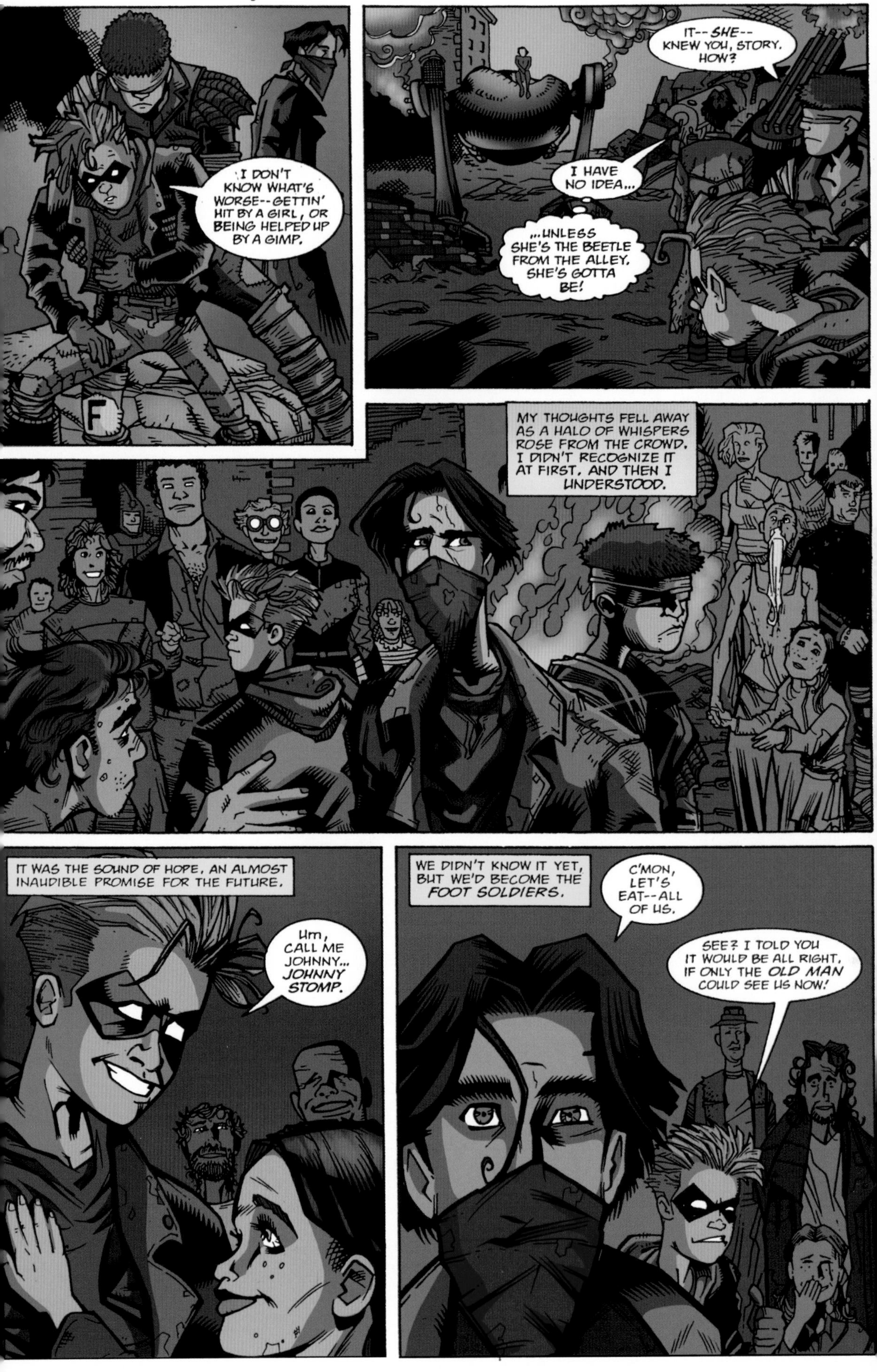
I DON'T KNOW WHAT'S WORSE--GETTIN' HIT BY A GIRL, OR BEING HELPED UP BY A GIMP.
IT-- SHE-- KNEW YOU, STORY. HOW?
I HAVE NO IDEA...
...UNLESS SHE'S THE BEETLE FROM THE ALLEY. SHE'S GOTTA BE!
MY THOUGHTS FELL AWAY AS A HALO OF WHISPERS ROSE FROM THE CROWD. I DIDN'T RECOGNIZE IT AT FIRST. AND THEN I UNDERSTOOD.
IT WAS THE SOUND OF HOPE. AN ALMOST INAUDIBLE PROMISE FOR THE FUTURE.
Um, CALL ME JOHNNY... JOHNNY STOMP.
WE DIDN'T KNOW IT YET, BUT WE'D BECOME THE FOOT SOLDIERS.
C'MON, LET'S EAT--ALL OF US.
SEE? I TOLD YOU IT WOULD BE ALL RIGHT. IF ONLY THE OLD MAN COULD SEE US NOW!

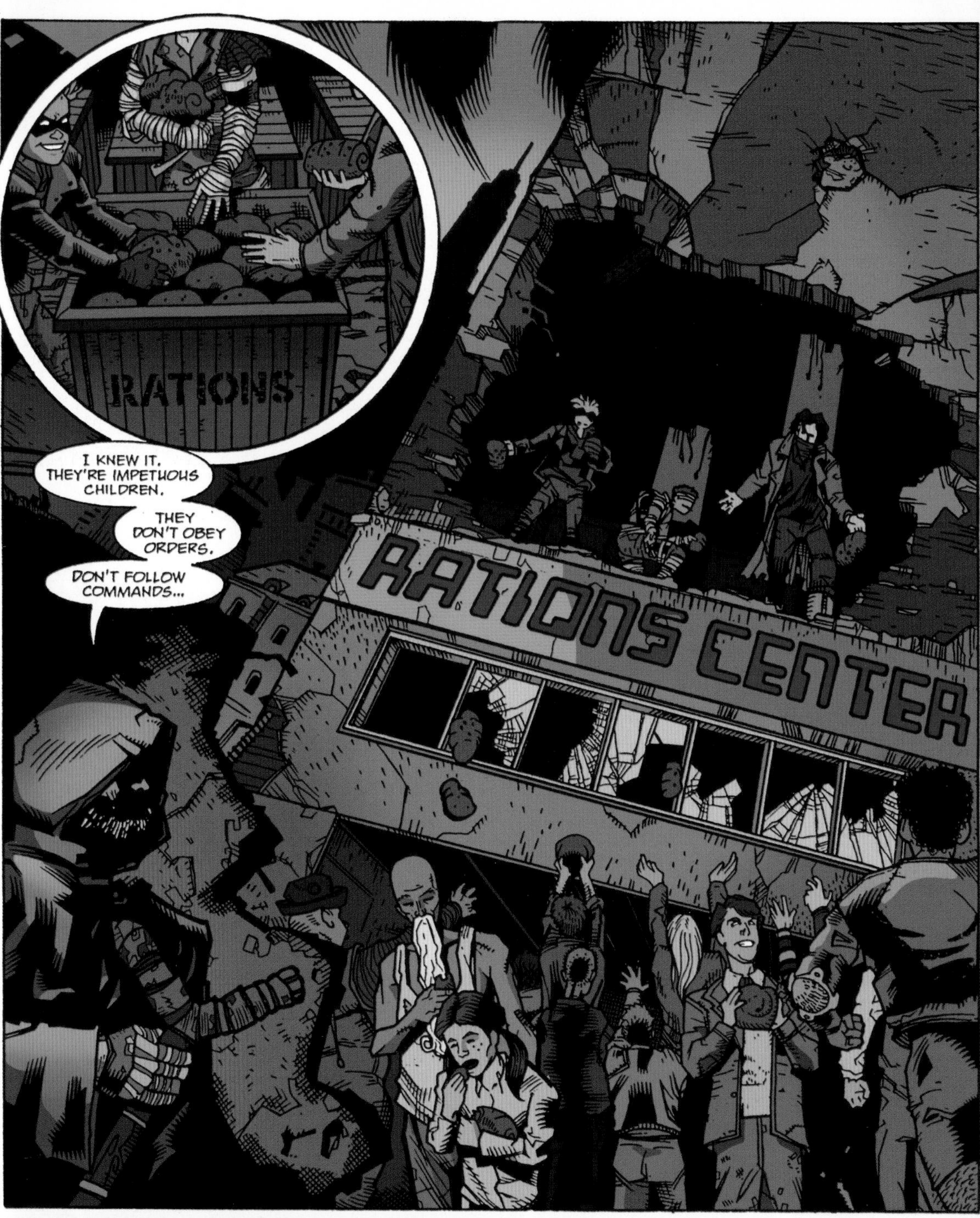
RATIONS
I KNEW IT. THEY'RE IMPETUOUS CHILDREN.
THEY DON'T OBEY ORDERS.
DON'T FOLLOW COMMANDS...
RATIONS CENTER

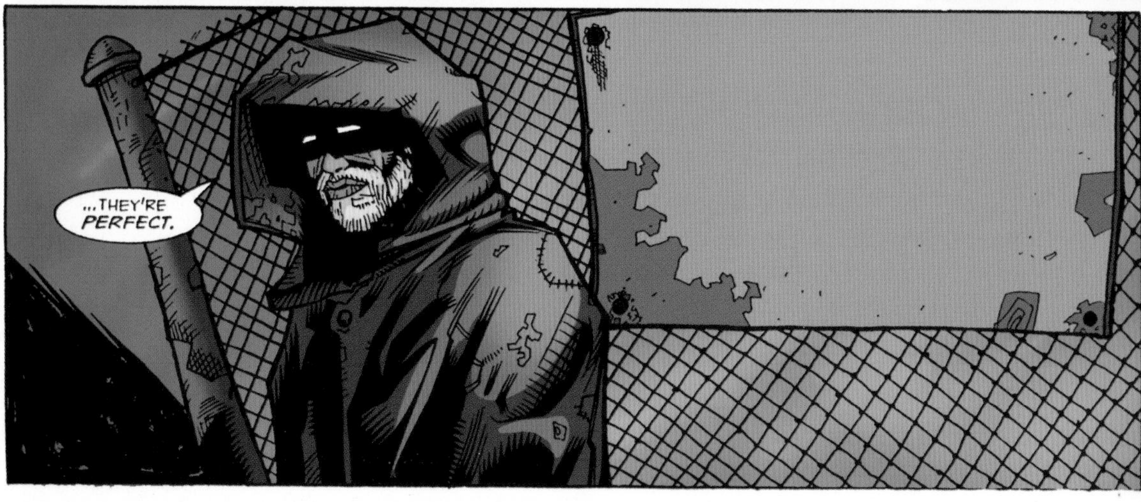
...THEY'RE *PERFECT.*

Story's Story

Chapter One

But it wasn't my story after all. It was our's. Johnny's. Rags's. Mine. And it was bigger than we were as well. We had become part of something far larger, a far greater struggle. One that would change the quality of our lives despite the fact that it would almost certainly decrease them. Not that there were any guarantees of long life in this city.

My father always said that life was not about finding the answers but of learning the questions. The first question I learned to ask was why my father had to die. The second was why, if I can read, I'm not one of the B.T.L.? And why, when I'm honest with myself, and I almost never am, do I want to be one of them? Again, no answers. But the questions do affect me. But that was before the old man with the glowing crutch showed up to give me enough questions for a lifetime. Who was he?

I had never seen this old man on the streets before. And I knew just about everyone that scraped their way to the factories. Or rotted away in the so-called hospitals we called "the dying rooms."

The old man was a stranger. That's either good reason to trust him or possibly the best reason not to. "New" doesn't work here. But while I knew everything that happened in the city, I had to admit that I had never been outside of it. The old man knew of a graveyard where all these super heroes were buried outside city limits. My father did not. And I thought he knew everything there was to know about the old heroes and about how they died.

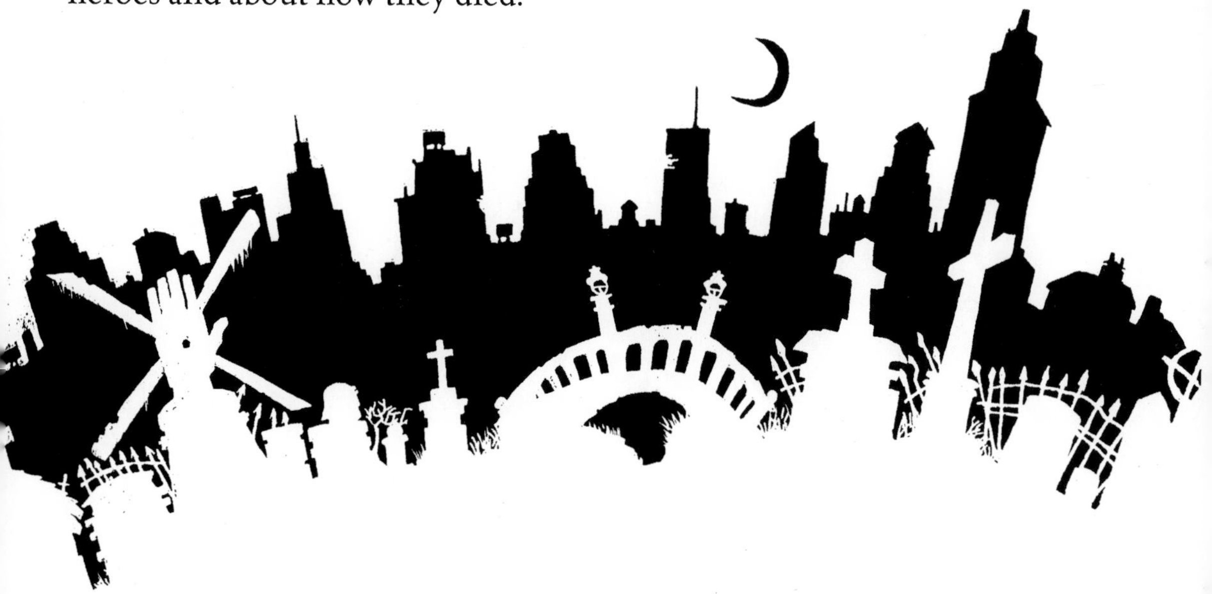

My father was a librarian and that's why I can read. He saved everything he could find. From encyclopedias to newspapers to comic books. He was like the junkyard man of myths. Anything other-worldly was of great worth to him. The misunderstood king of Atlantis who was neither friend nor foe to humanity, but often both. The child raised by wolves that was capable of speaking the language of the beasts. The soldier who would not kill but could not die. The man who walked in shadows and fought crimes darker still. My father taught all these stories to me. He tried to teach all these stories to me.

Now, with super hero boots on my feet, I wish I'd paid a little more attention. And what kind of hero starts out wanting to be one of the bad guys?

My Father's favorite story was about a man who came down from the city of gods. He had a walking stick that, when he struck the ground with it, transformed him into a god who could remake and change everything. This power, though, was available only for those who were pure of heart and courageous – the very characteristics the Old Man attributed to Johnny, myself, and Rags.

I had believed the stories were fiction. But what if they pointed to a greater reality? Is this the purpose of stories, the reason for myths? If the Old Man really had "that" walking stick, could he use it like a divining rod to find people with something heroic in them? Of course, he couldn't let it touch us, or we'd get the power ourselves and he wouldn't be able to find any others.

But I wanted to be a B.T.L. and I lied about the warning in the graveyard and yet, the crutch still chose me.

It still chose me.

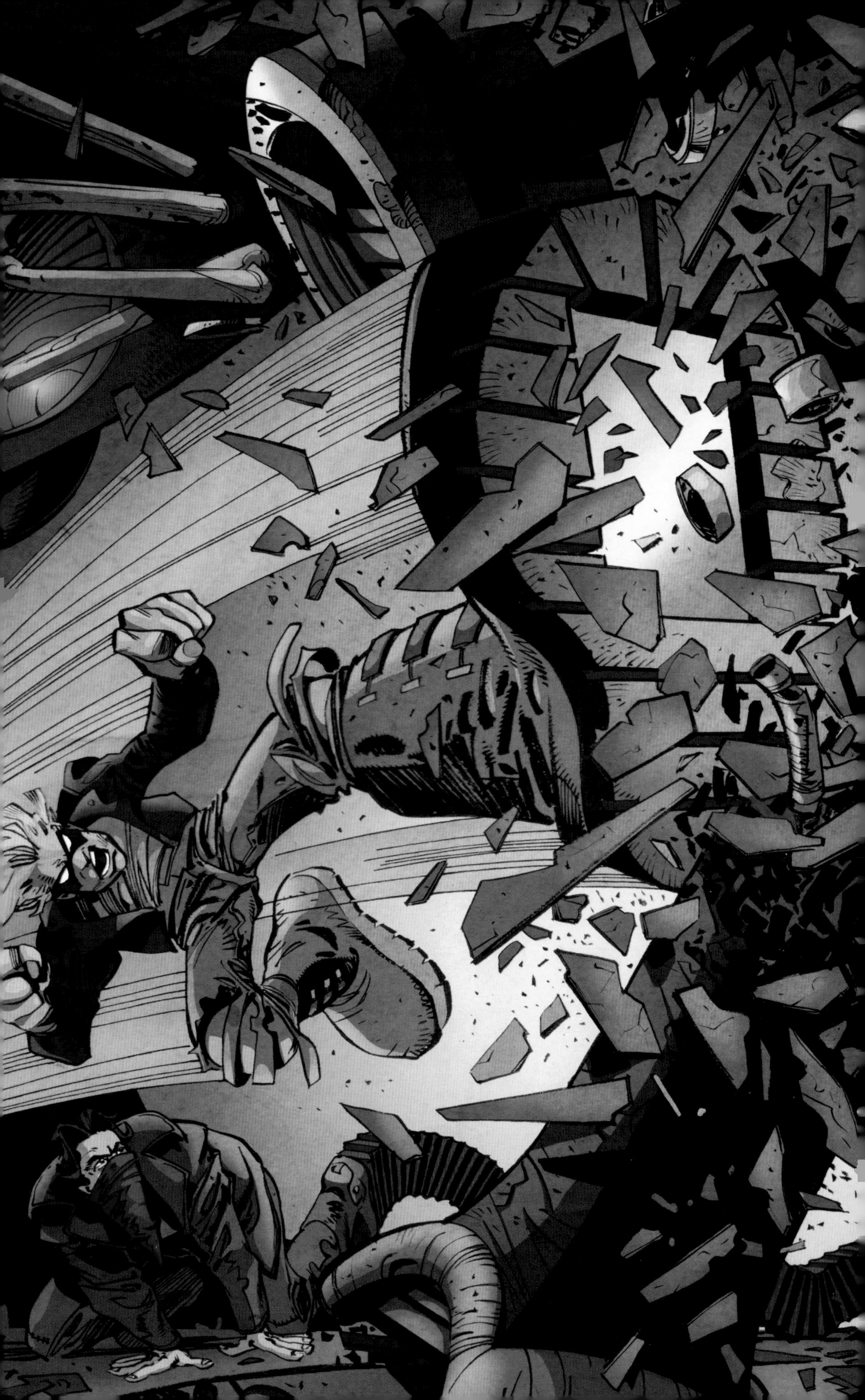

FIRST STEPS
CHAPTER TWO

"There was a graveyard of heroes for a reason," the boy sobbed. "Why didn't we heed its warning?"

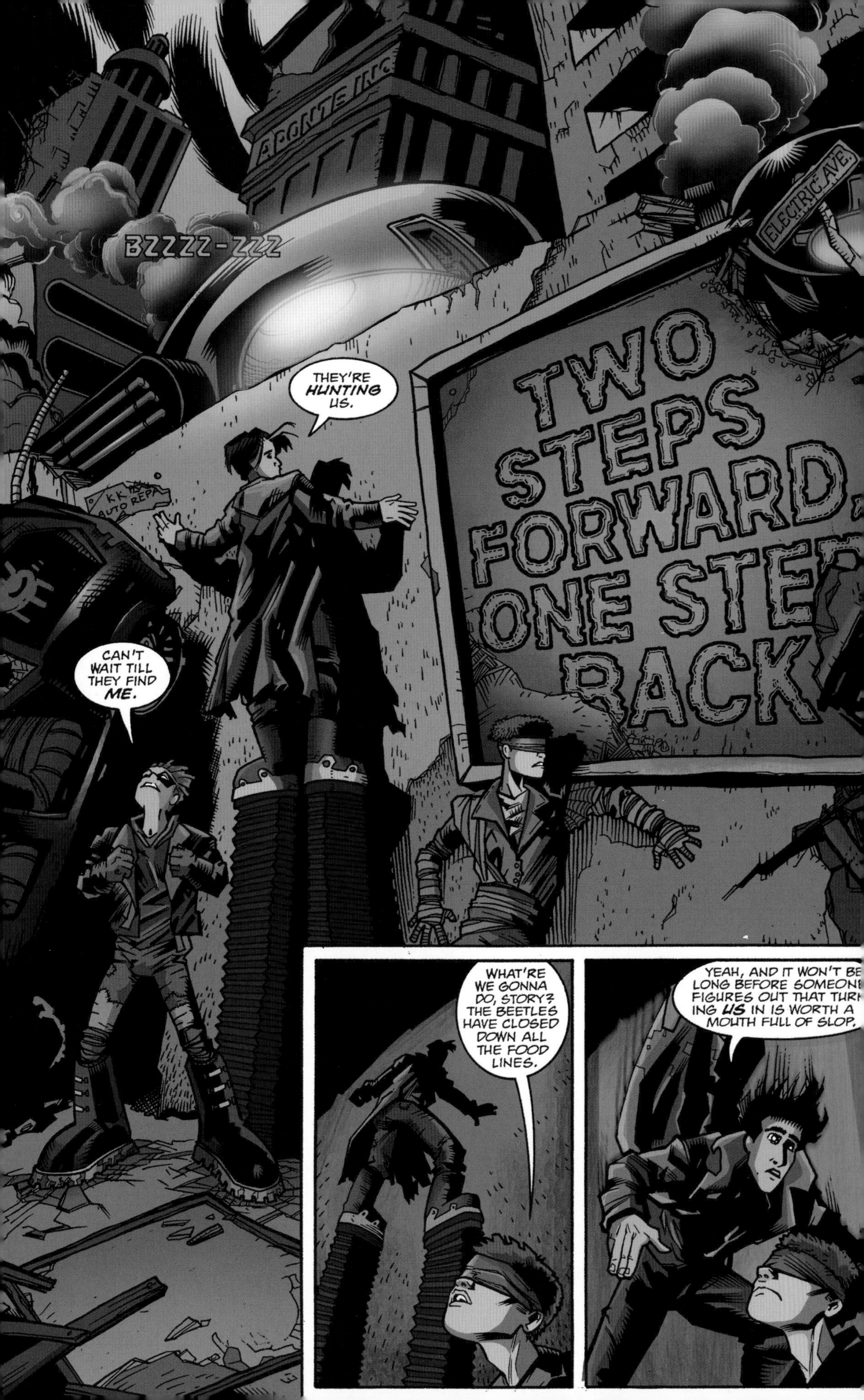
APONTE INC.
ELECTRIC AVE.
BZZZZ-ZZZ
THEY'RE *HUNTING* US.
TWO STEPS FORWARD, ONE STEP BACK
CAN'T WAIT TILL THEY FIND *ME*.
WHAT'RE WE GONNA DO, STORY? THE BEETLES HAVE CLOSED DOWN ALL THE FOOD LINES.
YEAH, AND IT WON'T BE LONG BEFORE SOMEONE FIGURES OUT THAT TURNING *US* IN IS WORTH A MOUTH FULL OF SLOP.

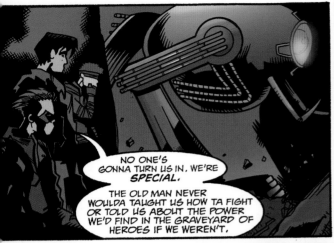

NO ONE'S GONNA TURN US IN, WE'RE *SPECIAL.*

THE OLD MAN NEVER WOULDA TAUGHT US HOW TA FIGHT OR TOLD US ABOUT THE POWER WE'D FIND IN THE GRAVEYARD OF HEROES IF WE WEREN'T.

IF WE SPLIT UP, I COULD TRY TO FIND...

WE SHOULD SPLIT UP, THAT'LL MAKE US HARDER TO TRACK.

I AGREE WITH STORY.

YOU *WOULD,* RAG-RUNT. WE SHOULD STICK TOGETHER--THE OLD MAN SAID SO.

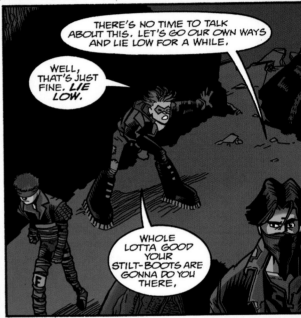

THERE'S NO TIME TO TALK ABOUT THIS. LET'S GO OUR OWN WAYS AND LIE LOW FOR A WHILE.

WELL, THAT'S JUST FINE. *LIE LOW.*

WHOLE LOTTA GOOD YOUR STILT-BOOTS ARE GONNA DO YOU THERE.

THE OLD MAN MUST'VE MADE A MISTAKE. *YOU'RE* NOTHIN' SPECIAL AT ALL.

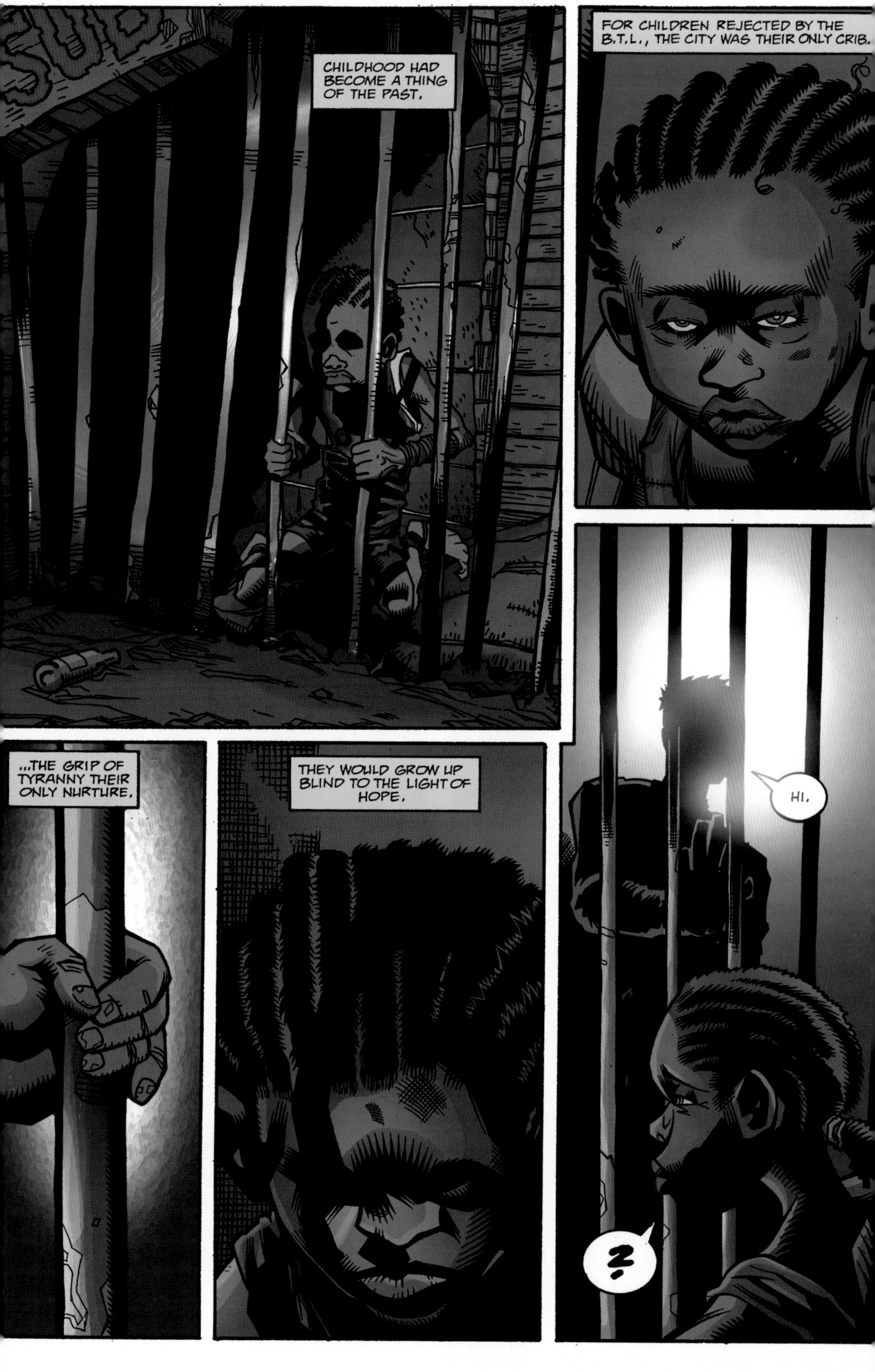
CHILDHOOD HAD BECOME A THING OF THE PAST.
FOR CHILDREN REJECTED BY THE B.T.L., THE CITY WAS THEIR ONLY CRIB.
...THE GRIP OF TYRANNY THEIR ONLY NURTURE.
THEY WOULD GROW UP BLIND TO THE LIGHT OF HOPE.
HI.
?

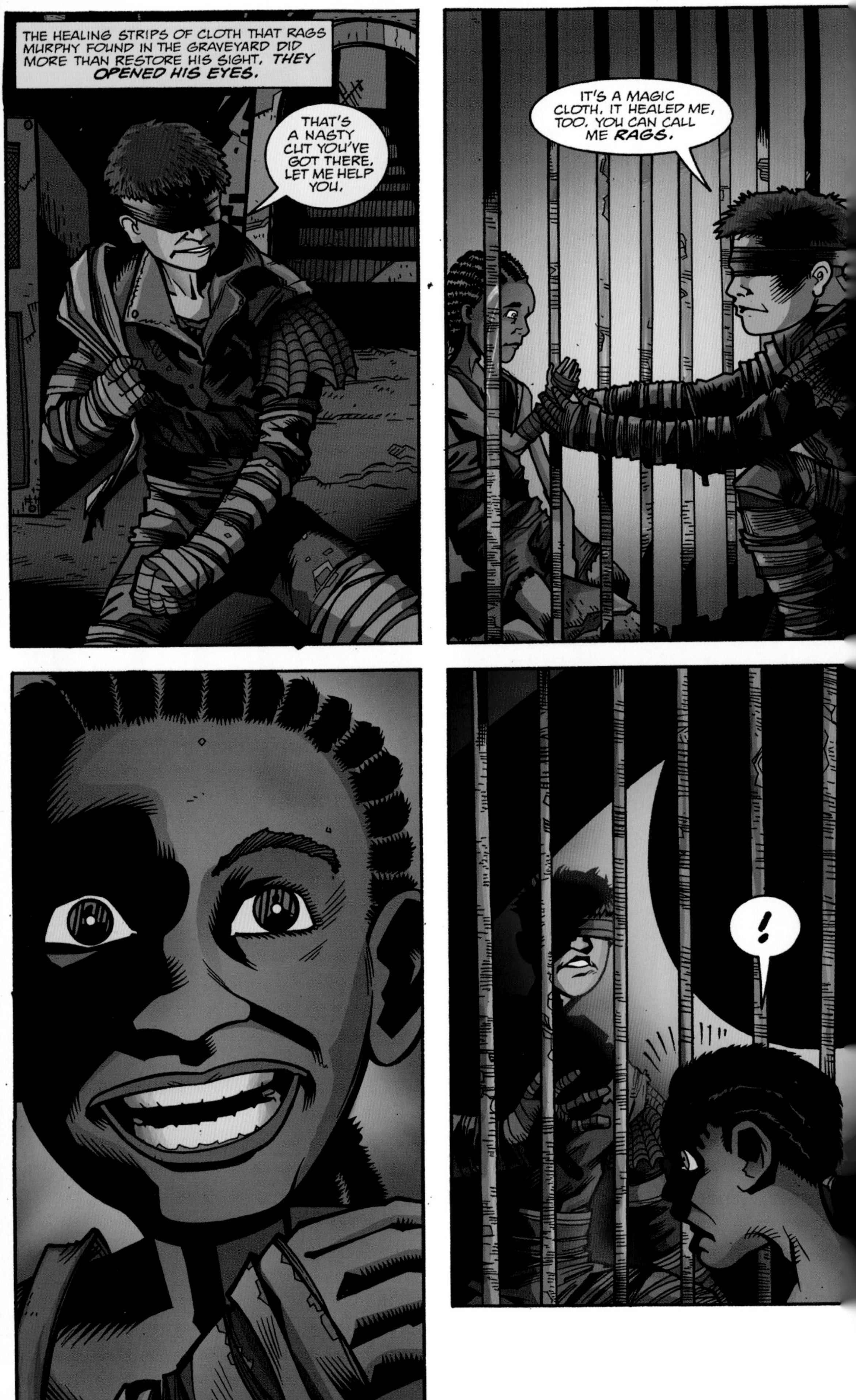
THE HEALING STRIPS OF CLOTH THAT RAGS MURPHY FOUND IN THE GRAVEYARD DID MORE THAN RESTORE HIS SIGHT, THEY OPENED HIS EYES.
THAT'S A NASTY CUT YOU'VE GOT THERE. LET ME HELP YOU.
IT'S A MAGIC CLOTH. IT HEALED ME, TOO. YOU CAN CALL ME RAGS.
!

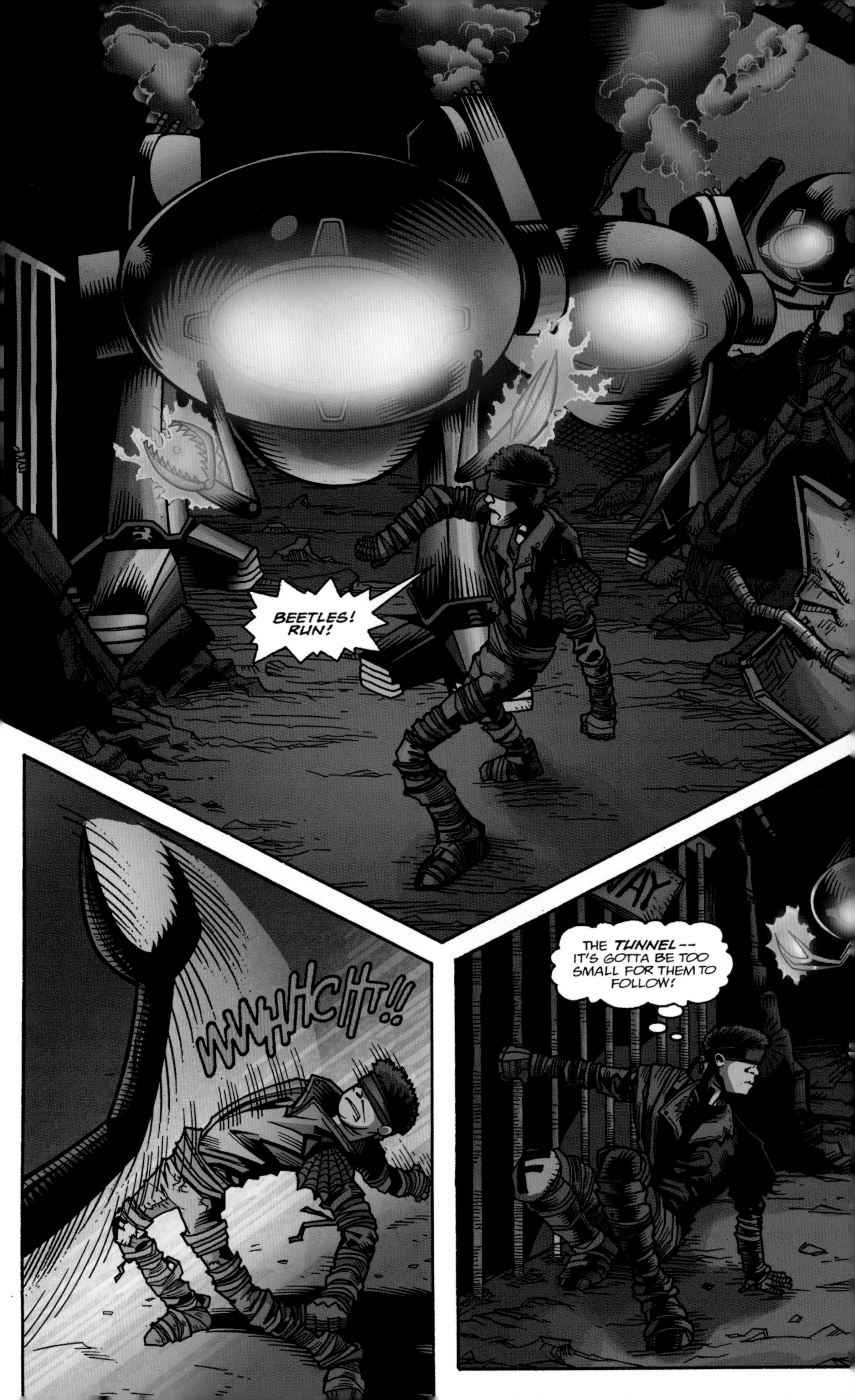
BEETLES! RUN!
WWHHCHT!!
THE TUNNEL-- IT'S GOTTA BE TOO SMALL FOR THEM TO FOLLOW!

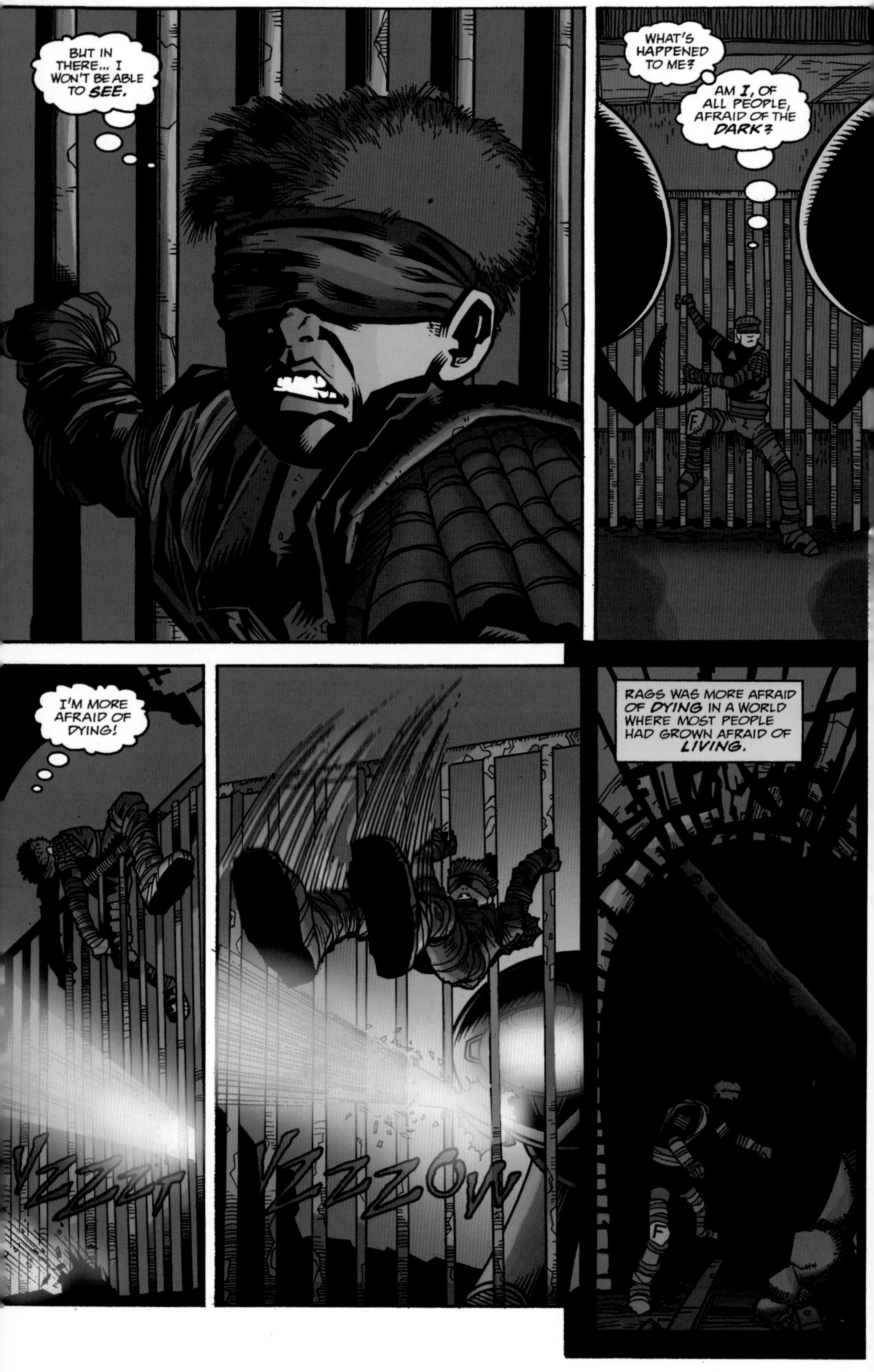
BUT IN THERE... I WON'T BE ABLE TO SEE.
WHAT'S HAPPENED TO ME?
AM I, OF ALL PEOPLE, AFRAID OF THE DARK?
I'M MORE AFRAID OF DYING!
VZZZT
VZZZOW
RAGS WAS MORE AFRAID OF DYING IN A WORLD WHERE MOST PEOPLE HAD GROWN AFRAID OF LIVING.

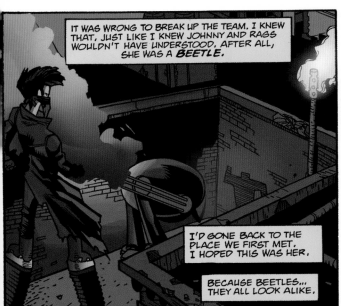

IT WAS WRONG TO BREAK UP THE TEAM. I KNEW THAT, JUST LIKE I KNEW JOHNNY AND RAGS WOULDN'T HAVE UNDERSTOOD. AFTER ALL, SHE WAS A *BEETLE*.

I'D GONE BACK TO THE PLACE WE FIRST MET. I HOPED THIS WAS HER.

BECAUSE BEETLES... THEY ALL LOOK ALIKE.

THE BEETLE YAWNED-- AND THERE *SHE* WAS.

YOU'RE GOING TO RUIN EVERYTHING, JUST LIKE *CHINA* SAID.

I KNOW YOU WERE *HUNGRY*... NOT REALLY A THREAT... IT WAS JUST A STOLEN LOAF...

WHY DO YOU KEEP *LOOKING* AT ME THAT WAY?

HER WORDS DIDN'T MAKE ANY SENSE. WHO WAS SHE TALKING TO?

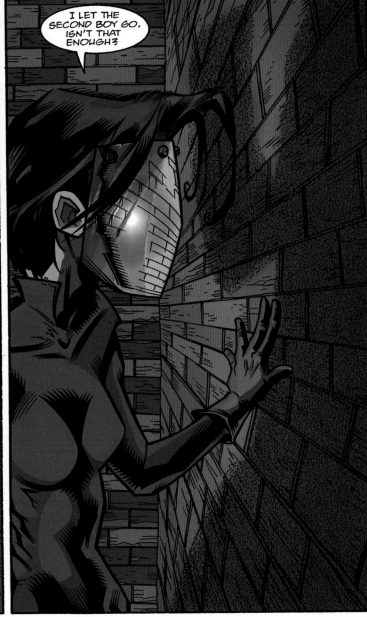

I LET THE SECOND BOY GO. ISN'T THAT ENOUGH?

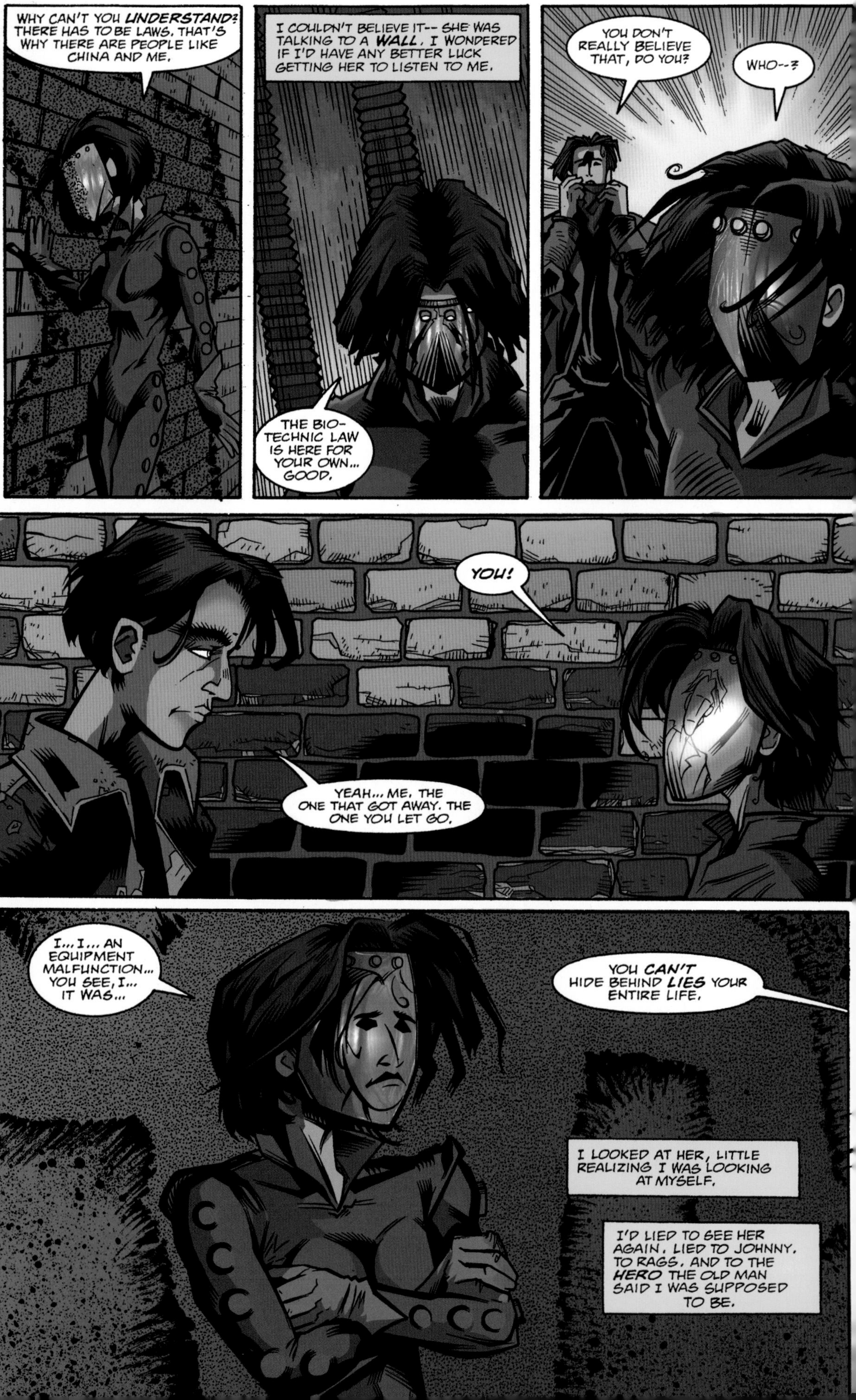
WHY CAN'T YOU UNDERSTAND? THERE HAS TO BE LAWS. THAT'S WHY THERE ARE PEOPLE LIKE CHINA AND ME.
I COULDN'T BELIEVE IT-- SHE WAS TALKING TO A WALL. I WONDERED IF I'D HAVE ANY BETTER LUCK GETTING HER TO LISTEN TO ME.
THE BIO-TECHNIC LAW IS HERE FOR YOUR OWN... GOOD.
YOU DON'T REALLY BELIEVE THAT, DO YOU?
WHO--?
YOU!
YEAH... ME. THE ONE THAT GOT AWAY. THE ONE YOU LET GO.
I... I... AN EQUIPMENT MALFUNCTION... YOU SEE, I... IT WAS...
YOU CAN'T HIDE BEHIND LIES YOUR ENTIRE LIFE.
I LOOKED AT HER, LITTLE REALIZING I WAS LOOKING AT MYSELF.
I'D LIED TO SEE HER AGAIN. LIED TO JOHNNY. TO RAGS. AND TO THE HERO THE OLD MAN SAID I WAS SUPPOSED TO BE.

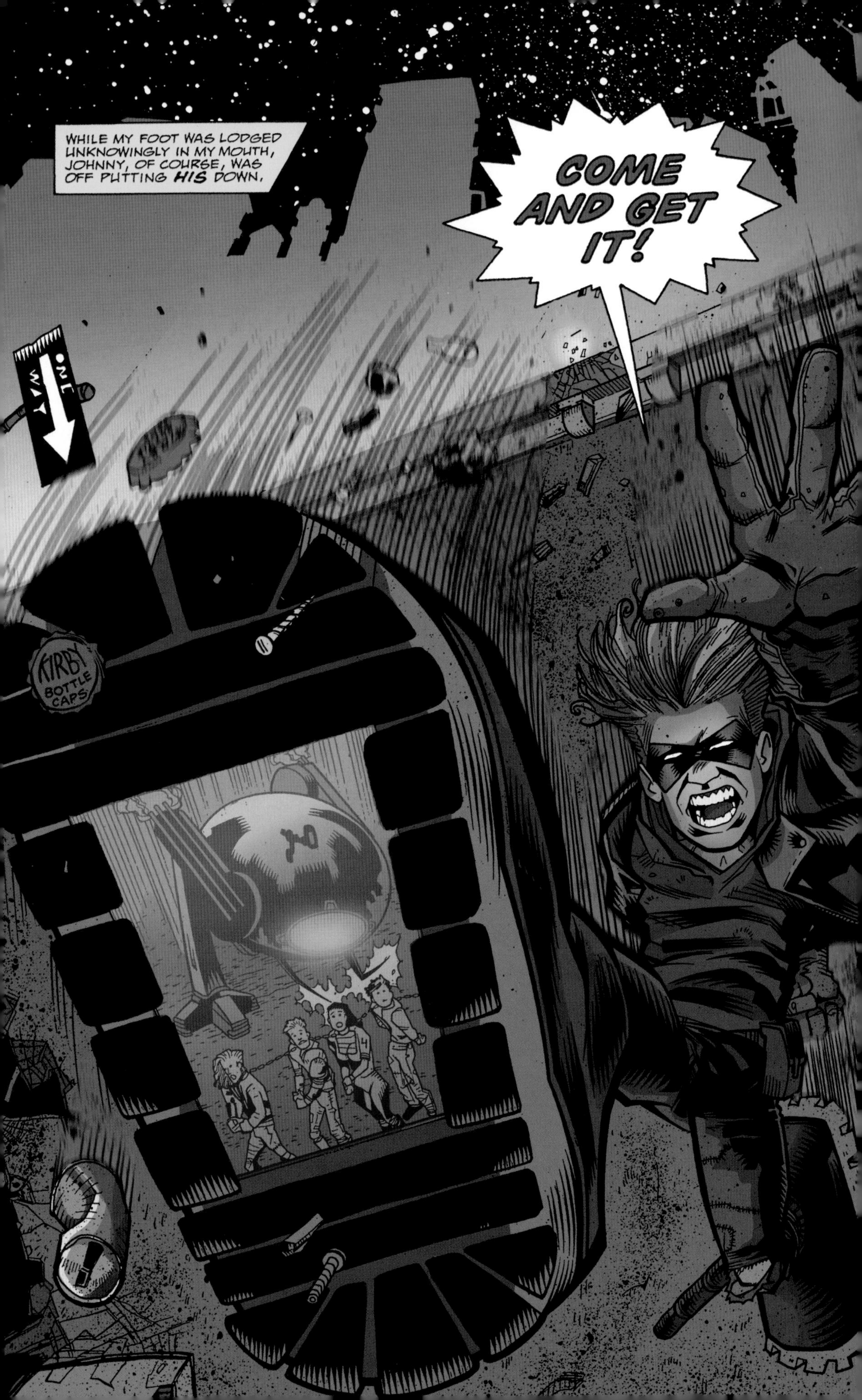
WHILE MY FOOT WAS LODGED UNKNOWINGLY IN MY MOUTH, JOHNNY, OF COURSE, WAS OFF PUTTING HIS DOWN.
COME AND GET IT!
ONE WAY
KIRBY BOTTLE CAPS

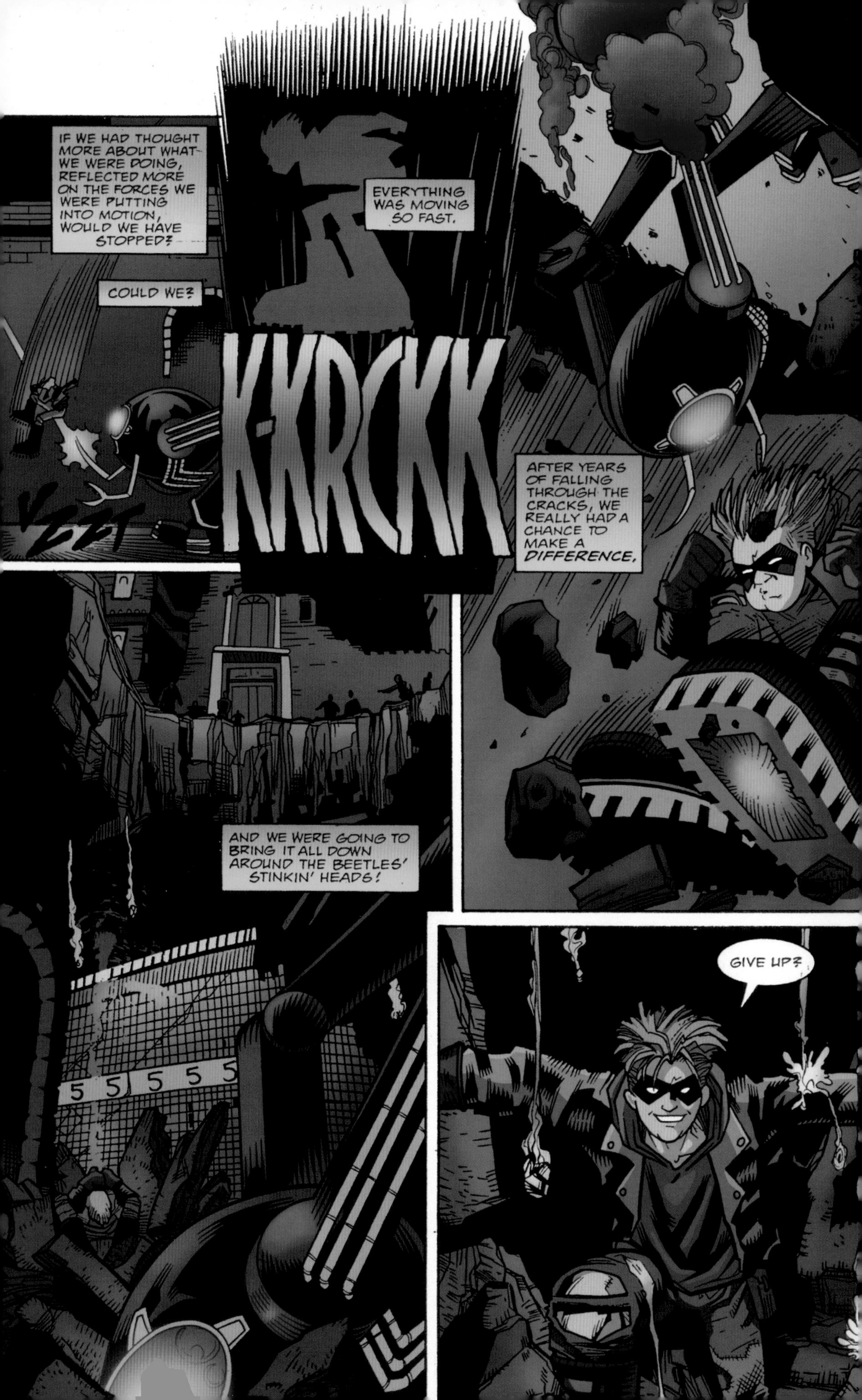

IF WE HAD THOUGHT MORE ABOUT WHAT WE WERE DOING, REFLECTED MORE ON THE FORCES WE WERE PUTTING INTO MOTION, WOULD WE HAVE STOPPED?
COULD WE?
VEET
EVERYTHING WAS MOVING SO FAST.
K-KRCKK
AFTER YEARS OF FALLING THROUGH THE CRACKS, WE REALLY HAD A CHANCE TO MAKE A *DIFFERENCE.*
AND WE WERE GOING TO BRING IT ALL DOWN AROUND THE BEETLES' STINKIN' HEADS!
55555
GIVE UP?

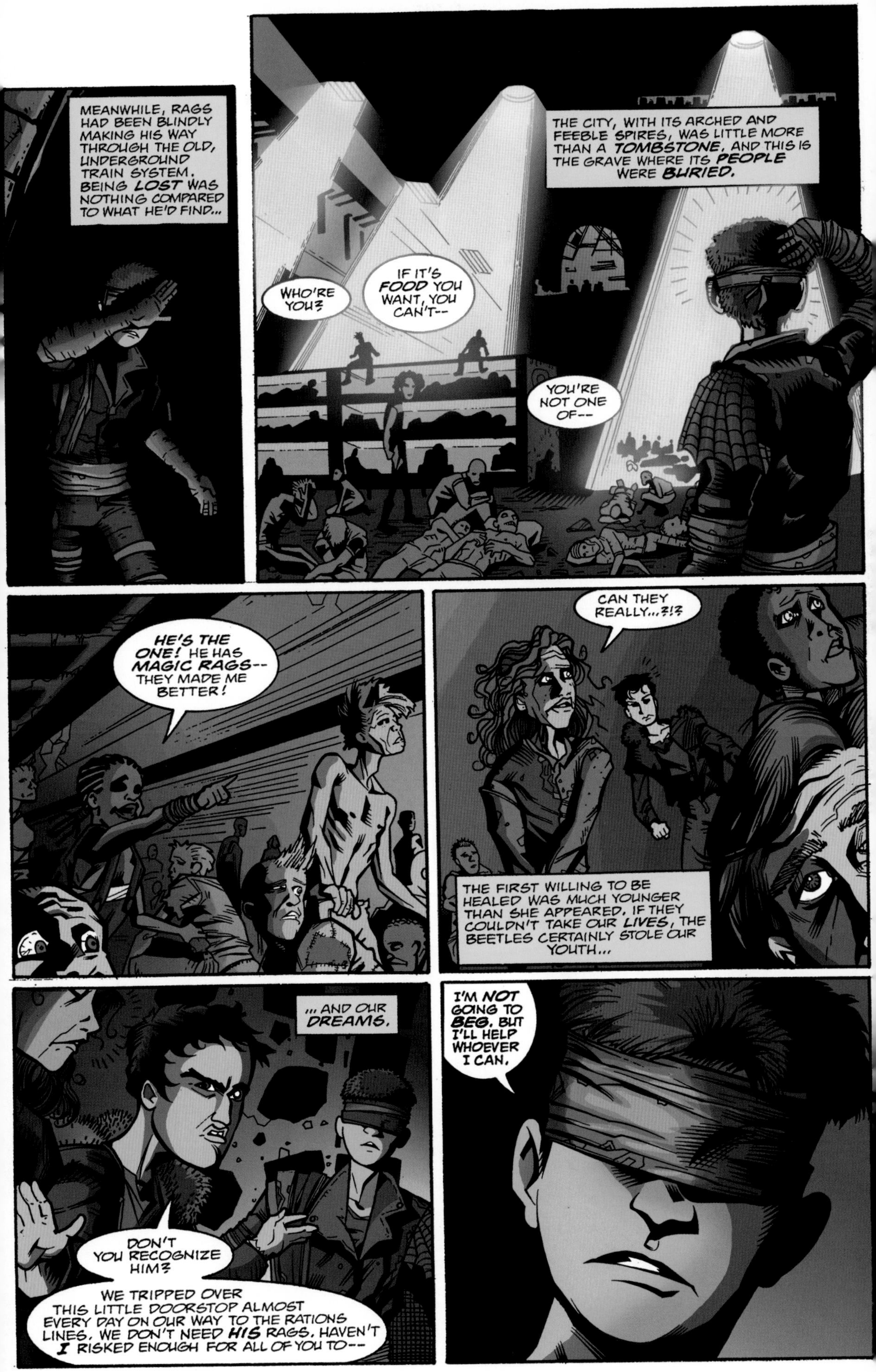
MEANWHILE, RAGS HAD BEEN BLINDLY MAKING HIS WAY THROUGH THE OLD, UNDERGROUND TRAIN SYSTEM. BEING LOST WAS NOTHING COMPARED TO WHAT HE'D FIND...
THE CITY, WITH ITS ARCHED AND FEEBLE SPIRES, WAS LITTLE MORE THAN A TOMBSTONE, AND THIS IS THE GRAVE WHERE ITS PEOPLE WERE BURIED.
WHO'RE YOU?
IF IT'S FOOD YOU WANT, YOU CAN'T--
YOU'RE NOT ONE OF--
HE'S THE ONE! HE HAS MAGIC RAGS-- THEY MADE ME BETTER!
CAN THEY REALLY...?!?
THE FIRST WILLING TO BE HEALED WAS MUCH YOUNGER THAN SHE APPEARED. IF THEY COULDN'T TAKE OUR LIVES, THE BEETLES CERTAINLY STOLE OUR YOUTH...
...AND OUR DREAMS.
DON'T YOU RECOGNIZE HIM?
WE TRIPPED OVER THIS LITTLE DOORSTOP ALMOST EVERY DAY ON OUR WAY TO THE RATIONS LINES. WE DON'T NEED HIS RAGS. HAVEN'T I RISKED ENOUGH FOR ALL OF YOU TO--
I'M NOT GOING TO BEG. BUT I'LL HELP WHOEVER I CAN.

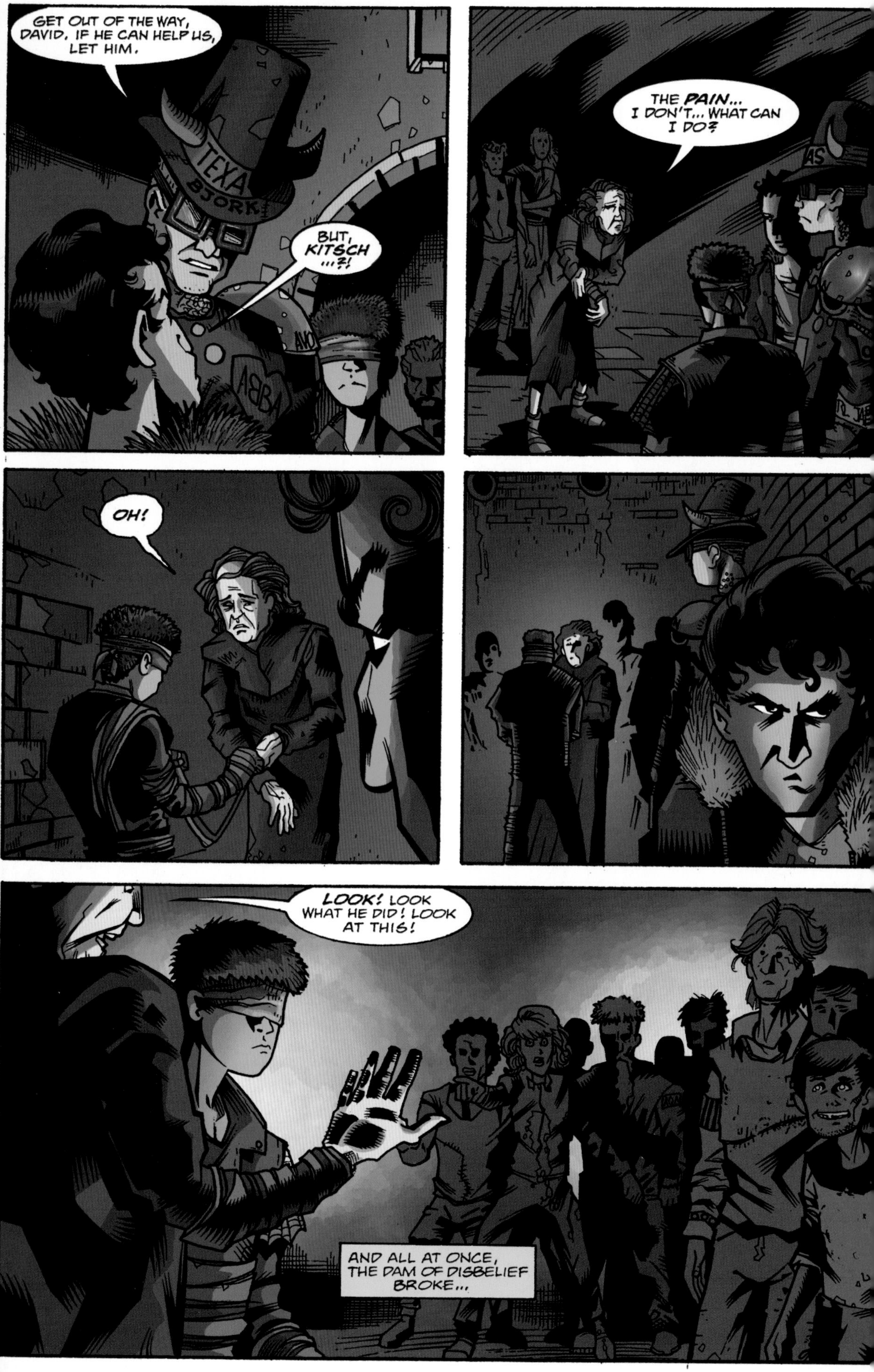
GET OUT OF THE WAY, DAVID. IF HE CAN HELP US, LET HIM.
BUT, KITSCH ...?!
TEXA
BJORK
ABBA
THE PAIN... I DON'T... WHAT CAN I DO?
OH!
LOOK! LOOK WHAT HE DID! LOOK AT THIS!
AND ALL AT ONCE, THE DAM OF DISBELIEF BROKE...

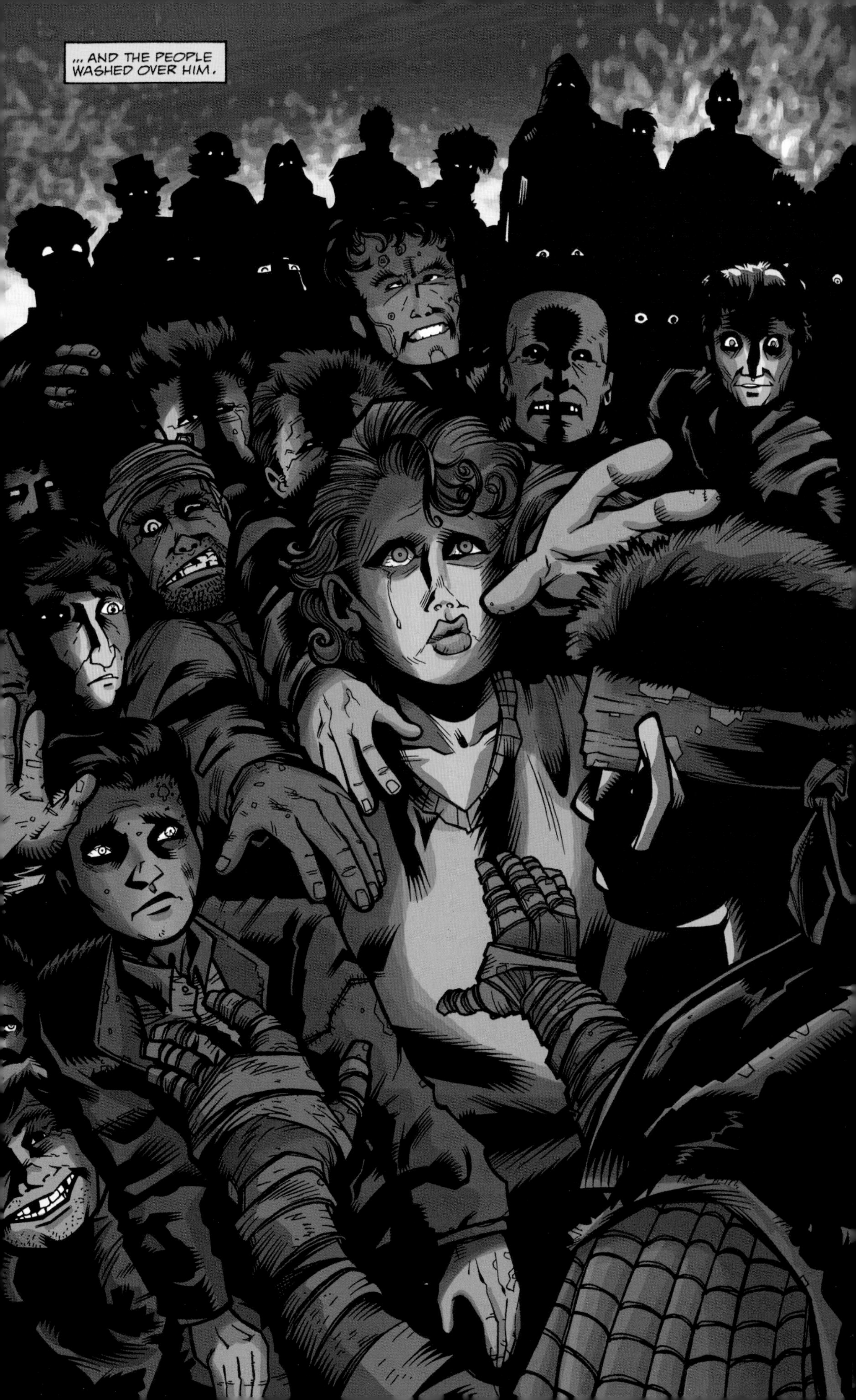
... AND THE PEOPLE WASHED OVER HIM.

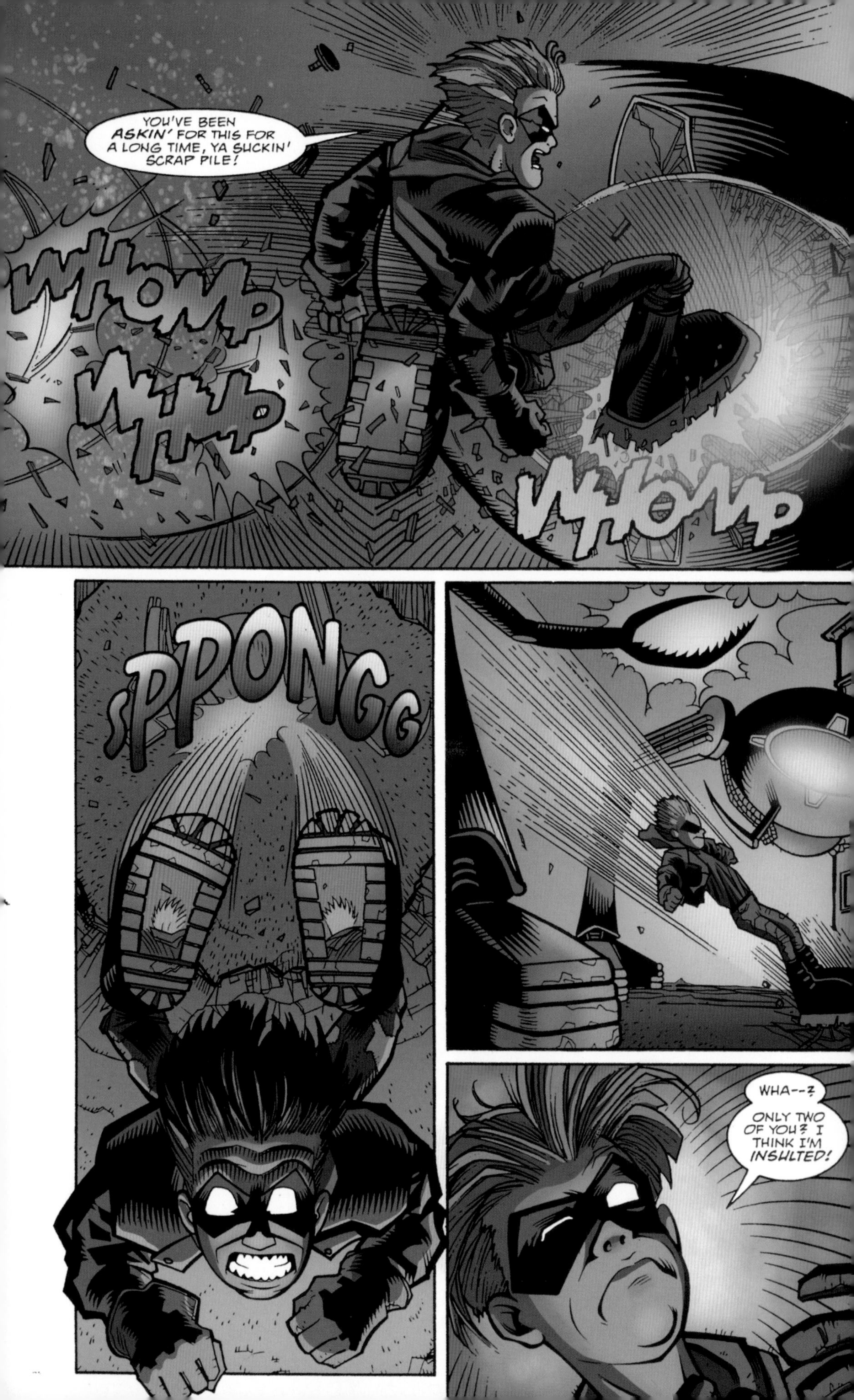
YOU'VE BEEN ASKIN' FOR THIS FOR A LONG TIME, YA SUCKIN' SCRAP PILE!
WHOMP
WHUMP
WHOMP
SPPONGG
WHA--?
ONLY TWO OF YOU? I THINK I'M INSULTED!

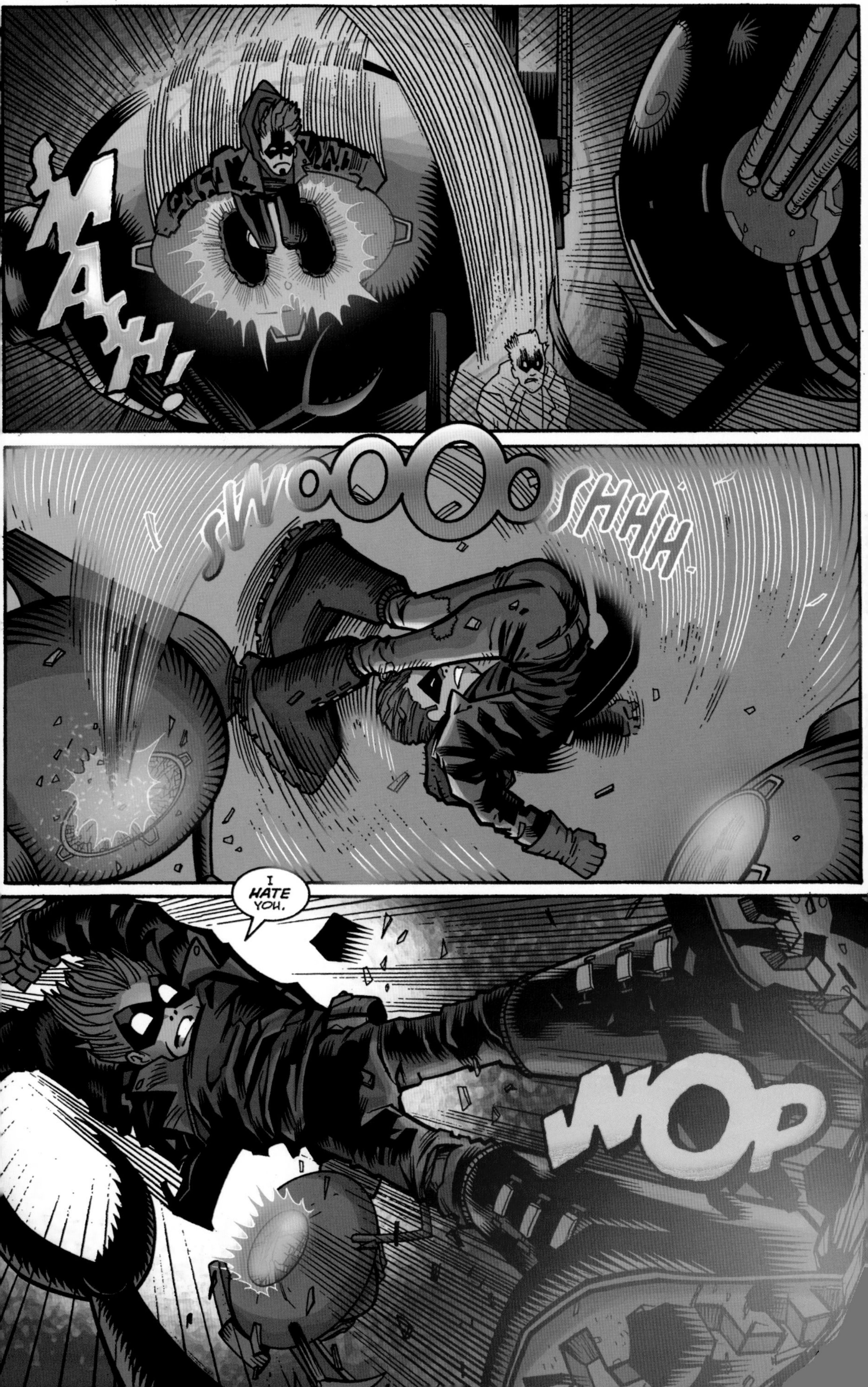
WAH!
SWOOOOSHHH
I HATE YOU.
WOP

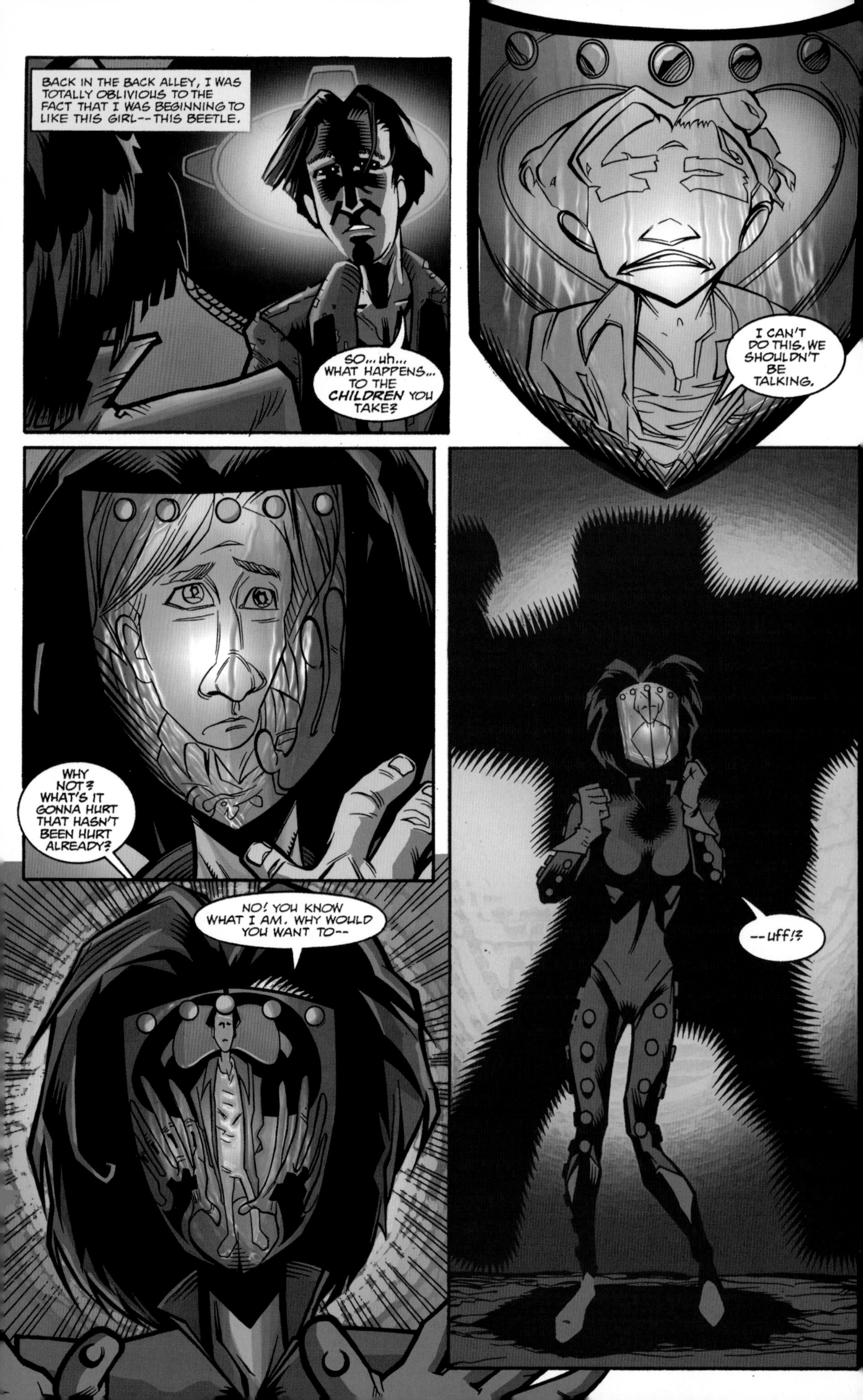
BACK IN THE BACK ALLEY, I WAS TOTALLY OBLIVIOUS TO THE FACT THAT I WAS BEGINNING TO LIKE THIS GIRL--THIS BEETLE.
SO...uh... WHAT HAPPENS... TO THE CHILDREN YOU TAKE?
I CAN'T DO THIS. WE SHOULDN'T BE TALKING.
WHY NOT? WHAT'S IT GONNA HURT THAT HASN'T BEEN HURT ALREADY?
NO! YOU KNOW WHAT I AM. WHY WOULD YOU WANT TO--
--uff!?

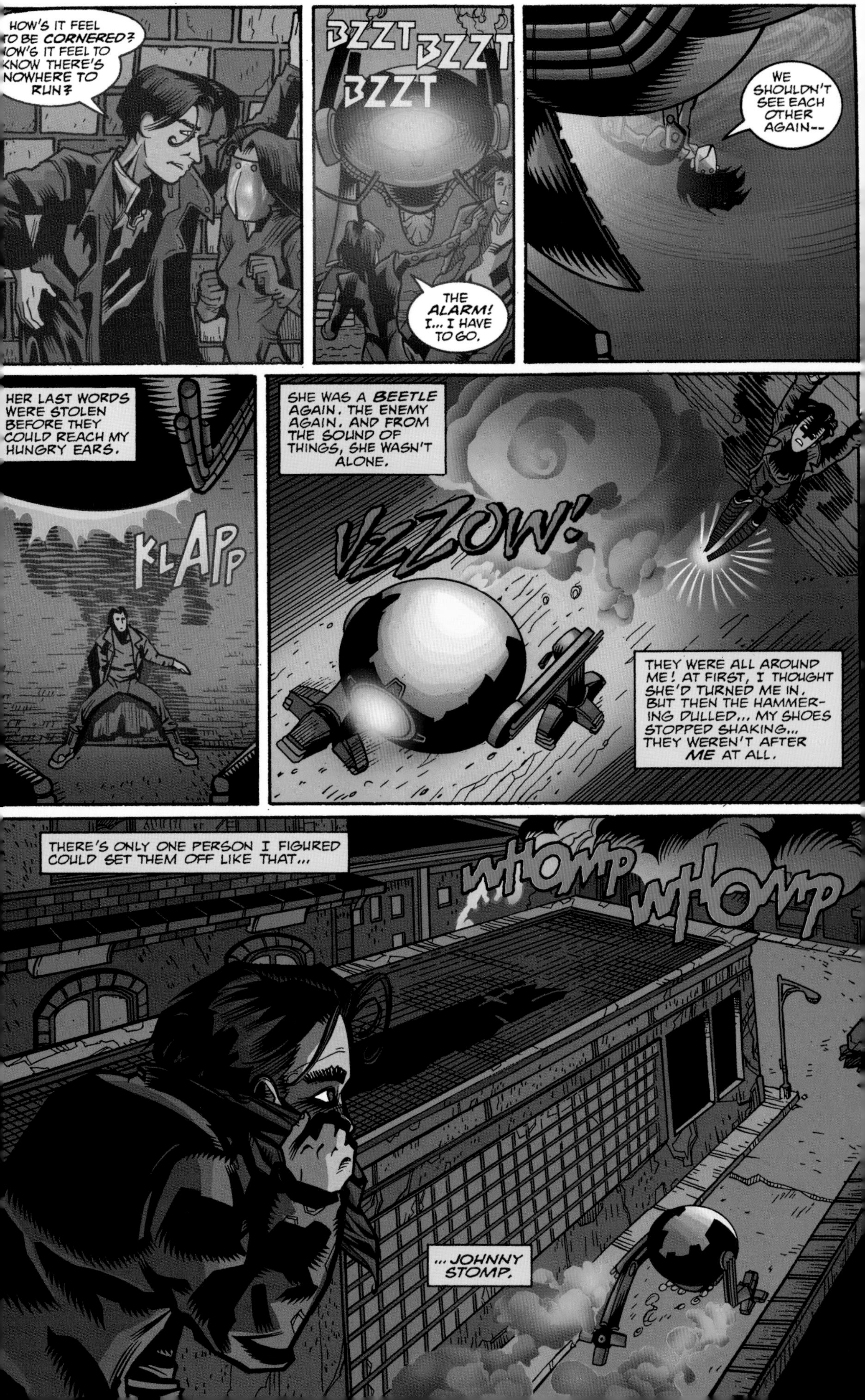
HOW'S IT FEEL TO BE CORNERED? HOW'S IT FEEL TO KNOW THERE'S NOWHERE TO RUN?
BZZT BZZT BZZT
THE ALARM! I... I HAVE TO GO.
WE SHOULDN'T SEE EACH OTHER AGAIN--
HER LAST WORDS WERE STOLEN BEFORE THEY COULD REACH MY HUNGRY EARS.
KLAPP
SHE WAS A BEETLE AGAIN. THE ENEMY AGAIN. AND FROM THE SOUND OF THINGS, SHE WASN'T ALONE.
VEZOW!
THEY WERE ALL AROUND ME! AT FIRST, I THOUGHT SHE'D TURNED ME IN. BUT THEN THE HAMMERING DULLED... MY SHOES STOPPED SHAKING... THEY WEREN'T AFTER ME AT ALL.
THERE'S ONLY ONE PERSON I FIGURED COULD SET THEM OFF LIKE THAT...
WHOMP WHOMP
...JOHNNY STOMP.

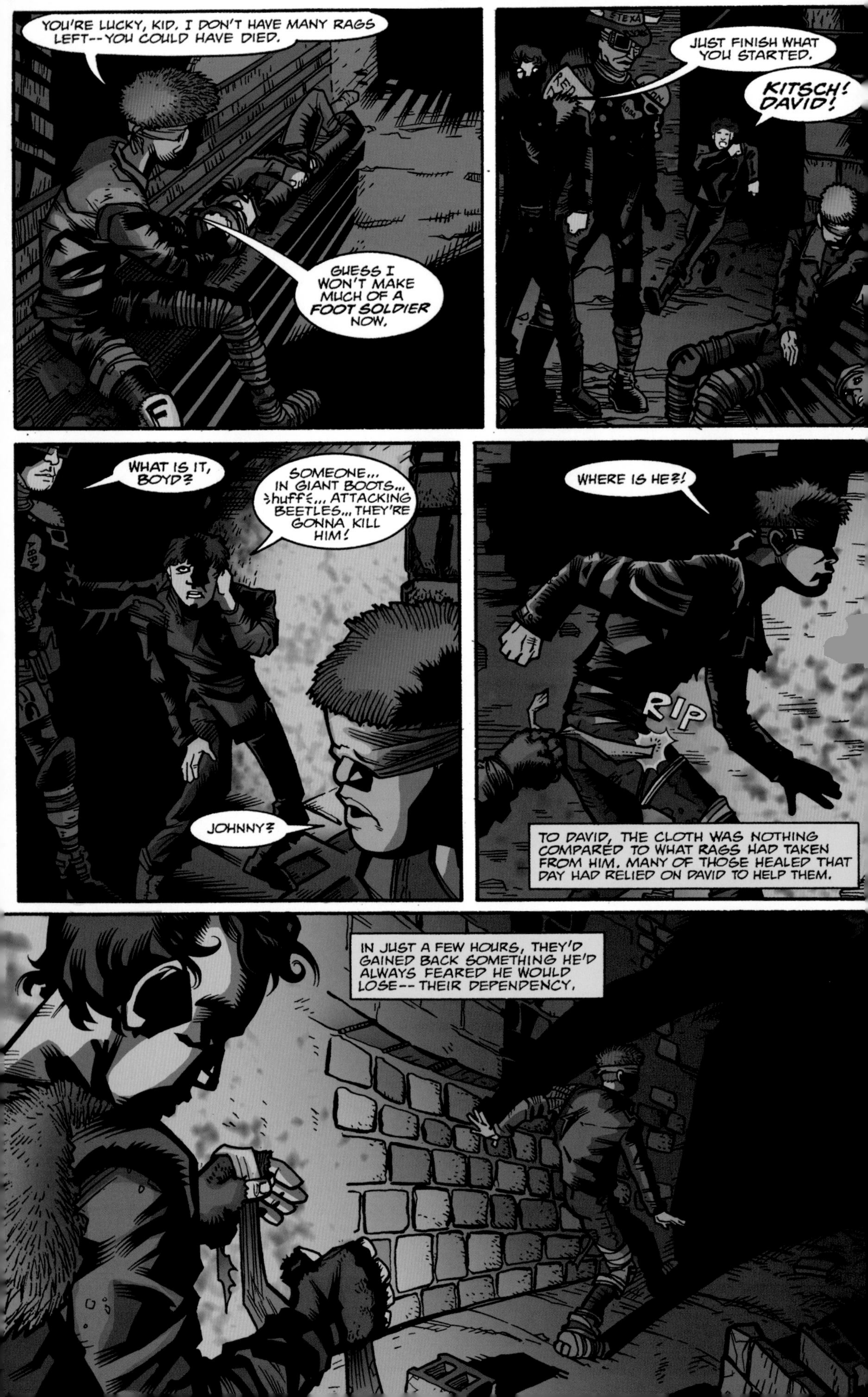
YOU'RE LUCKY, KID. I DON'T HAVE MANY RAGS LEFT--YOU COULD HAVE DIED.
GUESS I WON'T MAKE MUCH OF A FOOT SOLDIER NOW.
JUST FINISH WHAT YOU STARTED.
KITSCH! DAVID!
WHAT IS IT, BOYD?
SOMEONE... IN GIANT BOOTS... huff... ATTACKING BEETLES... THEY'RE GONNA KILL HIM!
JOHNNY?
WHERE IS HE?!
RIP
TO DAVID, THE CLOTH WAS NOTHING COMPARED TO WHAT RAGS HAD TAKEN FROM HIM. MANY OF THOSE HEALED THAT DAY HAD RELIED ON DAVID TO HELP THEM.
IN JUST A FEW HOURS, THEY'D GAINED BACK SOMETHING HE'D ALWAYS FEARED HE WOULD LOSE-- THEIR DEPENDENCY.

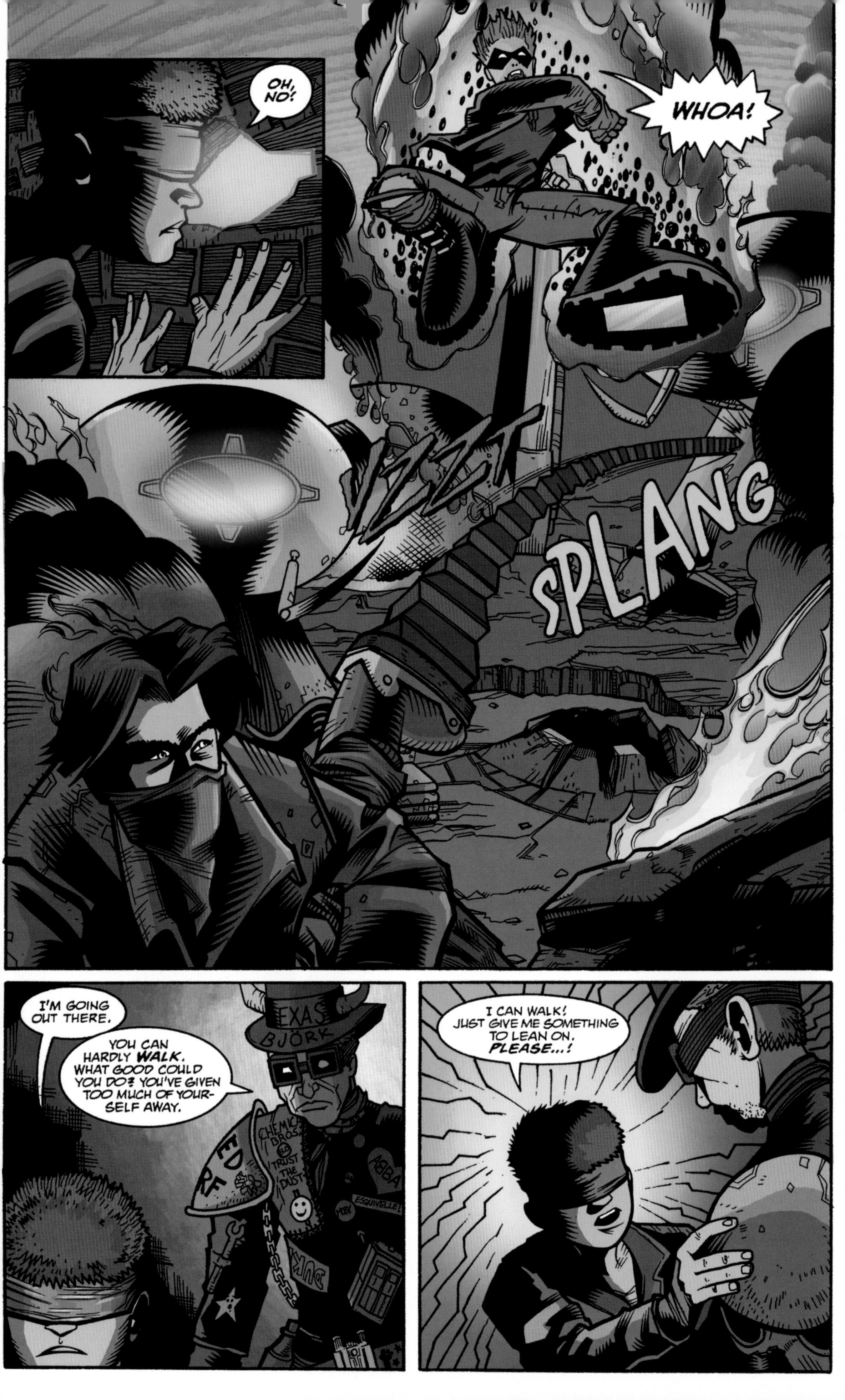
OH, NO!
WHOA!
SPLANG
I'M GOING OUT THERE.
YOU CAN HARDLY WALK. WHAT GOOD COULD YOU DO? YOU'VE GIVEN TOO MUCH OF YOURSELF AWAY.
BJÖRK
ABBA
TRUST THE DUST
I CAN WALK! JUST GIVE ME SOMETHING TO LEAN ON. PLEASE...!

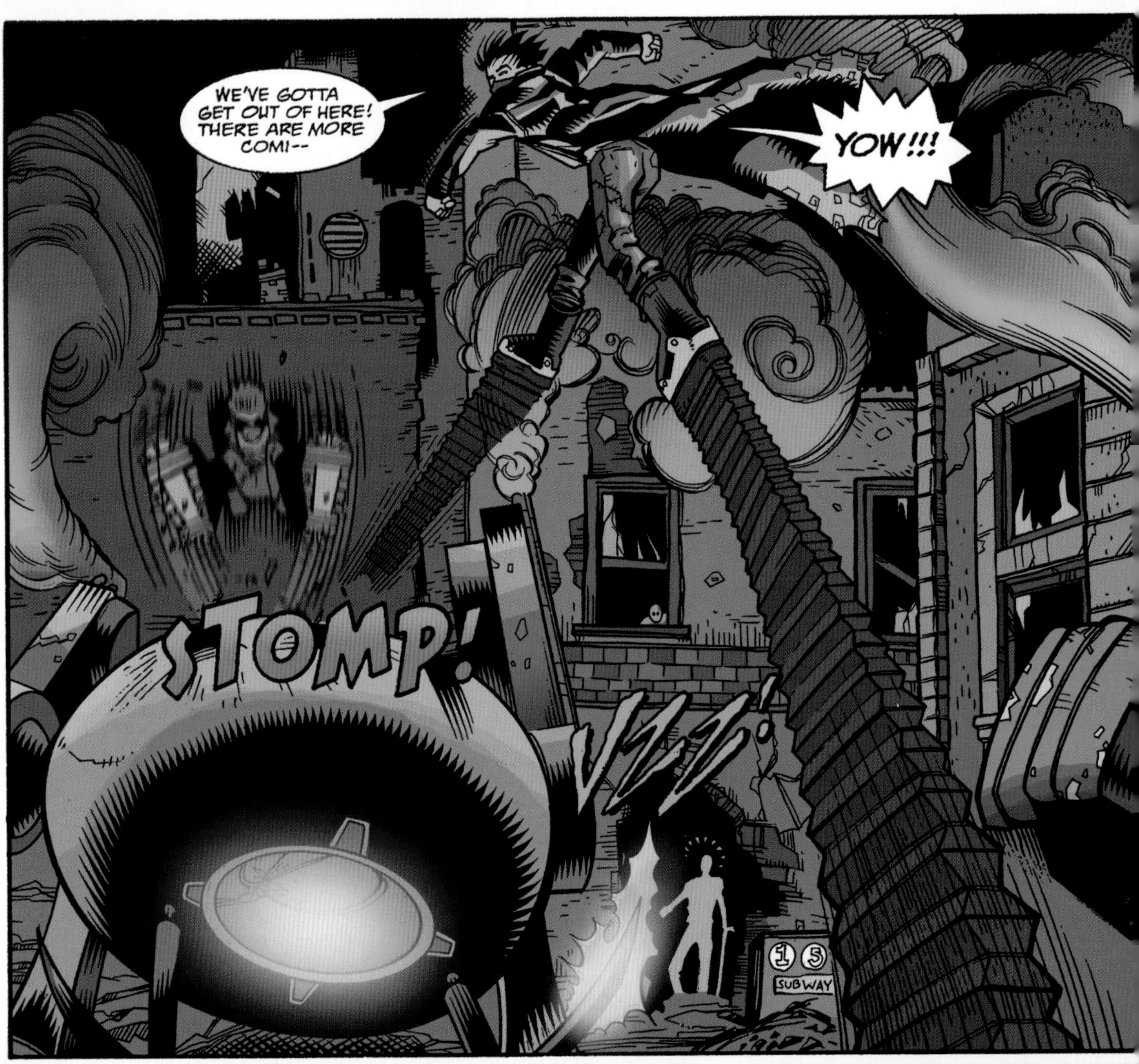
WE'VE GOTTA GET OUT OF HERE! THERE ARE MORE COMI--
YOW!!!
STOMP!
VZZ!
15
SUBWAY

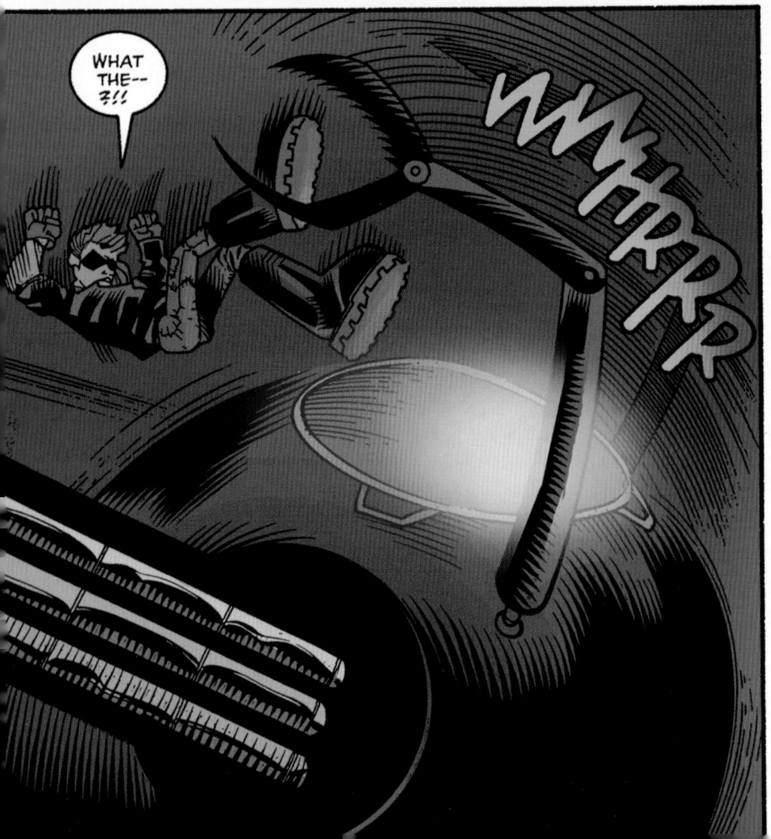
WHAT THE-- ?!!
WWHIRRR

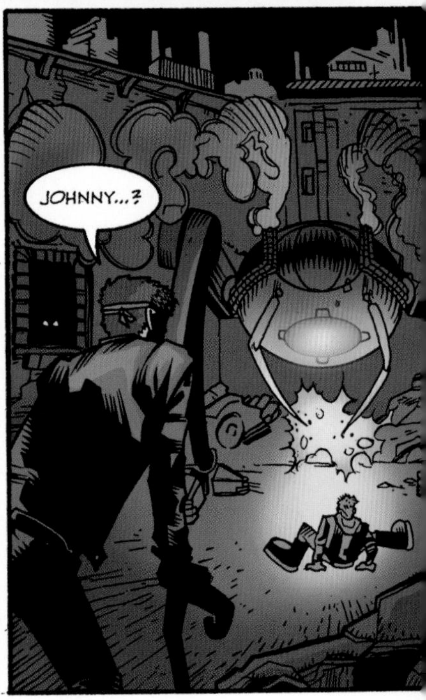
JOHNNY...?

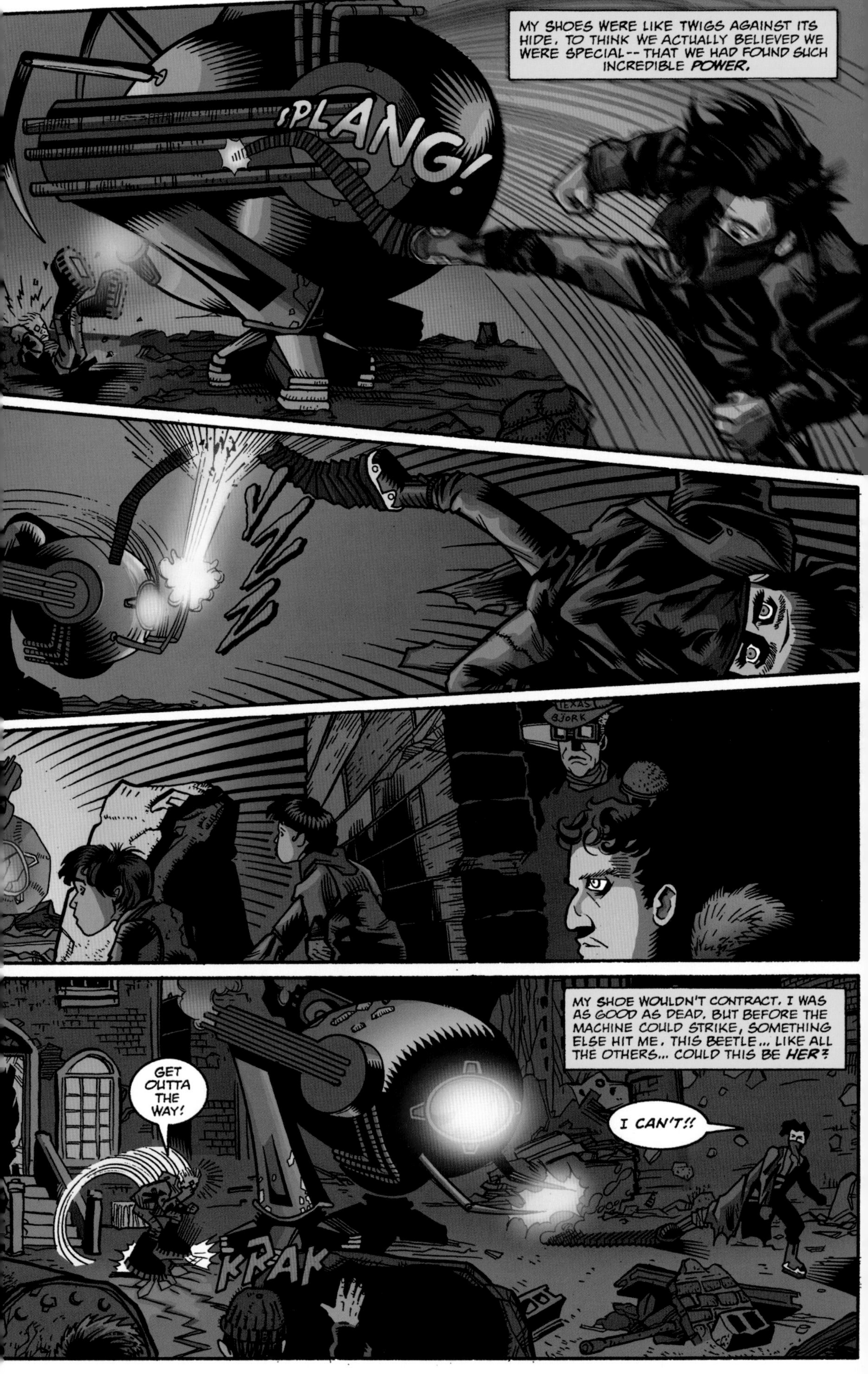
MY SHOES WERE LIKE TWIGS AGAINST ITS HIDE. TO THINK WE ACTUALLY BELIEVED WE WERE SPECIAL-- THAT WE HAD FOUND SUCH INCREDIBLE POWER.
SPLANG!
VMMM
TEXAS
BJORK
MY SHOE WOULDN'T CONTRACT. I WAS AS GOOD AS DEAD. BUT BEFORE THE MACHINE COULD STRIKE, SOMETHING ELSE HIT ME. THIS BEETLE... LIKE ALL THE OTHERS... COULD THIS BE HER?
GET OUTTA THE WAY!
I CAN'T!!
KRAK

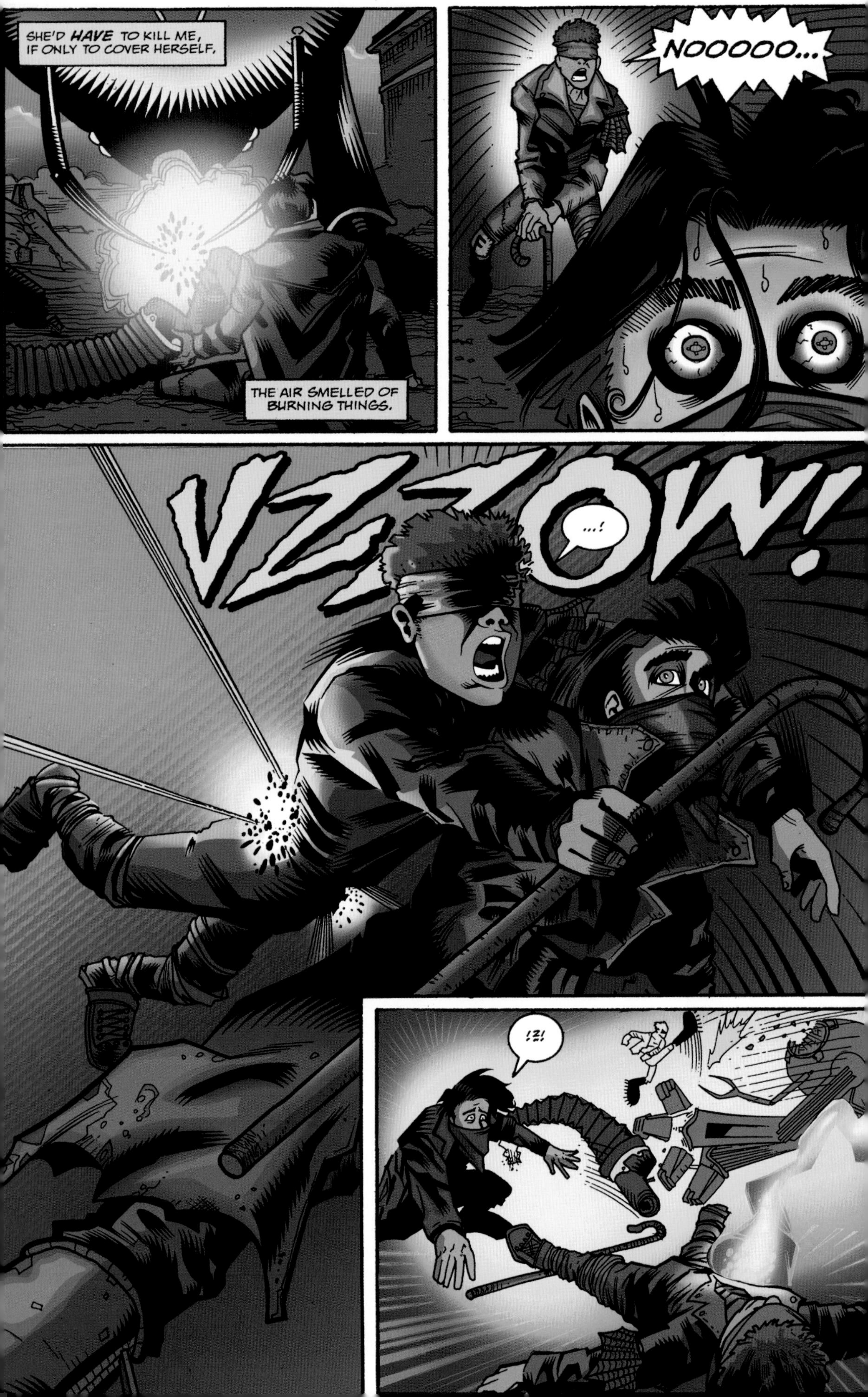
SHE'D **HAVE** TO KILL ME, IF ONLY TO COVER HERSELF.
THE AIR SMELLED OF BURNING THINGS.
NOOOOO...
VZZOW!
...!
!?!

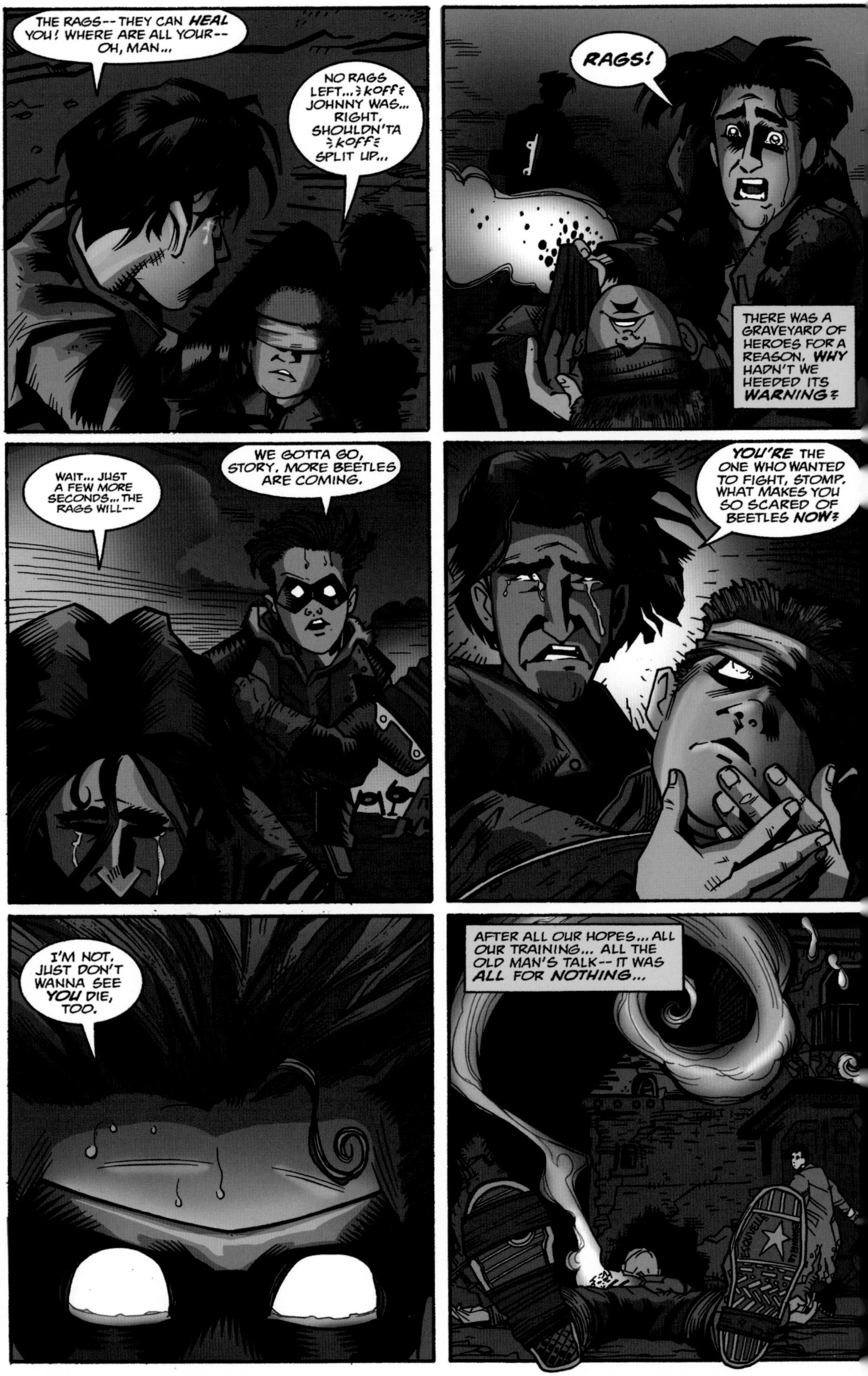
THE RAGS-- THEY CAN HEAL YOU! WHERE ARE ALL YOUR-- OH, MAN...
NO RAGS LEFT... koff JOHNNY WAS... RIGHT. SHOULDN'TA koff SPLIT UP...
RAGS!
THERE WAS A GRAVEYARD OF HEROES FOR A REASON. WHY HADN'T WE HEEDED ITS WARNING?
WAIT... JUST A FEW MORE SECONDS... THE RAGS WILL--
WE GOTTA GO, STORY. MORE BEETLES ARE COMING.
YOU'RE THE ONE WHO WANTED TO FIGHT, STOMP. WHAT MAKES YOU SO SCARED OF BEETLES NOW?
I'M NOT. JUST DON'T WANNA SEE YOU DIE, TOO.
AFTER ALL OUR HOPES... ALL OUR TRAINING... ALL THE OLD MAN'S TALK-- IT WAS ALL FOR NOTHING...

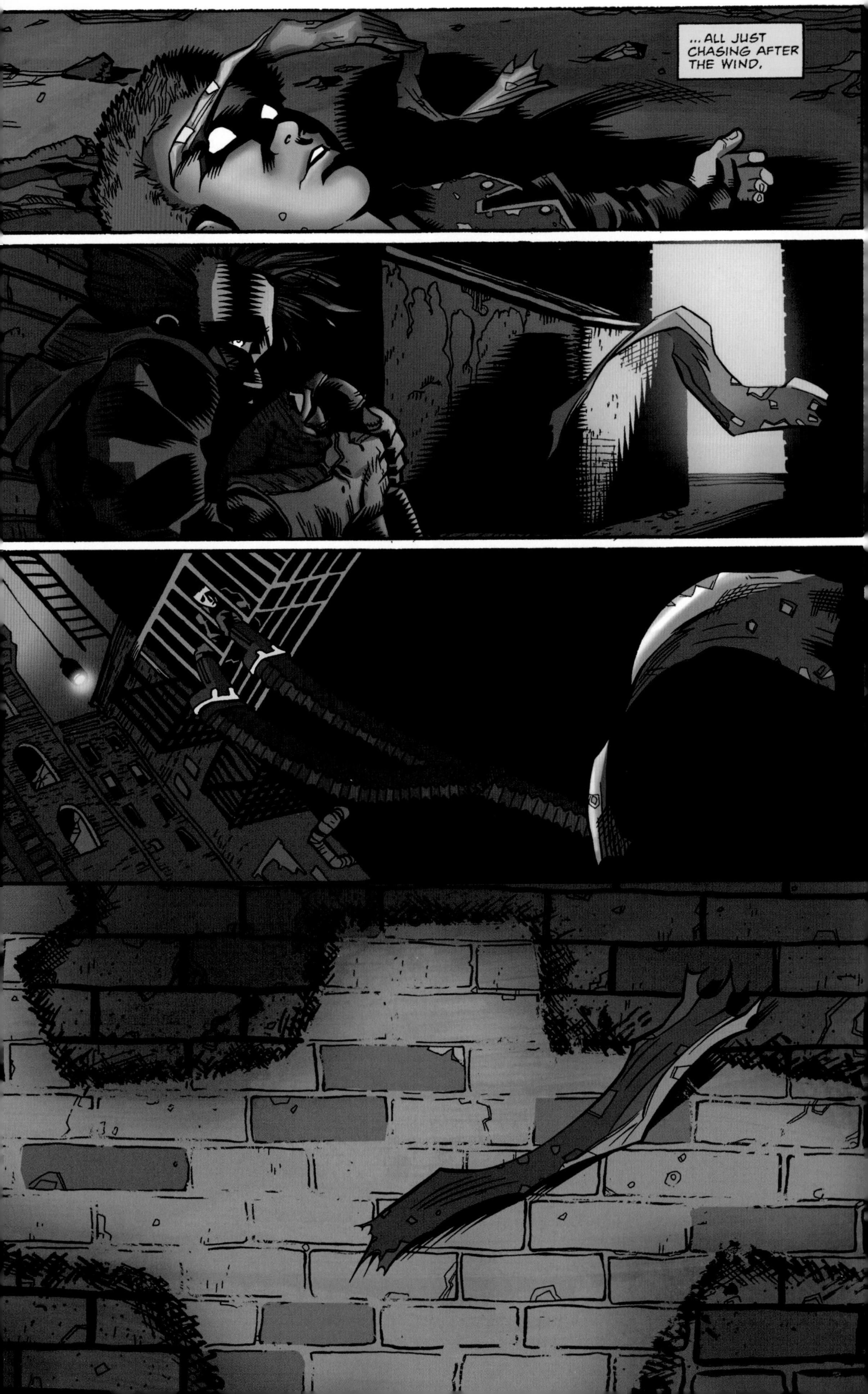
...ALL JUST CHASING AFTER THE WIND.

Story's Story

Chapter Two

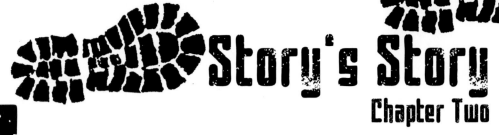

Rags was dead and we were next. Somehow, when I put these boots on it felt as if I could not or would not die. That somehow, because I was chosen and because of this power, I… we were impervious to harm.

Of course the truth was that the power we found did nothing but remove us from our safety zone. Well, maybe safety is the wrong word. But Rags wasn't a beggar anymore. He no longer depended on those around him, people who really had nothing to give, to take care of him.

I wasn't scamming on the streets for extra loaves from my usual suppliers. Or rescuing babies from Beetles for a chance to get a few extra ration tokens or a favor for me to call upon at some point in the future.

And Johnny wasn't, I don't know, spitting down on the B.T.L. from rusted fire escapes anymore.

Our old ways of doing things had lost their reason. Everything had changed, whether we had the boots on or not. The power changed us. Being told we were special changed us. We put these boots on our feet – but it was our eyes that changed along with them. Our minds and spirits as well.

The Old Man marked the graves we were supposed to dig in. Why did he choose boots? Why did he choose such lame powers? I wanted the sword of the gods. Or the ability to rip the Beetles apart at a glance. Instead, all I got were automatic elevator shoes–the ability to

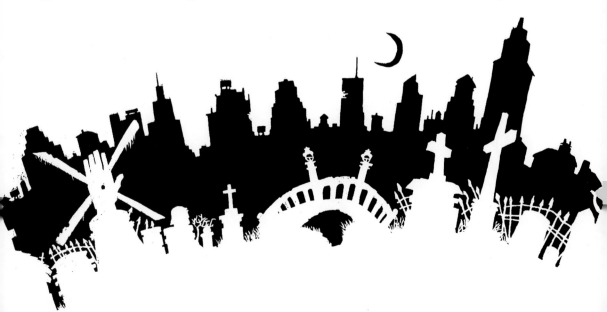

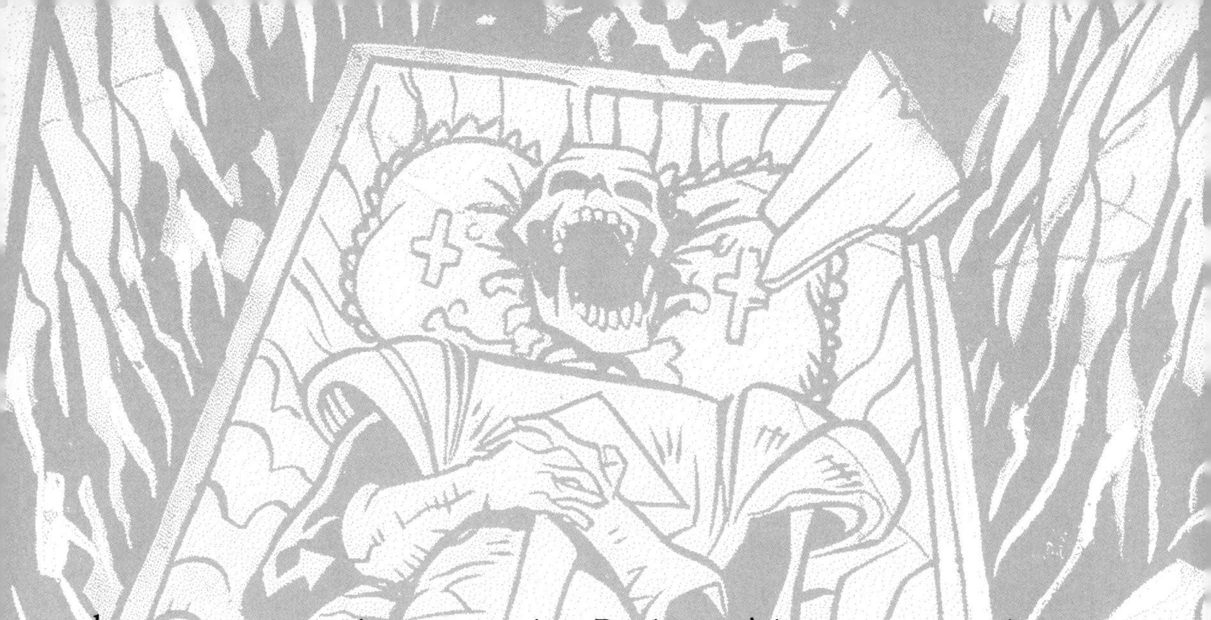

change my perspective at any point. But it wasn't just my perspective either. That's what I've been saying. We all changed.

How could someone like Rags, someone who had begged on the streets, dependent on someone else his entire life, suddenly throw himself in front of a Beetle's blast and die for me? It wasn't for his well-being. Or his best interest. So why did he do it?

He had given the bandages we had found in the crypt to a number of people. He had given his power away, so he didn't even have it when he became so heroic. Perhaps the only answer that makes any sense at is that once heroism is put on, unlike a pair of boots, it's difficult to take off.

When the Old Man chose Rags to be one of us, what did he see in a beggar who was lame and blind? Maybe he didn't see Rags at all. Maybe he saw what Rags had been begging for, crying out for. Maybe what Rags was asking for was to be someone else, to have a different life? And when he died, it was out of gratitude for those few days when his wish came true.

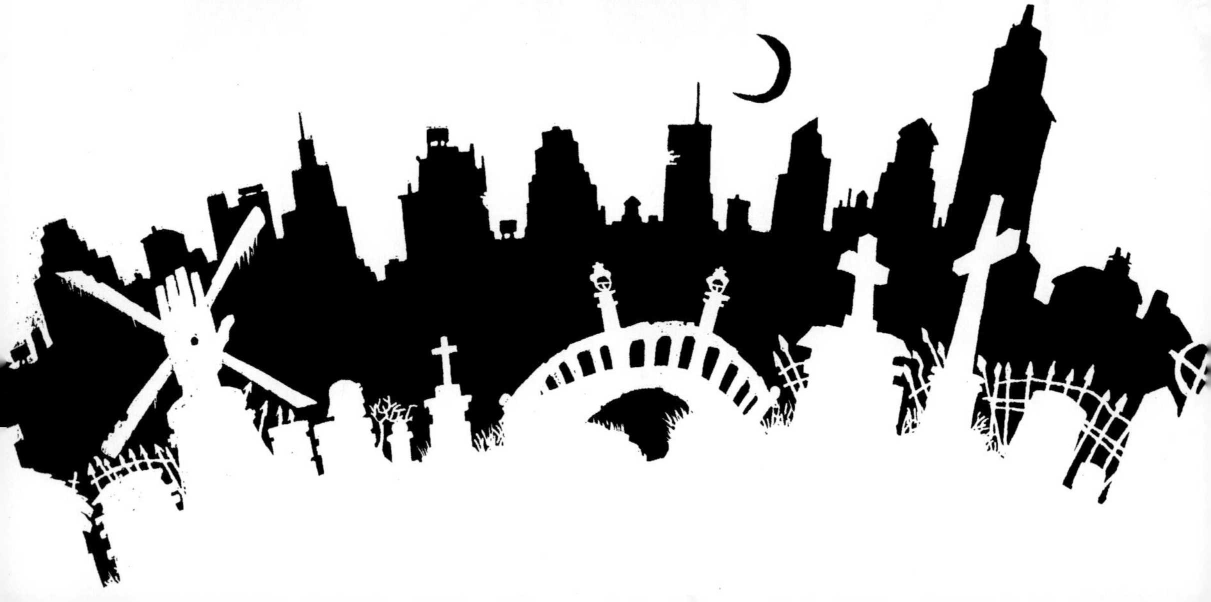

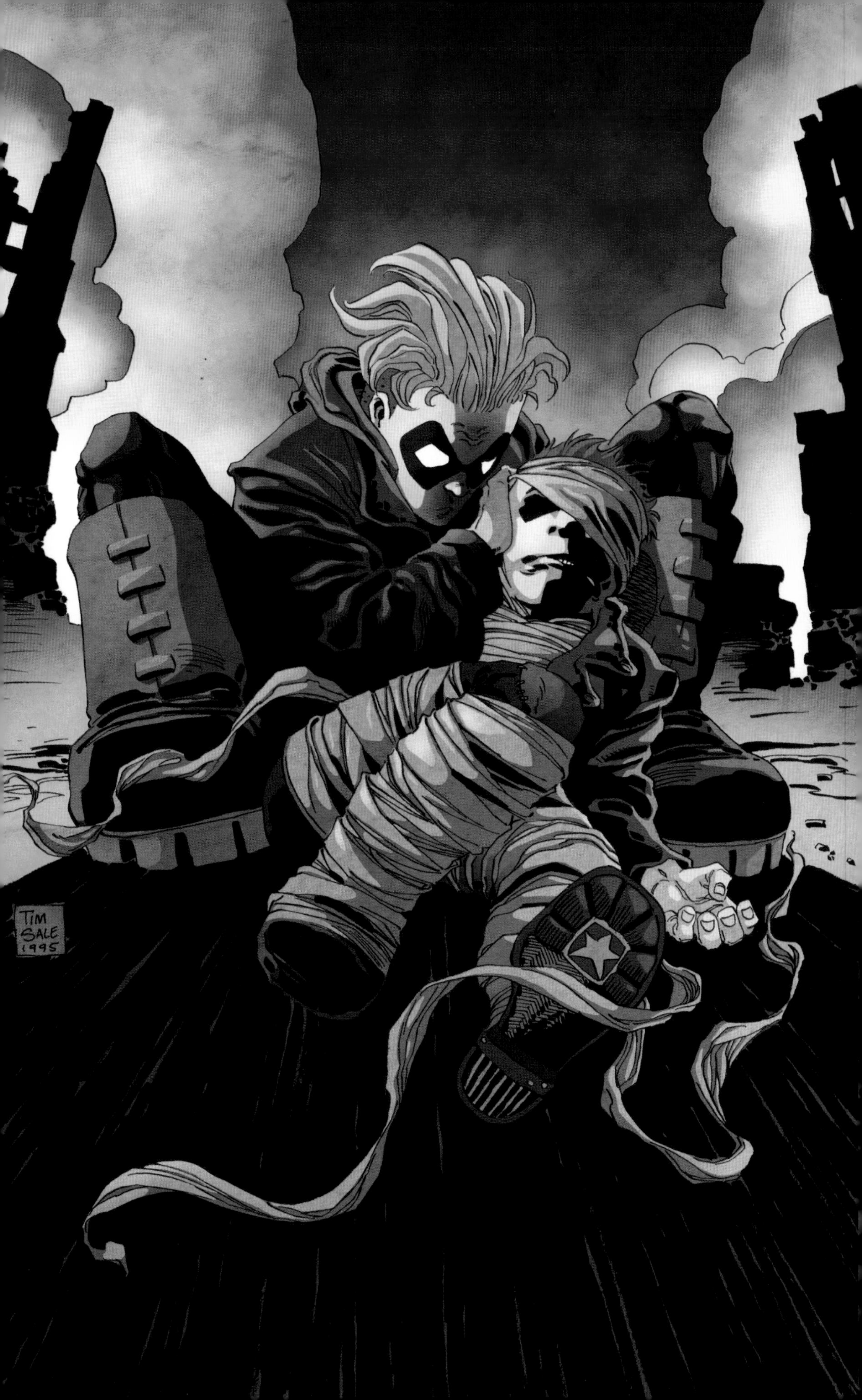
TIM SALE 1995

FiRST STEPS
CHAPTER THREE

"All I see is a beautiful Flower hiding behind an ugly wall," Story said to the girl in the mask. "And it's time for the walls to come down."

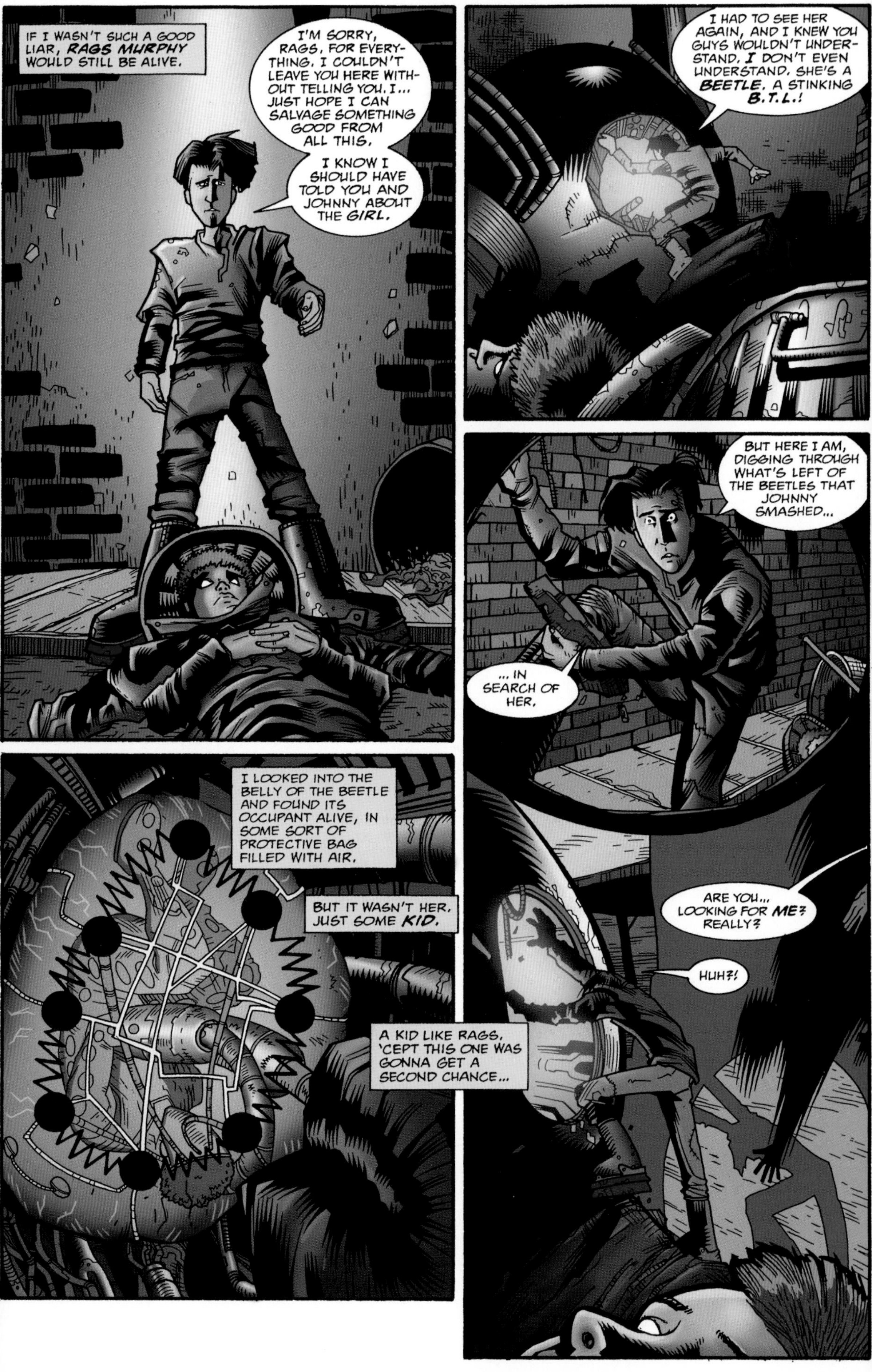

IF I WASN'T SUCH A GOOD LIAR, RAGS MURPHY WOULD STILL BE ALIVE.
I'M SORRY, RAGS, FOR EVERYTHING. I COULDN'T LEAVE YOU HERE WITHOUT TELLING YOU. I... JUST HOPE I CAN SALVAGE SOMETHING GOOD FROM ALL THIS.
I KNOW I SHOULD HAVE TOLD YOU AND JOHNNY ABOUT THE GIRL.
I HAD TO SEE HER AGAIN, AND I KNEW YOU GUYS WOULDN'T UNDERSTAND. I DON'T EVEN UNDERSTAND. SHE'S A BEETLE. A STINKING B.T.L.!
BUT HERE I AM, DIGGING THROUGH WHAT'S LEFT OF THE BEETLES THAT JOHNNY SMASHED...
...IN SEARCH OF HER.
I LOOKED INTO THE BELLY OF THE BEETLE AND FOUND ITS OCCUPANT ALIVE, IN SOME SORT OF PROTECTIVE BAG FILLED WITH AIR.
BUT IT WASN'T HER. JUST SOME KID.
A KID LIKE RAGS, 'CEPT THIS ONE WAS GONNA GET A SECOND CHANCE...
ARE YOU... LOOKING FOR ME? REALLY?
HUH?!

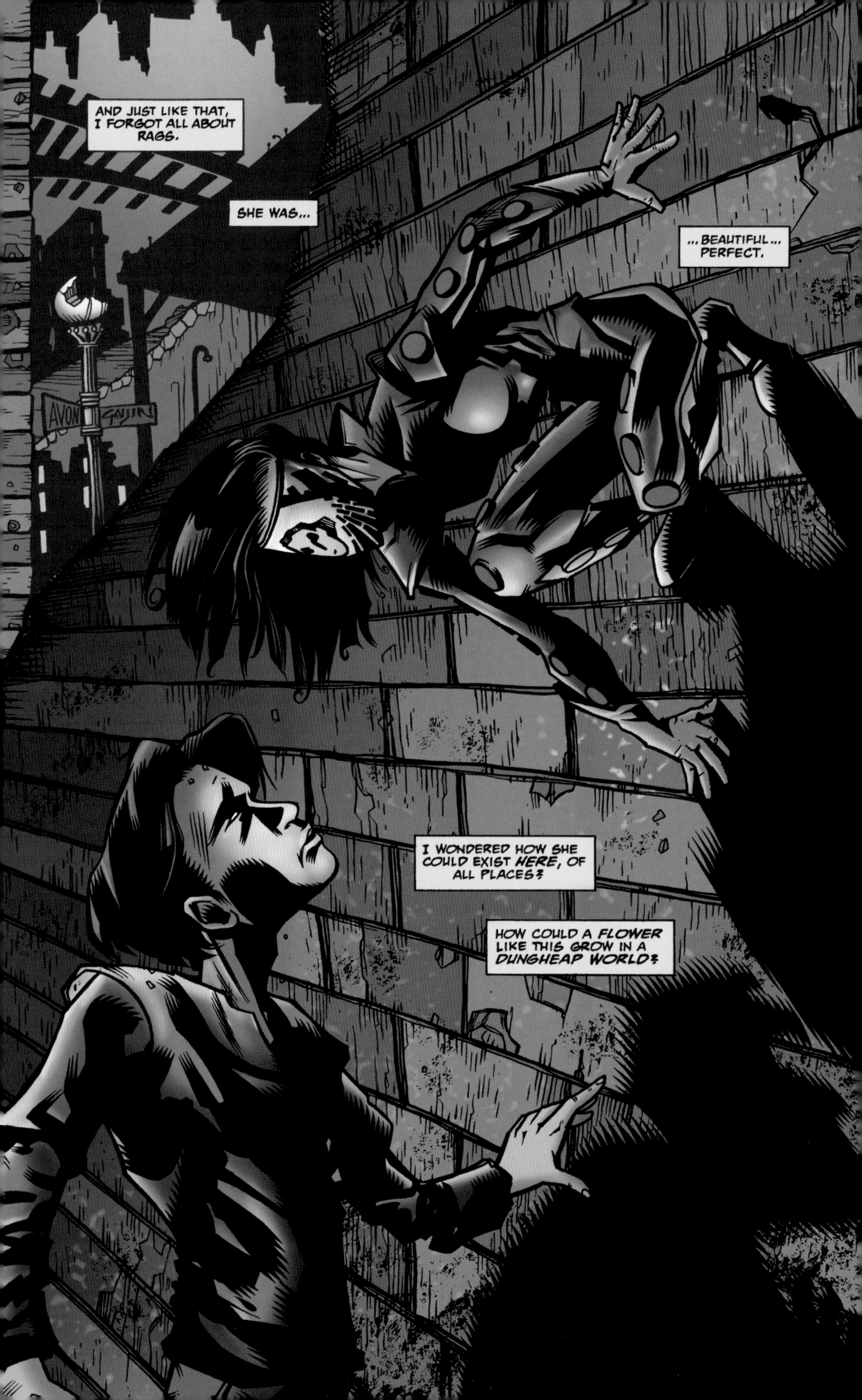

AND JUST LIKE THAT, I FORGOT ALL ABOUT RAGS.
SHE WAS...
...BEAUTIFUL... PERFECT.
AVON
I WONDERED HOW SHE COULD EXIST *HERE*, OF ALL PLACES?
HOW COULD A *FLOWER* LIKE THIS GROW IN A *DUNGHEAP WORLD*?

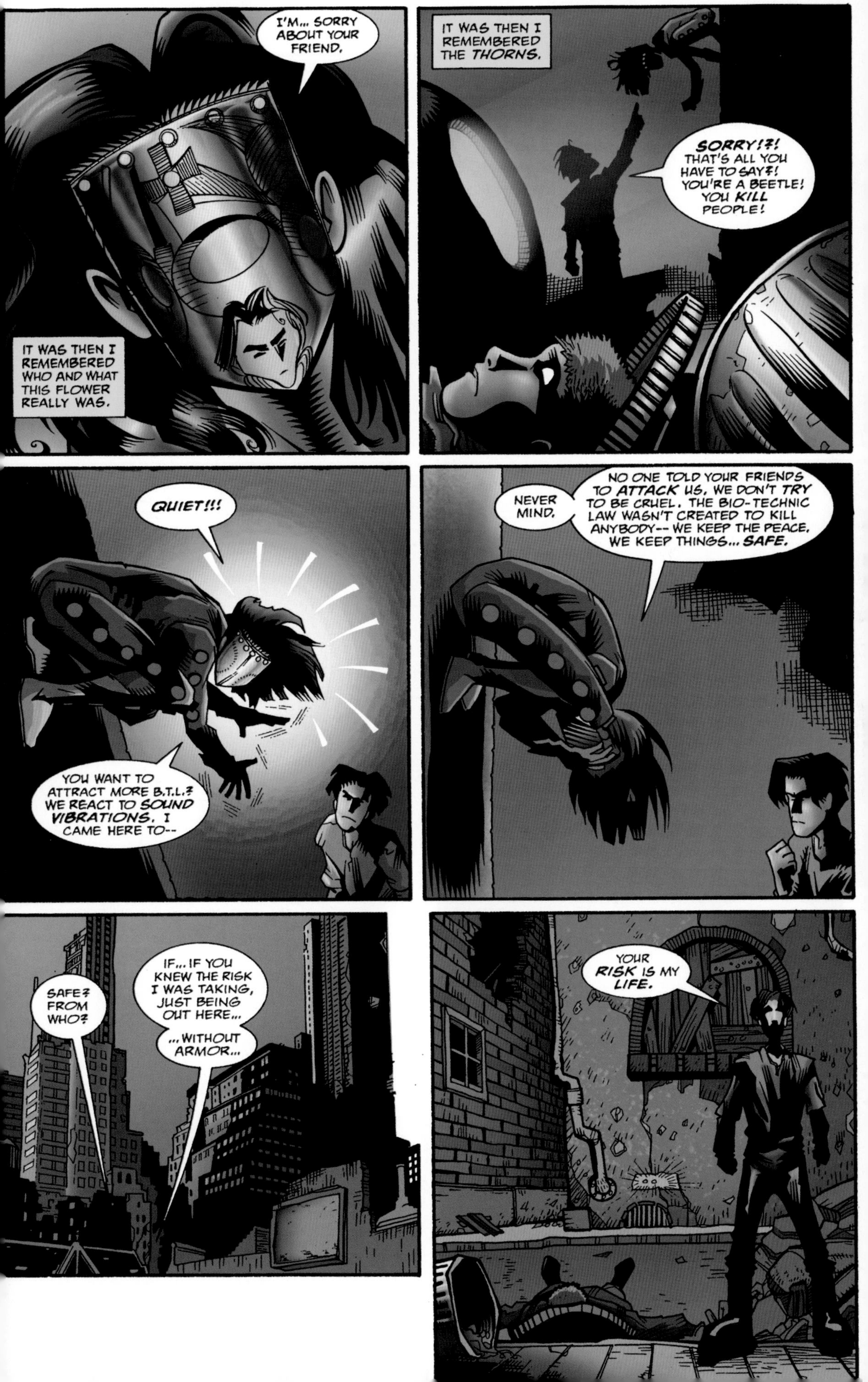
I'M... SORRY ABOUT YOUR FRIEND.
IT WAS THEN I REMEMBERED WHO AND WHAT THIS FLOWER REALLY WAS.
IT WAS THEN I REMEMBERED THE THORNS.
SORRY!?! THAT'S ALL YOU HAVE TO SAY?! YOU'RE A BEETLE! YOU KILL PEOPLE!
QUIET!!!
YOU WANT TO ATTRACT MORE B.T.L.? WE REACT TO SOUND VIBRATIONS. I CAME HERE TO--
NEVER MIND.
NO ONE TOLD YOUR FRIENDS TO ATTACK US. WE DON'T TRY TO BE CRUEL. THE BIO-TECHNIC LAW WASN'T CREATED TO KILL ANYBODY-- WE KEEP THE PEACE. WE KEEP THINGS... SAFE.
SAFE? FROM WHO?
IF... IF YOU KNEW THE RISK I WAS TAKING, JUST BEING OUT HERE...
...WITHOUT ARMOR...
YOUR RISK IS MY LIFE.

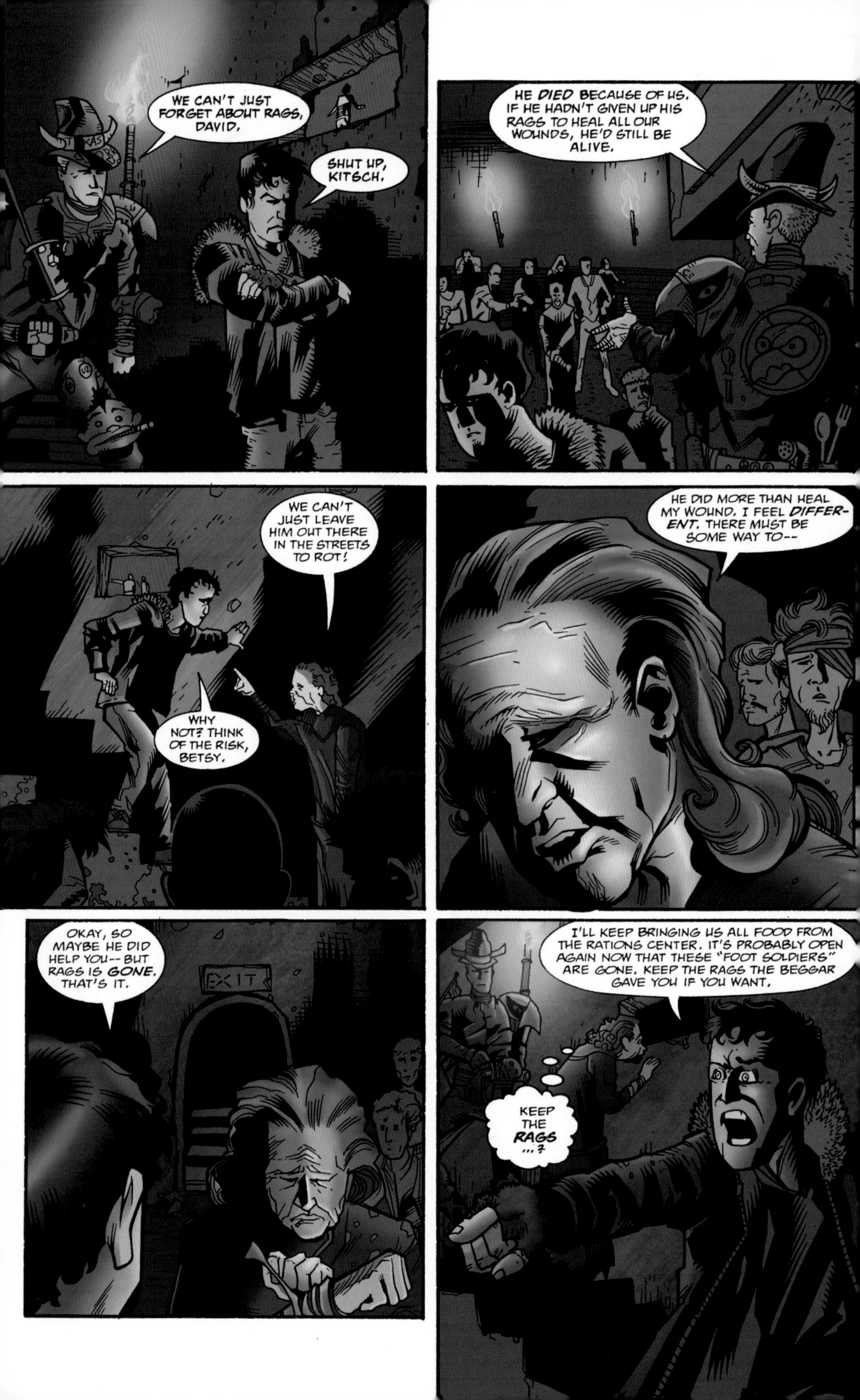

WE CAN'T JUST FORGET ABOUT RAGS, DAVID.
SHUT UP, KITSCH.
HE DIED BECAUSE OF US. IF HE HADN'T GIVEN UP HIS RAGS TO HEAL ALL OUR WOUNDS, HE'D STILL BE ALIVE.
WE CAN'T JUST LEAVE HIM OUT THERE IN THE STREETS TO ROT!
WHY NOT? THINK OF THE RISK, BETSY.
HE DID MORE THAN HEAL MY WOUND. I FEEL DIFFERENT. THERE MUST BE SOME WAY TO--
OKAY, SO MAYBE HE DID HELP YOU-- BUT RAGS IS GONE. THAT'S IT.
EXIT
I'LL KEEP BRINGING US ALL FOOD FROM THE RATIONS CENTER. IT'S PROBABLY OPEN AGAIN NOW THAT THESE "FOOT SOLDIERS" ARE GONE. KEEP THE RAGS THE BEGGAR GAVE YOU IF YOU WANT.
KEEP THE RAGS ...?

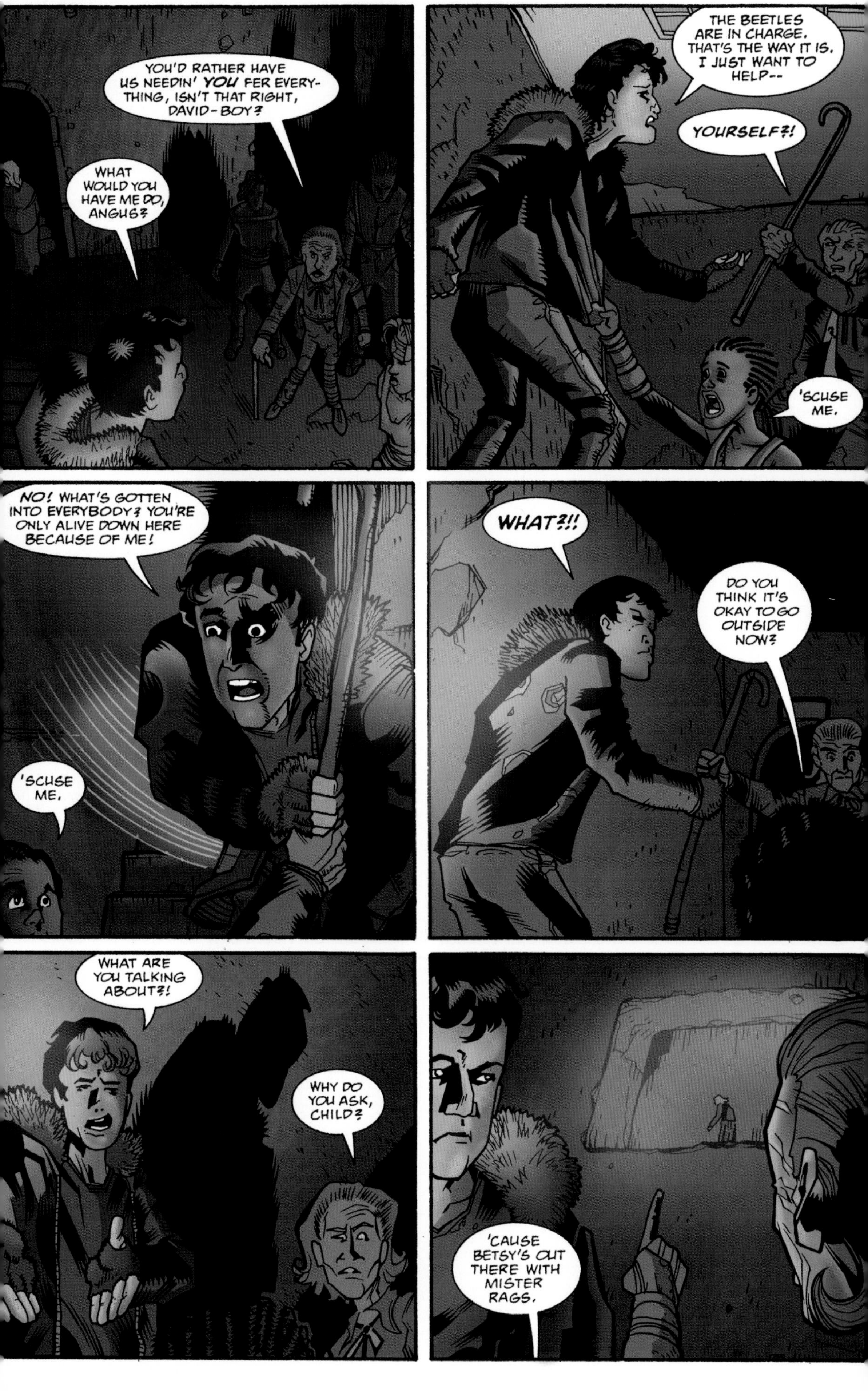
YOU'D RATHER HAVE US NEEDIN' YOU FER EVERY-THING, ISN'T THAT RIGHT, DAVID-BOY?
WHAT WOULD YOU HAVE ME DO, ANGUS?
THE BEETLES ARE IN CHARGE. THAT'S THE WAY IT IS. I JUST WANT TO HELP--
YOURSELF?!
'SCUSE ME.
NO! WHAT'S GOTTEN INTO EVERYBODY? YOU'RE ONLY ALIVE DOWN HERE BECAUSE OF ME!
'SCUSE ME.
WHAT?!!
DO YOU THINK IT'S OKAY TO GO OUTSIDE NOW?
WHAT ARE YOU TALKING ABOUT?!
WHY DO YOU ASK, CHILD?
'CAUSE BETSY'S OUT THERE WITH MISTER RAGS.

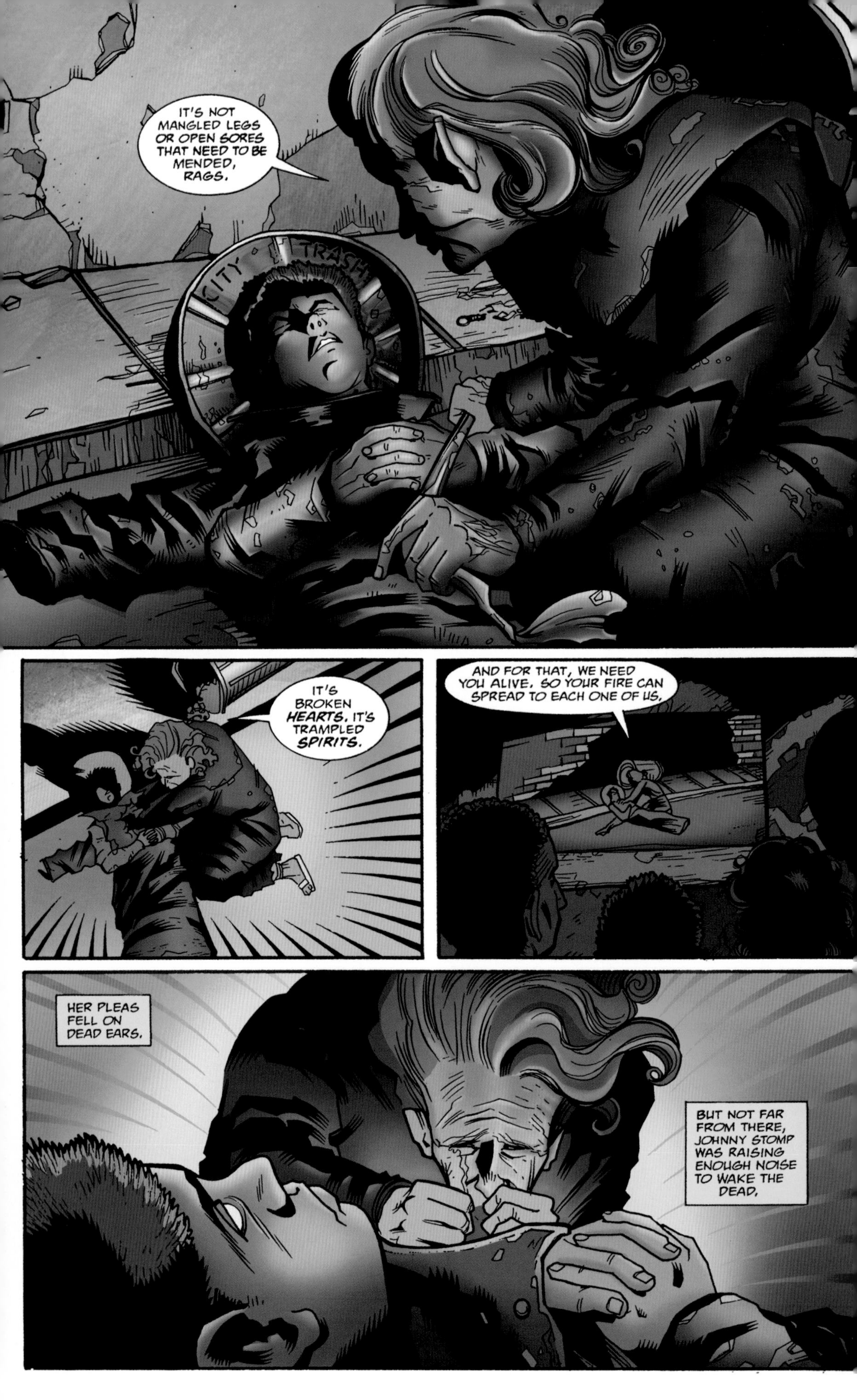
IT'S NOT MANGLED LEGS OR OPEN SORES THAT NEED TO BE MENDED, RAGS.
CITY TRASH
IT'S BROKEN HEARTS. IT'S TRAMPLED SPIRITS.
AND FOR THAT, WE NEED YOU ALIVE. SO YOUR FIRE CAN SPREAD TO EACH ONE OF US.
HER PLEAS FELL ON DEAD EARS.
BUT NOT FAR FROM THERE, JOHNNY STOMP WAS RAISING ENOUGH NOISE TO WAKE THE DEAD.

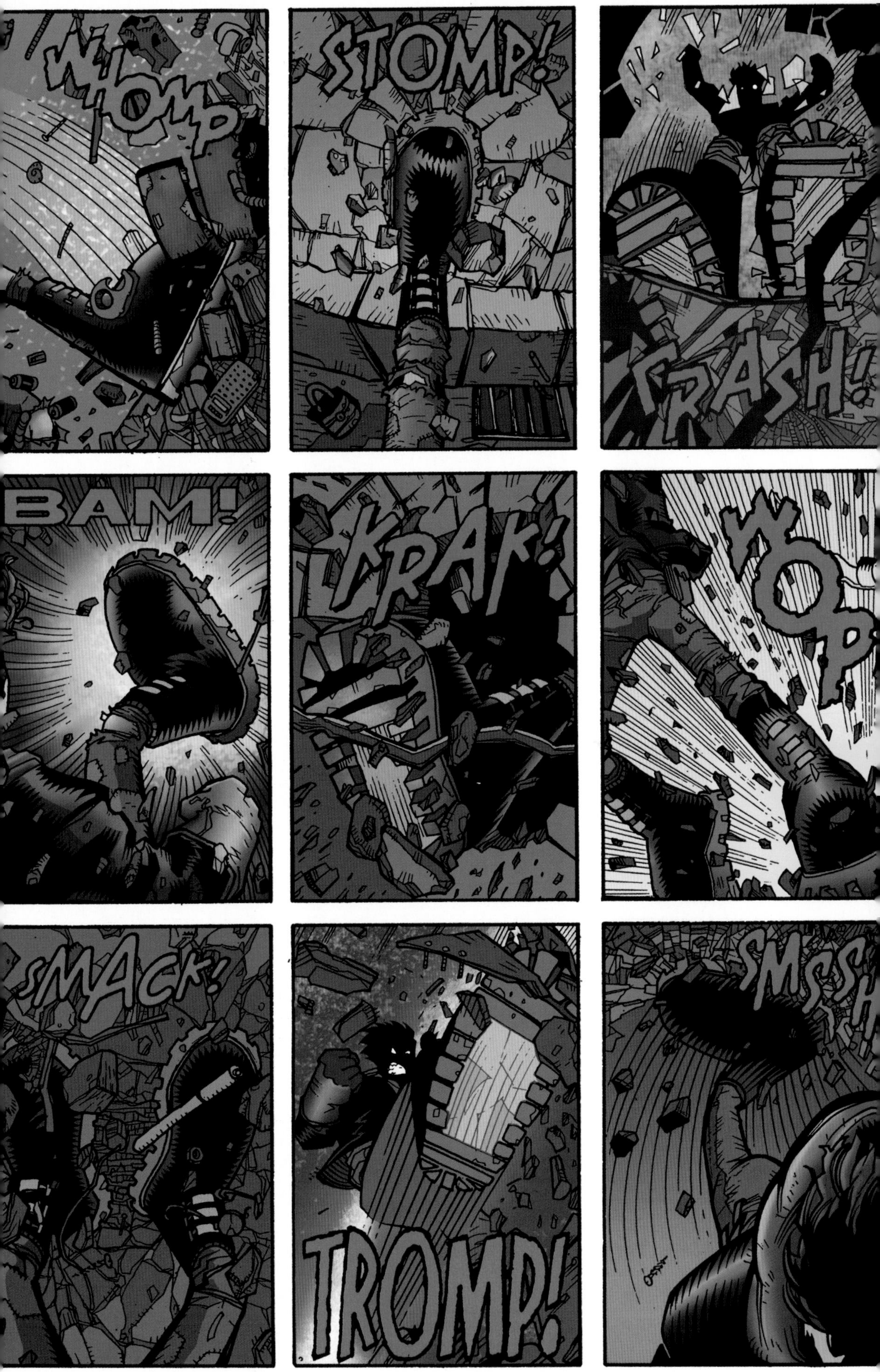
WHOMP
STOMP!
CRASH!
BAM!
KRAK!
WOP
SMACK!
TROMP!
SMSH

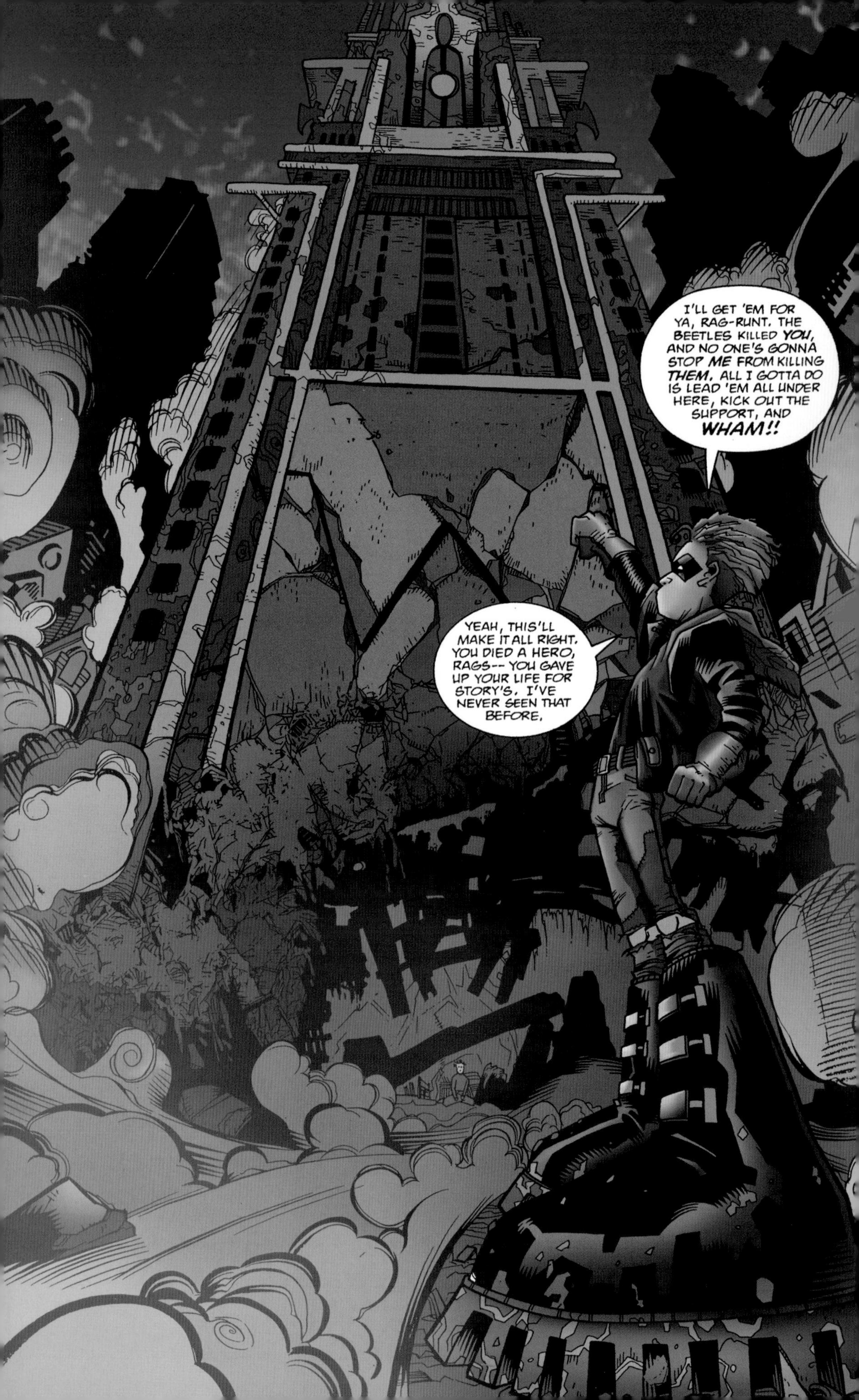
I'LL GET 'EM FOR YA, RAG-RUNT. THE BEETLES KILLED YOU, AND NO ONE'S GONNA STOP ME FROM KILLING THEM. ALL I GOTTA DO IS LEAD 'EM ALL UNDER HERE, KICK OUT THE SUPPORT, AND WHAM!!
YEAH, THIS'LL MAKE IT ALL RIGHT. YOU DIED A HERO, RAGS-- YOU GAVE UP YOUR LIFE FOR STORY'S. I'VE NEVER SEEN THAT BEFORE.

SO AS JOHNNY BUSIED HIMSELF PLANNING THE DOWNFALL OF THE B.T.L., MY OPINION OF ONE OF THEM IN PARTICULAR WAS RISING.

I'VE ALMOST GOT YOUR BOOT FIXED.

YOU'VE BEEN TRAINED HOW TO REPAIR THINGS AND STUFF?!

YEAH, OF COURSE. HERE, IT'S AMAZING THIS "SHOE" STILL WORKS, IT LOOKS OLDER THAN DIRT.

HA!

IF ONLY YOU KNEW WHERE I FOUND IT!

YOU'RE NOT A VERY GOOD BEETLE, ARE YOU? I MEAN, NOT THAT THERE ARE ANY GOOD BEETLES.

WHAT MAKES YOU SAY THAT?

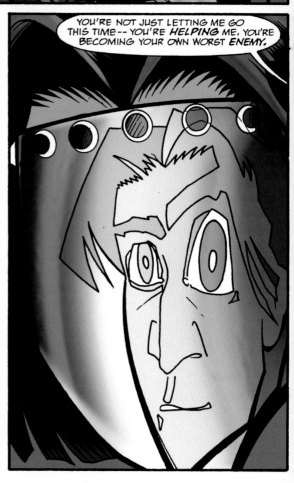

YOU'RE NOT JUST LETTING ME GO THIS TIME-- YOU'RE HELPING ME, YOU'RE BECOMING YOUR OWN WORST ENEMY.

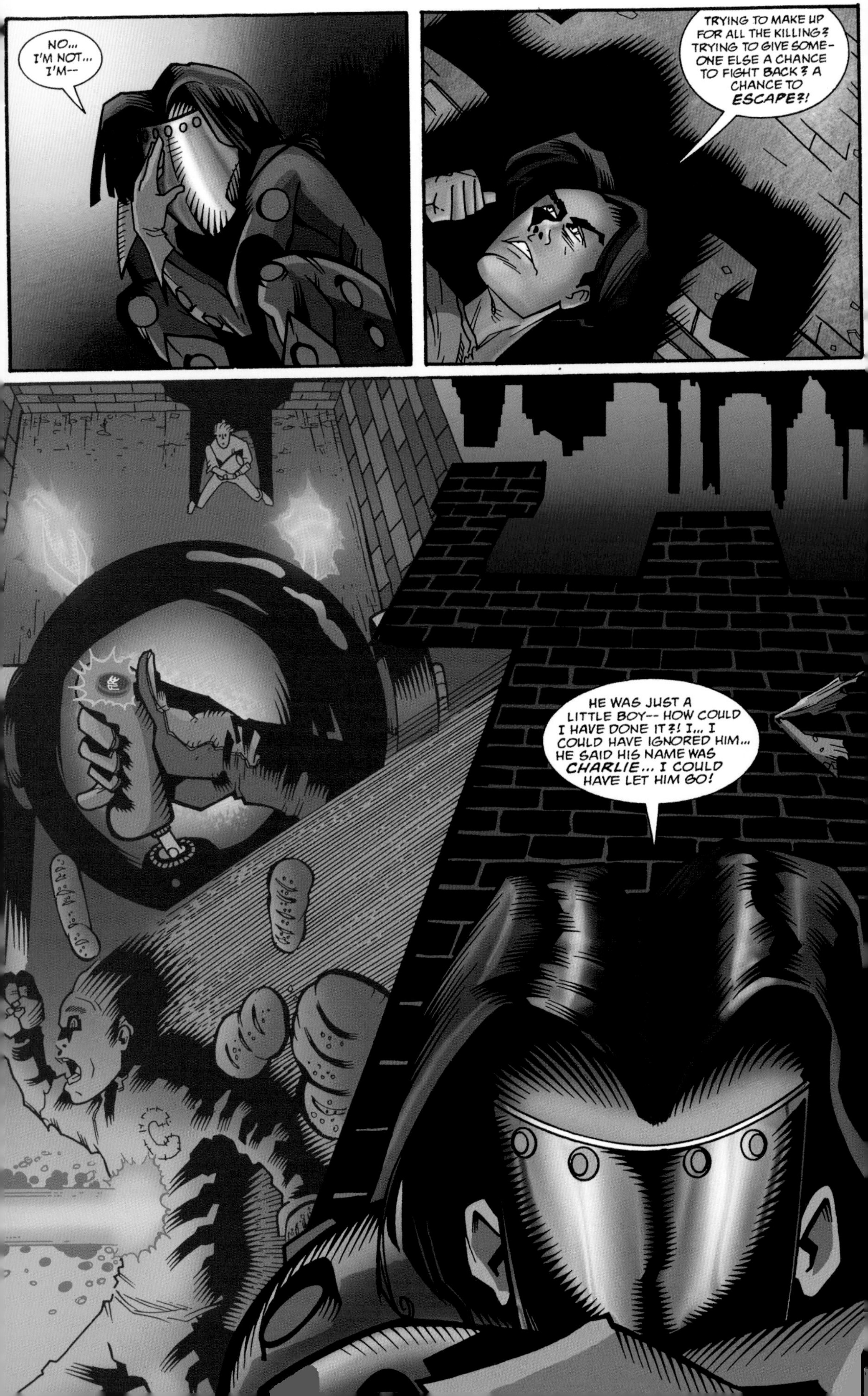
NO... I'M NOT... I'M--
TRYING TO MAKE UP FOR ALL THE KILLING? TRYING TO GIVE SOME-ONE ELSE A CHANCE TO FIGHT BACK? A CHANCE TO ESCAPE?!
HE WAS JUST A LITTLE BOY-- HOW COULD I HAVE DONE IT?! I... I COULD HAVE IGNORED HIM... HE SAID HIS NAME WAS CHARLIE... I COULD HAVE LET HIM GO!

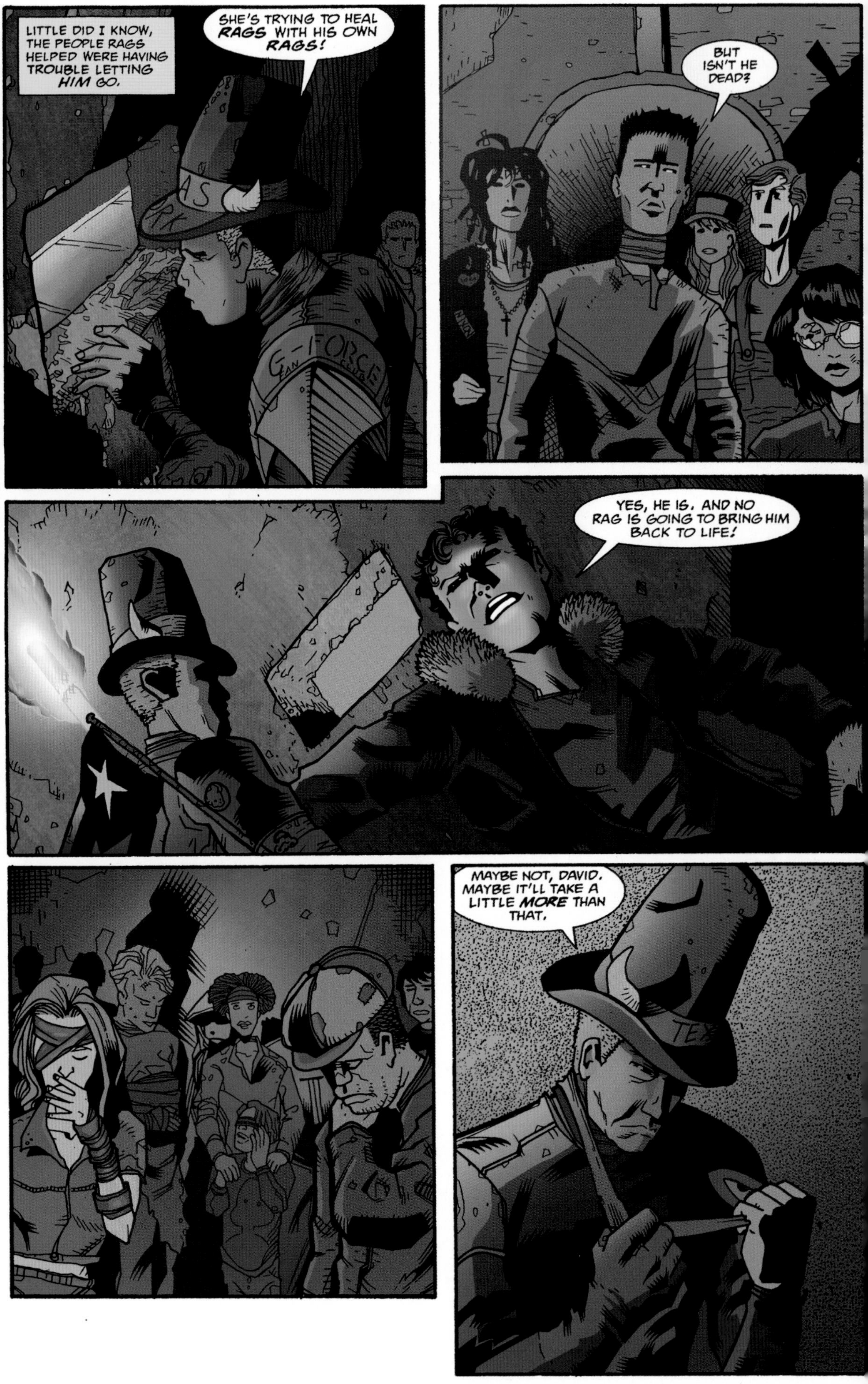

LITTLE DID I KNOW, THE PEOPLE RAGS HELPED WERE HAVING TROUBLE LETTING *HIM* GO.
SHE'S TRYING TO HEAL *RAGS* WITH HIS OWN *RAGS!*
BUT ISN'T HE DEAD?
YES, HE IS. AND NO RAG IS GOING TO BRING HIM BACK TO LIFE!
MAYBE NOT, DAVID. MAYBE IT'LL TAKE A LITTLE *MORE* THAN THAT.

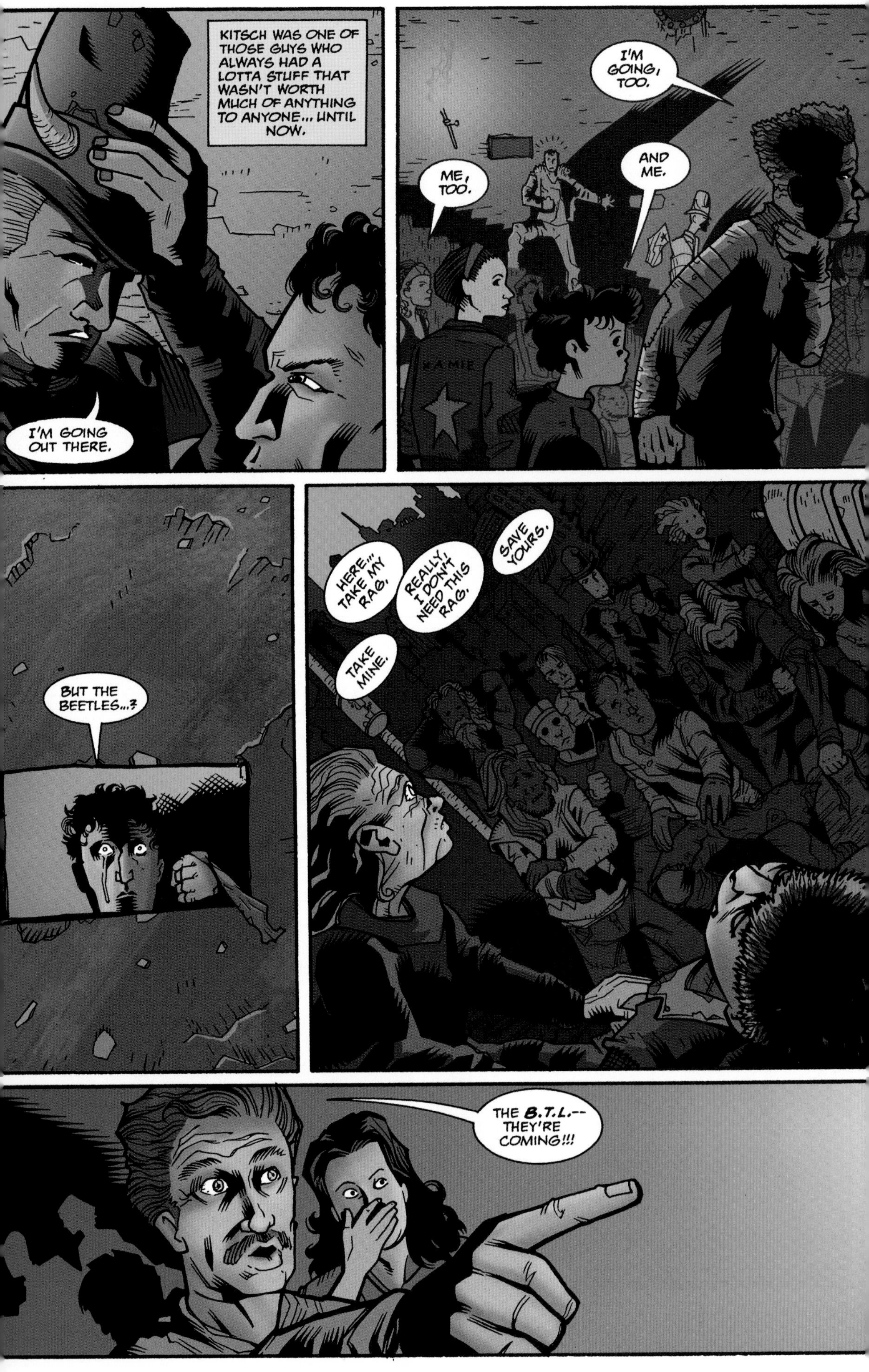
KITSCH WAS ONE OF THOSE GUYS WHO ALWAYS HAD A LOTTA STUFF THAT WASN'T WORTH MUCH OF ANYTHING TO ANYONE... UNTIL NOW.
I'M GOING OUT THERE.
I'M GOING, TOO.
ME, TOO.
AND ME.
BUT THE BEETLES...?
HERE... TAKE MY RAG.
REALLY, I DON'T NEED THIS RAG.
SAVE YOURS.
TAKE MINE.
THE B.T.L.-- THEY'RE COMING!!!

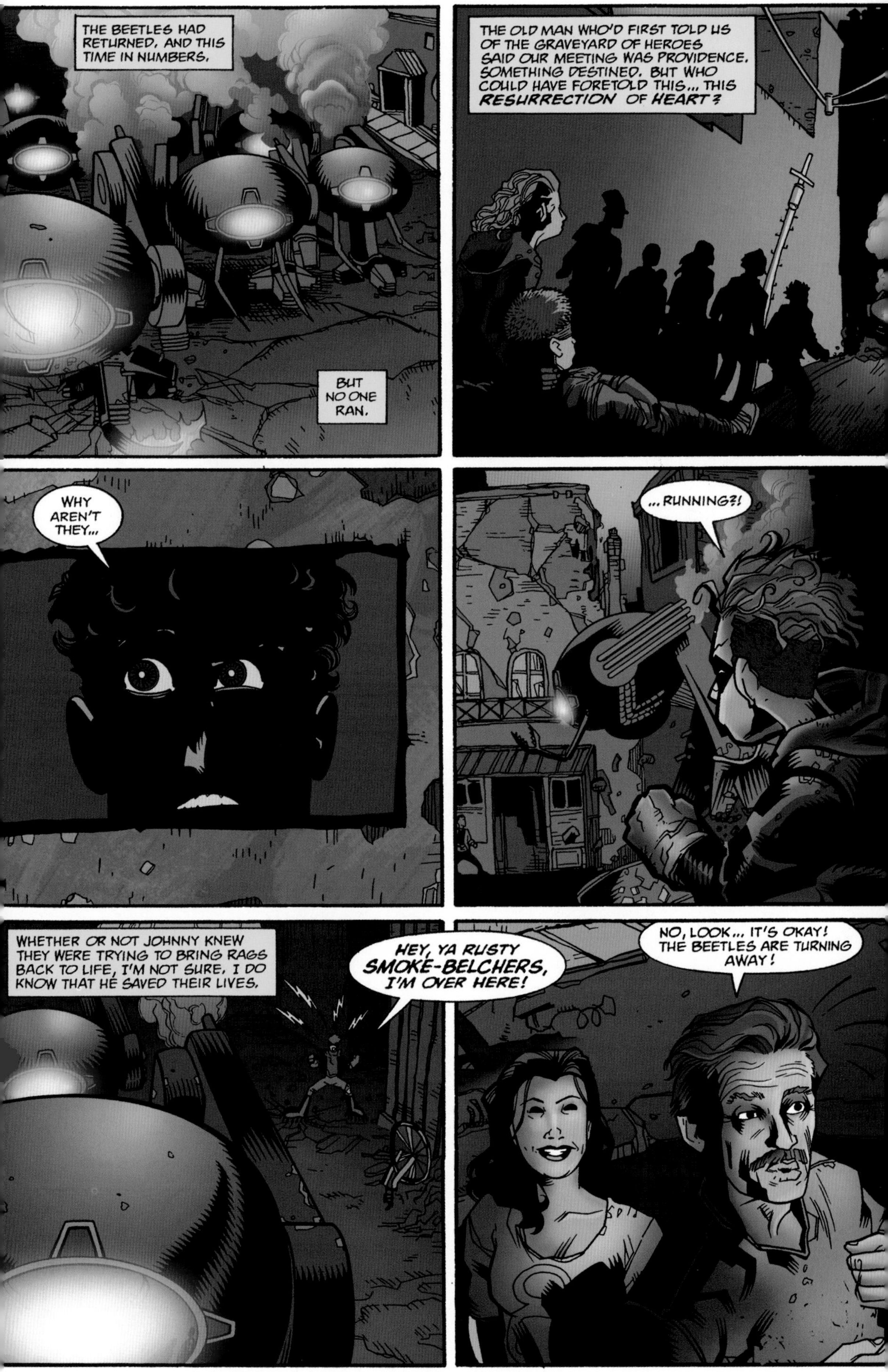

THE BEETLES HAD RETURNED, AND THIS TIME IN NUMBERS.
BUT NO ONE RAN.
THE OLD MAN WHO'D FIRST TOLD US OF THE GRAVEYARD OF HEROES SAID OUR MEETING WAS PROVIDENCE. SOMETHING DESTINED. BUT WHO COULD HAVE FORETOLD THIS... THIS RESURRECTION OF HEART?
WHY AREN'T THEY...
...RUNNING?!
WHETHER OR NOT JOHNNY KNEW THEY WERE TRYING TO BRING RAGS BACK TO LIFE, I'M NOT SURE. I DO KNOW THAT HE SAVED THEIR LIVES.
HEY, YA RUSTY SMOKE-BELCHERS, I'M OVER HERE!
NO, LOOK... IT'S OKAY! THE BEETLES ARE TURNING AWAY!

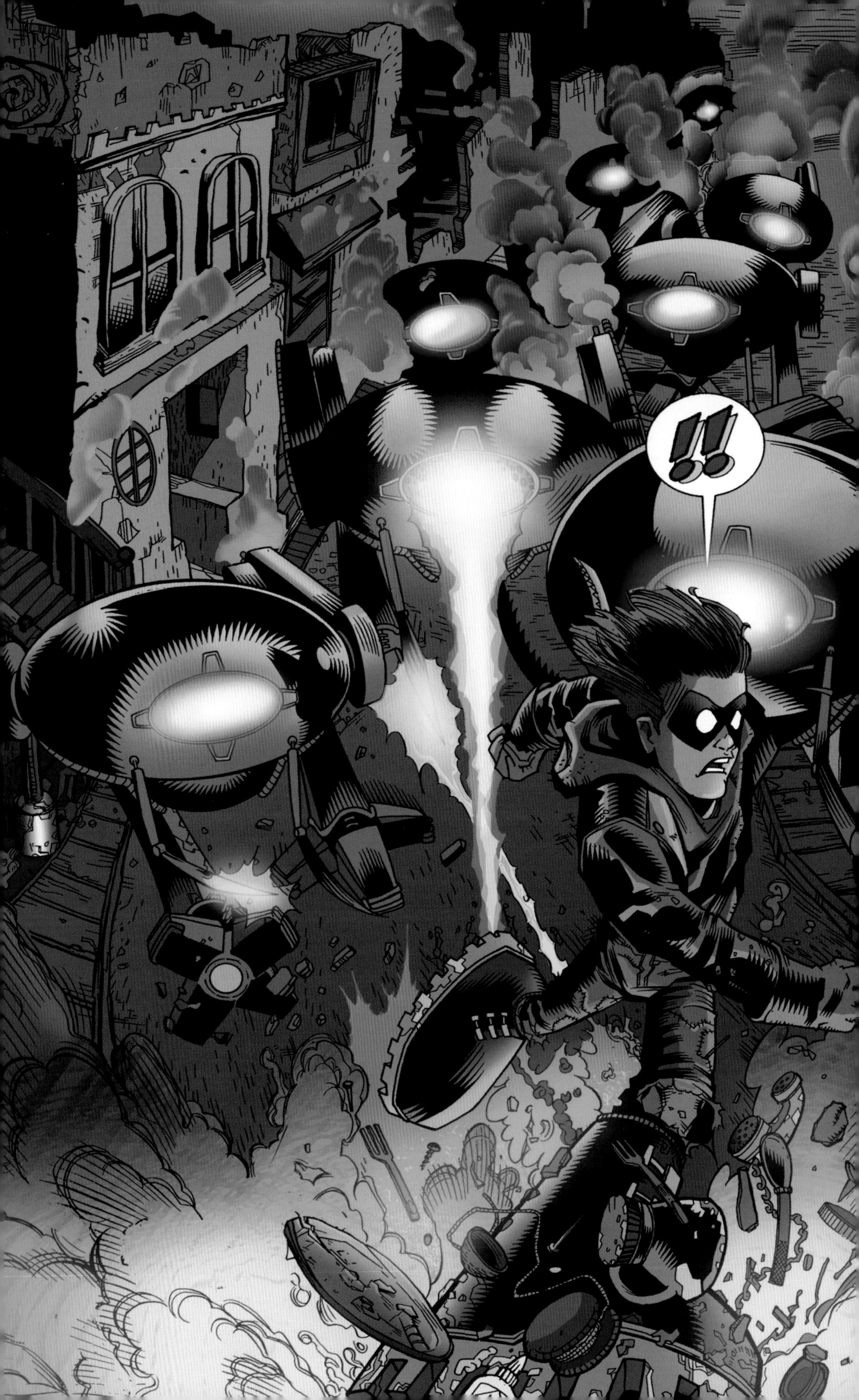
!!

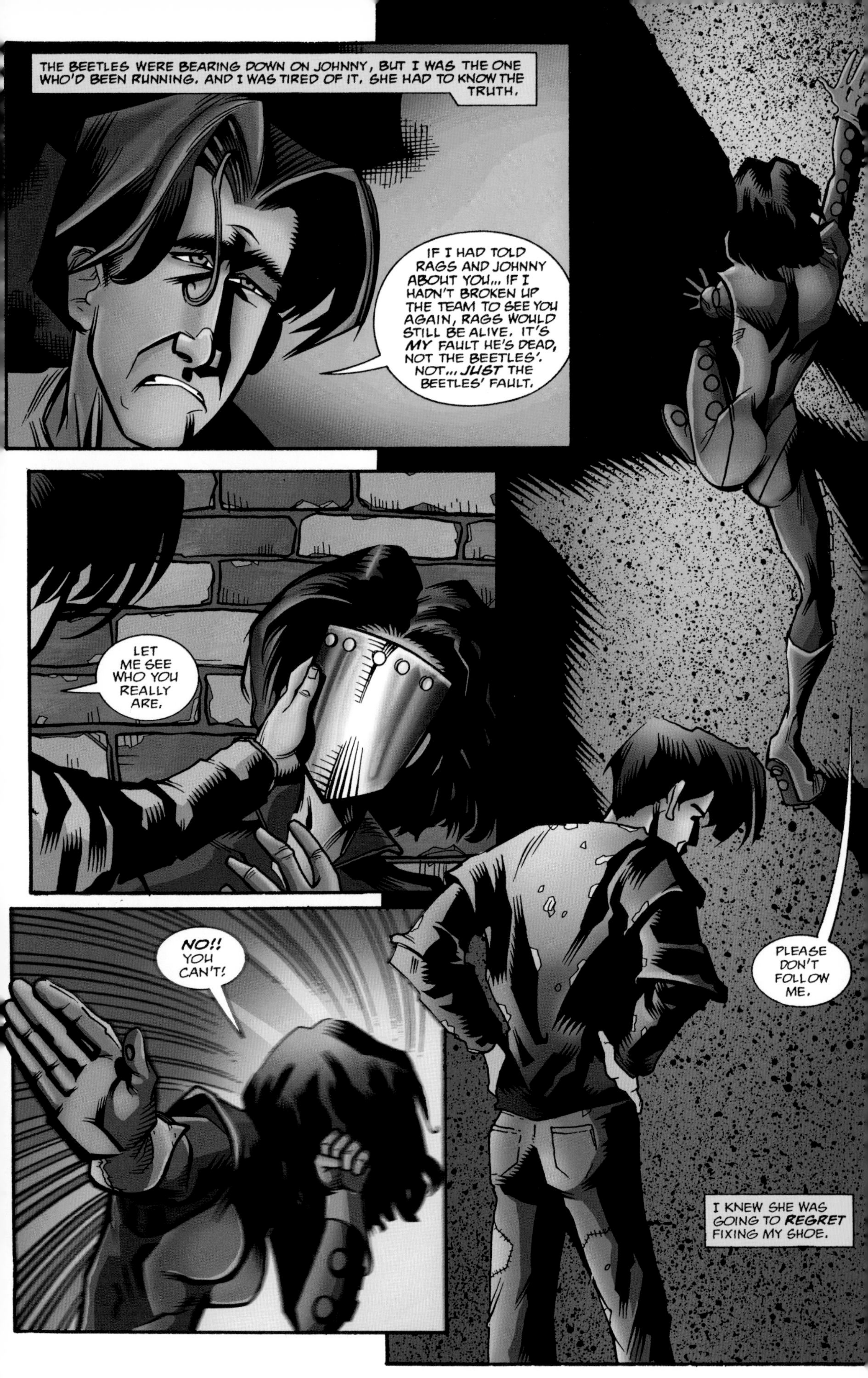
THE BEETLES WERE BEARING DOWN ON JOHNNY, BUT I WAS THE ONE WHO'D BEEN RUNNING. AND I WAS TIRED OF IT. SHE HAD TO KNOW THE TRUTH.
IF I HAD TOLD RAGS AND JOHNNY ABOUT YOU... IF I HADN'T BROKEN UP THE TEAM TO SEE YOU AGAIN, RAGS WOULD STILL BE ALIVE. IT'S MY FAULT HE'S DEAD, NOT THE BEETLES'. NOT... JUST THE BEETLES' FAULT.
LET ME SEE WHO YOU REALLY ARE.
NO!! YOU CAN'T!
PLEASE DON'T FOLLOW ME.
I KNEW SHE WAS GOING TO REGRET FIXING MY SHOE.

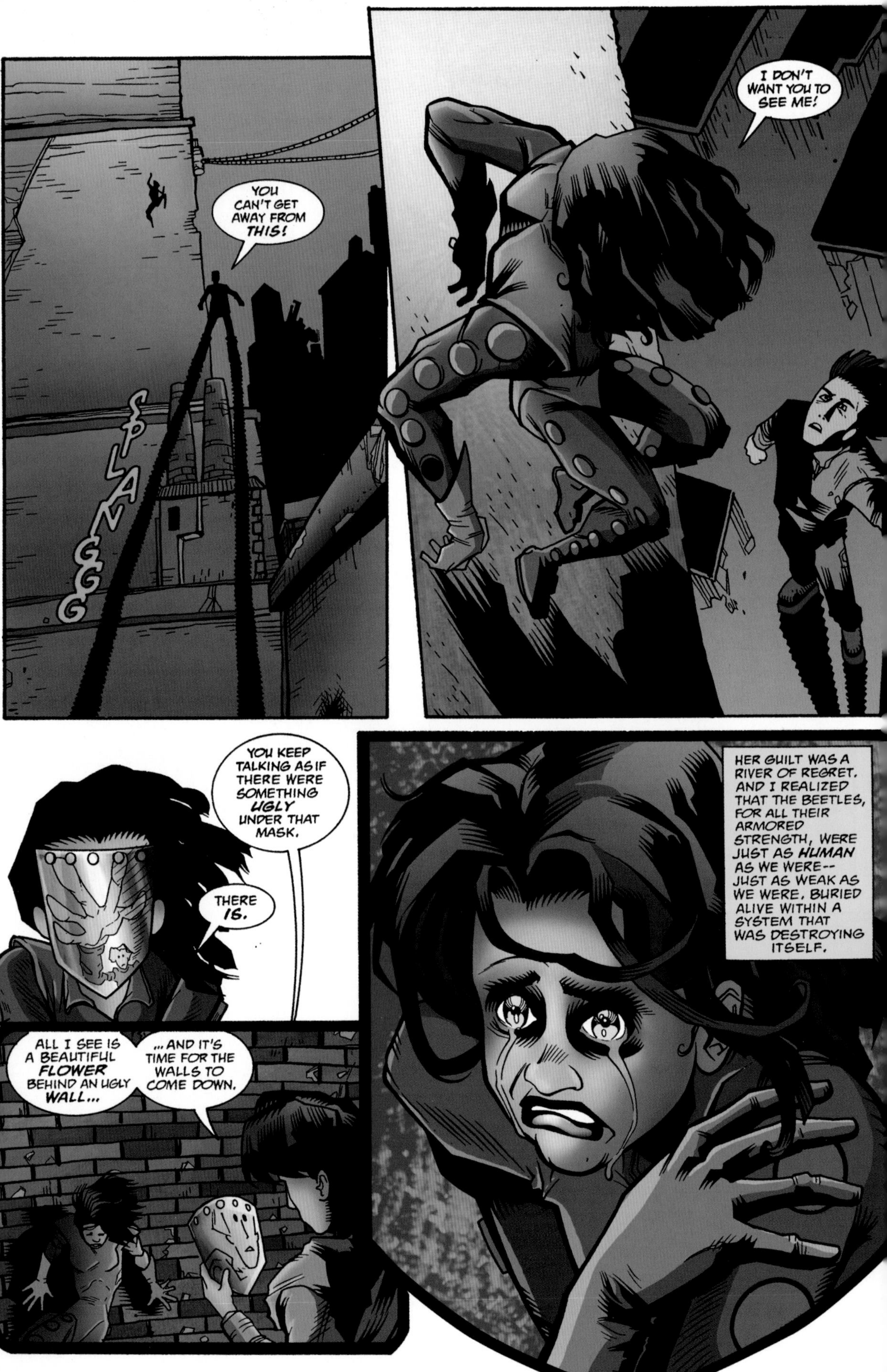
YOU CAN'T GET AWAY FROM THIS!
SPLANGGG
I DON'T WANT YOU TO SEE ME!
YOU KEEP TALKING AS IF THERE WERE SOMETHING UGLY UNDER THAT MASK.
THERE IS.
ALL I SEE IS A BEAUTIFUL FLOWER BEHIND AN UGLY WALL...
...AND IT'S TIME FOR THE WALLS TO COME DOWN.
HER GUILT WAS A RIVER OF REGRET. AND I REALIZED THAT THE BEETLES, FOR ALL THEIR ARMORED STRENGTH, WERE JUST AS HUMAN AS WE WERE-- JUST AS WEAK AS WE WERE, BURIED ALIVE WITHIN A SYSTEM THAT WAS DESTROYING ITSELF.

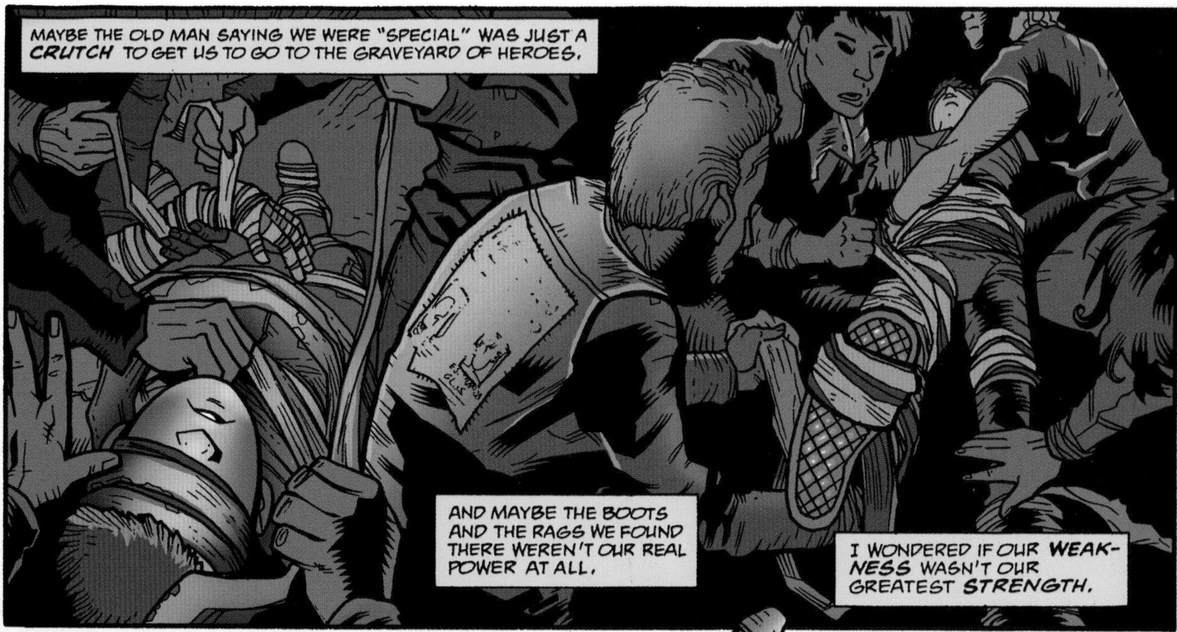
MAYBE THE OLD MAN SAYING WE WERE "SPECIAL" WAS JUST A CRUTCH TO GET US TO GO TO THE GRAVEYARD OF HEROES.
AND MAYBE THE BOOTS AND THE RAGS WE FOUND THERE WEREN'T OUR REAL POWER AT ALL.
I WONDERED IF OUR WEAKNESS WASN'T OUR GREATEST STRENGTH.

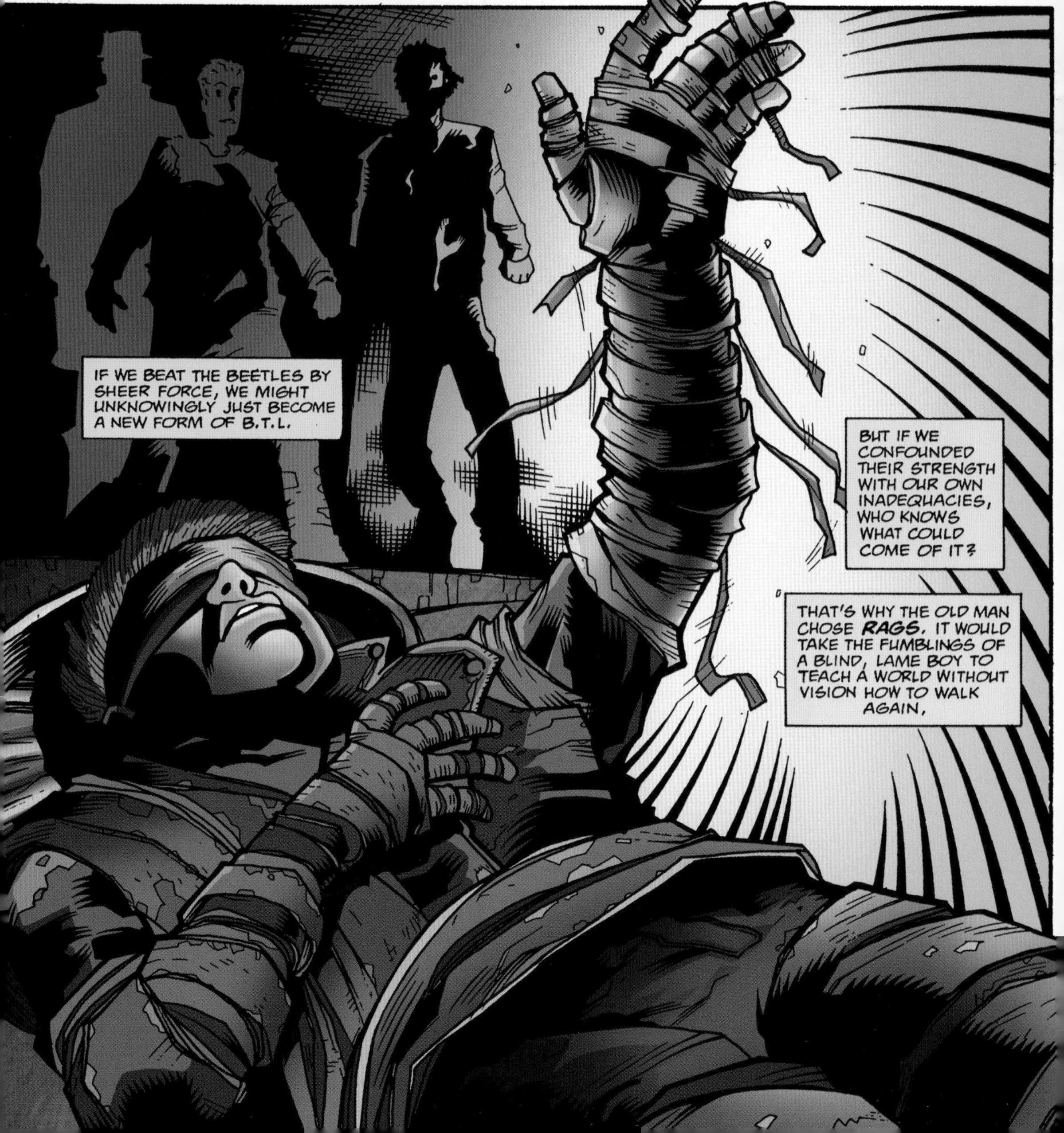
IF WE BEAT THE BEETLES BY SHEER FORCE, WE MIGHT UNKNOWINGLY JUST BECOME A NEW FORM OF B.T.L.
BUT IF WE CONFOUNDED THEIR STRENGTH WITH OUR OWN INADEQUACIES, WHO KNOWS WHAT COULD COME OF IT?
THAT'S WHY THE OLD MAN CHOSE RAGS. IT WOULD TAKE THE FUMBLINGS OF A BLIND, LAME BOY TO TEACH A WORLD WITHOUT VISION HOW TO WALK AGAIN.

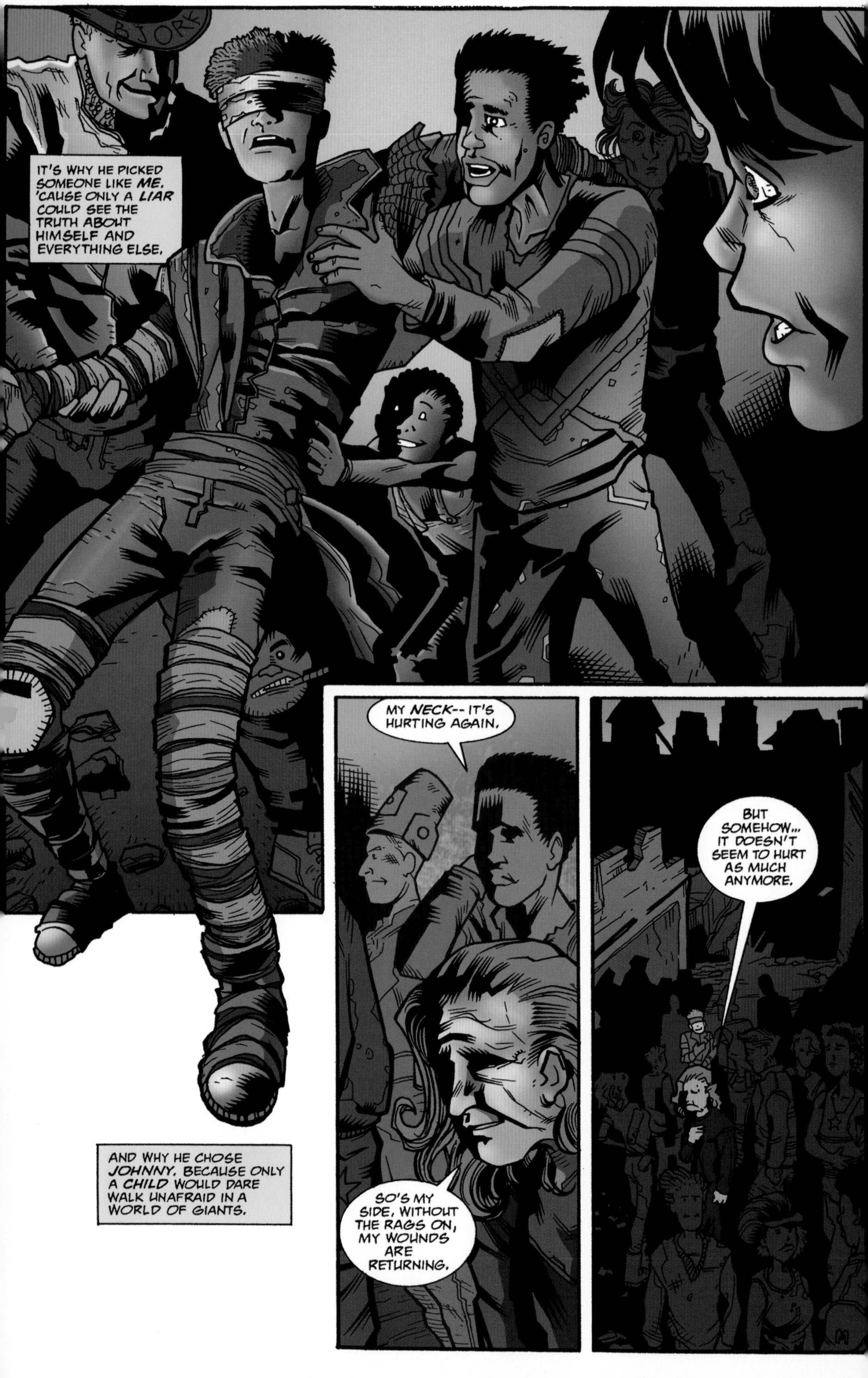
IT'S WHY HE PICKED SOMEONE LIKE *ME*. 'CAUSE ONLY A *LIAR* COULD SEE THE TRUTH ABOUT HIMSELF AND EVERYTHING ELSE.
AND WHY HE CHOSE *JOHNNY*. BECAUSE ONLY A *CHILD* WOULD DARE WALK UNAFRAID IN A WORLD OF GIANTS.
MY *NECK*-- IT'S HURTING AGAIN.
SO'S MY SIDE. WITHOUT THE RAGS ON, MY WOUNDS ARE RETURNING.
BUT SOMEHOW... IT DOESN'T SEEM TO HURT AS MUCH ANYMORE.

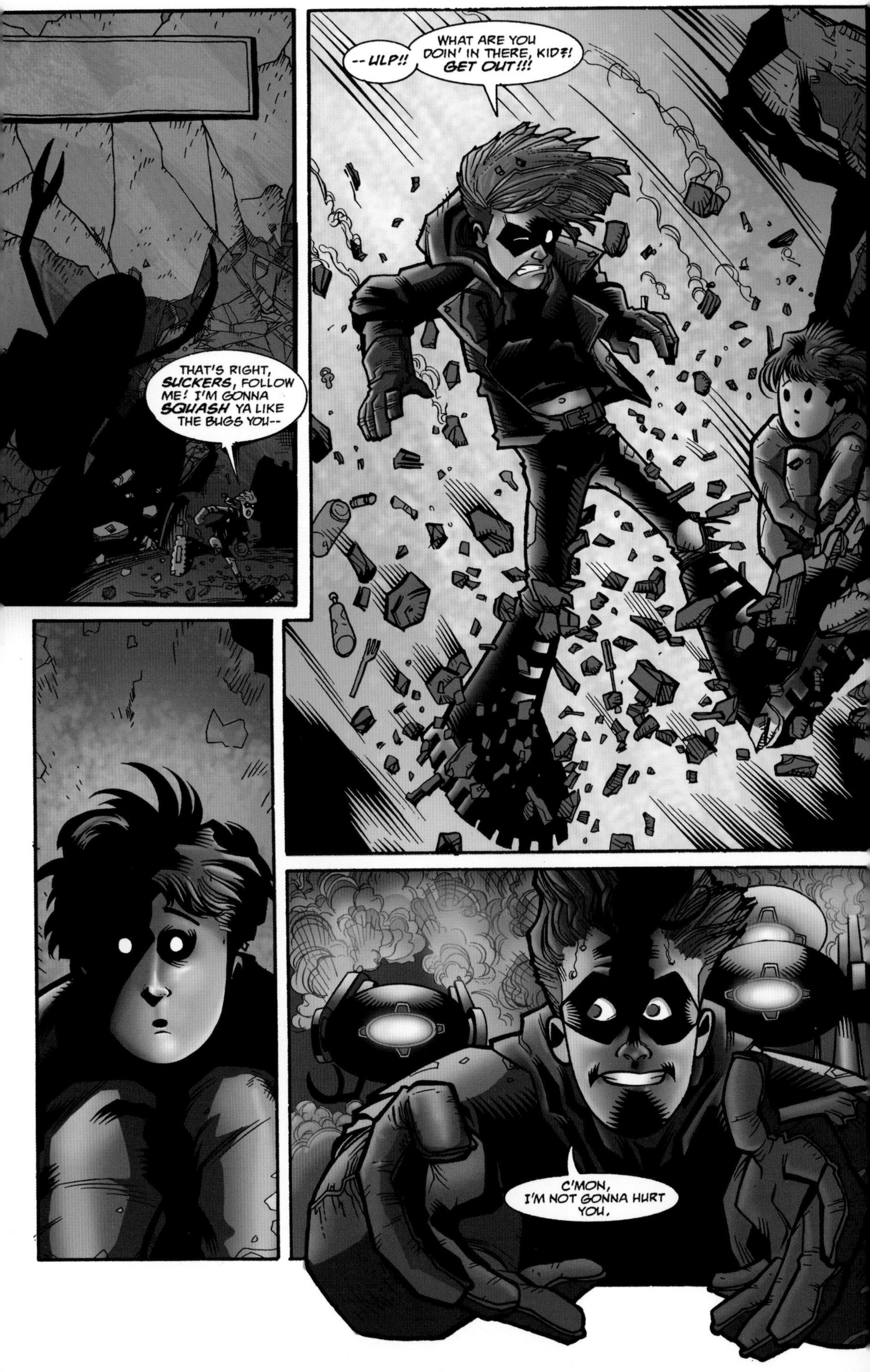
THAT'S RIGHT, SUCKERS, FOLLOW ME! I'M GONNA SQUASH YA LIKE THE BUGS YOU--
--ULP!!
WHAT ARE YOU DOIN' IN THERE, KID?! GET OUT!!!
C'MON, I'M NOT GONNA HURT YOU.

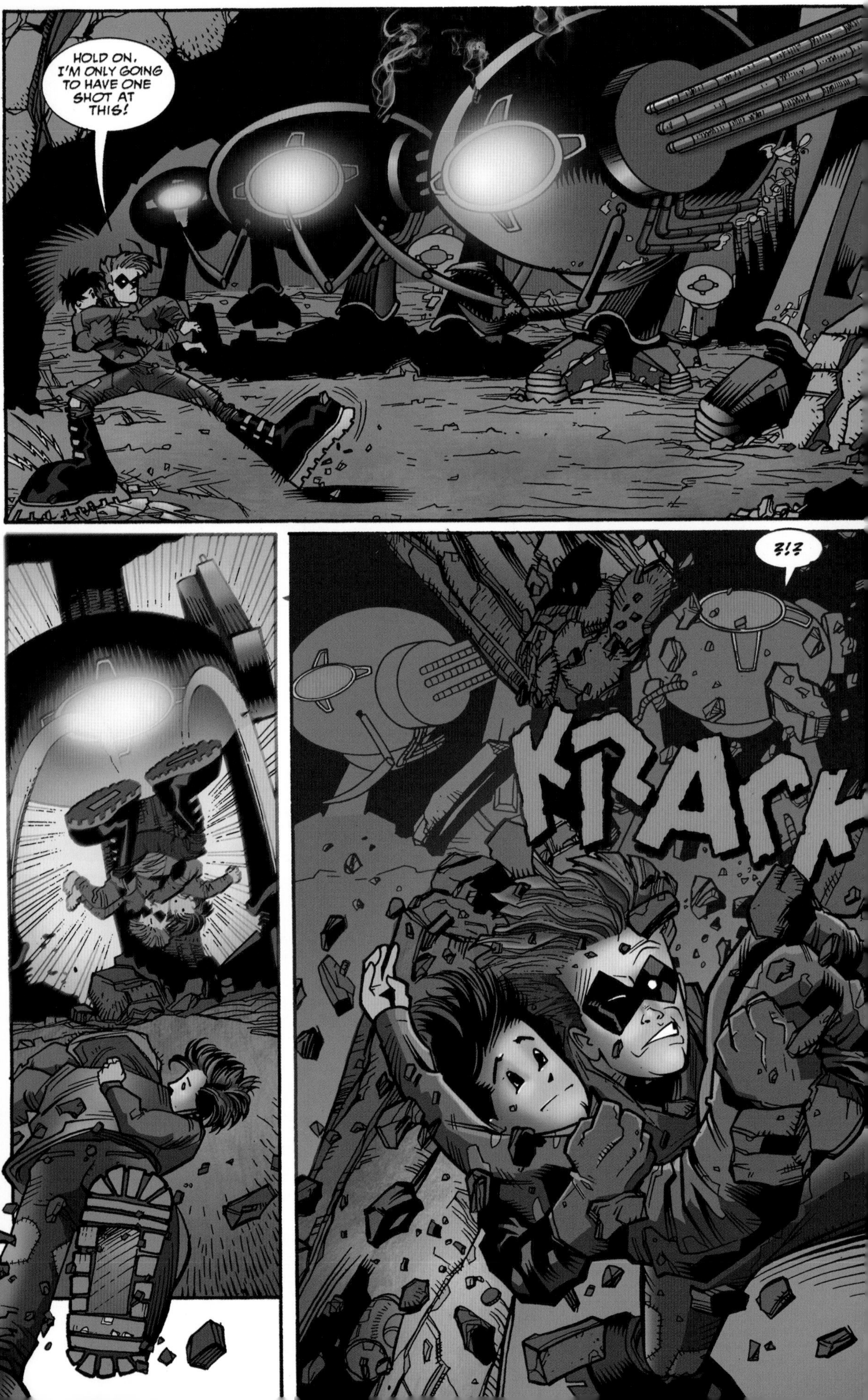
HOLD ON. I'M ONLY GOING TO HAVE ONE SHOT AT THIS!
?!?
KRACK

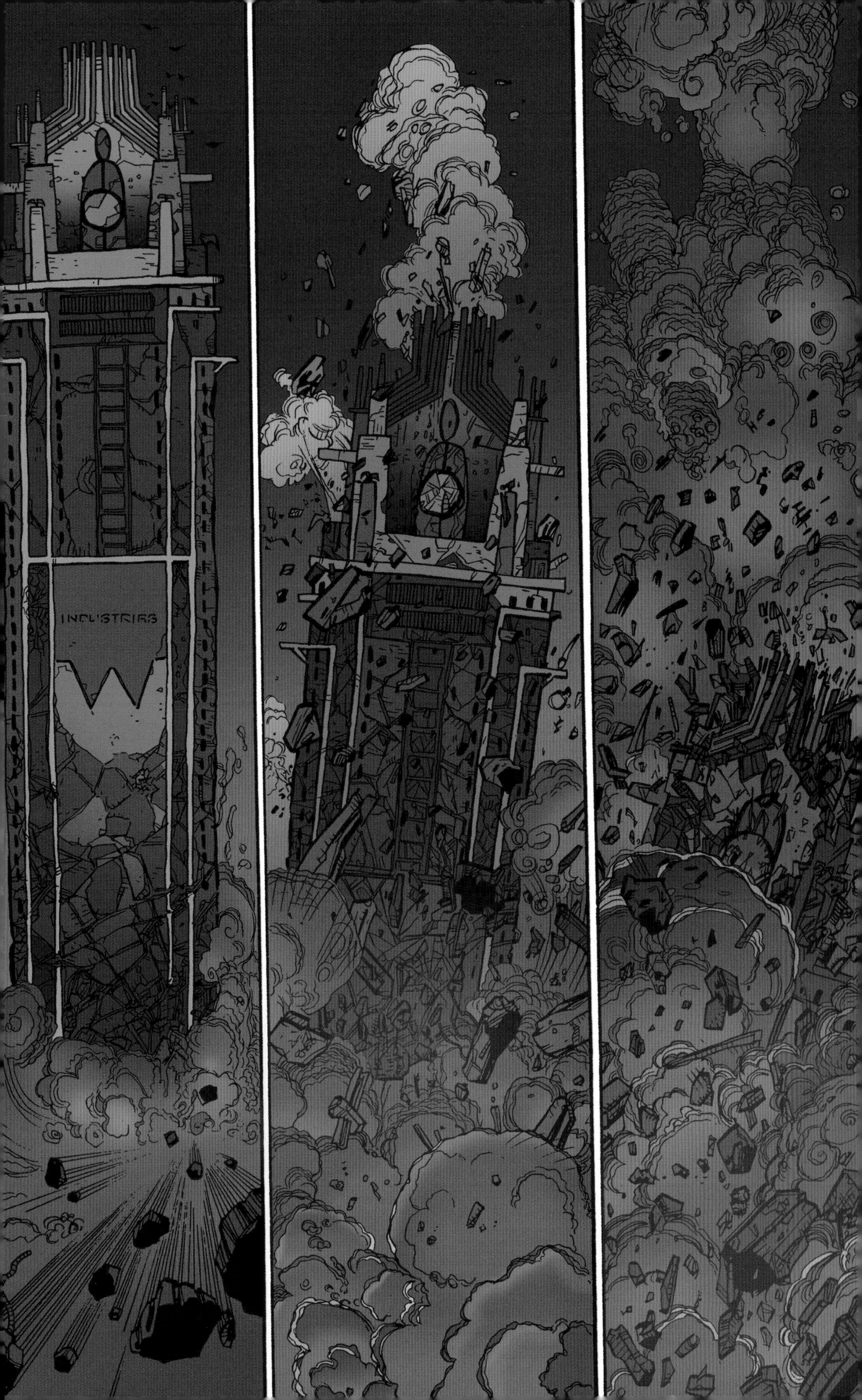
INDUSTRIES

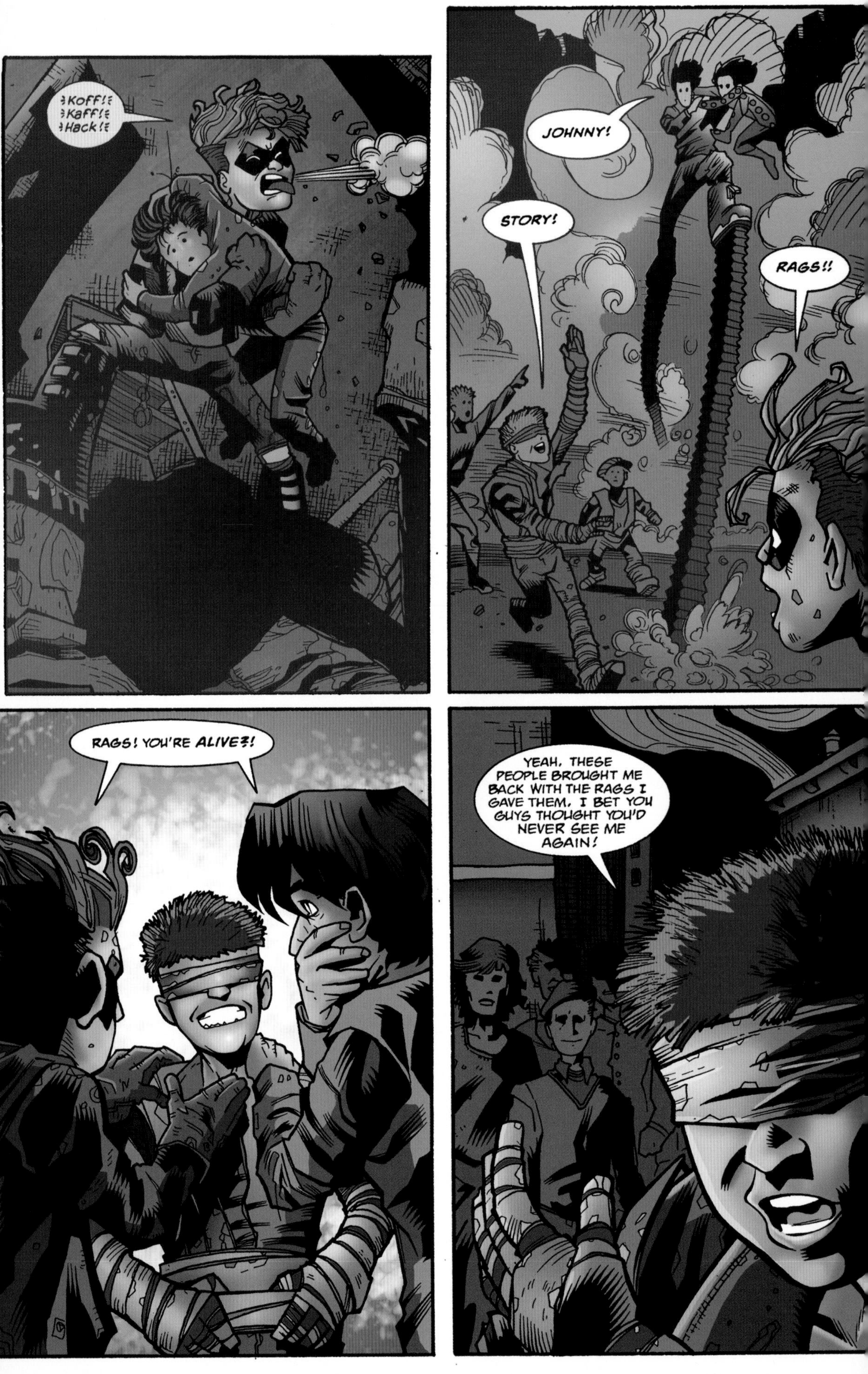
Koff! Kaff! Hack!
JOHNNY!
STORY!
RAGS!!
RAGS! YOU'RE ALIVE?!
YEAH, THESE PEOPLE BROUGHT ME BACK WITH THE RAGS I GAVE THEM. I BET YOU GUYS THOUGHT YOU'D NEVER SEE ME AGAIN!

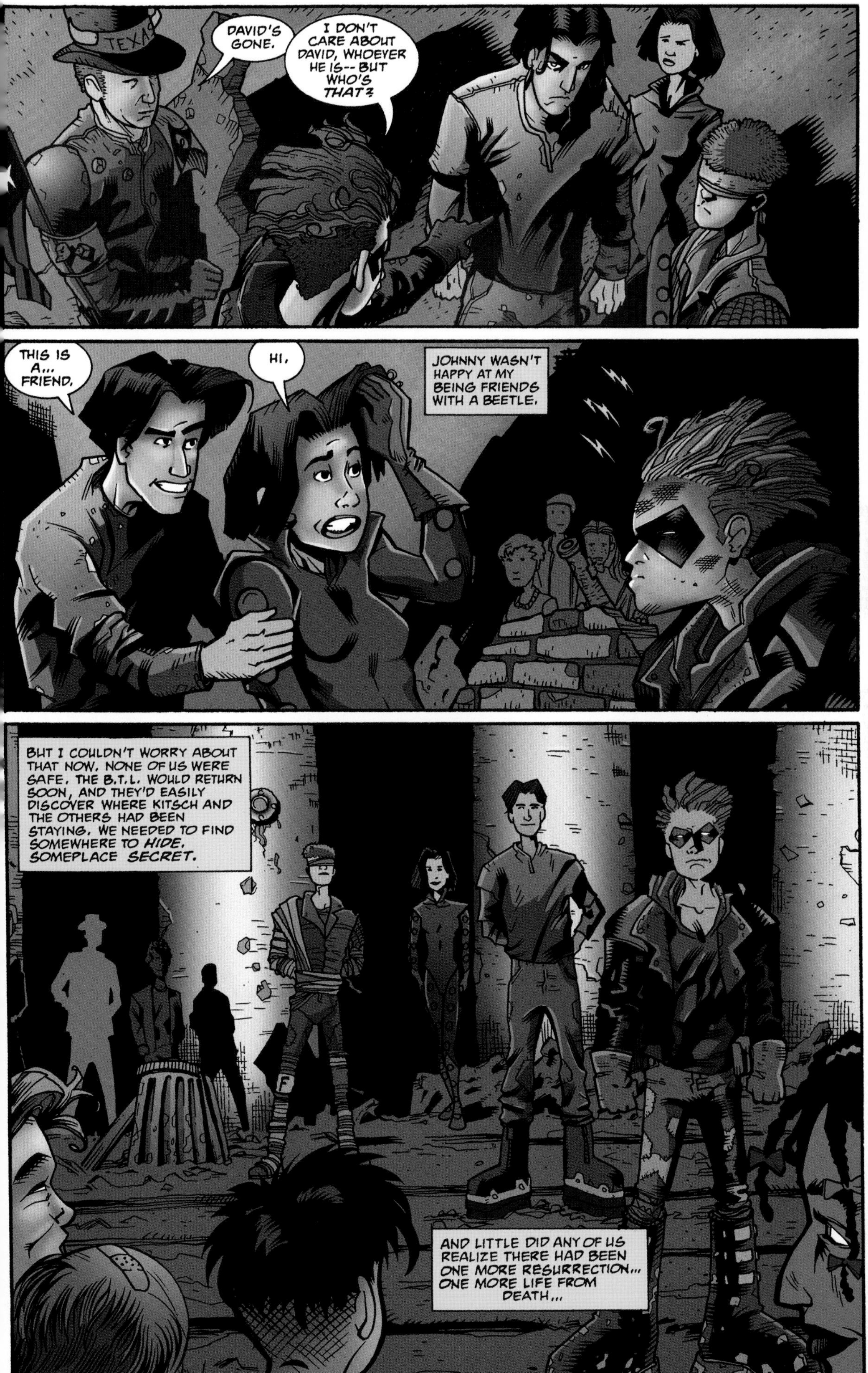
DAVID'S GONE.
I DON'T CARE ABOUT DAVID, WHOEVER HE IS-- BUT WHO'S THAT?
THIS IS A... FRIEND.
HI.
JOHNNY WASN'T HAPPY AT MY BEING FRIENDS WITH A BEETLE.
BUT I COULDN'T WORRY ABOUT THAT NOW. NONE OF US WERE SAFE. THE B.T.L. WOULD RETURN SOON, AND THEY'D EASILY DISCOVER WHERE KITSCH AND THE OTHERS HAD BEEN STAYING. WE NEEDED TO FIND SOMEWHERE TO HIDE. SOMEPLACE SECRET.
AND LITTLE DID ANY OF US REALIZE THERE HAD BEEN ONE MORE RESURRECTION... ONE MORE LIFE FROM DEATH...

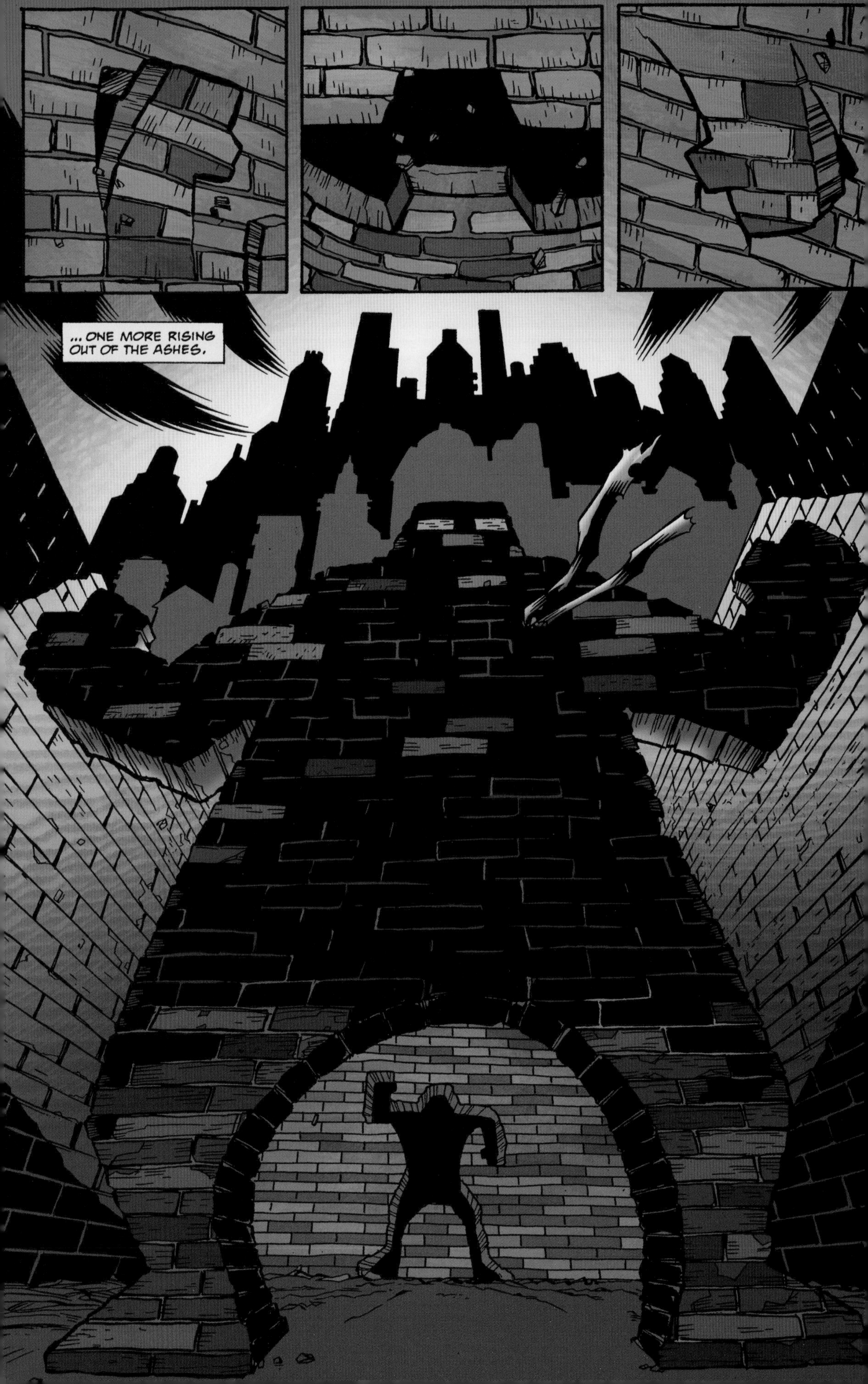
...ONE MORE RISING OUT OF THE ASHES.

Story's Story

Chapter Three

Rags was alive. He was dead. And now he was alive again. Was there anything that could stop us now? Was there any wall we could not bring down?

Even Flower was amazed at what was happening, what we were all caught up in. And she was convinced that if the other B.T.L. pilots knew about what was happening in our world, they would leave their's to save it.

Everything carried a sense of hope now. If Rags could come back to life, then even Death had lost its fearsomeness. And that meant that every tragedy might, in some amazing way we could not understand, lead to an even greater victory.

I had met a Beetle pilot. And instead of wanting to kill her, I wanted to get to know her. I wanted to tell her that I knew what it's like to be lied to.

The old man had nothing to do with this. How could he know this would happen?

There was an X scratched on the graves we were supposed to dig in, all except for the one we found Rags's healing bandages in. The miracle of Rags's new sight was beyond the old man's design. I don't know what grave Rags was supposed to get power from, but this power we found in Lion's crypt was more than a resurrection for Rags, it was a coming back to life for the people of this city.

All they ever did was wait for death. But Rags healed them in a

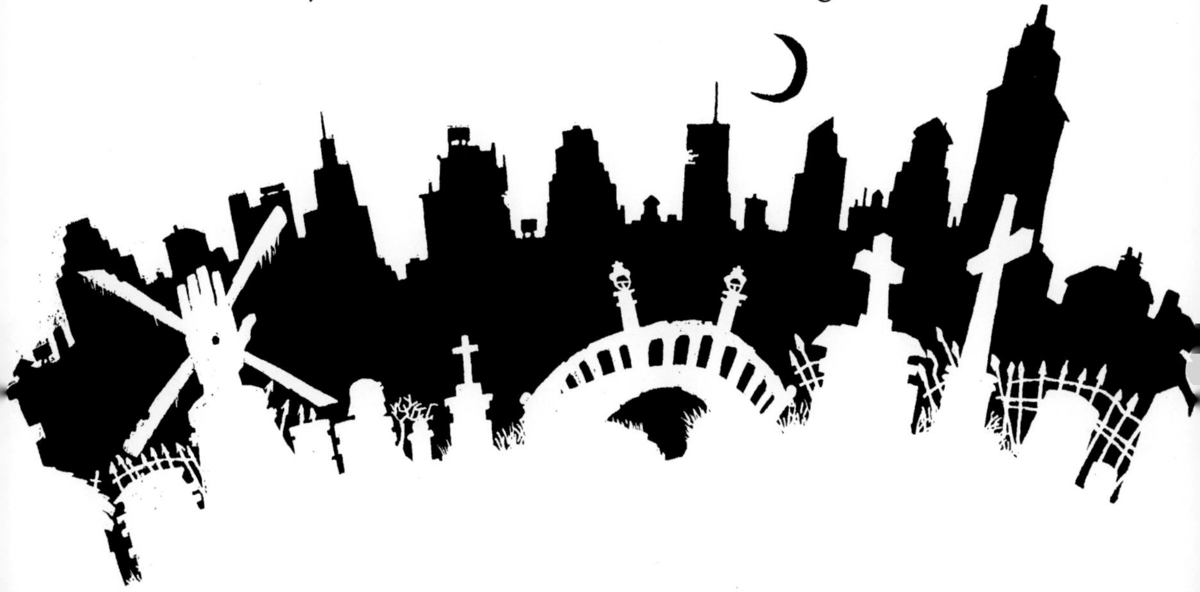

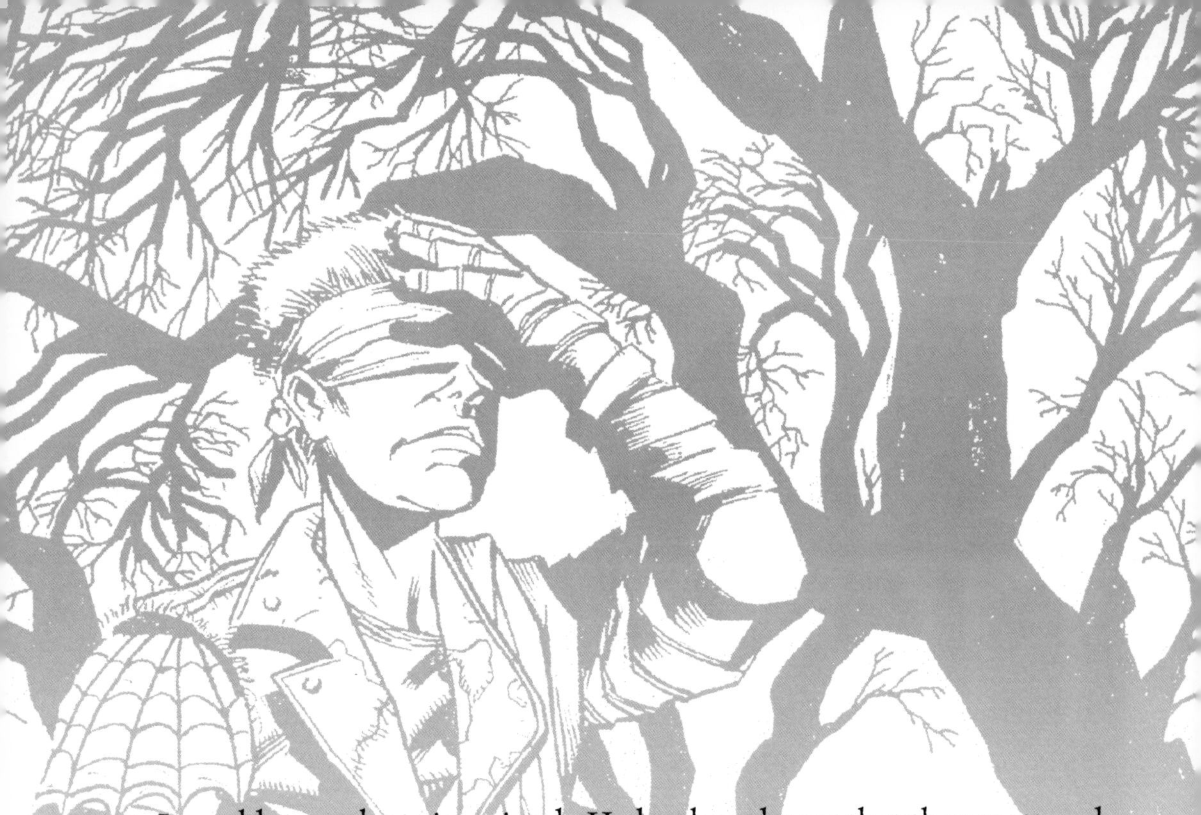

way I would never have imagined. He let them know that they mattered. That they were special. And then, somehow empowered them to give their new power up to save him.

I wonder if the same would be true for Johnny and I. If a day comes when we'll have to quit fighting. Or if we had to step out of our boots, could we? Would we? It's obvious from where we found this power that no hero lives forever.

Perhaps this is what the old man and his crutch saw in Rags in the first place. Maybe the bandages absorbed some of who Rags was, and passed that onto the people he healed.

I should have thought this through before. If the bandages can bring Rags back to life, why didn't they do that for Mr. Lion?

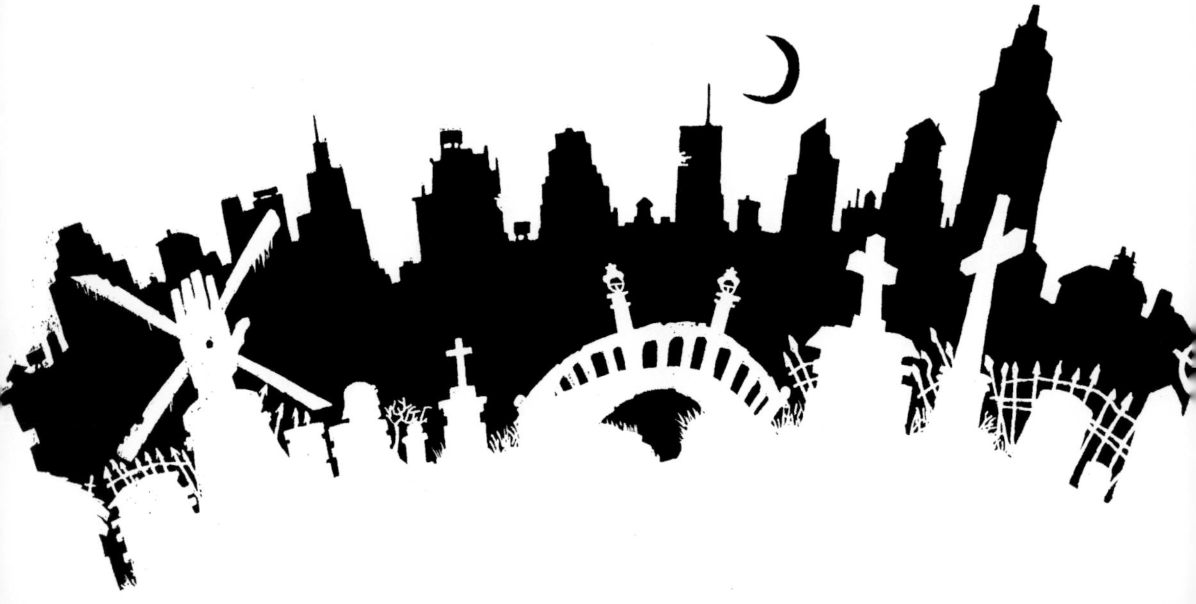

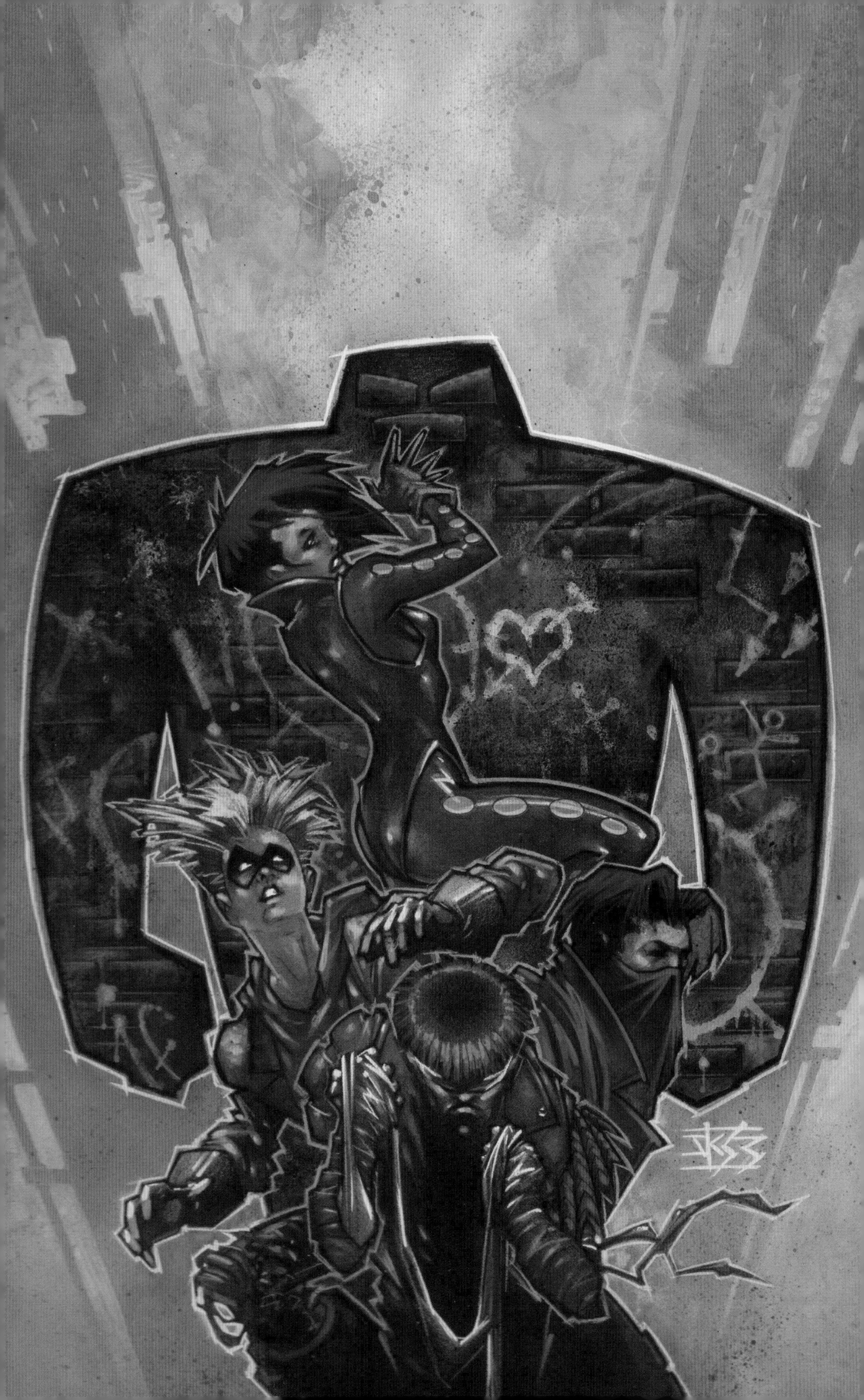

FIRST STEPS
CHAPTER FOUR

"One of us had come back from the dead. Another had once been an enemy. Still another had been inanimate brick. I don't think there's a wall that exists that we can't bring down," said Story to those who would not believe that the Foot Soldiers could make a difference.

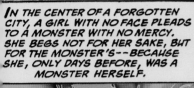

IN THE CENTER OF A FORGOTTEN CITY, A GIRL WITH NO FACE PLEADS TO A MONSTER WITH NO MERCY. SHE BEGS NOT FOR HER SAKE, BUT FOR THE MONSTER'S—BECAUSE SHE, ONLY DAYS BEFORE, WAS A MONSTER HERSELF.

I KNOW YOU CAN HEAR ME, BUT YOU NEED TO *LISTEN.*

SOMETHING'S WRONG, CHINA. WE MAY BE *KILLING* THE VERY PEOPLE WE'RE SUPPOSED TO BE *PROTECTING.*

WHAT IF THE B.T.L. IS A *LIE?*

I'VE MET SOMEONE WHO'S MAKING ME SEE THINGS A LITTLE DIFFERENTLY.

HE'S NOT ALL THAT DIFFERENT FROM US. I LIKE HIM.

HE'S A FOOT SOLDIER. YEAH... ONE OF *THEM.* BUT THEY'RE NOT LIKE WE'VE BEEN TOLD.

MAYBE THEY'RE NOT THE ENEMY.

CLINK!

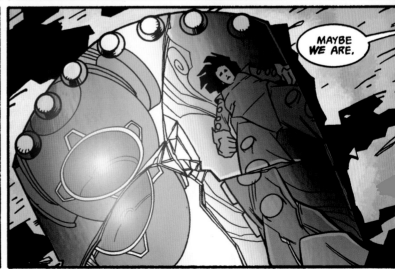

MAYBE *WE* ARE.

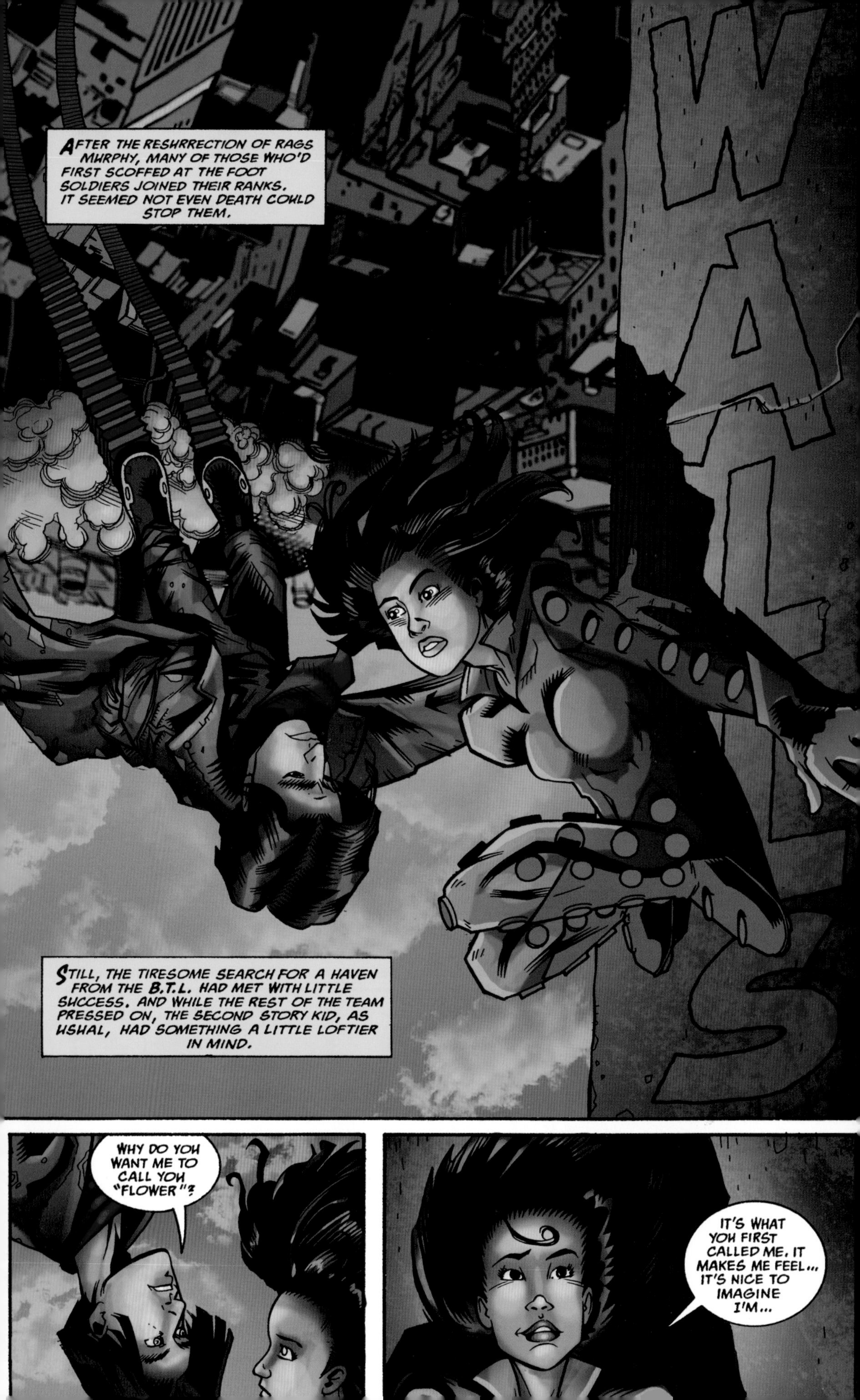
AFTER THE RESURRECTION OF RAGS MURPHY, MANY OF THOSE WHO'D FIRST SCOFFED AT THE FOOT SOLDIERS JOINED THEIR RANKS. IT SEEMED NOT EVEN DEATH COULD STOP THEM.
WALLS
STILL, THE TIRESOME SEARCH FOR A HAVEN FROM THE B.T.L. HAD MET WITH LITTLE SUCCESS. AND WHILE THE REST OF THE TEAM PRESSED ON, THE SECOND STORY KID, AS USUAL, HAD SOMETHING A LITTLE LOFTIER IN MIND.
WHY DO YOU WANT ME TO CALL YOU "FLOWER"?
IT'S WHAT YOU FIRST CALLED ME. IT MAKES ME FEEL... IT'S NICE TO IMAGINE I'M...

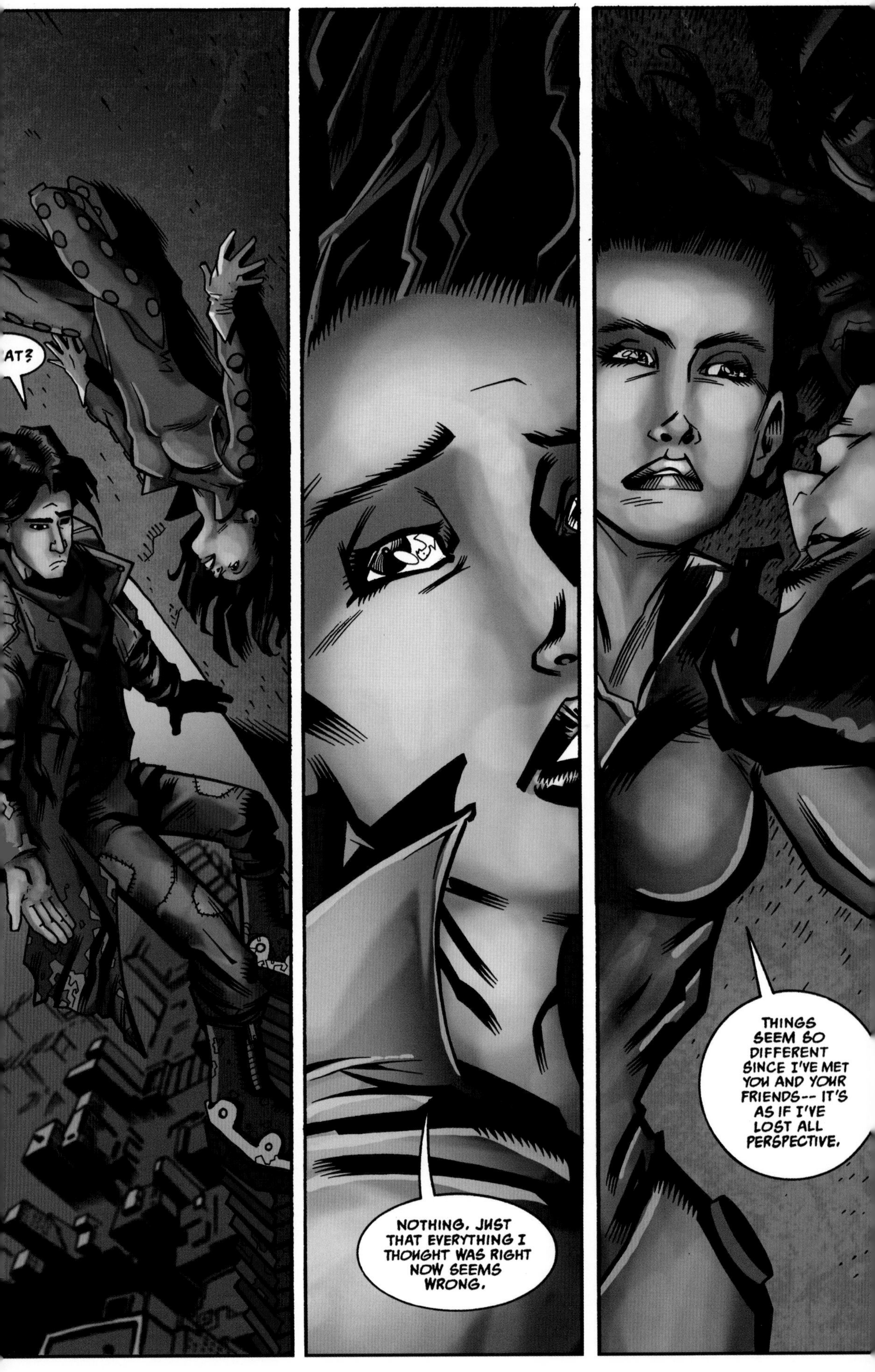
AT?
NOTHING. JUST THAT EVERYTHING I THOUGHT WAS RIGHT NOW SEEMS WRONG.
THINGS SEEM SO DIFFERENT SINCE I'VE MET YOU AND YOUR FRIENDS-- IT'S AS IF I'VE LOST ALL PERSPECTIVE.

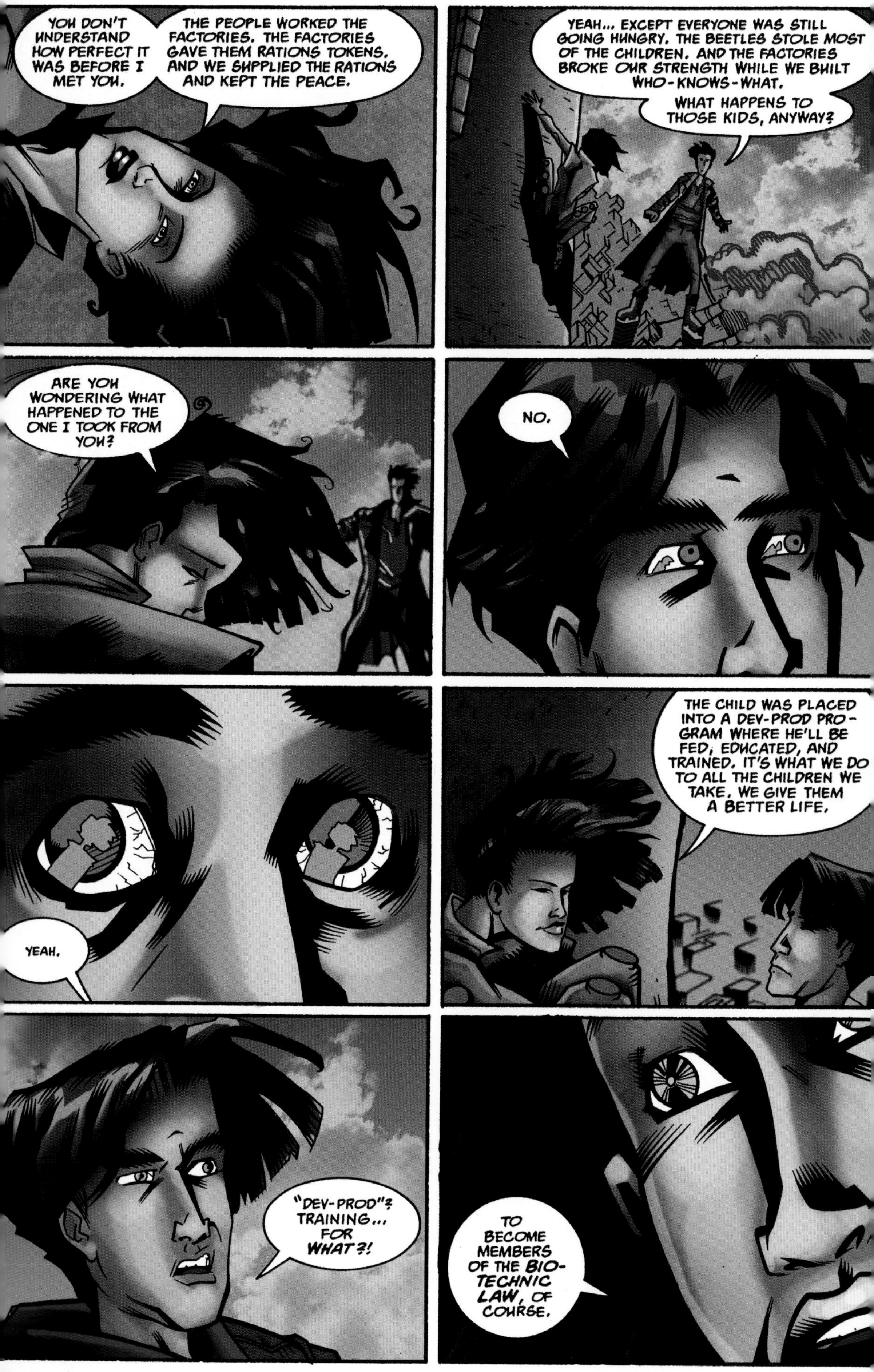
YOU DON'T UNDERSTAND HOW PERFECT IT WAS BEFORE I MET YOU.
THE PEOPLE WORKED THE FACTORIES. THE FACTORIES GAVE THEM RATIONS TOKENS. AND WE SUPPLIED THE RATIONS AND KEPT THE PEACE.
YEAH... EXCEPT EVERYONE WAS STILL GOING HUNGRY. THE BEETLES STOLE MOST OF THE CHILDREN. AND THE FACTORIES BROKE OUR STRENGTH WHILE WE BUILT WHO-KNOWS-WHAT.
WHAT HAPPENS TO THOSE KIDS, ANYWAY?
ARE YOU WONDERING WHAT HAPPENED TO THE ONE I TOOK FROM YOU?
NO.
YEAH.
THE CHILD WAS PLACED INTO A DEV-PROD PROGRAM WHERE HE'LL BE FED, EDUCATED, AND TRAINED. IT'S WHAT WE DO TO ALL THE CHILDREN WE TAKE. WE GIVE THEM A BETTER LIFE.
"DEV-PROD"? TRAINING... FOR *WHAT?!*
TO BECOME MEMBERS OF THE *BIO-TECHNIC LAW*, OF COURSE.

"YOU MEAN EVERYONE'S RUNNING FROM THEIR OWN *CHILDREN*?"

"I'M SORRY."

"THANK YOU VERY MUCH, THERE'S A LOT OF COMFORT IN KNOWING THE BEETLES ARE *SORRY*. LIKE I CAN REALLY BELIEVE THAT.

"SO, FOR ALL YOU KNOW...

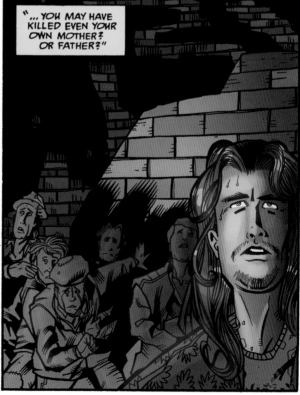

"... YOU MAY HAVE KILLED EVEN YOUR OWN MOTHER? OR FATHER?"

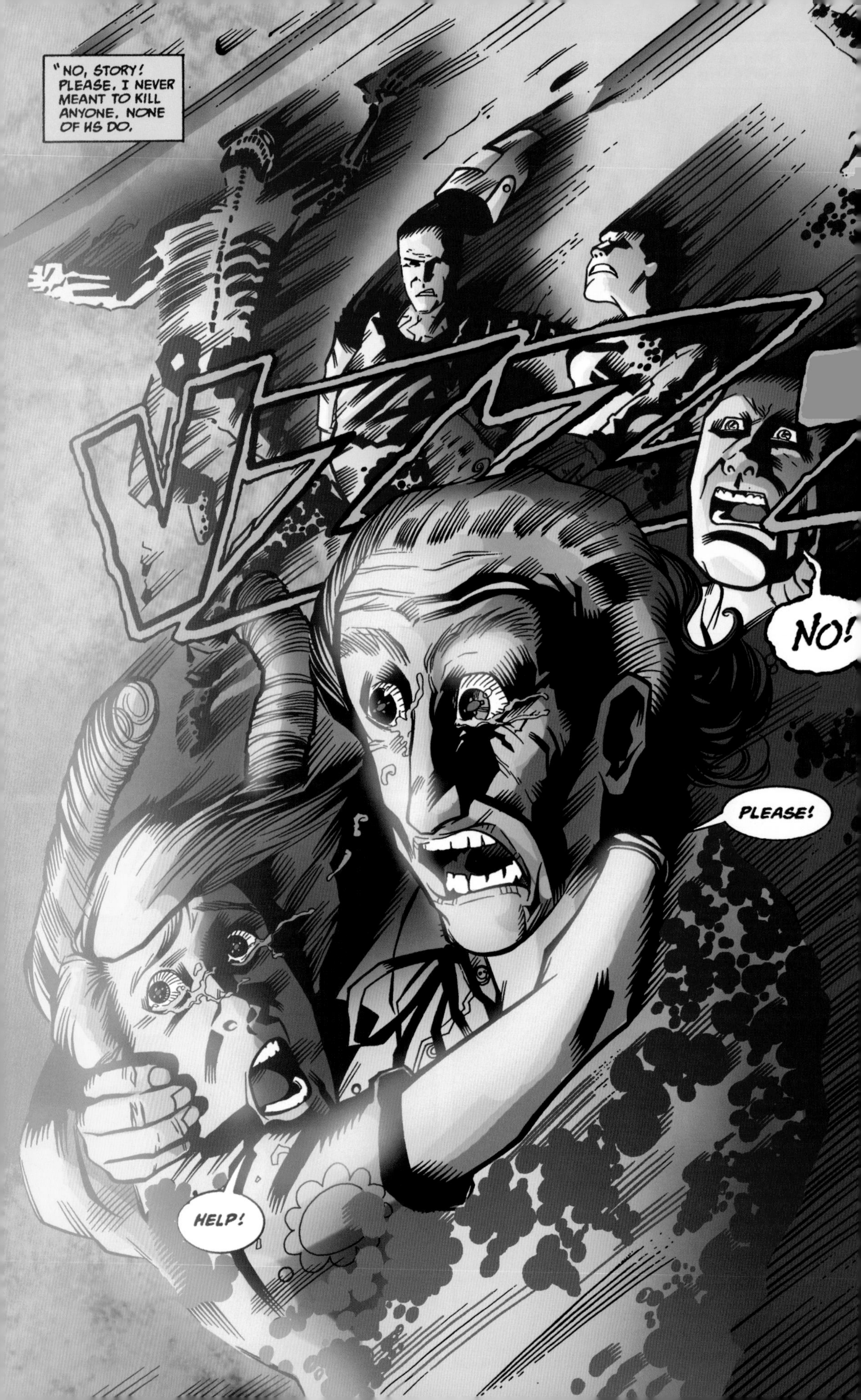
"NO, STORY! PLEASE. I NEVER MEANT TO KILL ANYONE. NONE OF US DO.
NO!
PLEASE!
HELP!

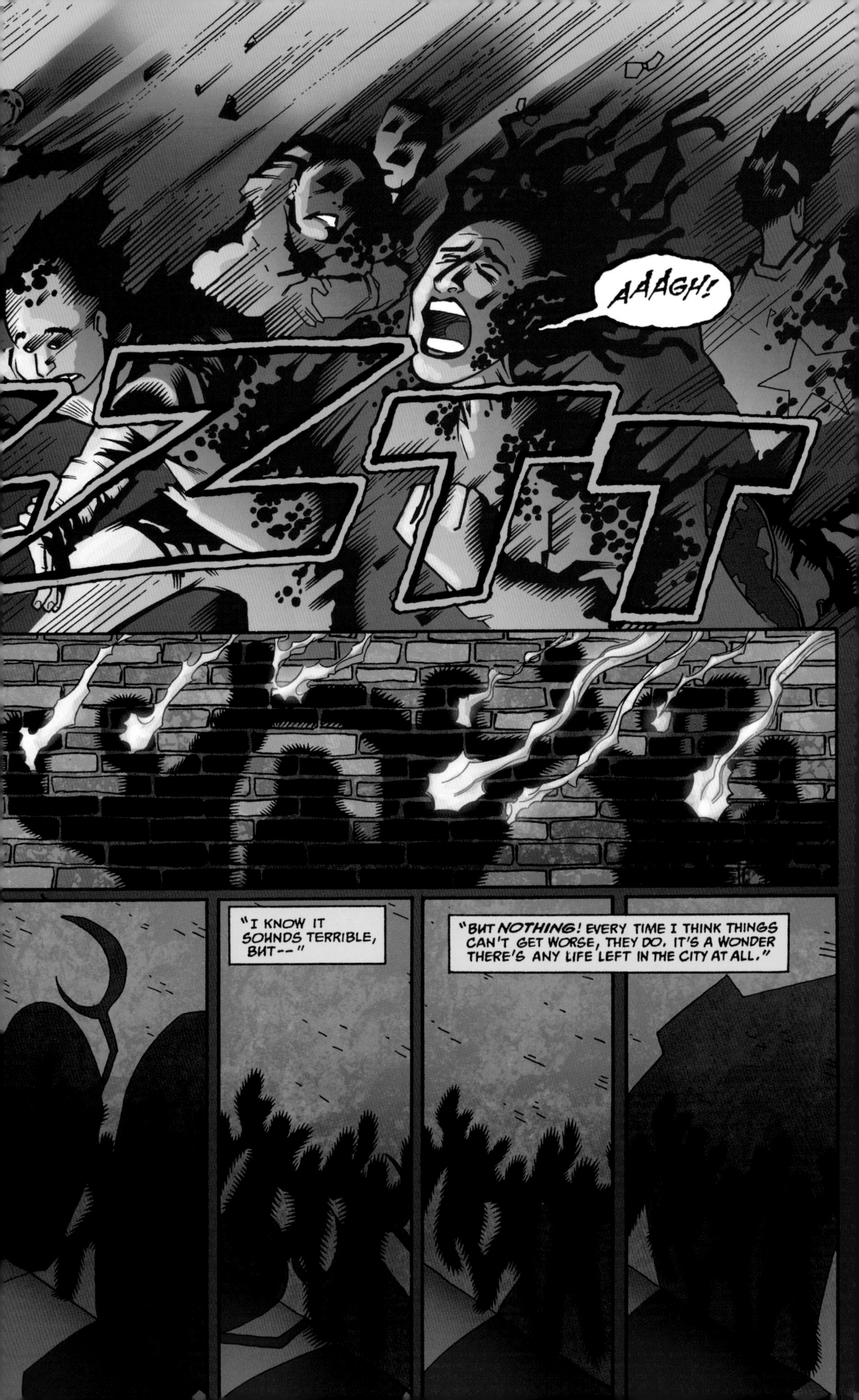
AAAGH!
ZZTTT
"I KNOW IT SOUNDS TERRIBLE, BUT--"
"BUT NOTHING! EVERY TIME I THINK THINGS CAN'T GET WORSE, THEY DO. IT'S A WONDER THERE'S ANY LIFE LEFT IN THE CITY AT ALL."

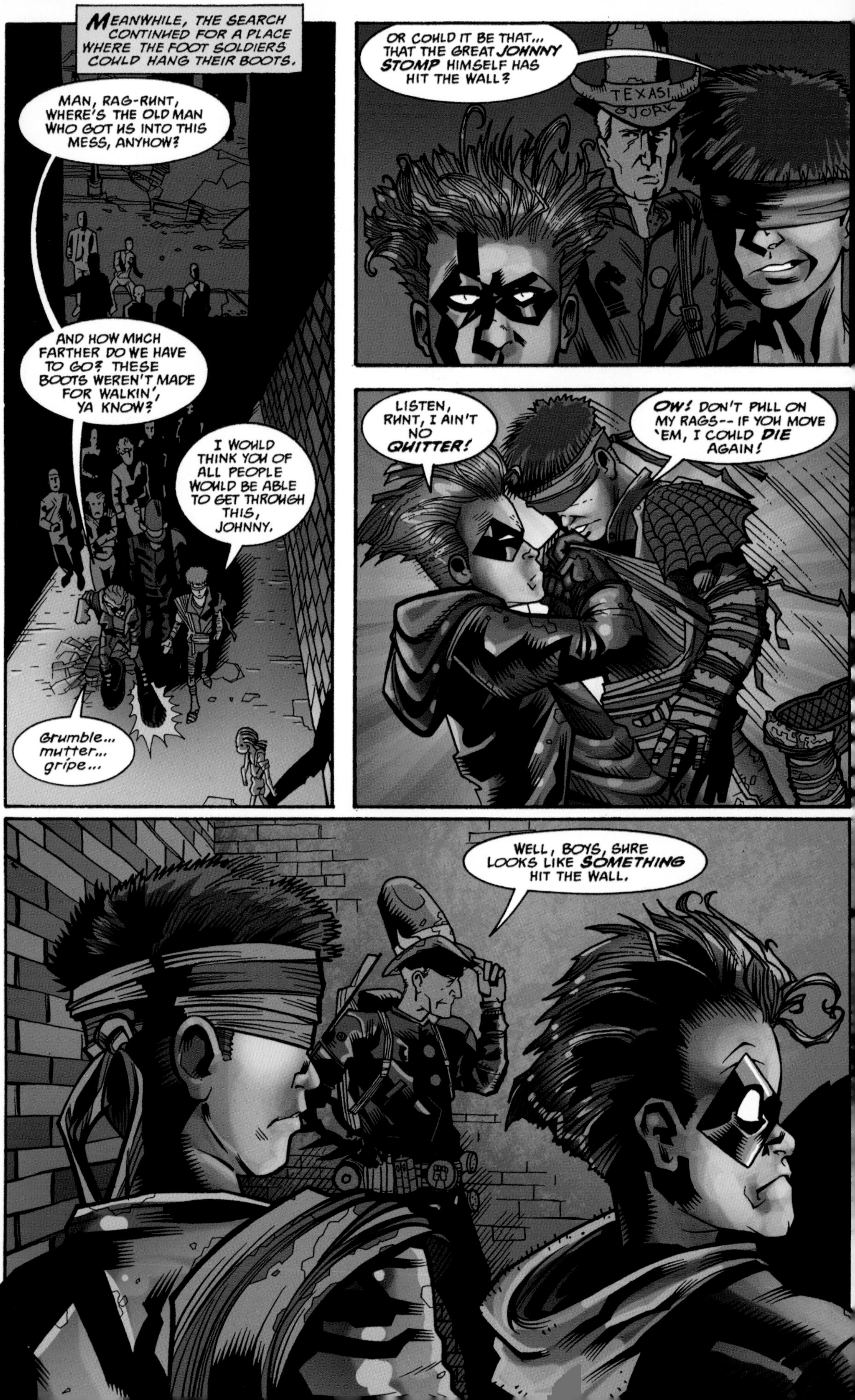
MEANWHILE, THE SEARCH CONTINUED FOR A PLACE WHERE THE FOOT SOLDIERS COULD HANG THEIR BOOTS.
MAN, RAG-RUNT, WHERE'S THE OLD MAN WHO GOT US INTO THIS MESS, ANYHOW?
AND HOW MUCH FARTHER DO WE HAVE TO GO? THESE BOOTS WEREN'T MADE FOR WALKIN', YA KNOW?
I WOULD THINK YOU OF ALL PEOPLE WOULD BE ABLE TO GET THROUGH THIS, JOHNNY.
Grumble... mutter... gripe...
OR COULD IT BE THAT... THAT THE GREAT JOHNNY STOMP HIMSELF HAS HIT THE WALL?
TEXAS
LISTEN, RUNT, I AIN'T NO QUITTER!
OW! DON'T PULL ON MY RAGS-- IF YOU MOVE 'EM, I COULD DIE AGAIN!
WELL, BOYS, SURE LOOKS LIKE SOMETHING HIT THE WALL.

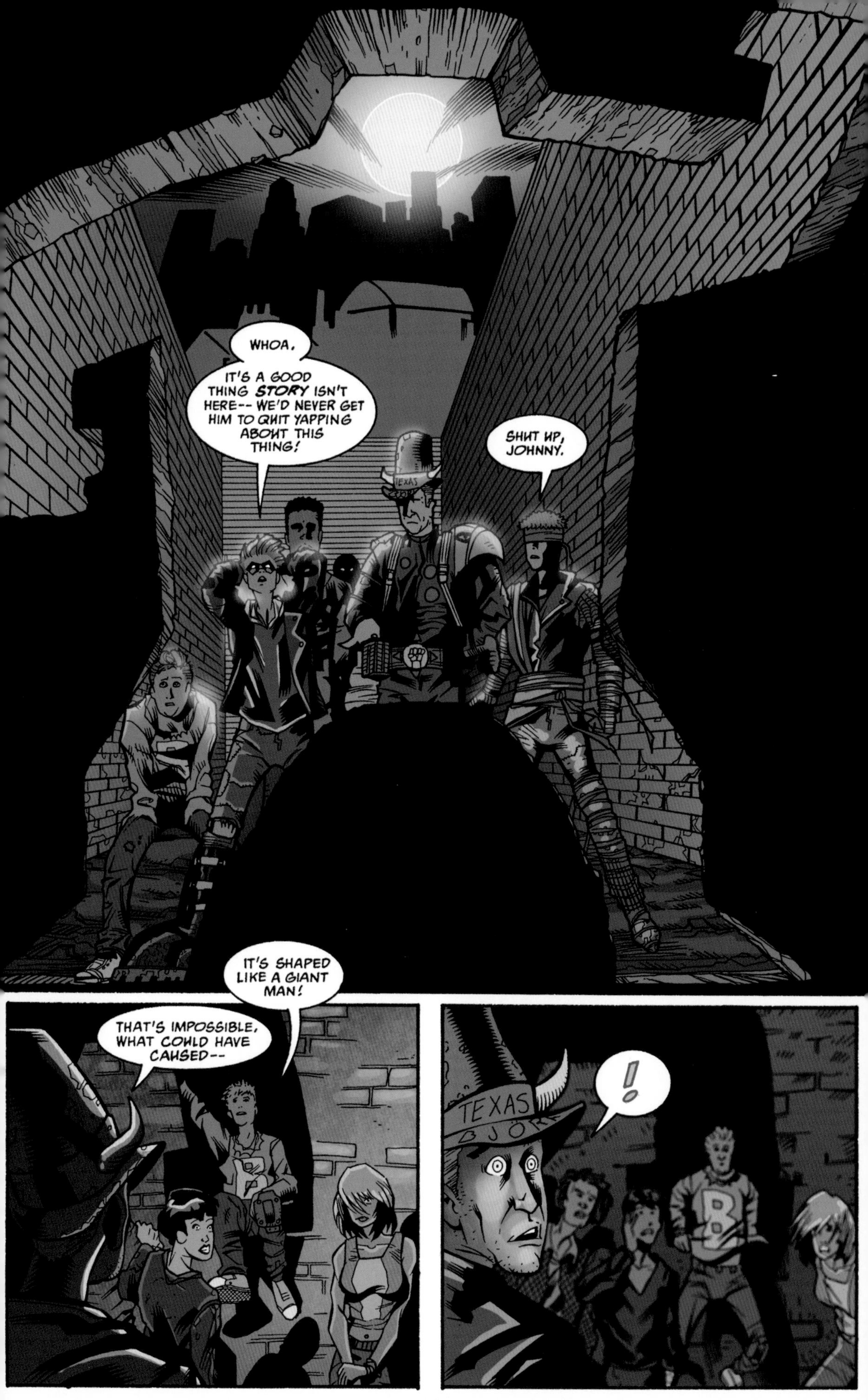
WHOA,
IT'S A GOOD THING STORY ISN'T HERE-- WE'D NEVER GET HIM TO QUIT YAPPING ABOUT THIS THING!
SHUT UP, JOHNNY.
TEXAS
IT'S SHAPED LIKE A GIANT MAN!
THAT'S IMPOSSIBLE, WHAT COULD HAVE CAUSED--
!
TEXAS
BJORK

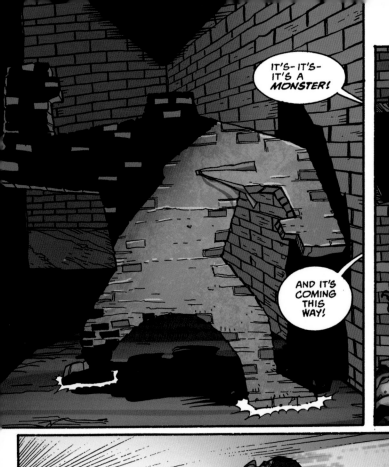

IT'S- IT'S- IT'S A *MONSTER!*

AND IT'S COMING THIS WAY!

IT MUST BE SOME NEW KINDA *BEETLE!*

NO, JOHNNY... *WAIT!* IT MIGHT BE--

WAITING IS FER WIMPS.

¡*Ooof!*¿

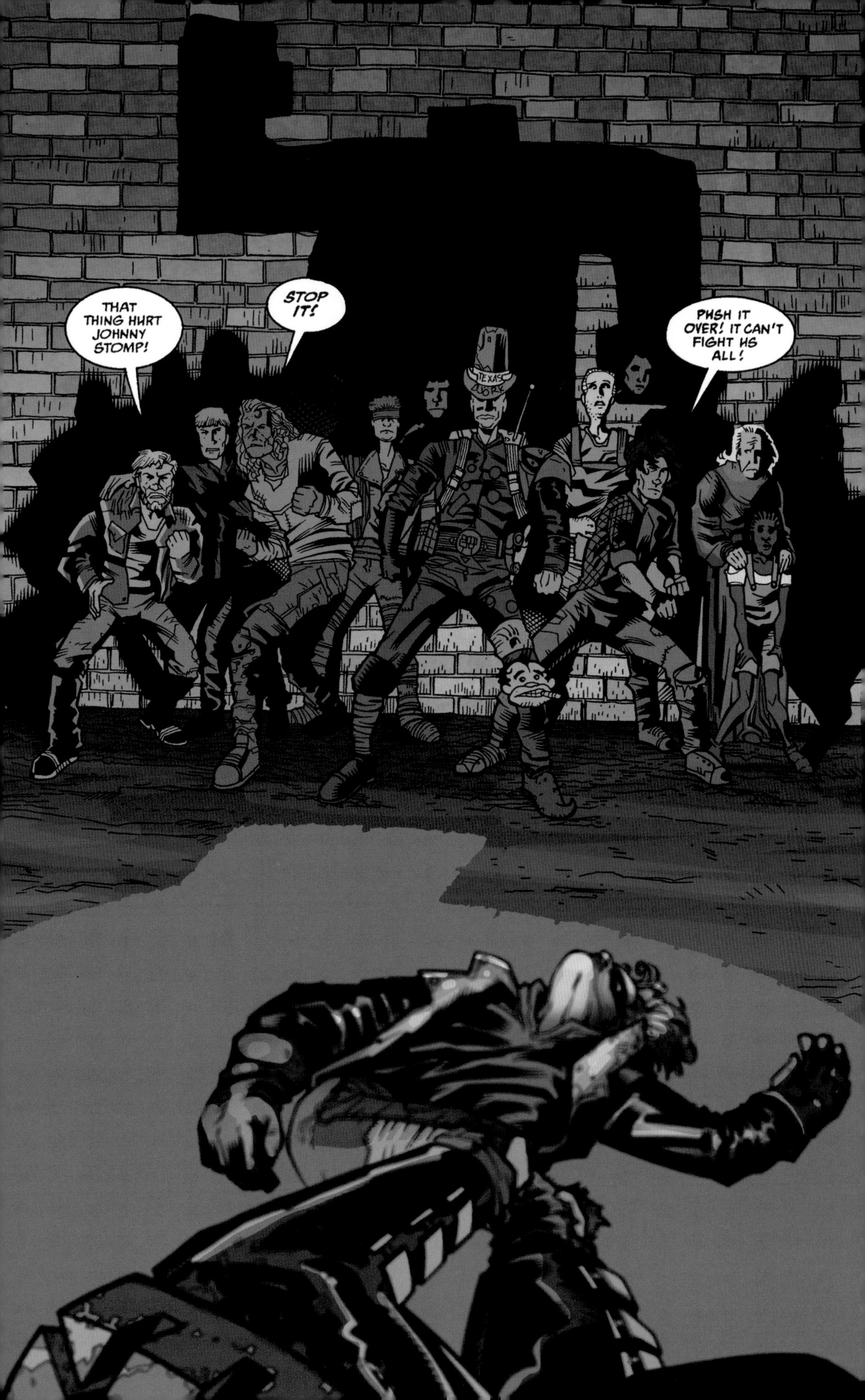
THAT THING HURT JOHNNY STOMP!
STOP IT!
TEXAS
PUSH IT OVER! IT CAN'T FIGHT US ALL!

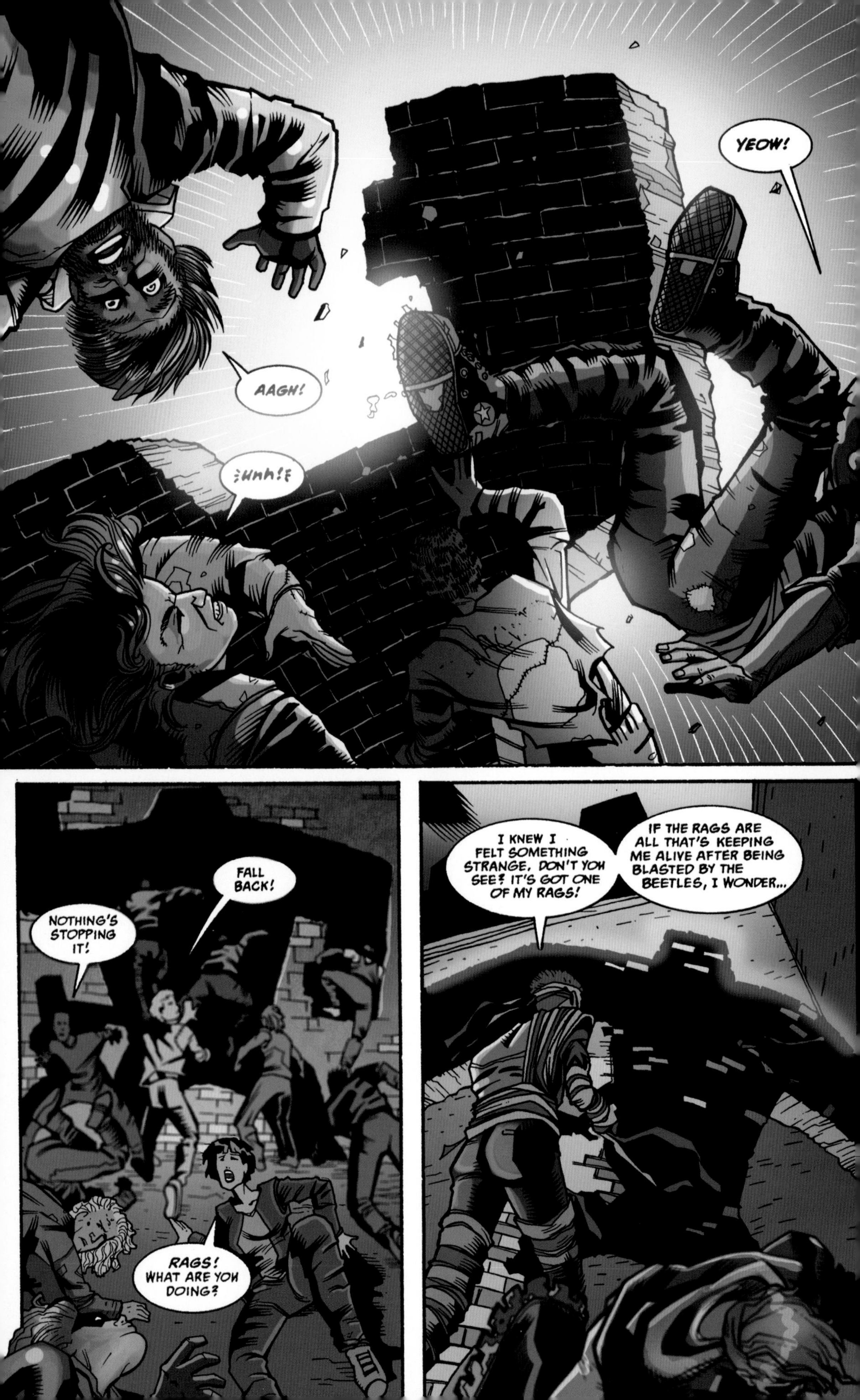
YEOW!
AAGH!
¡Unh!¡
FALL BACK!
NOTHING'S STOPPING IT!
RAGS! WHAT ARE YOU DOING?
I KNEW I FELT SOMETHING STRANGE. DON'T YOU SEE? IT'S GOT ONE OF MY RAGS!
IF THE RAGS ARE ALL THAT'S KEEPING ME ALIVE AFTER BEING BLASTED BY THE BEETLES, I WONDER...

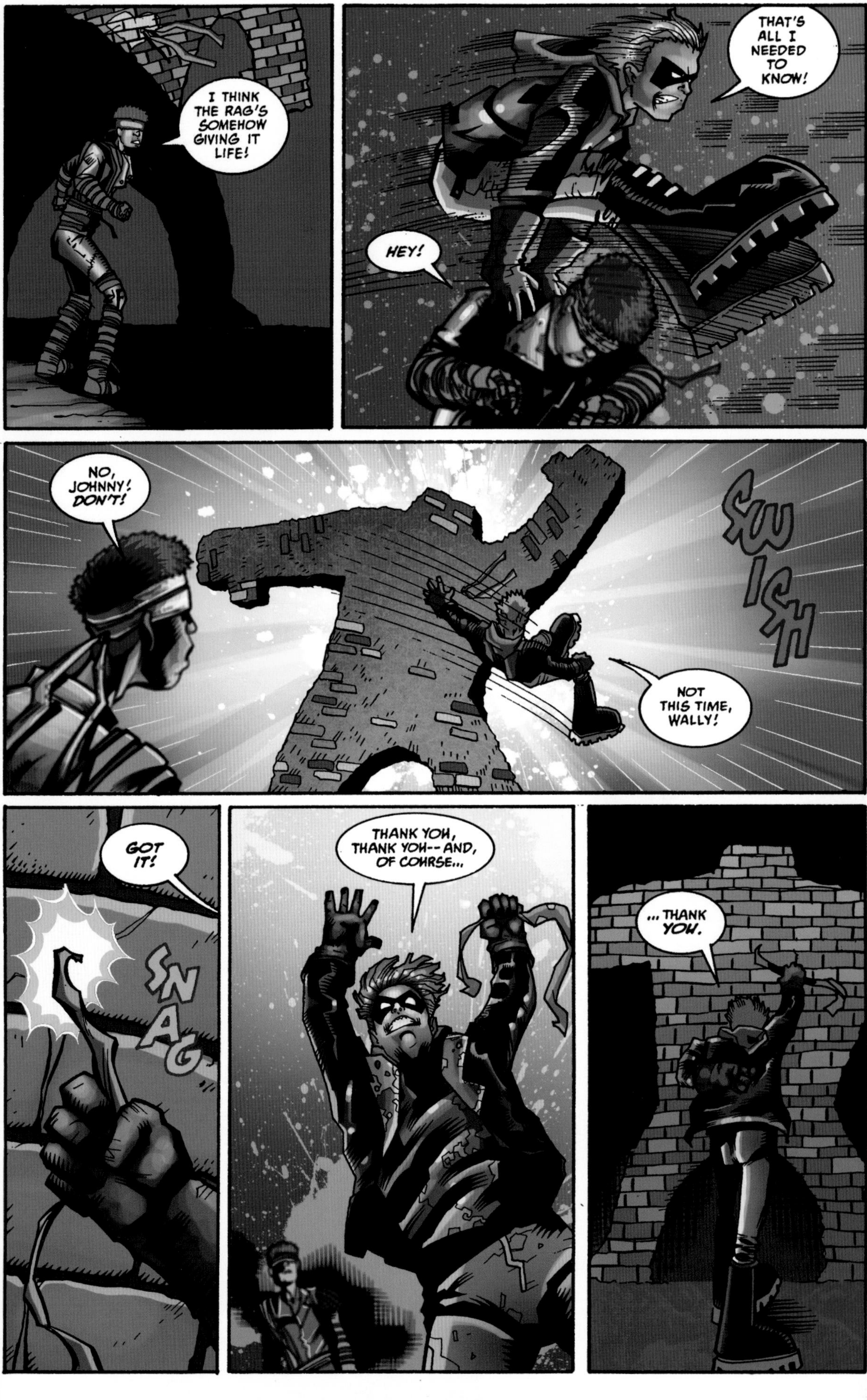
I THINK THE RAG'S SOMEHOW GIVING IT LIFE!
THAT'S ALL I NEEDED TO KNOW!
HEY!
NO, JOHNNY! DON'T!
SWISH
NOT THIS TIME, WALLY!
GOT IT!
SNAG
THANK YOU, THANK YOU-- AND, OF COURSE...
...THANK YOU.

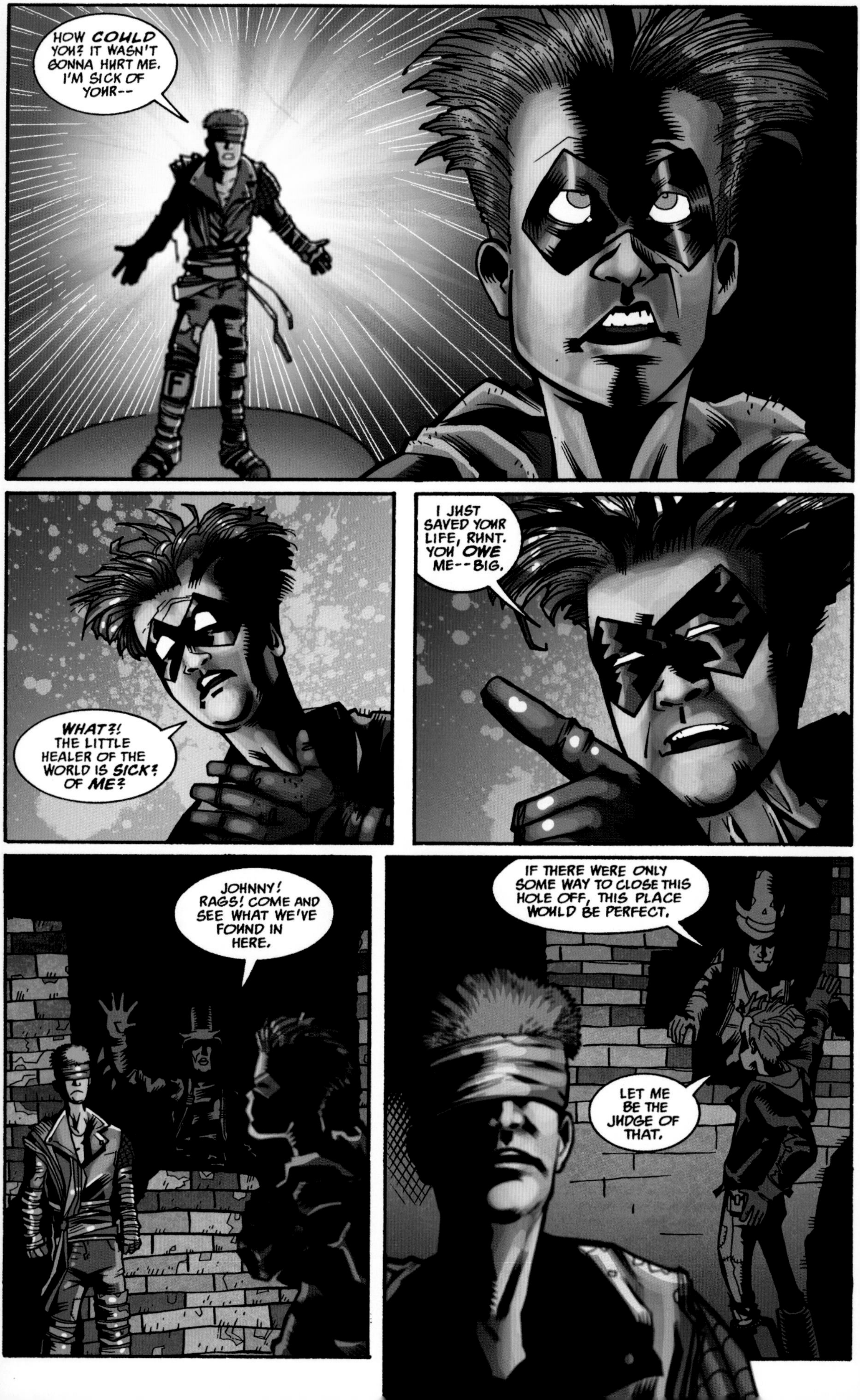
HOW COULD YOU? IT WASN'T GONNA HURT ME. I'M SICK OF YOUR--
WHAT?! THE LITTLE HEALER OF THE WORLD IS SICK? OF ME?
I JUST SAVED YOUR LIFE, RUNT. YOU OWE ME--BIG.
JOHNNY! RAGS! COME AND SEE WHAT WE'VE FOUND IN HERE.
IF THERE WERE ONLY SOME WAY TO CLOSE THIS HOLE OFF, THIS PLACE WOULD BE PERFECT.
LET ME BE THE JUDGE OF THAT.

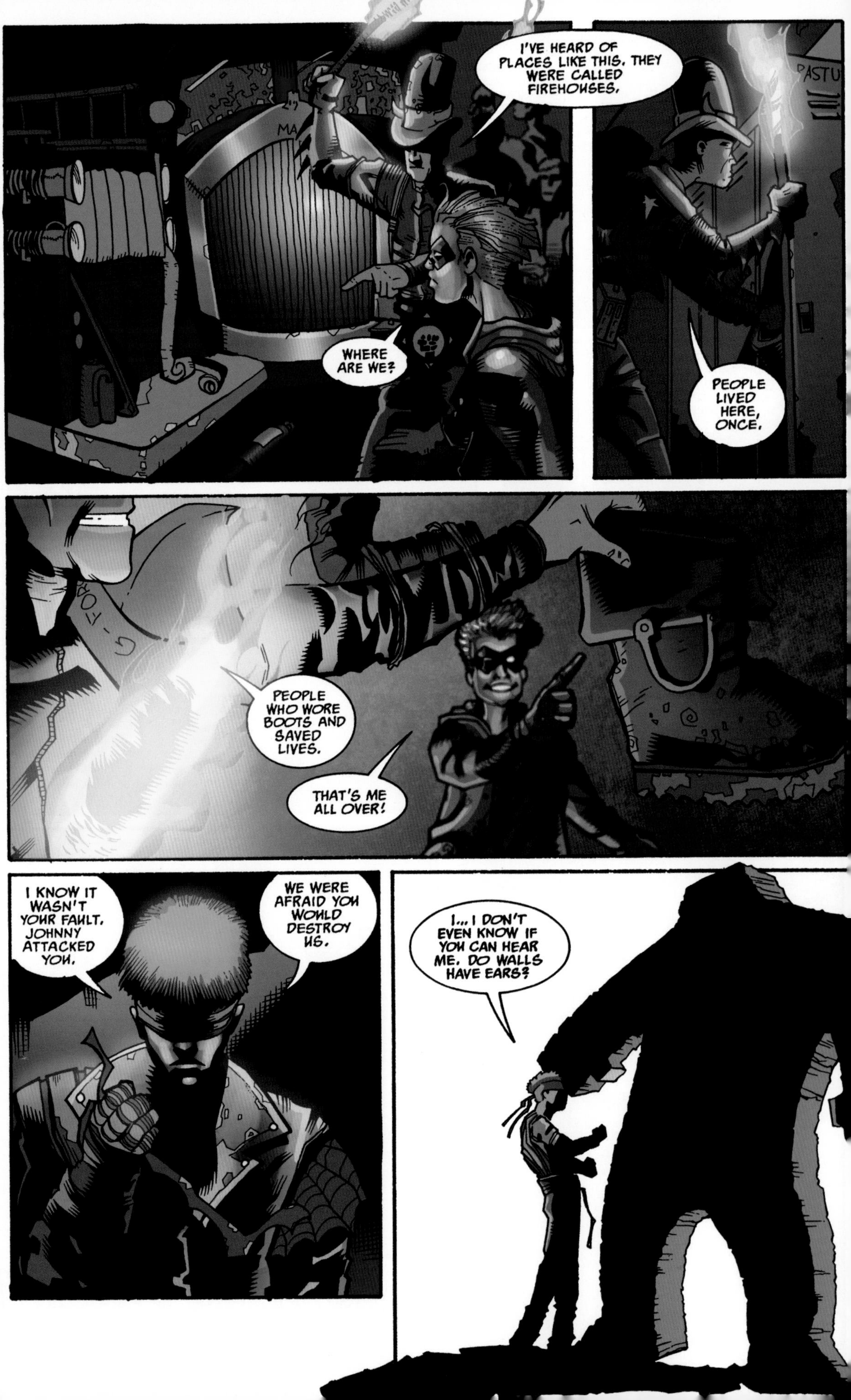
I'VE HEARD OF PLACES LIKE THIS. THEY WERE CALLED FIREHOUSES.
WHERE ARE WE?
PEOPLE LIVED HERE, ONCE.
PEOPLE WHO WORE BOOTS AND SAVED LIVES.
THAT'S ME ALL OVER!
I KNOW IT WASN'T YOUR FAULT. JOHNNY ATTACKED YOU.
WE WERE AFRAID YOU WOULD DESTROY US.
I... I DON'T EVEN KNOW IF YOU CAN HEAR ME. DO WALLS HAVE EARS?

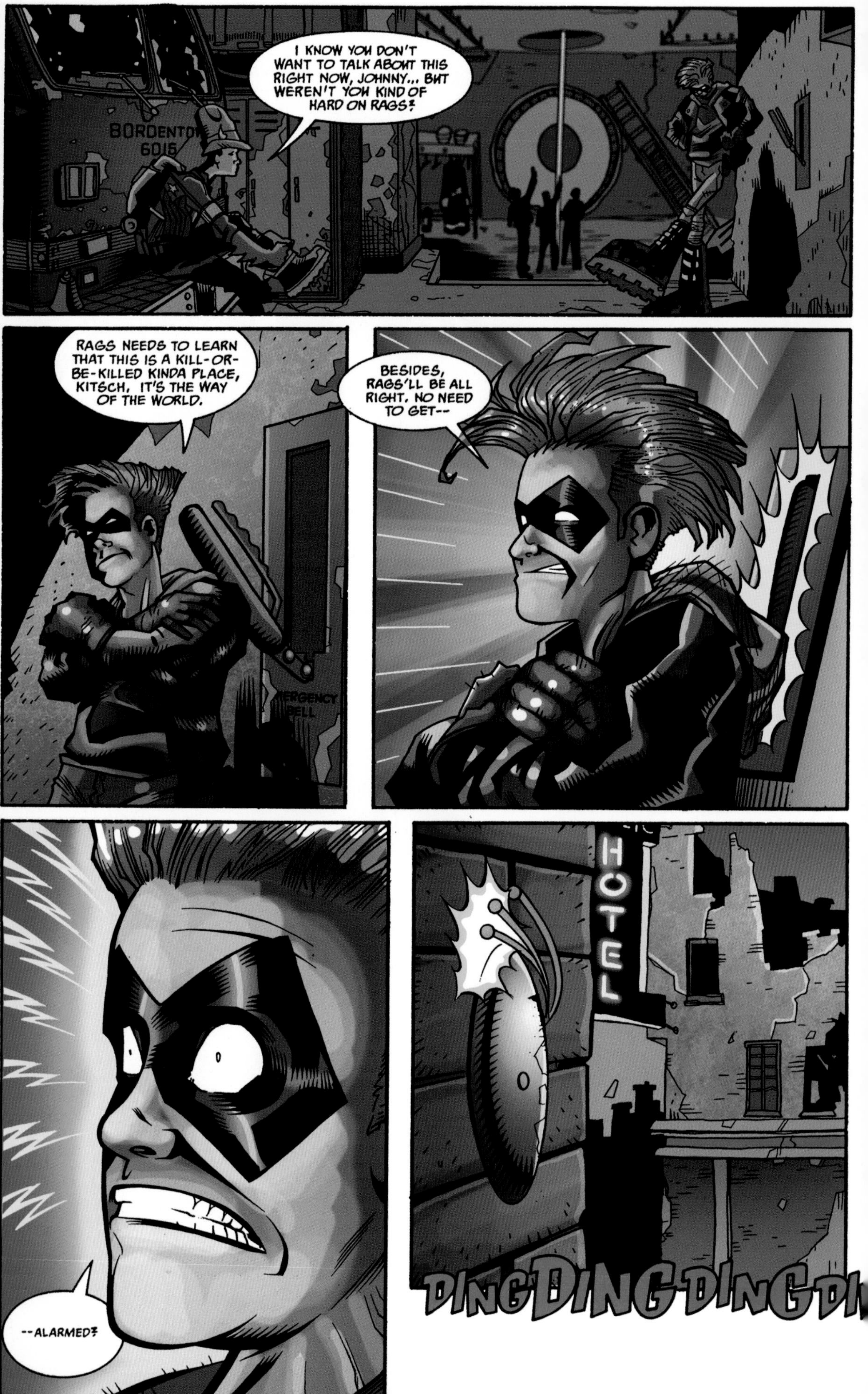
I KNOW YOU DON'T WANT TO TALK ABOUT THIS RIGHT NOW, JOHNNY... BUT WEREN'T YOU KIND OF HARD ON RAGS?
BORDENTOW
6015
RAGS NEEDS TO LEARN THAT THIS IS A KILL-OR-BE-KILLED KINDA PLACE, KITSCH. IT'S THE WAY OF THE WORLD.
MERGENCY BELL
BESIDES, RAGS'LL BE ALL RIGHT. NO NEED TO GET--
--ALARMED?
HOTEL
DINGDINGDINGDINGDI

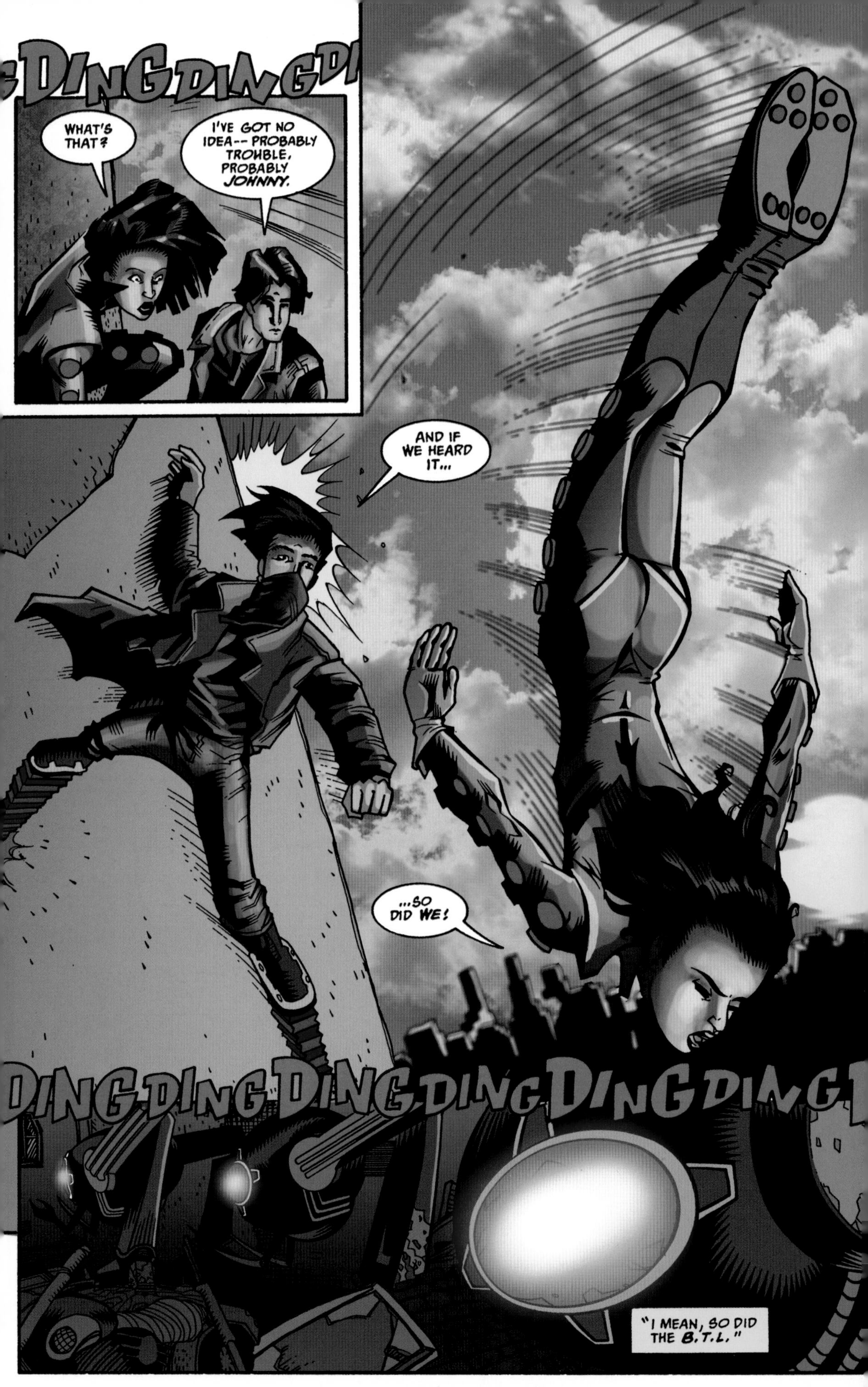

DINGDINGDING
WHAT'S THAT?
I'VE GOT NO IDEA-- PROBABLY TROUBLE, PROBABLY JOHNNY.
AND IF WE HEARD IT...
...SO DID WE!
DINGDINGDINGDINGDINGDING
"I MEAN, SO DID THE B.T.L."

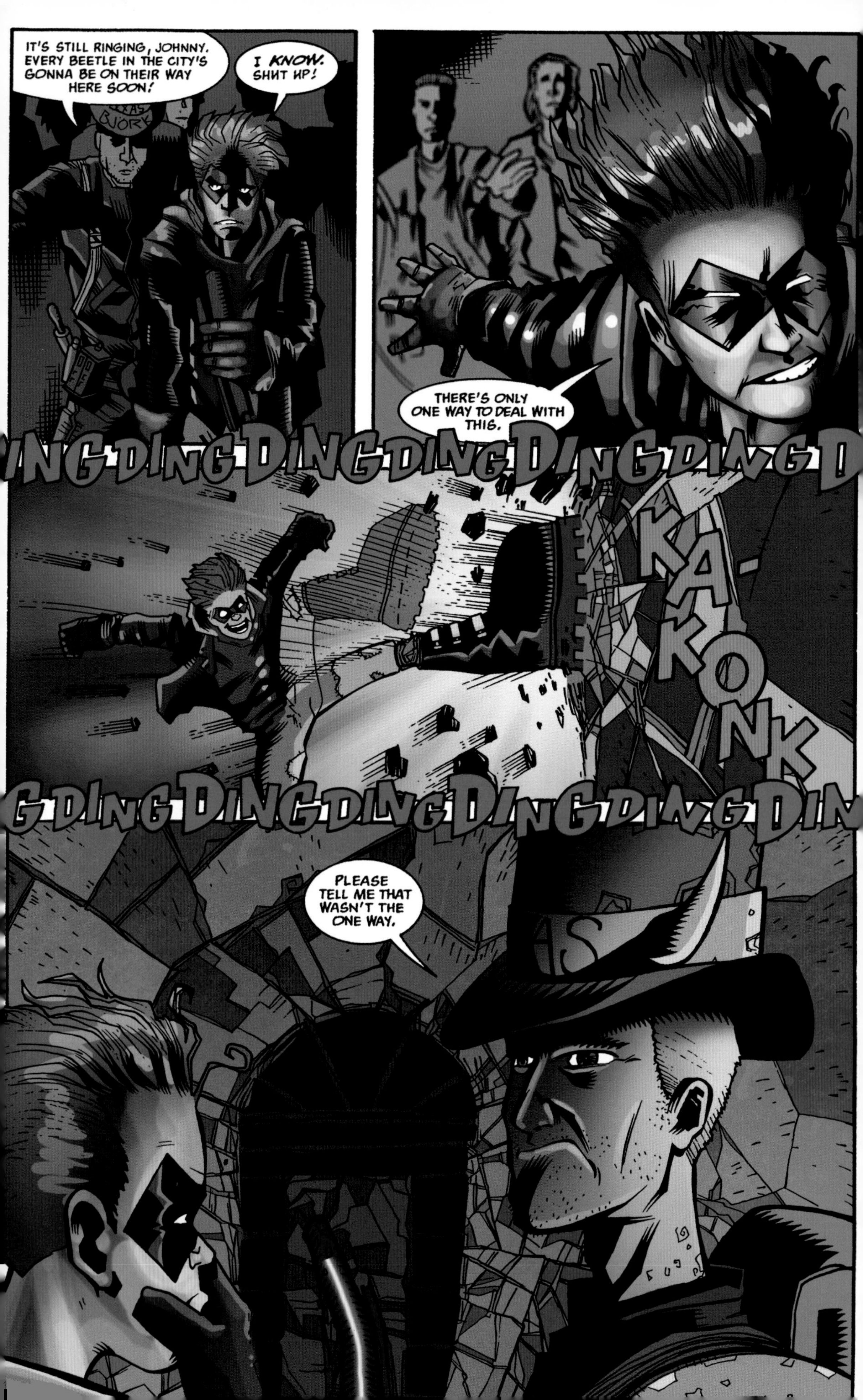
IT'S STILL RINGING, JOHNNY. EVERY BEETLE IN THE CITY'S GONNA BE ON THEIR WAY HERE SOON!
I KNOW. SHUT UP!
THERE'S ONLY ONE WAY TO DEAL WITH THIS.
INGDINGDINGDINGDINGDINGD
KA-KONK
GDINGDINGDINGDINGDINGDIN
PLEASE TELL ME THAT WASN'T THE ONE WAY.

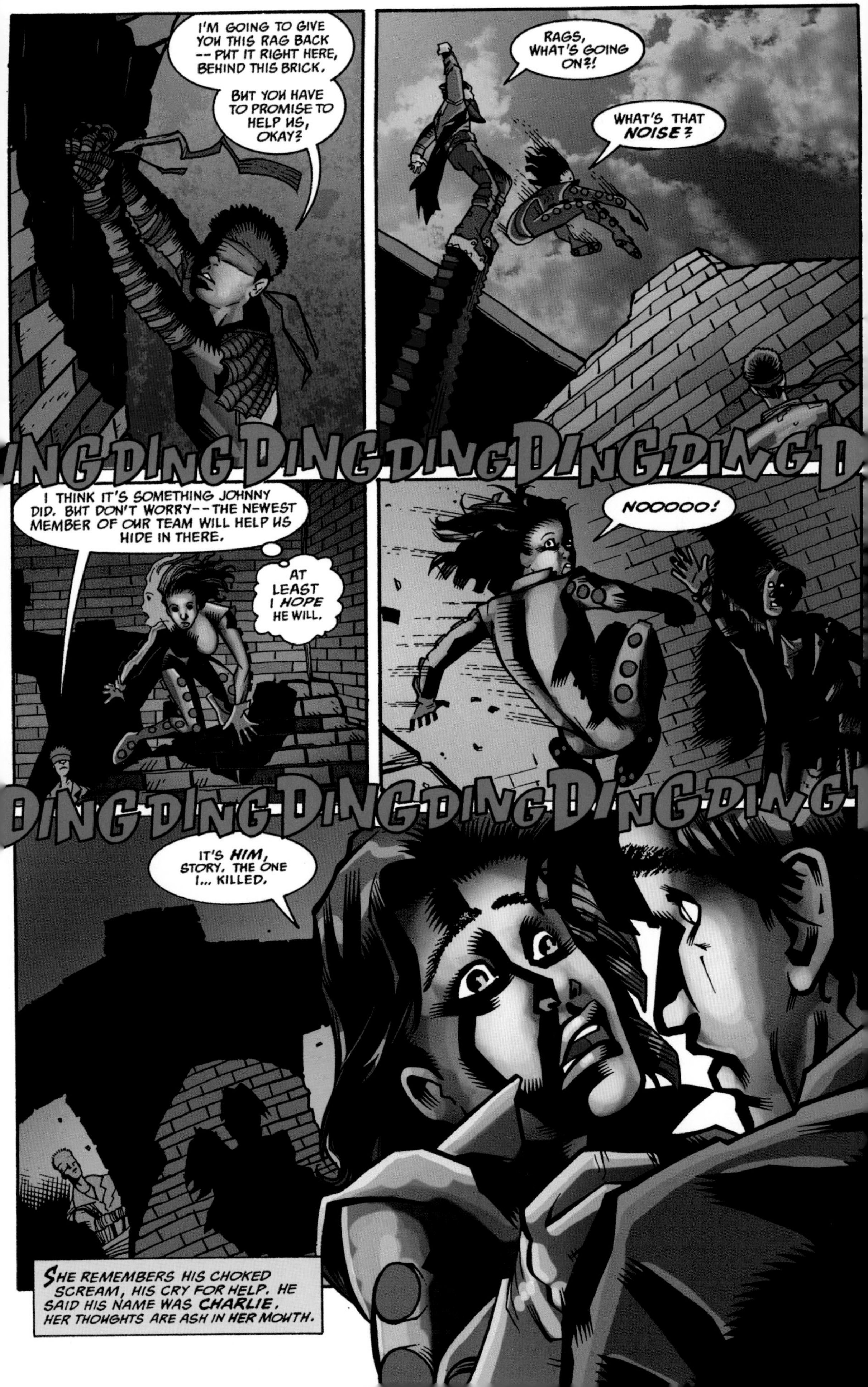
I'M GOING TO GIVE YOU THIS RAG BACK -- PUT IT RIGHT HERE, BEHIND THIS BRICK.
BUT YOU HAVE TO PROMISE TO HELP US, OKAY?
RAGS, WHAT'S GOING ON?!
WHAT'S THAT NOISE?
DINGDINGDINGDINGDINGDINGD
I THINK IT'S SOMETHING JOHNNY DID. BUT DON'T WORRY-- THE NEWEST MEMBER OF OUR TEAM WILL HELP US HIDE IN THERE.
AT LEAST I HOPE HE WILL.
NOOOOO!
DINGDINGDINGDINGDINGDING
IT'S HIM, STORY. THE ONE I... KILLED.
SHE REMEMBERS HIS CHOKED SCREAM, HIS CRY FOR HELP. HE SAID HIS NAME WAS CHARLIE. HER THOUGHTS ARE ASH IN HER MOUTH.

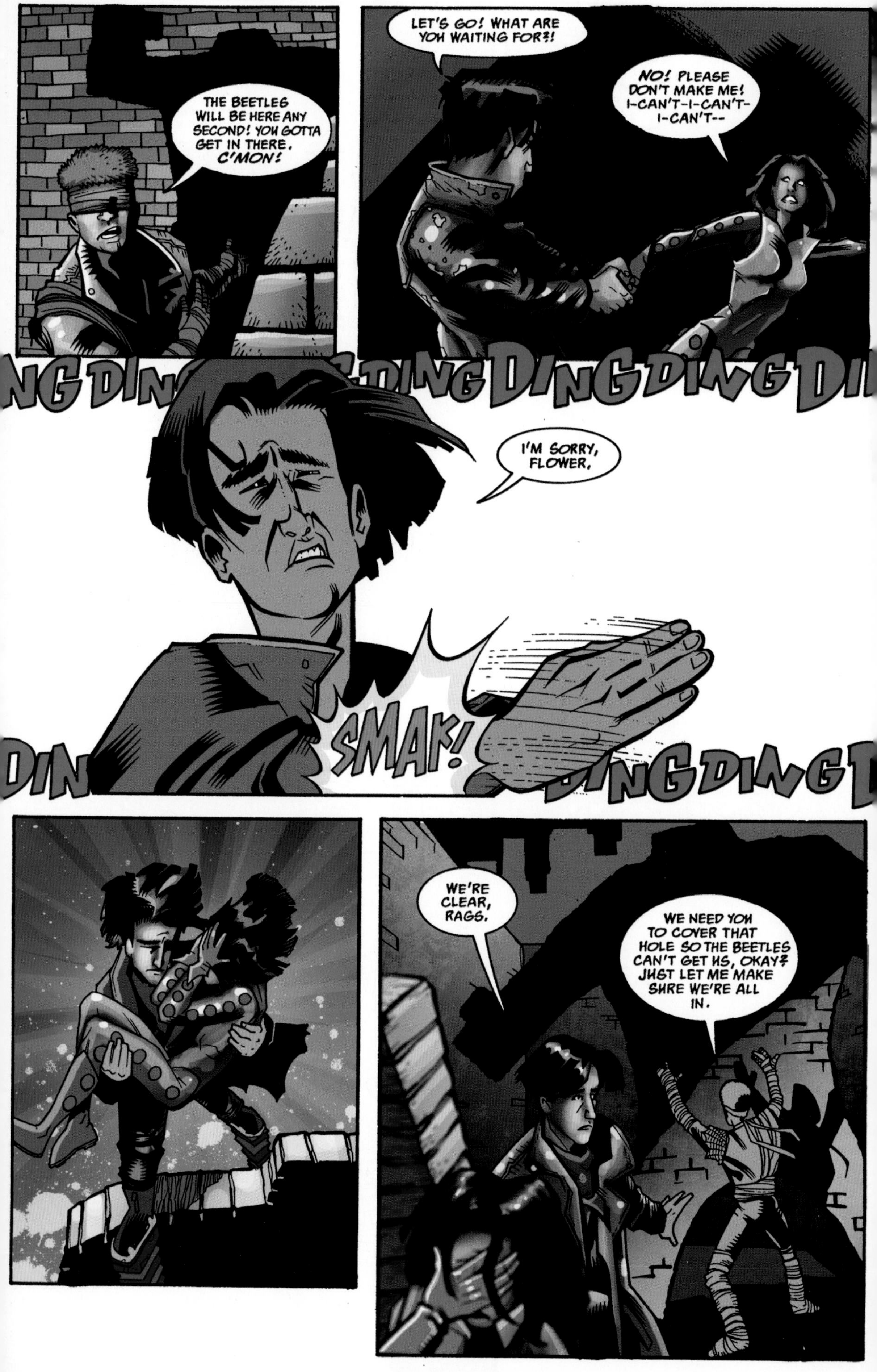
THE BEETLES WILL BE HERE ANY SECOND! YOU GOTTA GET IN THERE. C'MON!
LET'S GO! WHAT ARE YOU WAITING FOR?!
NO! PLEASE DON'T MAKE ME! I-CAN'T-I-CAN'T-I-CAN'T--
DING DING DING
I'M SORRY, FLOWER.
SMAK!
DING DING
WE'RE CLEAR, RAGS.
WE NEED YOU TO COVER THAT HOLE SO THE BEETLES CAN'T GET US, OKAY? JUST LET ME MAKE SURE WE'RE ALL IN.

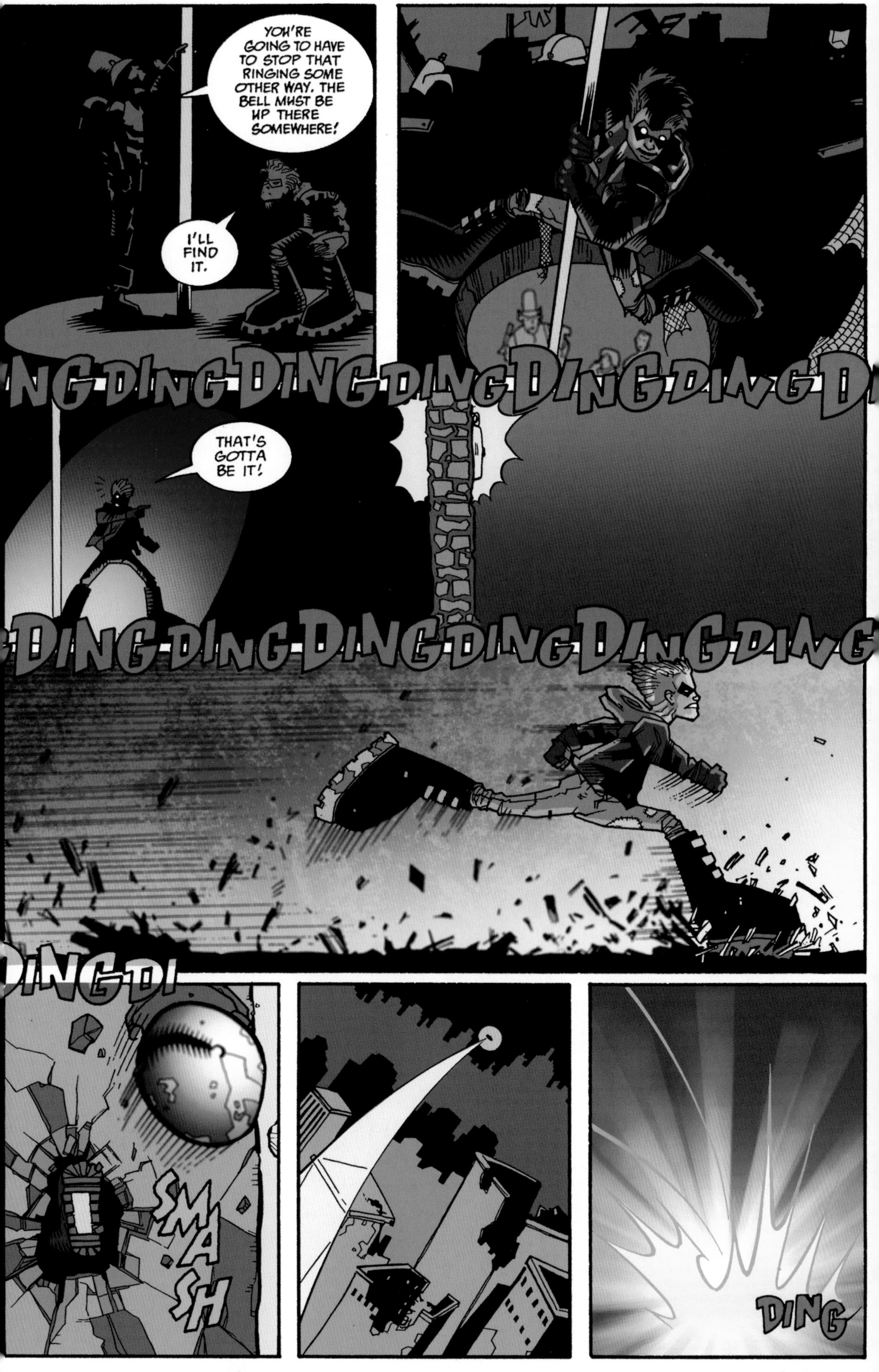
YOU'RE GOING TO HAVE TO STOP THAT RINGING SOME OTHER WAY. THE BELL MUST BE UP THERE SOMEWHERE!
I'LL FIND IT.
DING DING DING DING DING DING DING
THAT'S GOTTA BE IT!
DING DING DING DING DING DING DING
SMASH
DING

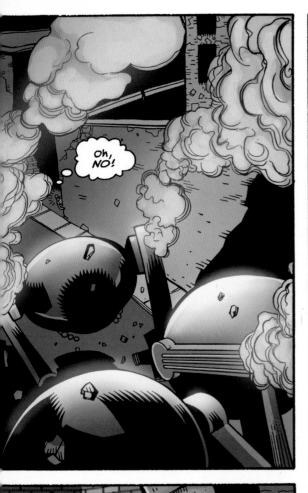

OH, NO!

GET IN THERE-- THEY'RE COMING! AND THERE'RE A LOT OF 'EM!

OKAY, WE'RE IN! REMEMBER WHAT I SAID-- THE BEETLES CAN'T KNOW WE'RE HERE.

BRRG   BRRG

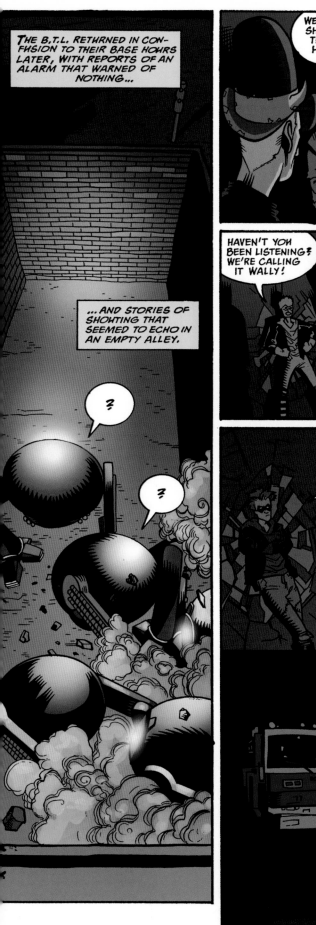

THE B.T.L. RETURNED IN CONFUSION TO THEIR BASE HOURS LATER, WITH REPORTS OF AN ALARM THAT WARNED OF NOTHING...

...AND STORIES OF SHOUTING THAT SEEMED TO ECHO IN AN EMPTY ALLEY.

?

?

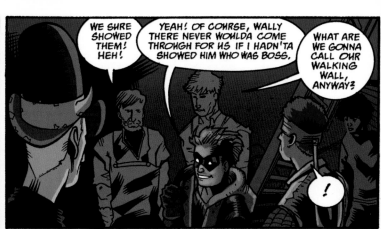

WE SURE SHOWED THEM! HEH!

YEAH! OF COURSE, WALLY THERE NEVER WOULDA COME THROUGH FOR US IF I HADN'TA SHOWED HIM WHO WAS BOSS.

WHAT ARE WE GONNA CALL OUR WALKING WALL, ANYWAY?

!

HAVEN'T YOU BEEN LISTENING? WE'RE CALLING IT WALLY!

HIS NAME IS CHARLIE.

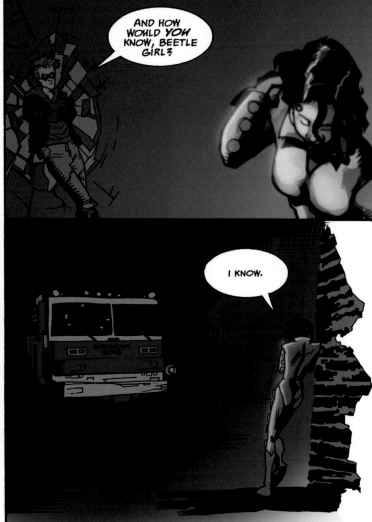

AND HOW WOULD YOU KNOW, BEETLE GIRL?

I KNOW.

LETTING YOUR FREEDOM RING A BIT TOO LOUDLY, EH, BOYS?

IT IS TIME FOR US TO MEET AGAIN. THERE IS MUCH MORE THAN QUICK ESCAPES AND DEFENSIVE TECHNIQUES TO LEARN.

THERE IS YOUR OWN POTENTIAL. THERE IS THE SECRET OF THE FACTORIES. THERE IS STRATEGY.

BUT, MOST OF ALL, YOU MUST KNOW WHO YOUR ENEMIES TRULY ARE.

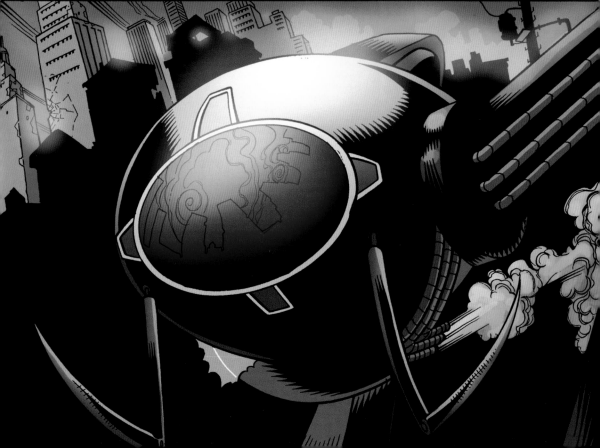

Story's Story

Chapter Four

There is something worse than being lied to. Something far worse than being on the streets and discovering you've been lied to your entire life.

It's being the one who told the lie.

Why did I lie about the warning in the crypt? Why didn't I tell Johnny and Rags about my being able to read? It's not like I'm so different from them, any less a victim of the B.T.L. than they are.

I was just a boy when the Beetles burnt down the libraries and the book stores. I think it was an attempt to keep us from getting any ideas. Or, at the very least, to cut us off from the ideas others have had before us.

The writings and therefore readings of any sort of material became associated only with the Bio-Technic Law years ago. To be educated is to be in their number. To be illiterate is to be on the streets. Or working the factories. Where once the A, B, Cs were the first letters learned in a larger alphabet, the very keys to language; now it begins and ends with the letters B.T.L. And there's a wall there. One, unlike Charlie, that won't move. Not without pushing it down.

Some may say that I'm reading too much into the events that my father told me, but that's the cost of being educated. You get ideas. The first to fall didn't die because they were older or it was harder for them to run. No, I think it was because they too had ideas, they too were aware of what was happening in the city. Those who could read were the first targets. Those who could reason had nothing to stand on before

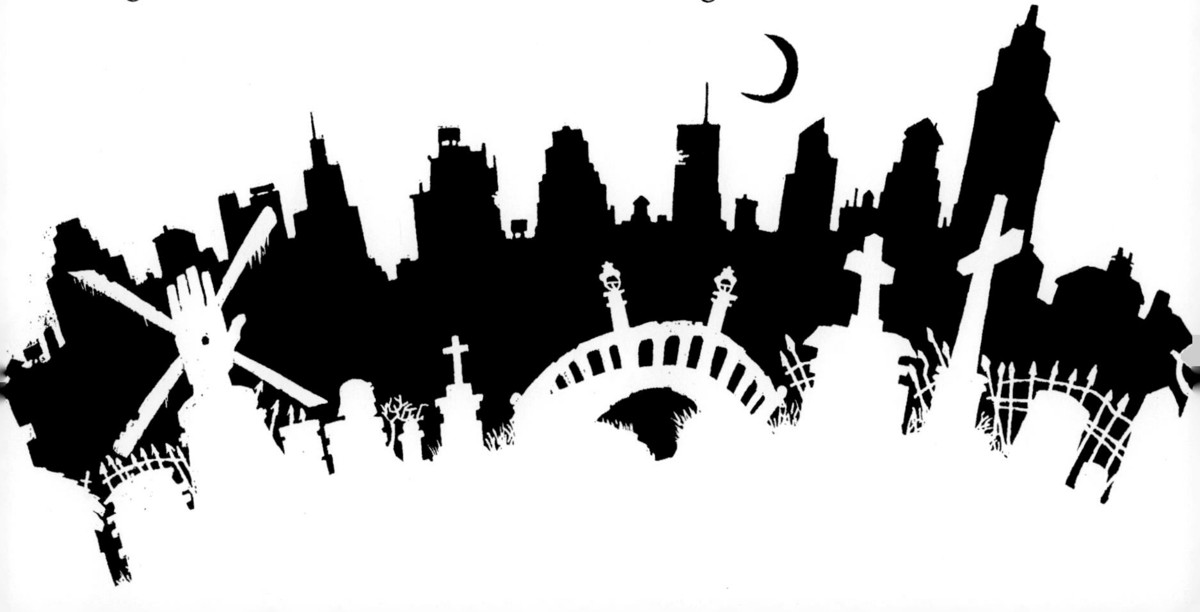

the unreasonable. The less educated among the nonmilitary personnel even dared to hope that with the culturally affluent amongst us gone, the B.T.L. might show mercy. So people turned on each other, on their neighbors, but not for being too smart for their own good. It was for being too smart for what was now considered the common good.

My father told me that he had seen this before, and more than once. He used to say it was the sad way of democracy.

The young turned on the old. The educated elite, those we should have looked up to for direction, became targets by more than just the Beetles. After a few months, if you admitted you could read, you were dead.

All dead, except for the old ones, the ones who dressed in vestments and read from the oldest of books. No one pointed a finger at them. My father refused to join them when he was asked. He never told me why, only that he was afraid of them. Somehow, after the "purges" of the educated amongst us, there were some that were considered like priests of a sort. Superstition and tradition kept them safe from the resentment that killed others of their stature and position within the city.

Looking back now, how could I know that they were still there, protected and hidden away, waiting for Rags to give them more power? How could I have known the deal they had made with Mr. Lion? Or that Lion was alive?

When we took those bandages that restored Rags his sight and mobility, we freed Lion. I freed Lion. An evil greater than any created or perpetuated by the B.T.L. You may think that because I am writing this, that it must mean that I, at least, lived through becoming one of the Old Man's Foot Soldiers.

I did not.

Heroes always die. They have to, like a right of passage. I don't think any of us realized how many times, and how many things we would have to die to.

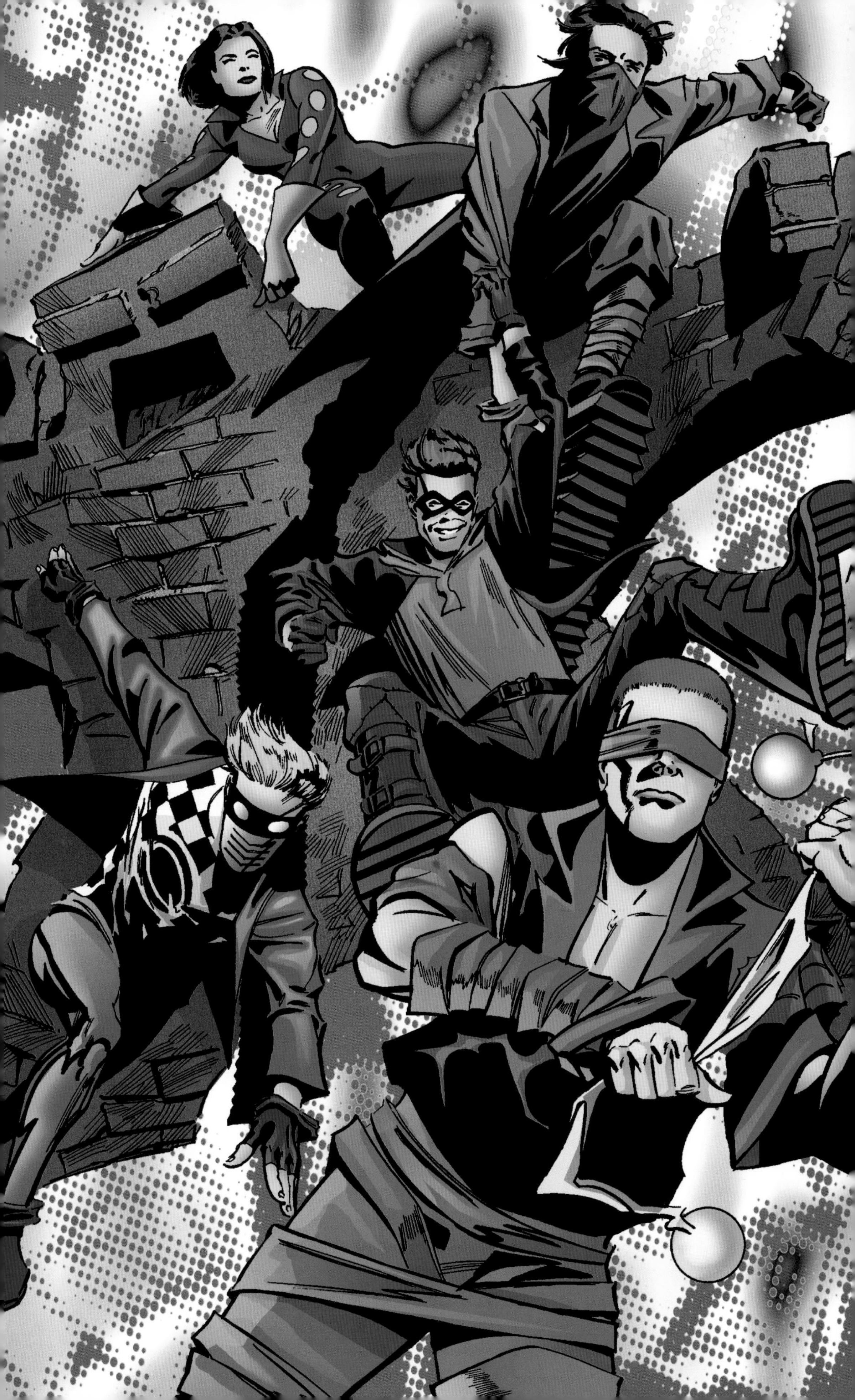

FiRST STEPS
SHORT STORIES

"What if they're not the enemy at all?"

The Flower pleaded to the Beetle…

"What if we are?"

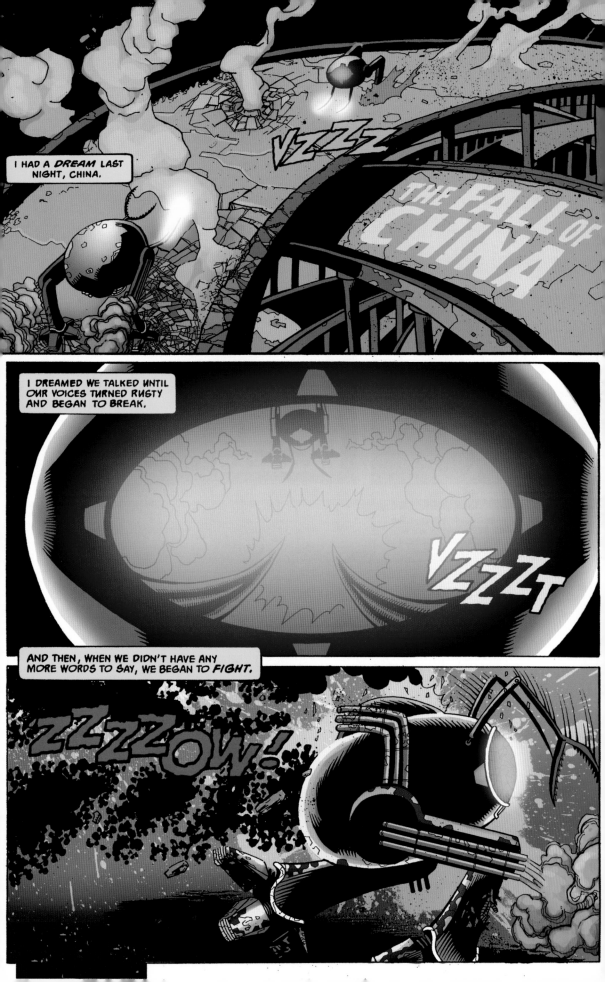

I HAD A *DREAM* LAST NIGHT, CHINA.

THE FALL OF CHINA

I DREAMED WE TALKED UNTIL OUR VOICES TURNED RUSTY AND BEGAN TO BREAK.

AND THEN, WHEN WE DIDN'T HAVE ANY MORE WORDS TO SAY, WE BEGAN TO *FIGHT*.

WE'VE GROWN UP TOGETHER, CHINA. TRAINED TOGETHER. YOU'RE LIKE A *SISTER* TO ME!

CRUNCH

KRAK

BUT LAST NIGHT NONE OF IT MADE A BIT OF DIFFERENCE.

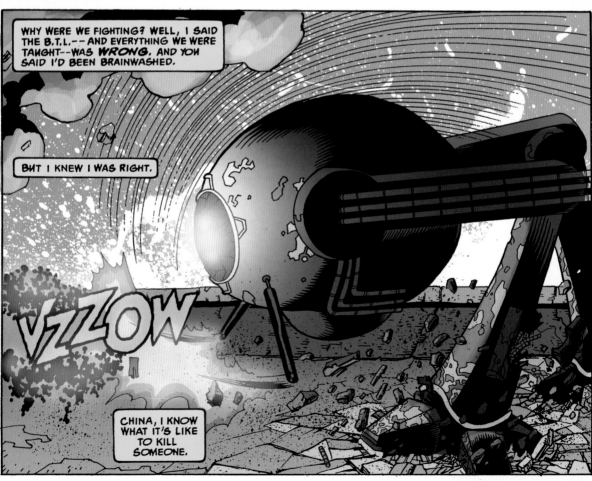

WHY WERE WE FIGHTING? WELL, I SAID THE B.T.L.--AND EVERYTHING WE WERE TAUGHT--WAS *WRONG*. AND YOU SAID I'D BEEN BRAINWASHED.

BUT I KNEW I WAS RIGHT.

VZZOW

CHINA, I KNOW WHAT IT'S LIKE TO KILL SOMEONE.

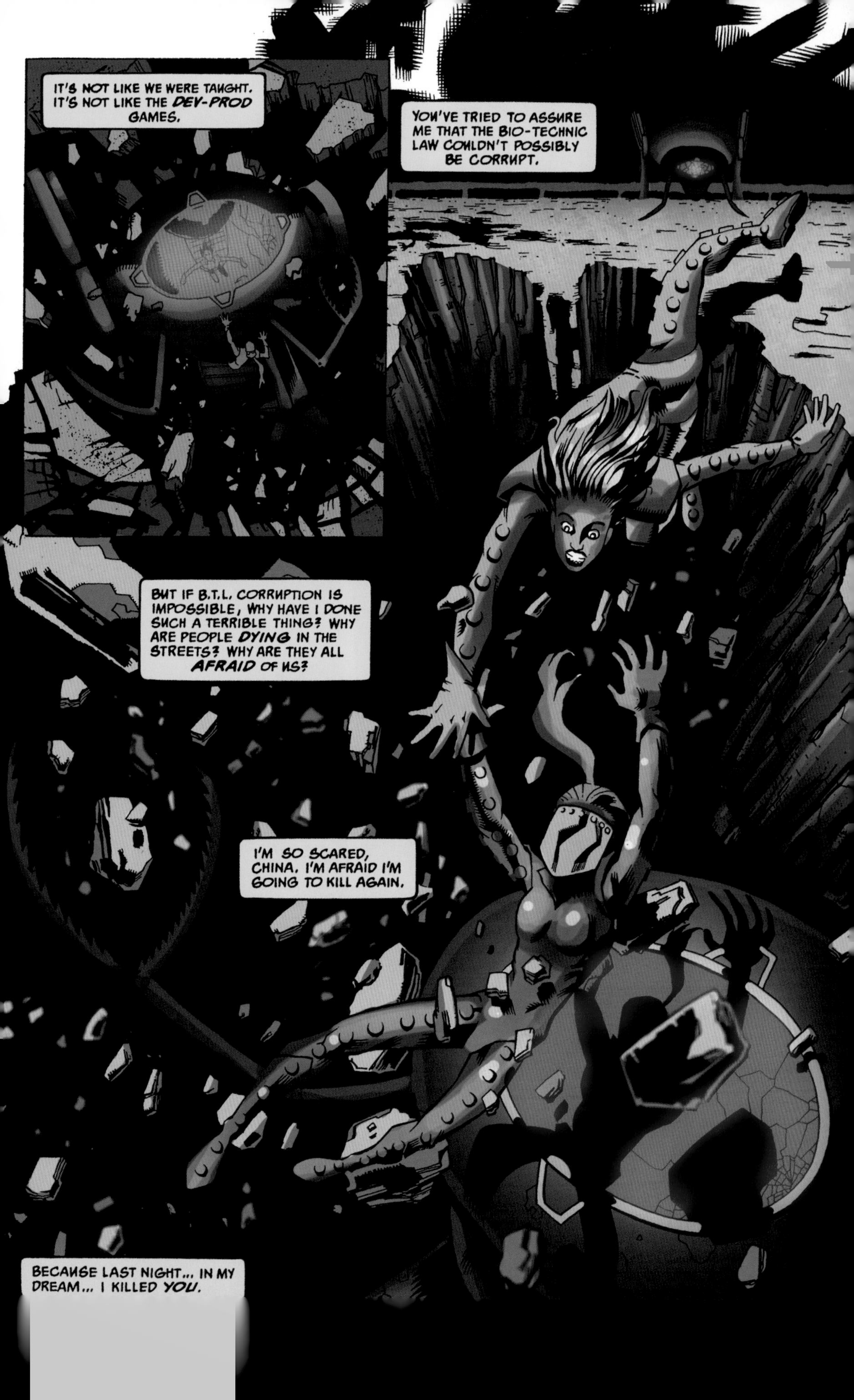
IT'S NOT LIKE WE WERE TAUGHT. IT'S NOT LIKE THE DEV-PROD GAMES.
YOU'VE TRIED TO ASSURE ME THAT THE BIO-TECHNIC LAW COULDN'T POSSIBLY BE CORRUPT.
BUT IF B.T.L. CORRUPTION IS IMPOSSIBLE, WHY HAVE I DONE SUCH A TERRIBLE THING? WHY ARE PEOPLE DYING IN THE STREETS? WHY ARE THEY ALL AFRAID OF US?
I'M SO SCARED, CHINA. I'M AFRAID I'M GOING TO KILL AGAIN.
BECAUSE LAST NIGHT... IN MY DREAM... I KILLED YOU.

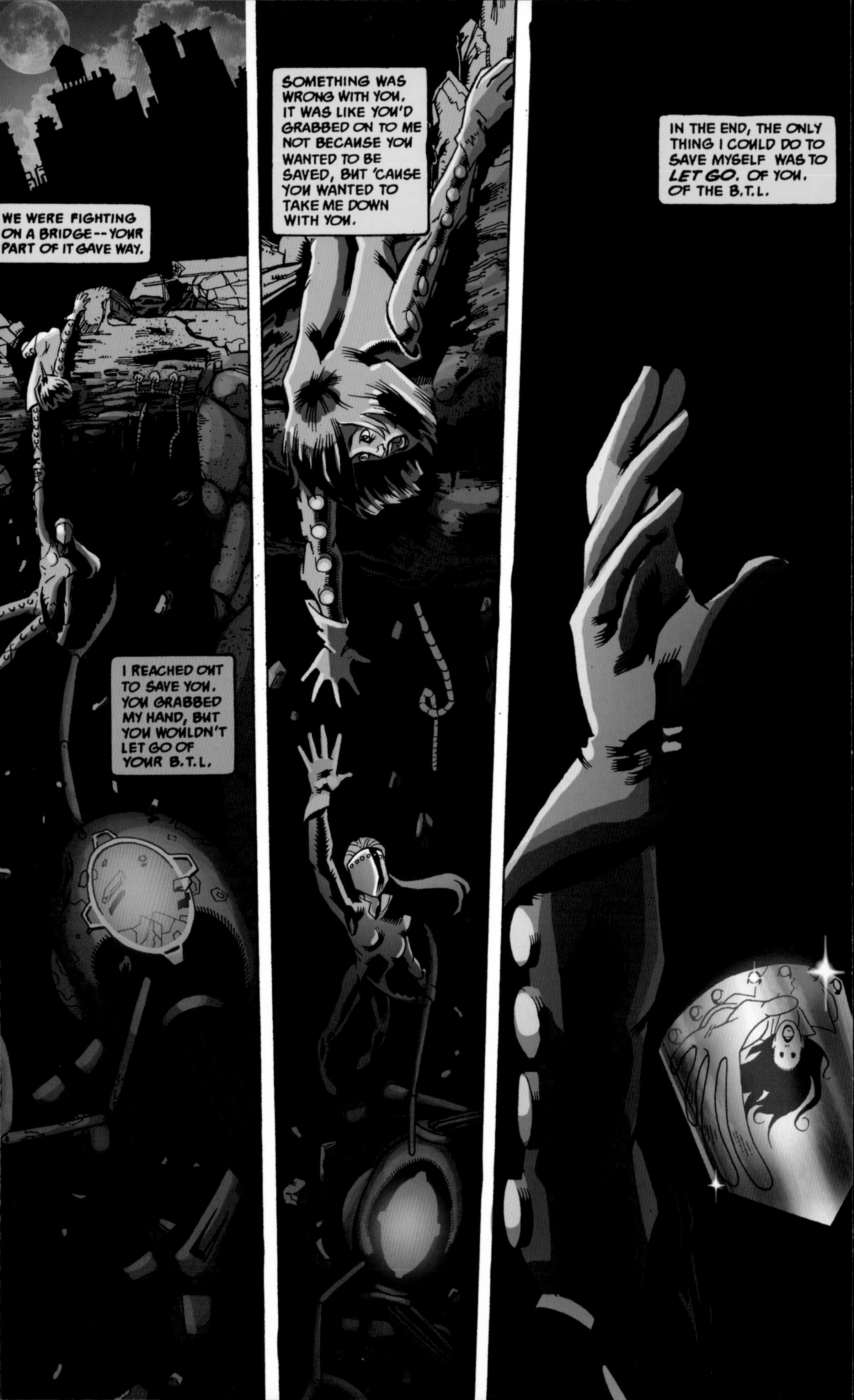
WE WERE FIGHTING ON A BRIDGE--YOUR PART OF IT GAVE WAY.
I REACHED OUT TO SAVE YOU. YOU GRABBED MY HAND, BUT YOU WOULDN'T LET GO OF YOUR B.T.L.
SOMETHING WAS WRONG WITH YOU. IT WAS LIKE YOU'D GRABBED ON TO ME NOT BECAUSE YOU WANTED TO BE SAVED, BUT 'CAUSE YOU WANTED TO TAKE ME DOWN WITH YOU.
IN THE END, THE ONLY THING I COULD DO TO SAVE MYSELF WAS TO *LET GO.* OF YOU. OF THE B.T.L.

I THINK IT WAS SOME SORT OF WAKE-UP CALL. AND IT TOOK WATCHING YOU FALL, STILL CLINGING TO YOUR B.T.L., TO OPEN MY EYES.

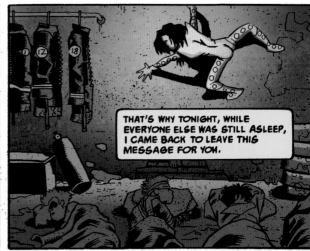

THAT'S WHY TONIGHT, WHILE EVERYONE ELSE WAS STILL ASLEEP, I CAME BACK TO LEAVE THIS MESSAGE FOR YOU.

I'M LEAVING THE B.T.L., AND I'M NEVER COMING BACK.

I'M GOING TO JOIN THE *FOOT SOLDIERS.*

I DON'T EXPECT YOU TO UNDERSTAND WHY...

...BUT I WISH YOU COULD.

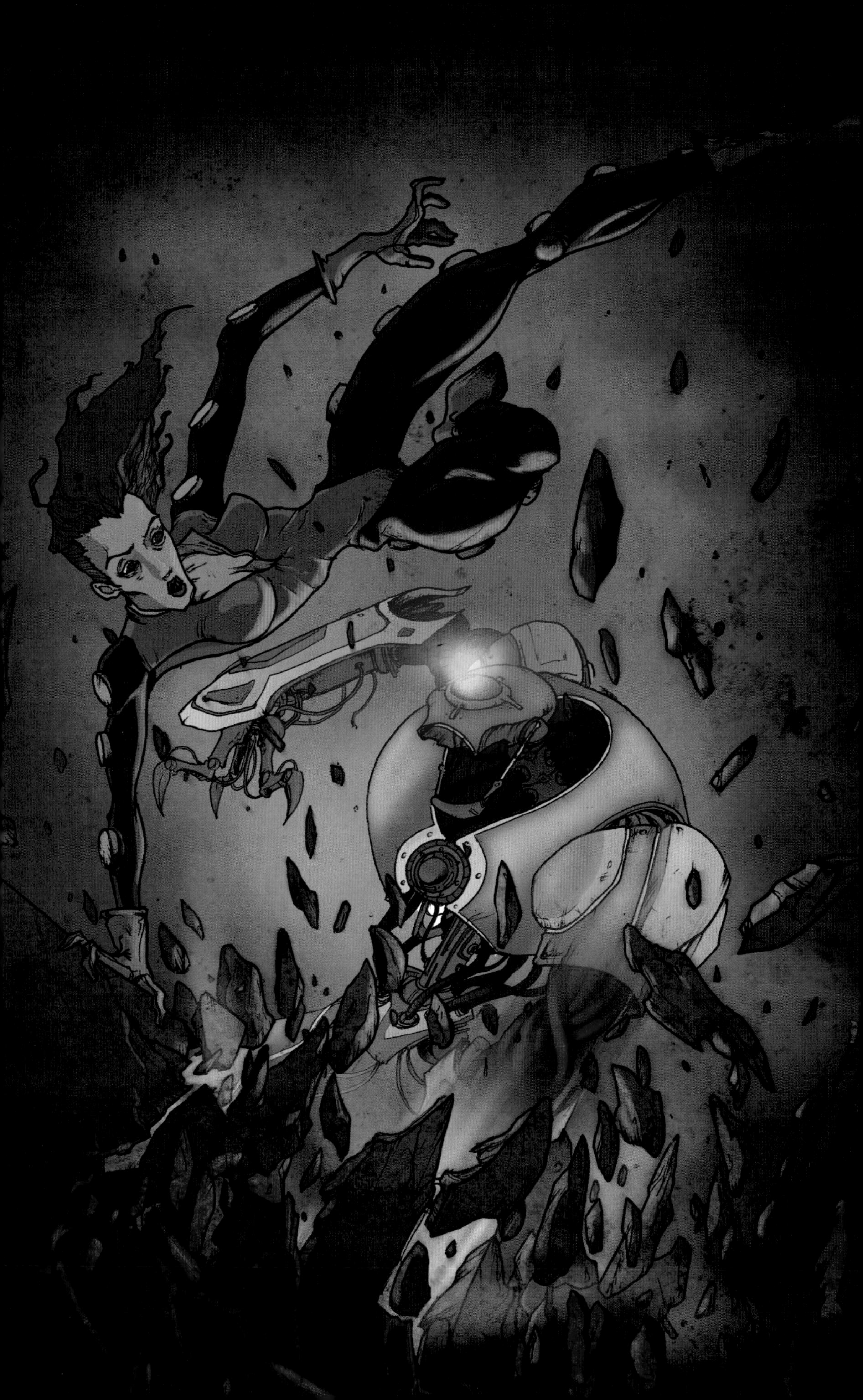

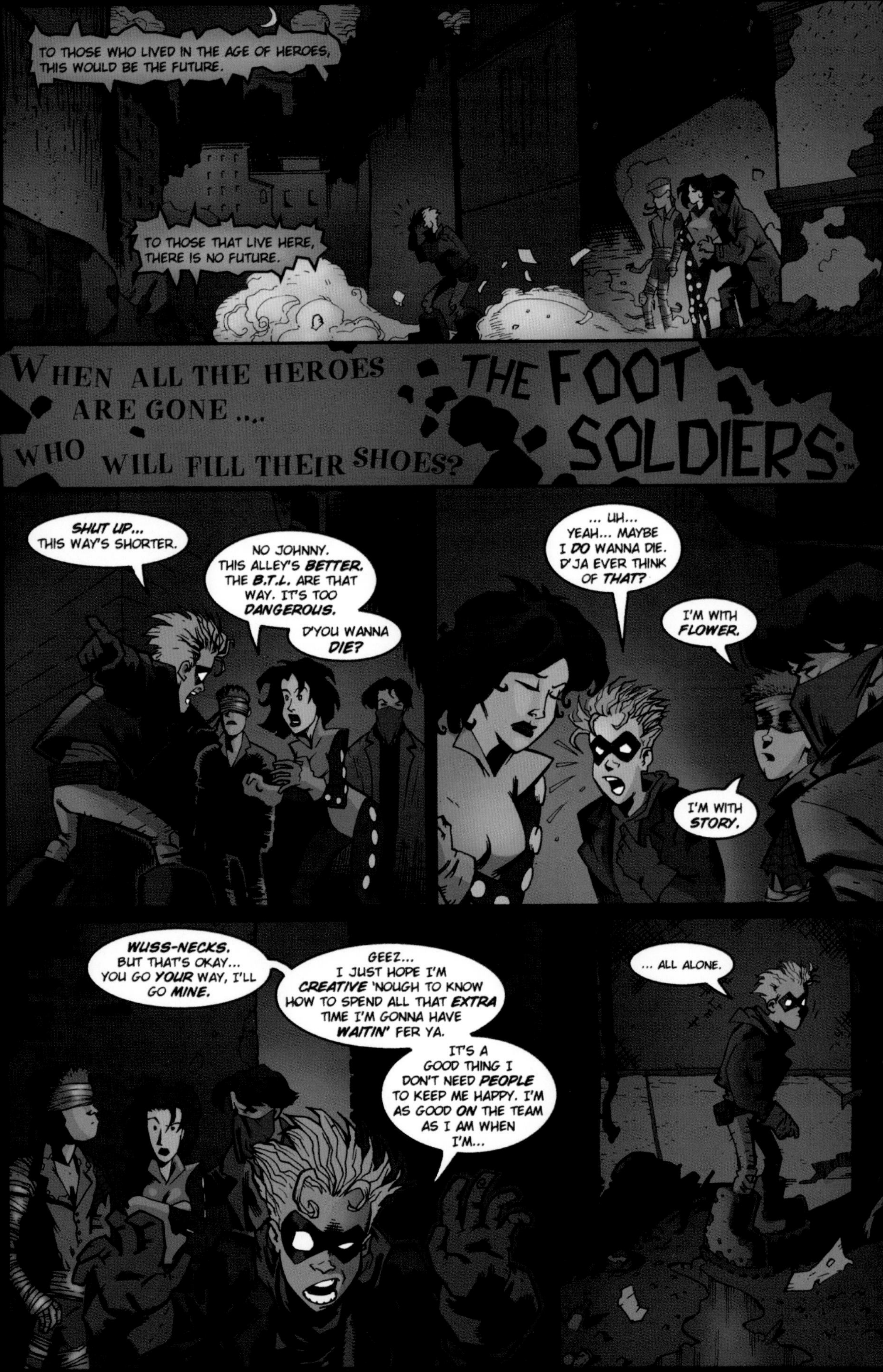
TO THOSE WHO LIVED IN THE AGE OF HEROES, THIS WOULD BE THE FUTURE.
TO THOSE THAT LIVE HERE, THERE IS NO FUTURE.
WHEN ALL THE HEROES ARE GONE ... WHO WILL FILL THEIR SHOES?
THE FOOT SOLDIERS™
SHUT UP... THIS WAY'S SHORTER.
NO JOHNNY. THIS ALLEY'S BETTER. THE B.T.L. ARE THAT WAY. IT'S TOO DANGEROUS.
D'YOU WANNA DIE?
... UH... YEAH... MAYBE I DO WANNA DIE. D'JA EVER THINK OF THAT?
I'M WITH FLOWER.
I'M WITH STORY.
WUSS-NECKS. BUT THAT'S OKAY... YOU GO YOUR WAY, I'LL GO MINE.
GEEZ... I JUST HOPE I'M CREATIVE 'NOUGH TO KNOW HOW TO SPEND ALL THAT EXTRA TIME I'M GONNA HAVE WAITIN' FER YA.
IT'S A GOOD THING I DON'T NEED PEOPLE TO KEEP ME HAPPY. I'M AS GOOD ON THE TEAM AS I AM WHEN I'M...
... ALL ALONE.

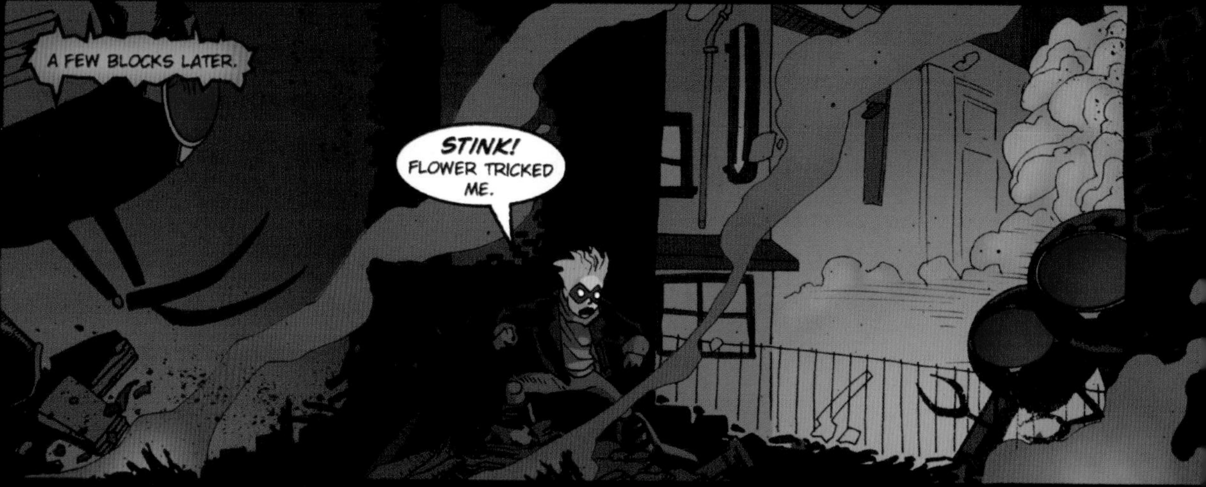
A FEW BLOCKS LATER.
STINK! FLOWER TRICKED ME.

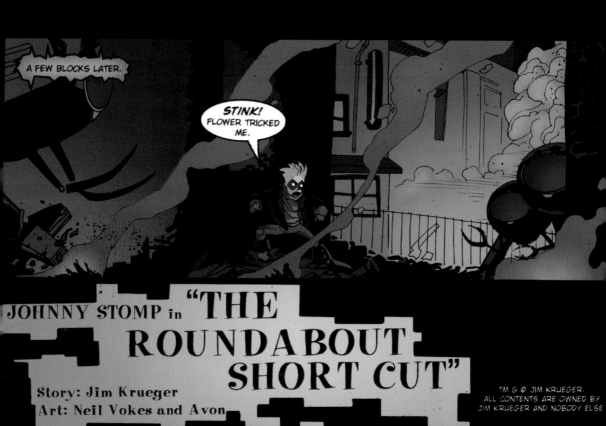

JOHNNY STOMP in "THE ROUNDABOUT SHORT CUT"

Story: Jim Krueger
Art: Neil Vokes and Avon

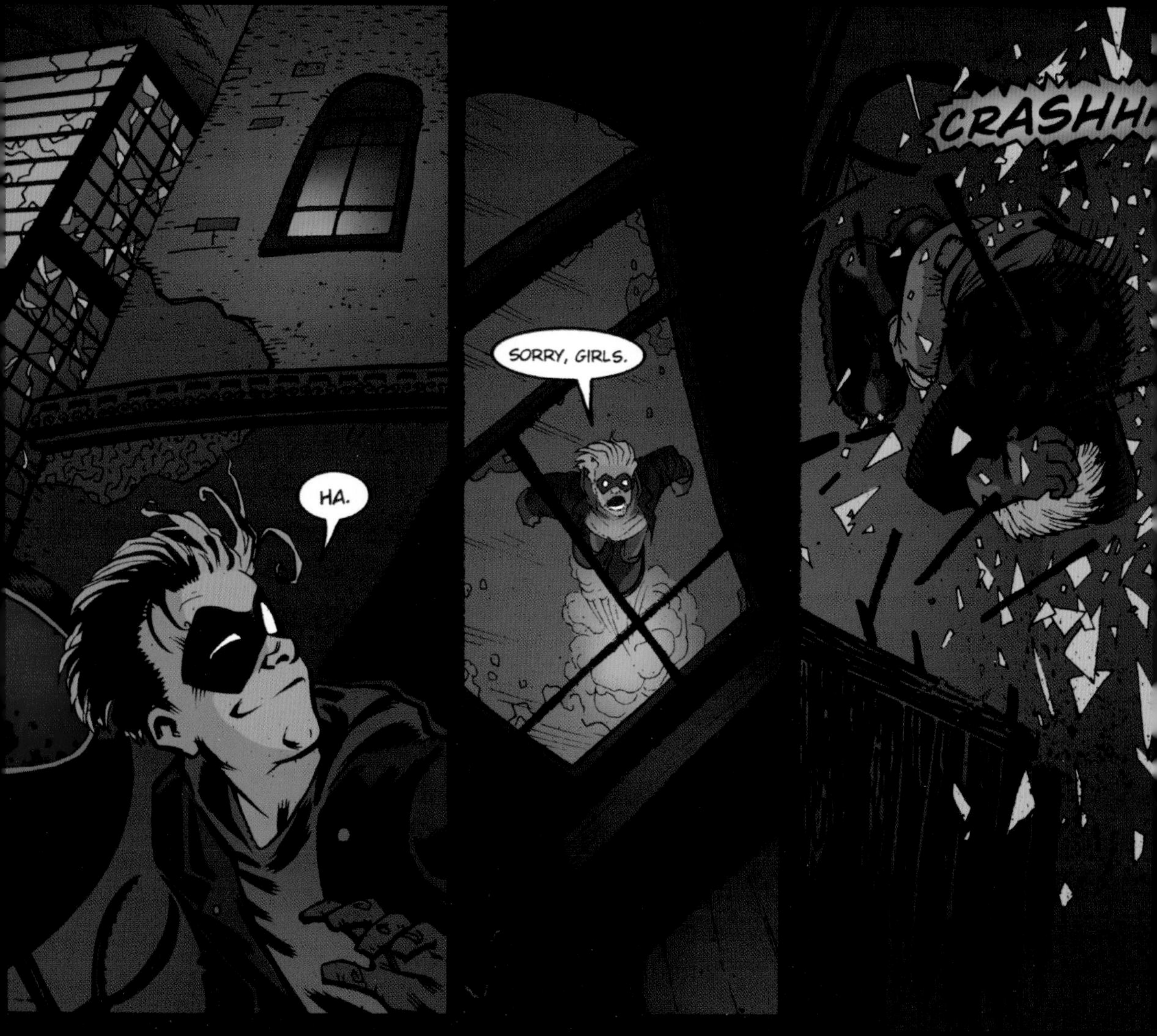
HA.
SORRY, GIRLS.
CRASHH

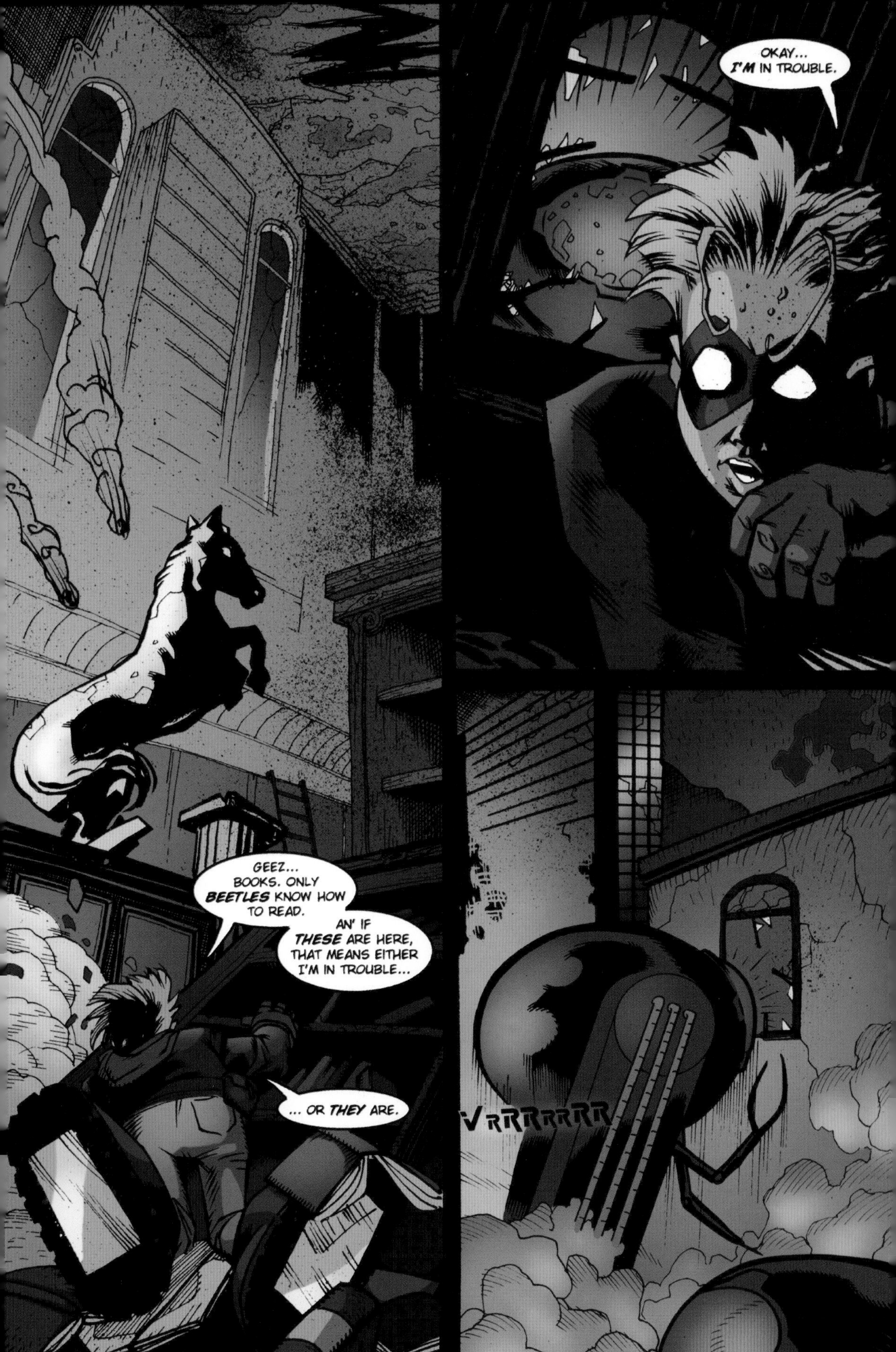
GEEZ... BOOKS. ONLY BEETLES KNOW HOW TO READ.
AN' IF THESE ARE HERE, THAT MEANS EITHER I'M IN TROUBLE...
... OR THEY ARE.
OKAY... I'M IN TROUBLE.
VRRRRRRRR

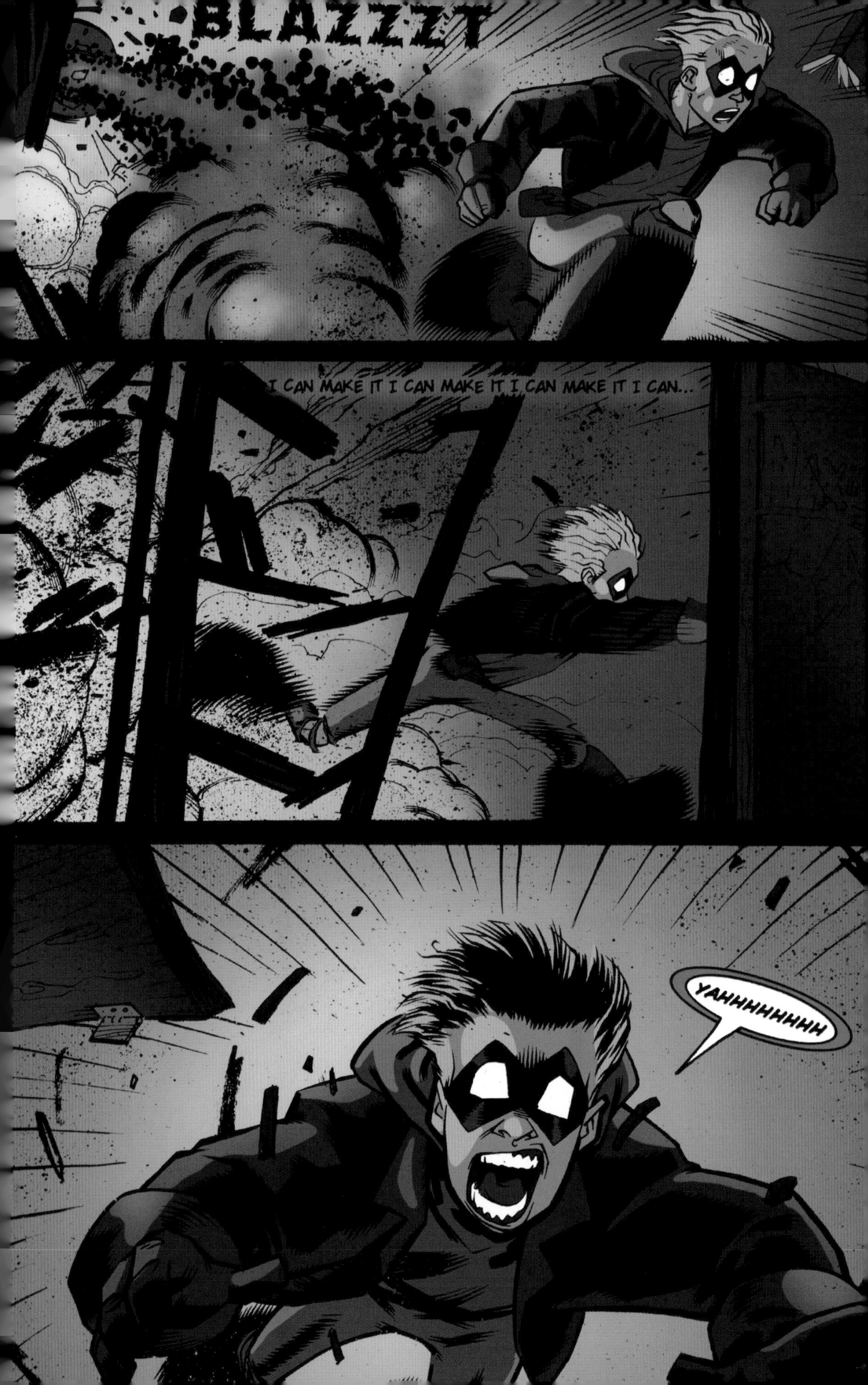
BLAZZZT
I CAN MAKE IT I CAN MAKE IT I CAN MAKE IT I CAN...
YAHHHHHHHH

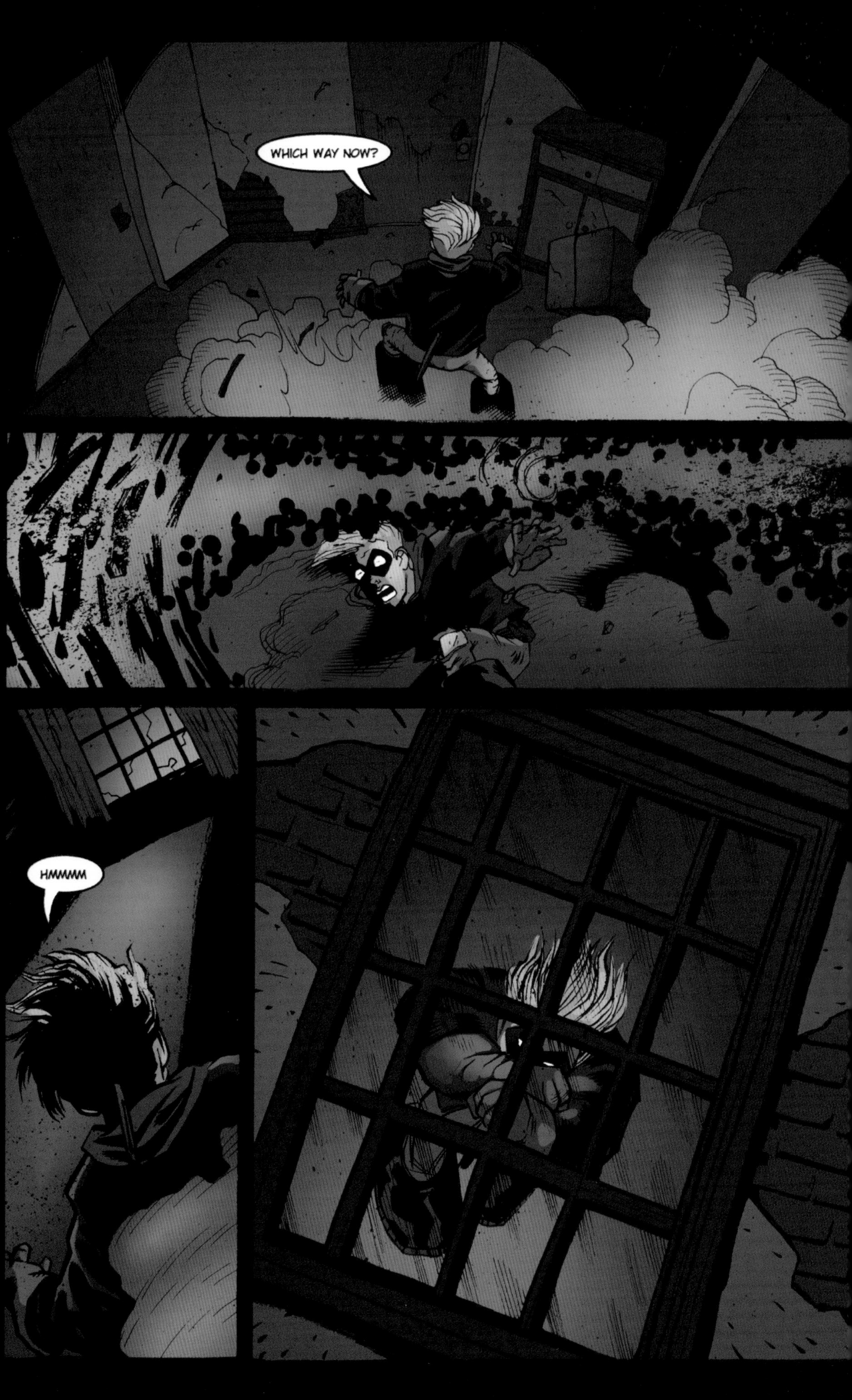
WHICH WAY NOW?
HMMMM

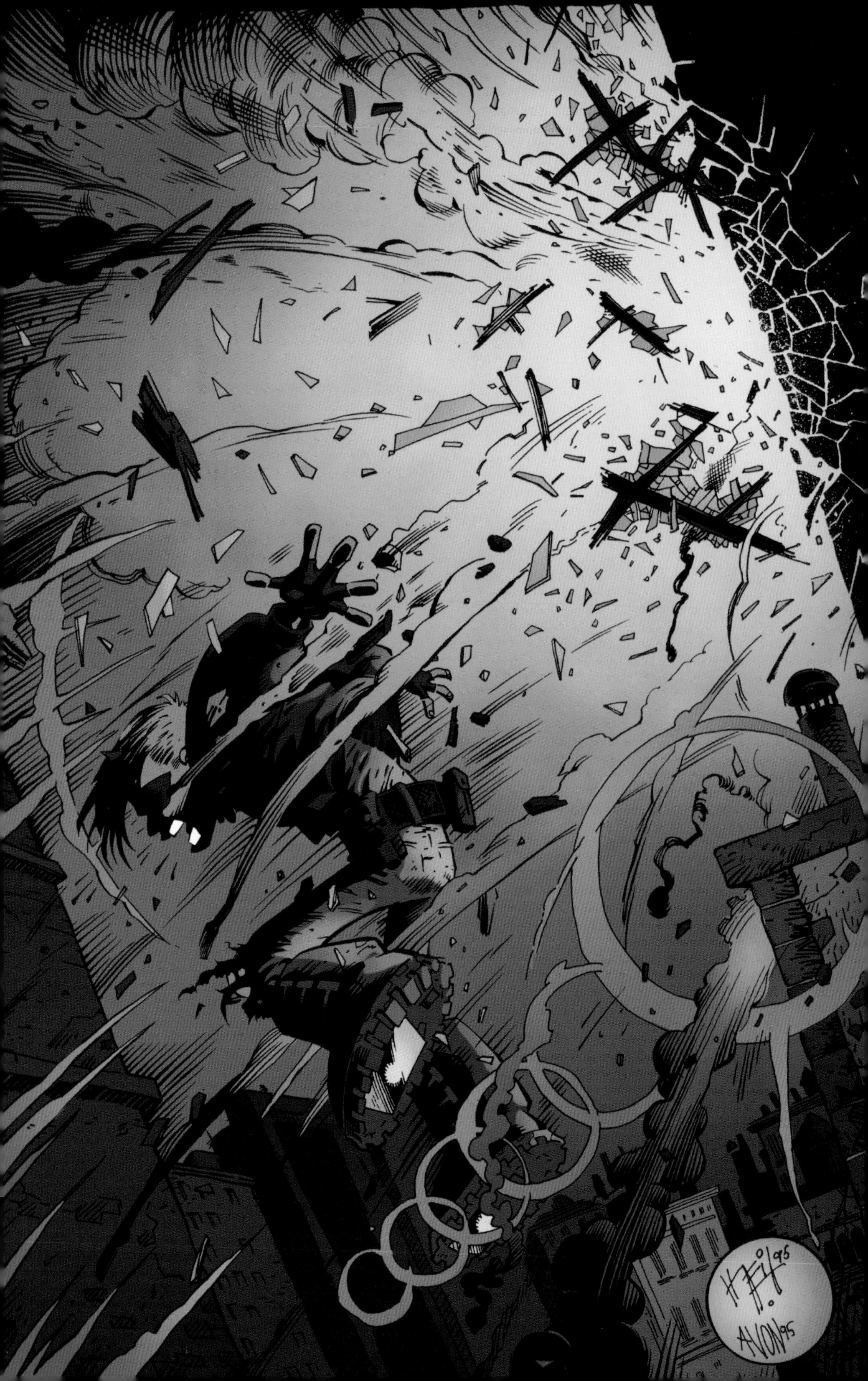

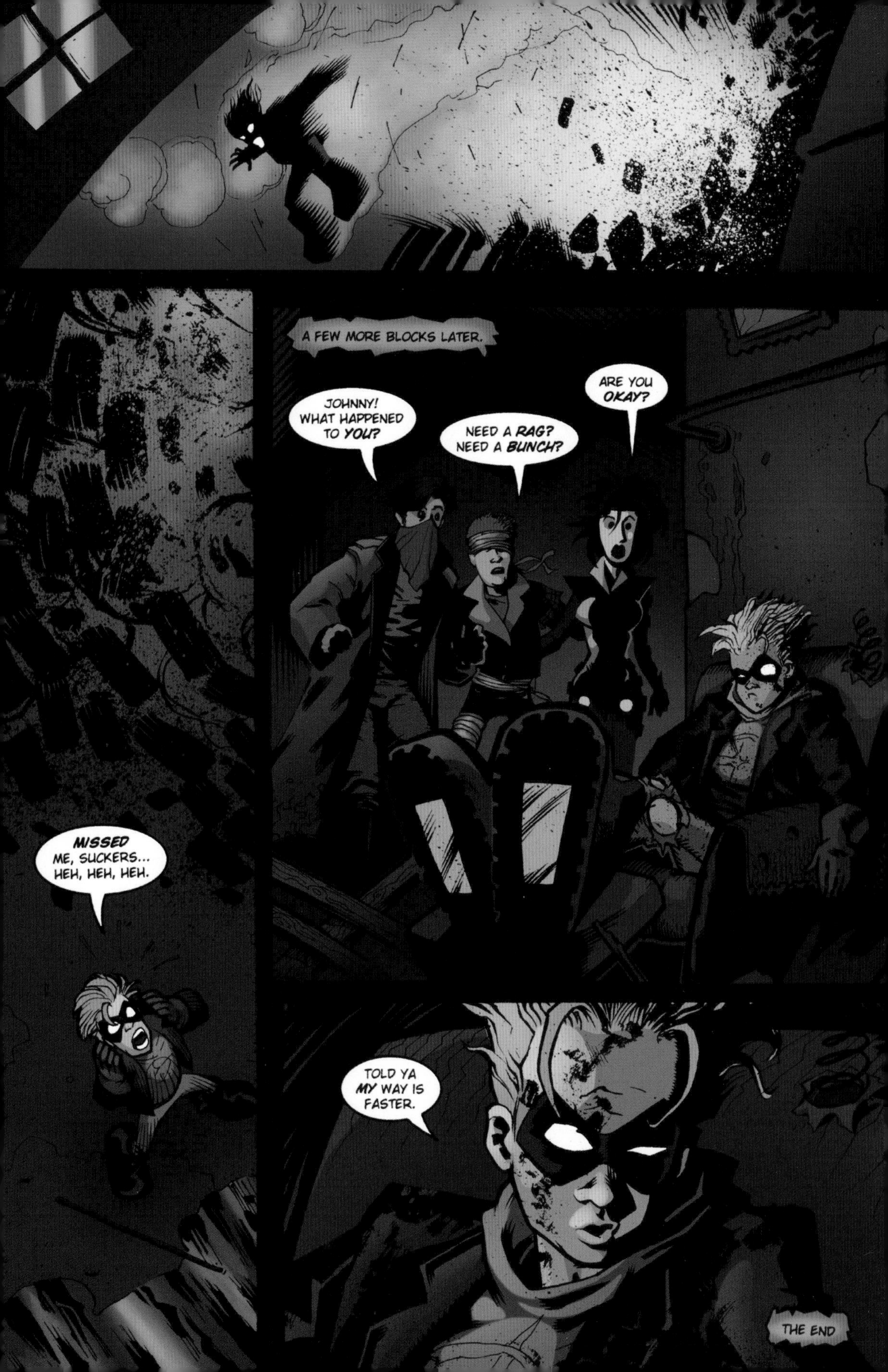
A FEW MORE BLOCKS LATER.
JOHNNY! WHAT HAPPENED TO YOU?
NEED A RAG? NEED A BUNCH?
ARE YOU OKAY?
MISSED ME, SUCKERS... HEH, HEH, HEH.
TOLD YA MY WAY IS FASTER.
THE END

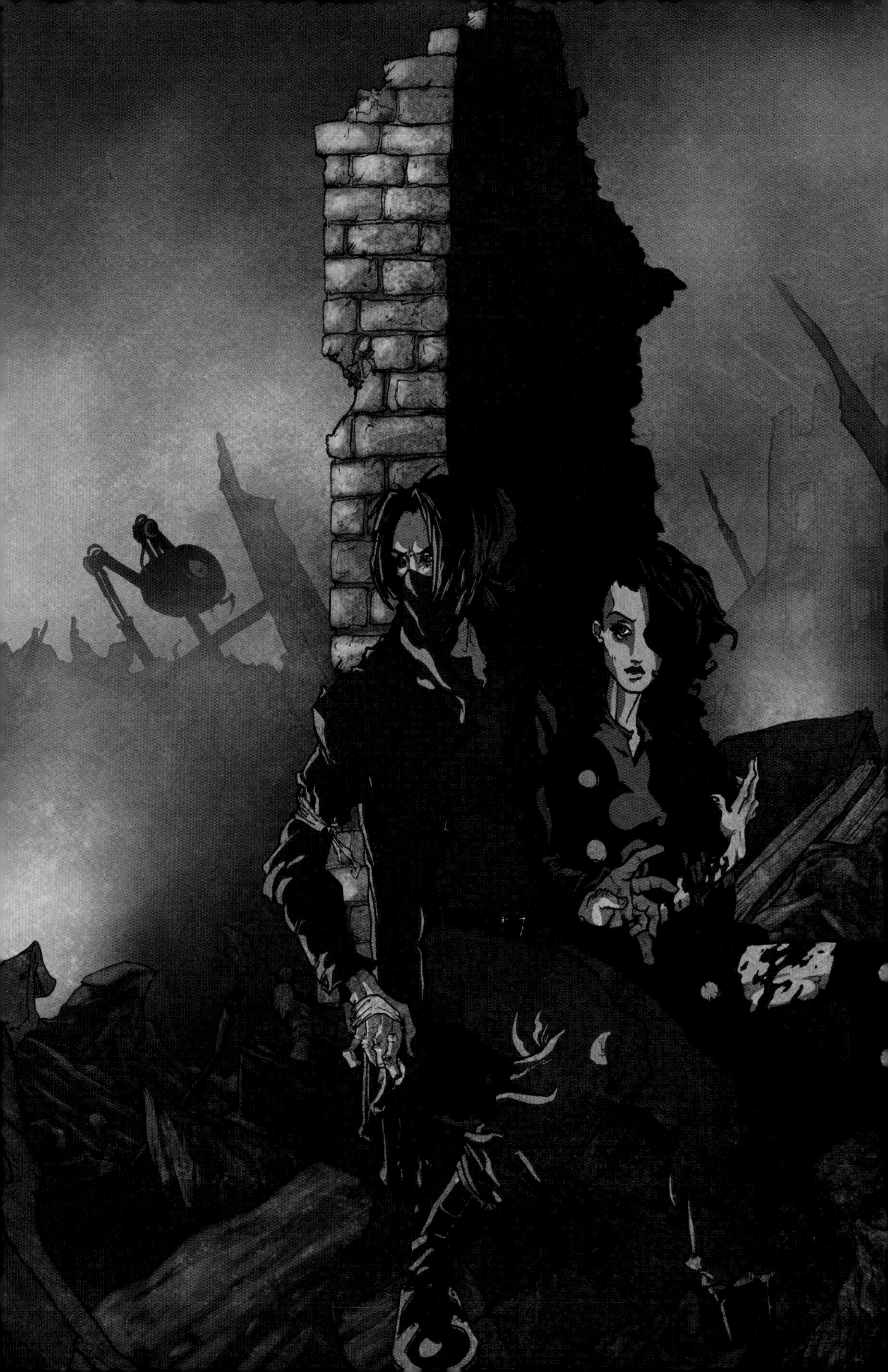

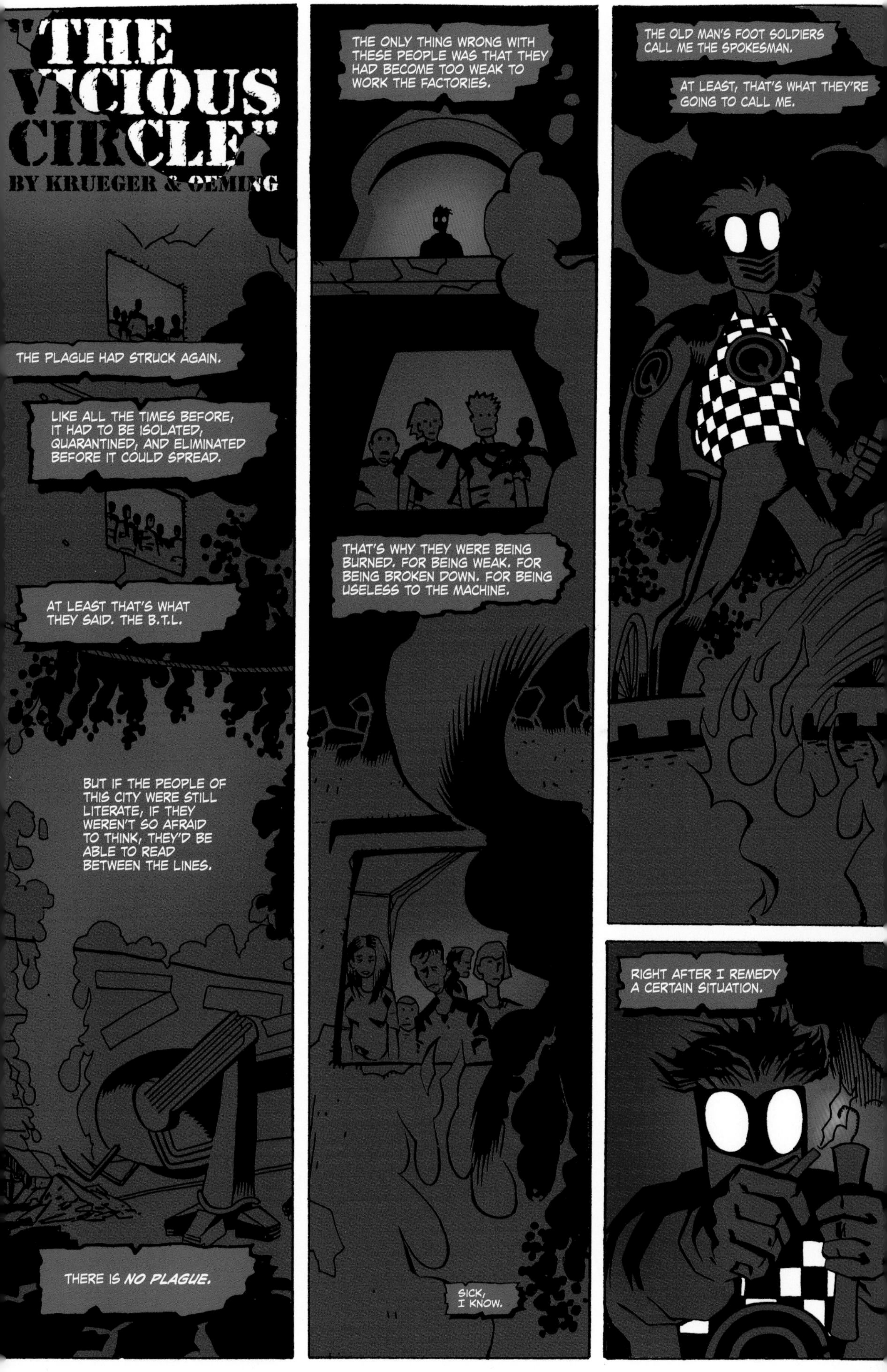
"THE VICIOUS CIRCLE"
BY KRUEGER & OEMING
THE PLAGUE HAD STRUCK AGAIN.
LIKE ALL THE TIMES BEFORE, IT HAD TO BE ISOLATED, QUARANTINED, AND ELIMINATED BEFORE IT COULD SPREAD.
AT LEAST THAT'S WHAT THEY SAID. THE B.T.L.
BUT IF THE PEOPLE OF THIS CITY WERE STILL LITERATE, IF THEY WEREN'T SO AFRAID TO THINK, THEY'D BE ABLE TO READ BETWEEN THE LINES.
THERE IS NO PLAGUE.
THE ONLY THING WRONG WITH THESE PEOPLE WAS THAT THEY HAD BECOME TOO WEAK TO WORK THE FACTORIES.
THAT'S WHY THEY WERE BEING BURNED. FOR BEING WEAK. FOR BEING BROKEN DOWN. FOR BEING USELESS TO THE MACHINE.
SICK, I KNOW.
THE OLD MAN'S FOOT SOLDIERS CALL ME THE SPOKESMAN.
AT LEAST, THAT'S WHAT THEY'RE GOING TO CALL ME.
RIGHT AFTER I REMEDY A CERTAIN SITUATION.

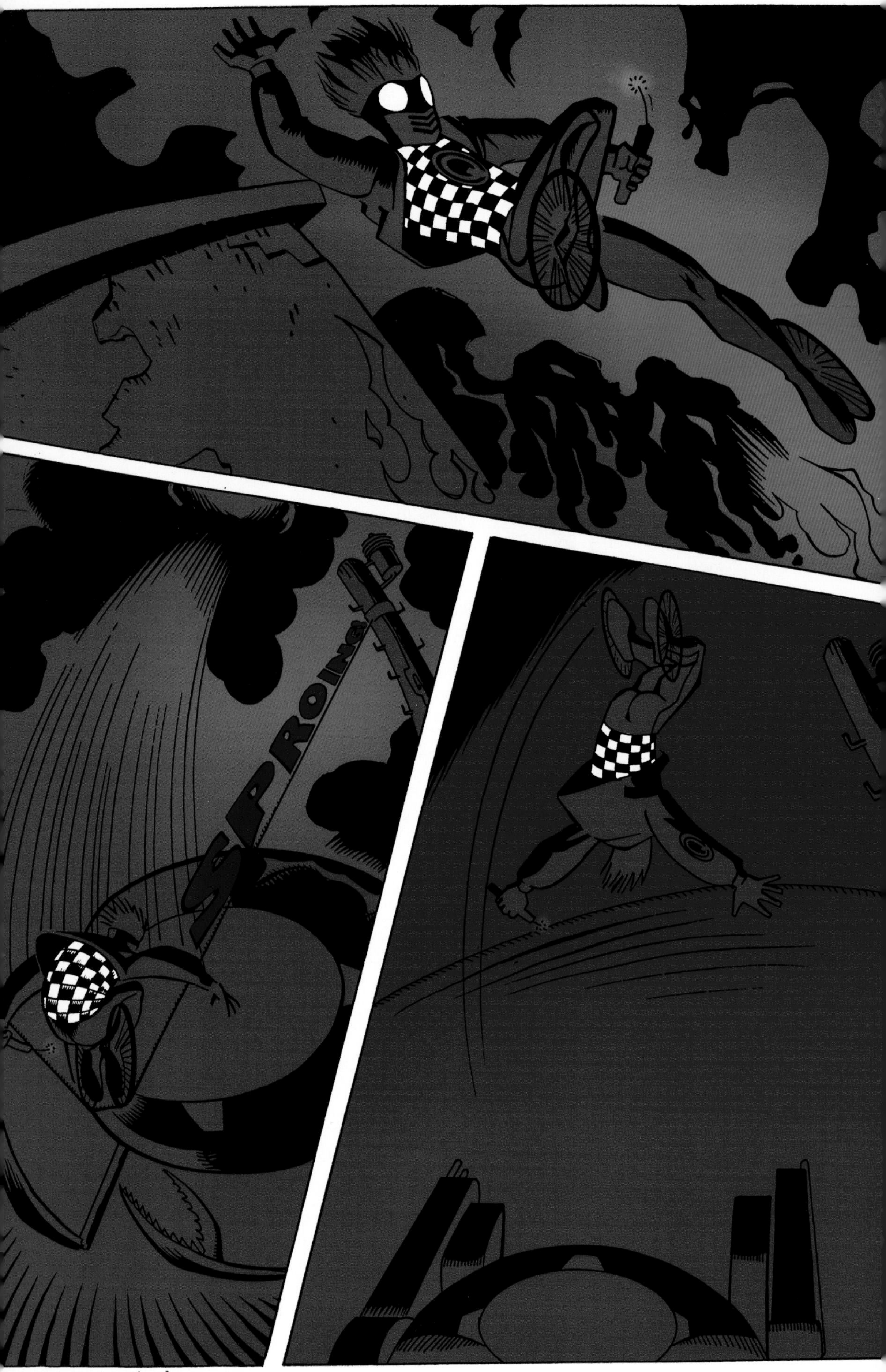
SPROING

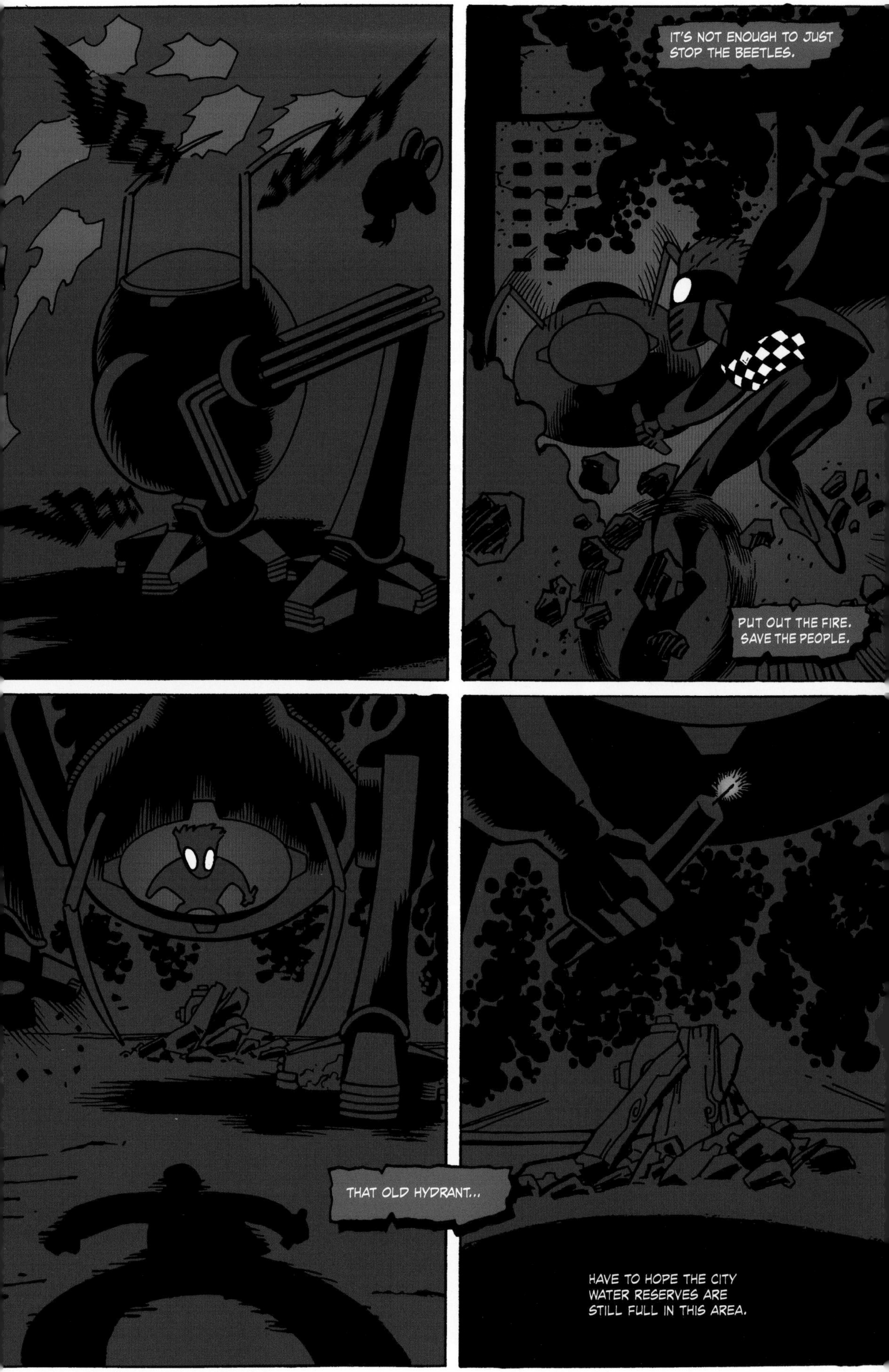
IT'S NOT ENOUGH TO JUST STOP THE BEETLES.
PUT OUT THE FIRE. SAVE THE PEOPLE.
THAT OLD HYDRANT...
HAVE TO HOPE THE CITY WATER RESERVES ARE STILL FULL IN THIS AREA.

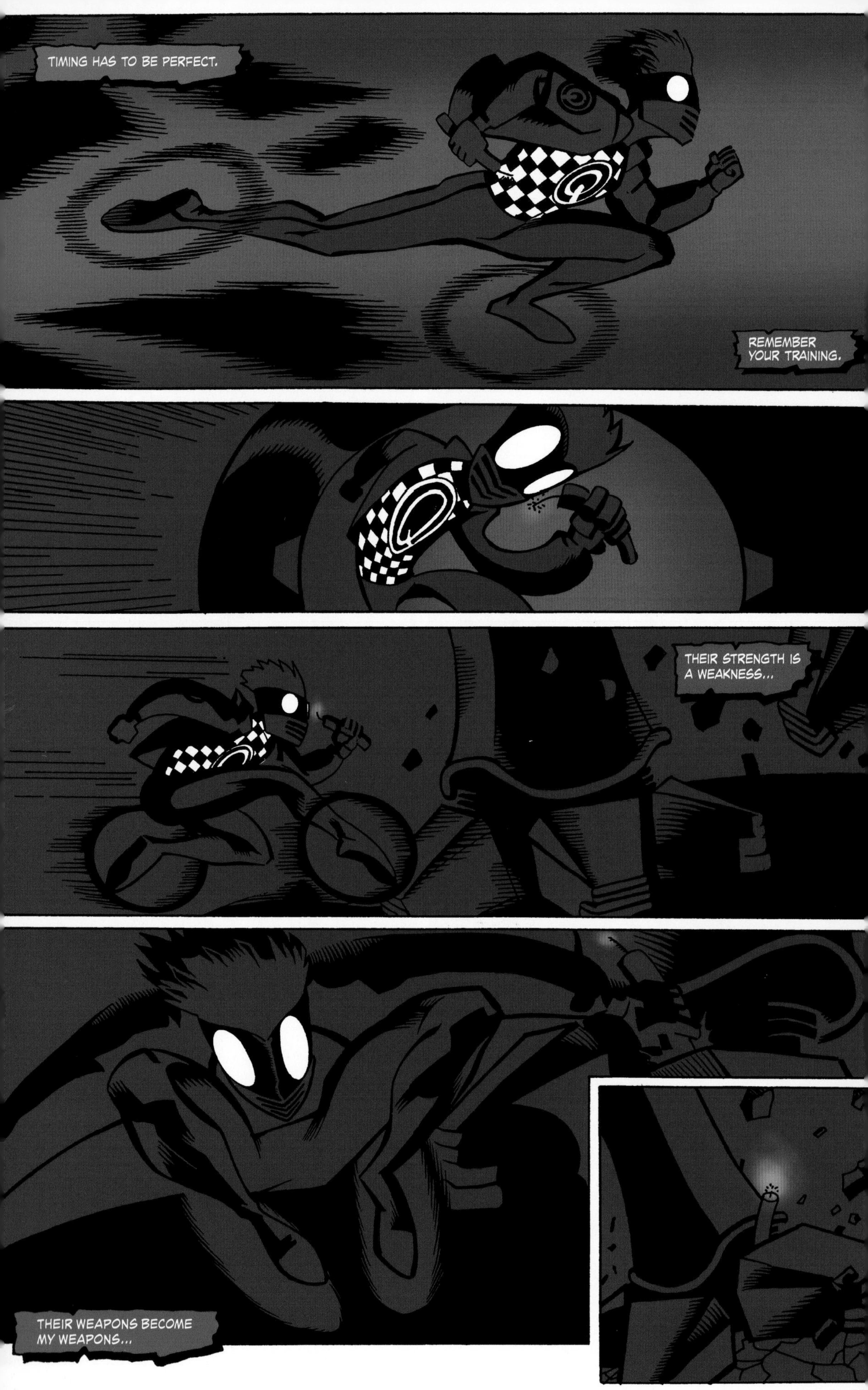
TIMING HAS TO BE PERFECT.
REMEMBER YOUR TRAINING.
THEIR STRENGTH IS A WEAKNESS...
THEIR WEAPONS BECOME MY WEAPONS...

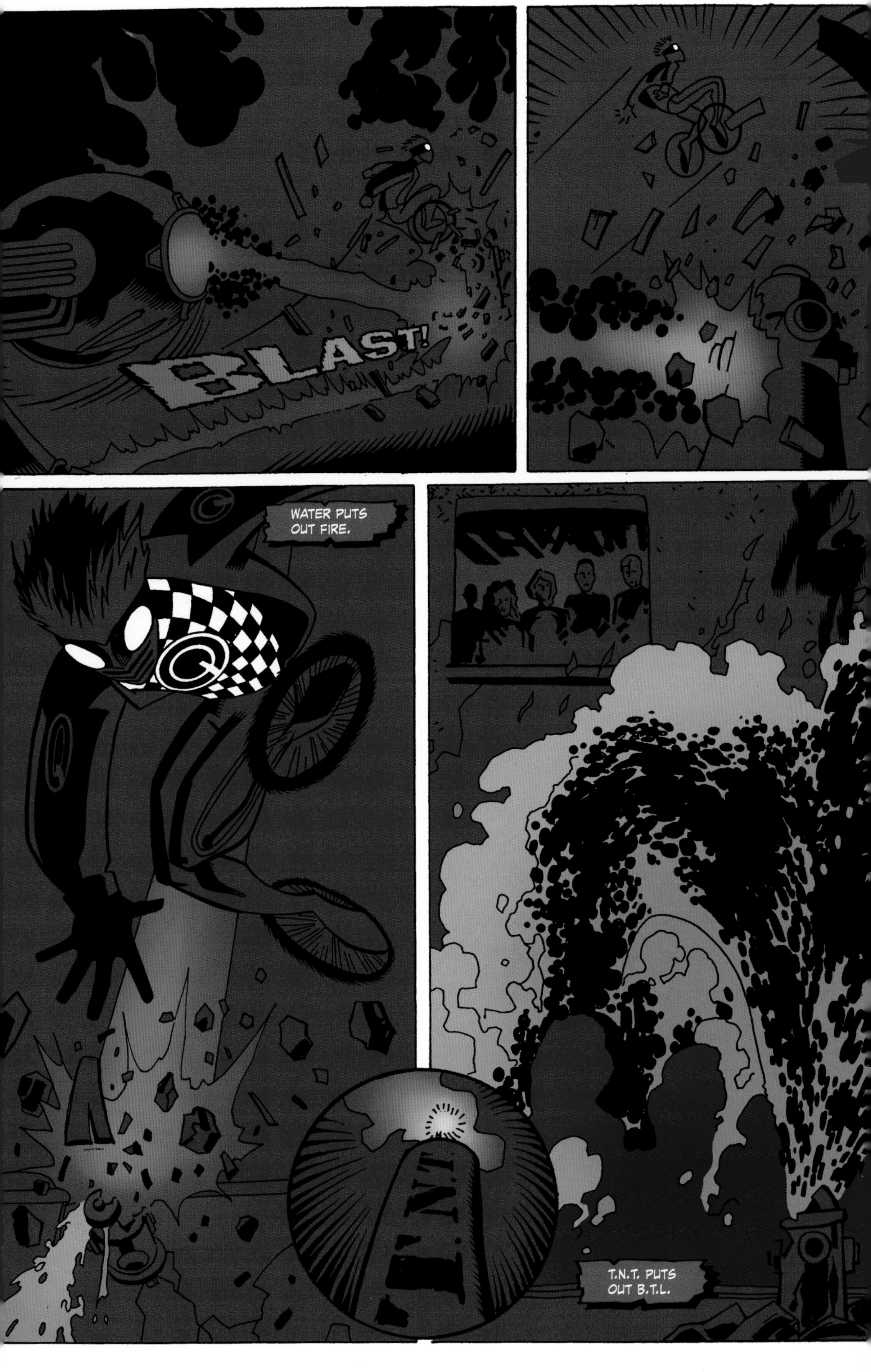
BLAST!
WATER PUTS OUT FIRE.
T.N.T.
T.N.T. PUTS OUT B.T.L.

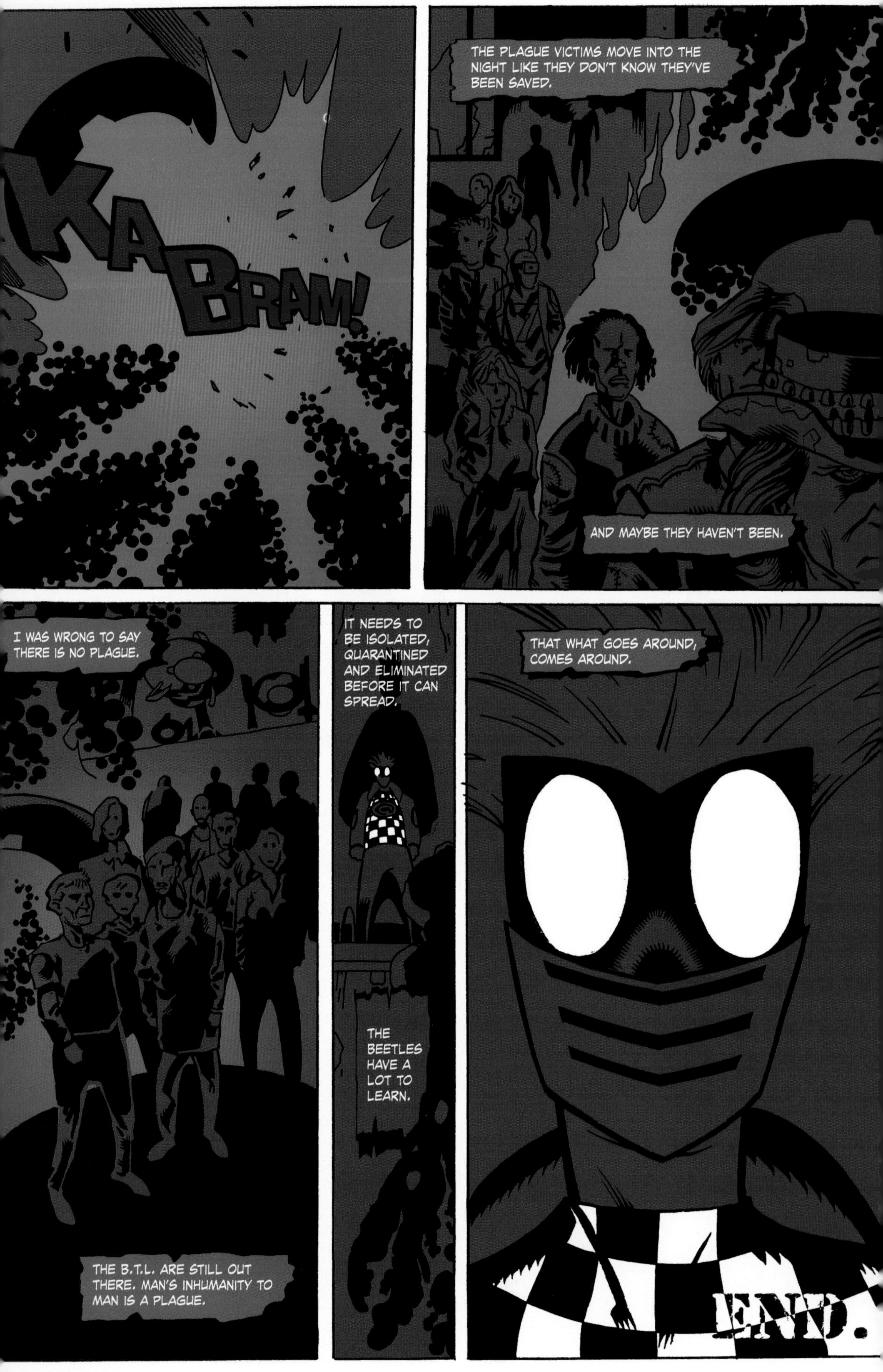
KA-BRAM!
THE PLAGUE VICTIMS MOVE INTO THE NIGHT LIKE THEY DON'T KNOW THEY'VE BEEN SAVED.
AND MAYBE THEY HAVEN'T BEEN.
I WAS WRONG TO SAY THERE IS NO PLAGUE.
THE B.T.L. ARE STILL OUT THERE. MAN'S INHUMANITY TO MAN IS A PLAGUE.
IT NEEDS TO BE ISOLATED, QUARANTINED AND ELIMINATED BEFORE IT CAN SPREAD.
THE BEETLES HAVE A LOT TO LEARN.
THAT WHAT GOES AROUND, COMES AROUND.
END.

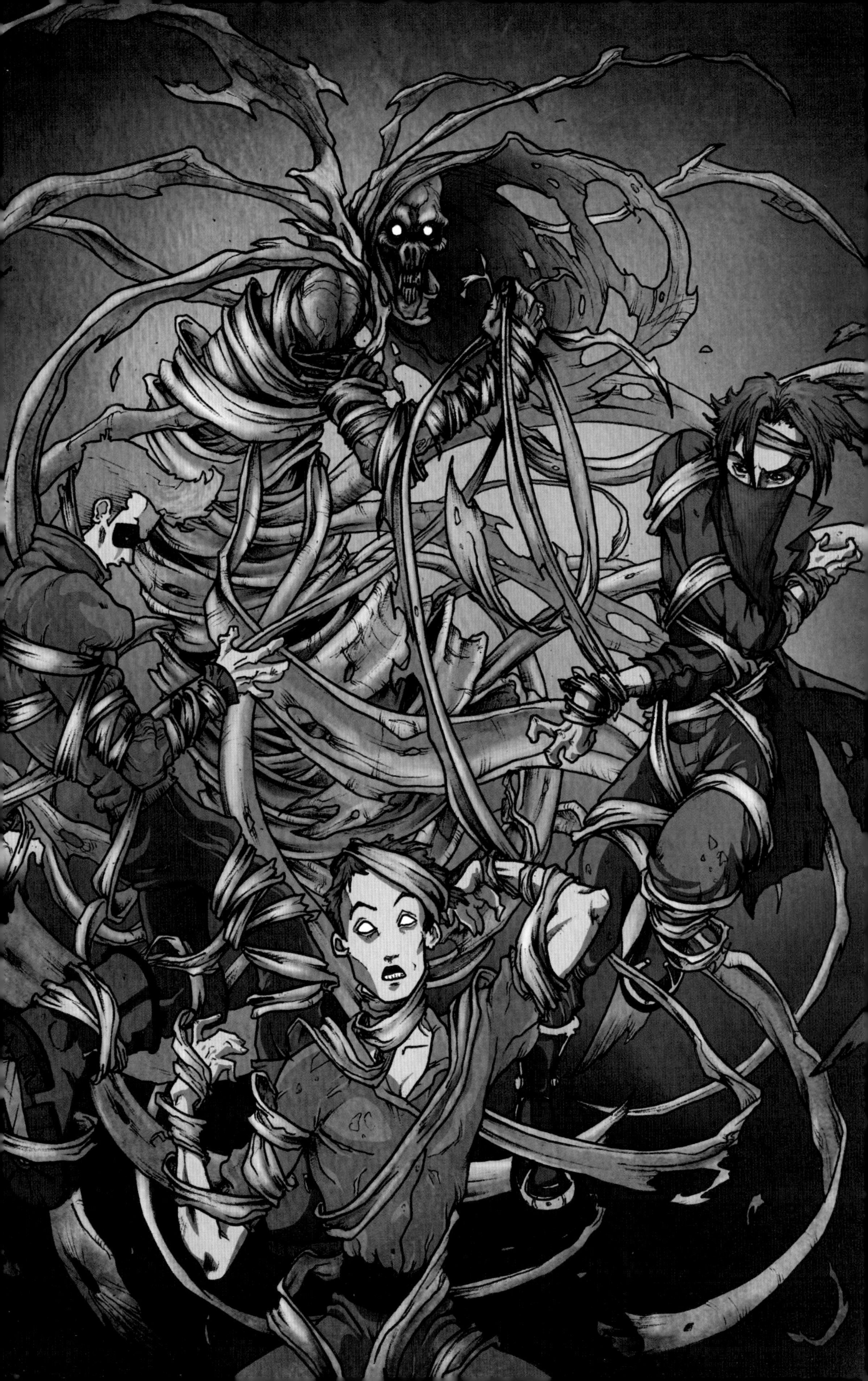

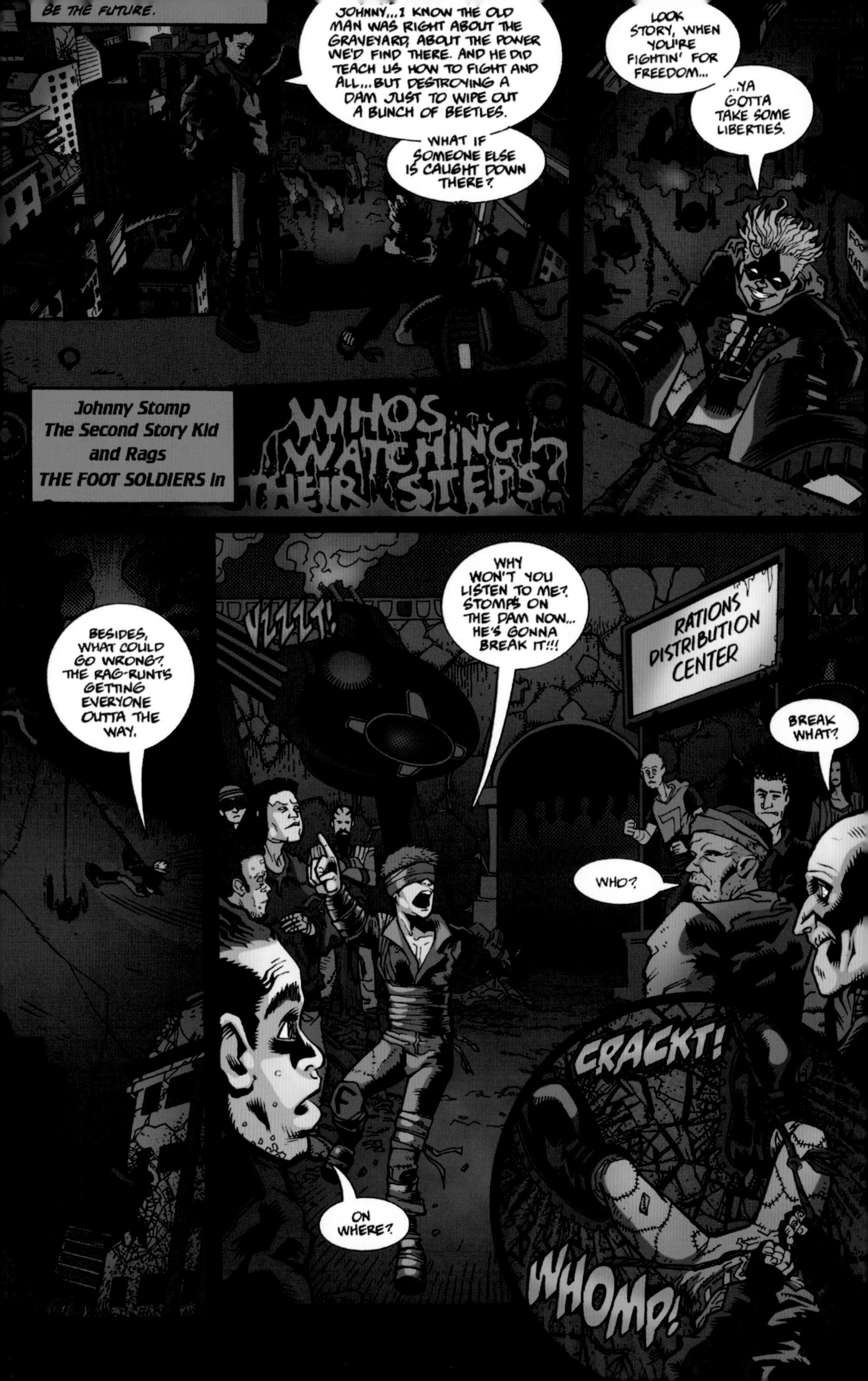
BE THE FUTURE.
JOHNNY...I KNOW THE OLD MAN WAS RIGHT ABOUT THE GRAVEYARD, ABOUT THE POWER WE'D FIND THERE. AND HE DID TEACH US HOW TO FIGHT AND ALL...BUT DESTROYING A DAM JUST TO WIPE OUT A BUNCH OF BEETLES.
WHAT IF SOMEONE ELSE IS CAUGHT DOWN THERE?
LOOK STORY, WHEN YOU'RE FIGHTIN' FOR FREEDOM...
...YA GOTTA TAKE SOME LIBERTIES.
Johnny Stomp
The Second Story Kid
and Rags
THE FOOT SOLDIERS in
WHO'S WATCHING THEIR STEPS?
BESIDES, WHAT COULD GO WRONG? THE RAG-RUNT'S GETTING EVERYONE OUTTA THE WAY.
VZZZT!
WHY WON'T YOU LISTEN TO ME? STOMP'S ON THE DAM NOW... HE'S GONNA BREAK IT!!!
RATIONS DISTRIBUTION CENTER
BREAK WHAT?
WHO?
ON WHERE?
CRACKT!
WHOMP!

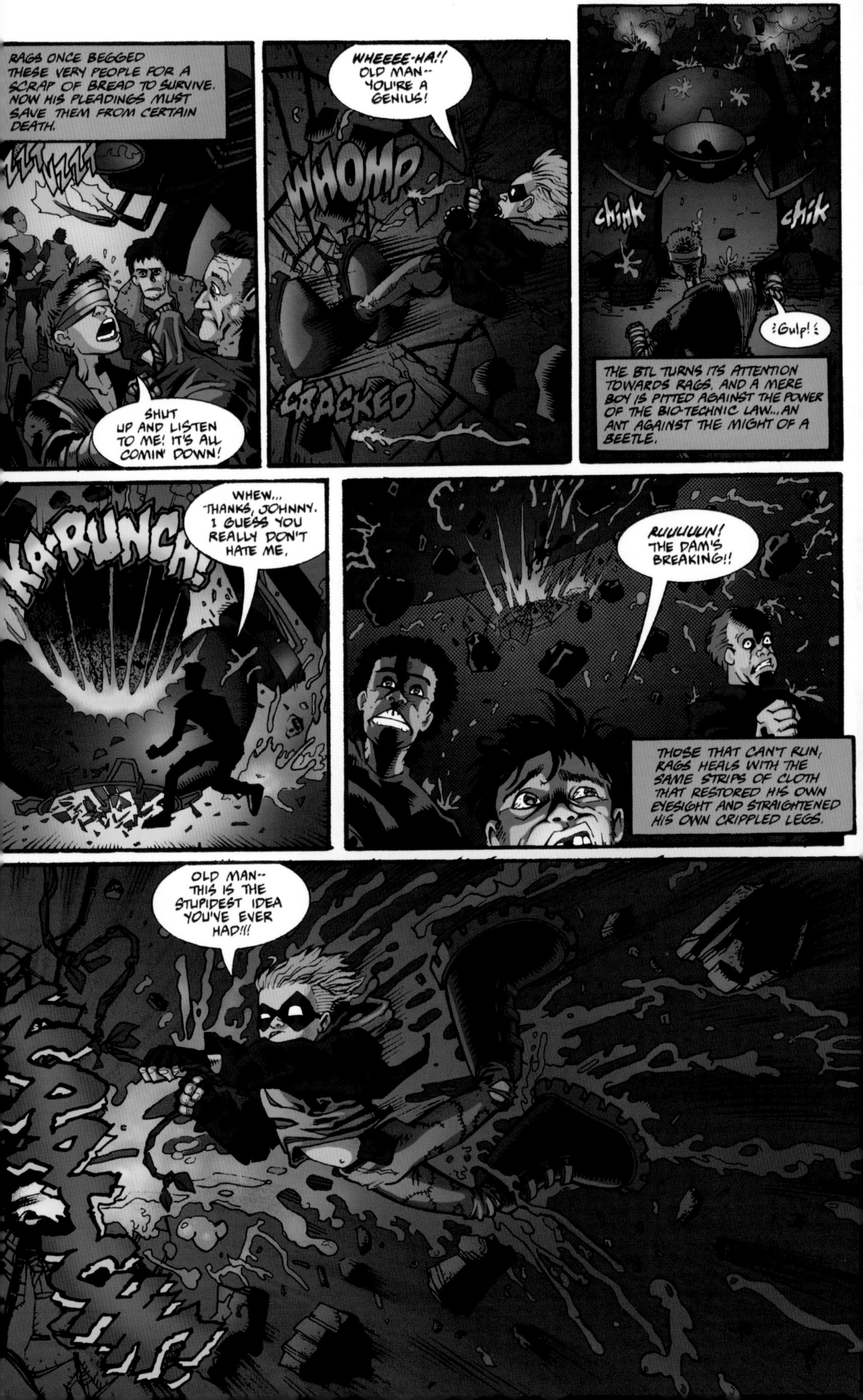
RAGS ONCE BEGGED THESE VERY PEOPLE FOR A SCRAP OF BREAD TO SURVIVE. NOW HIS PLEADINGS MUST SAVE THEM FROM CERTAIN DEATH.
SHUT UP AND LISTEN TO ME! IT'S ALL COMIN' DOWN!
WHEEEE-HA!! OLD MAN-- YOU'RE A GENIUS!
WHOMP
CRACKED
CHINK
CHIK
GULP!
THE BTL TURNS ITS ATTENTION TOWARDS RAGS, AND A MERE BOY IS PITTED AGAINST THE POWER OF THE BIO-TECHNIC LAW... AN ANT AGAINST THE MIGHT OF A BEETLE.
KA-RUNCH!
WHEW... THANKS, JOHNNY. I GUESS YOU REALLY DON'T HATE ME.
RUUUUUN! THE DAM'S BREAKING!!
THOSE THAT CAN'T RUN, RAGS HEALS WITH THE SAME STRIPS OF CLOTH THAT RESTORED HIS OWN EYESIGHT AND STRAIGHTENED HIS OWN CRIPPLED LEGS.
OLD MAN-- THIS IS THE STUPIDEST IDEA YOU'VE EVER HAD!!!

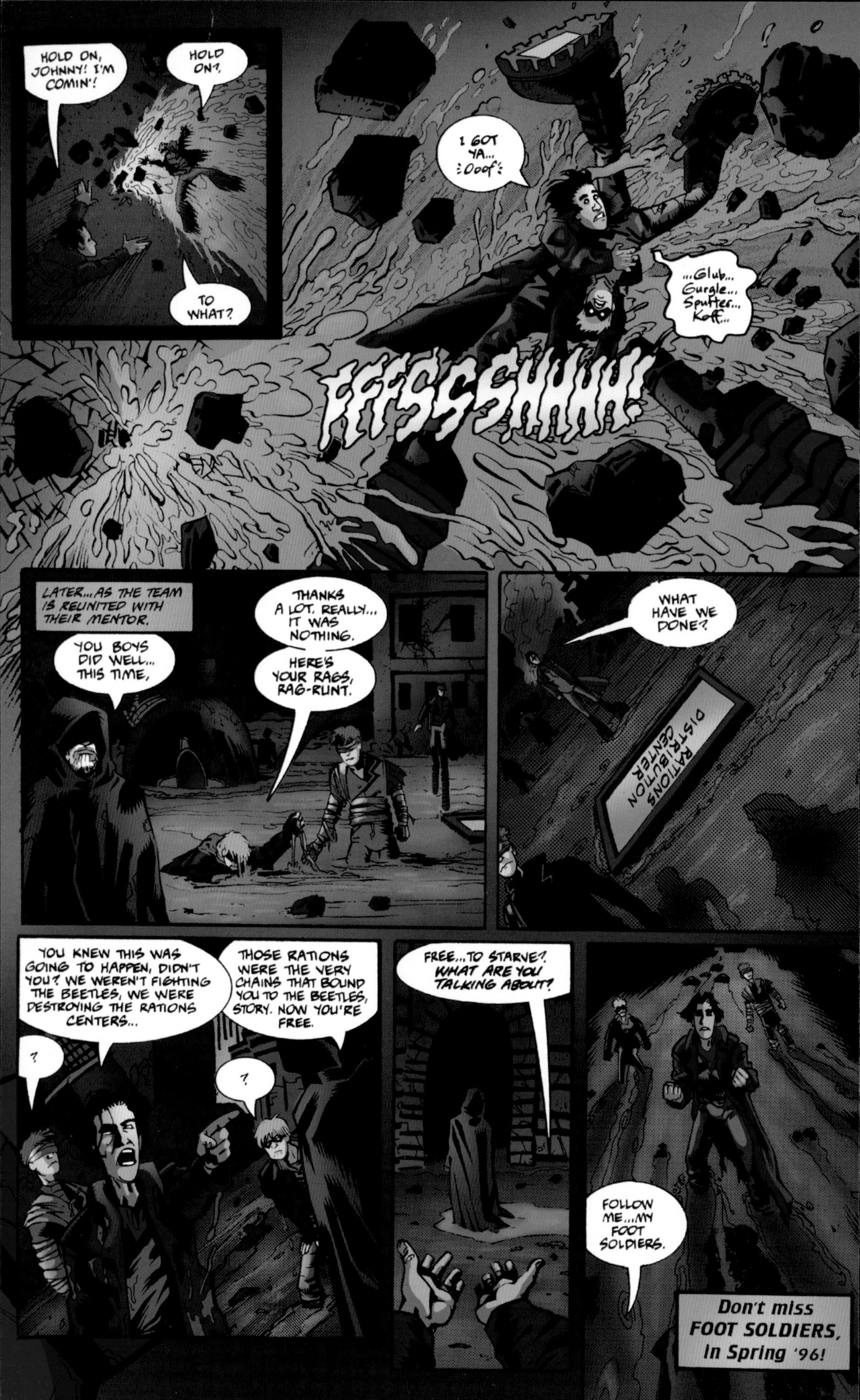
HOLD ON, JOHNNY! I'M COMIN'!
HOLD ON?
TO WHAT?
I GOT YA... Ooof
...Glub... Gurgle... Sputter... Koff...
FFFSSSHHHH!
LATER...AS THE TEAM IS REUNITED WITH THEIR MENTOR.
YOU BOYS DID WELL... THIS TIME,
THANKS A LOT. REALLY... IT WAS NOTHING.
HERE'S YOUR RAGS, RAG-RUNT.
WHAT HAVE WE DONE?
RATIONS DISTRIBUTION CENTER
YOU KNEW THIS WAS GOING TO HAPPEN, DIDN'T YOU? WE WEREN'T FIGHTING THE BEETLES, WE WERE DESTROYING THE RATIONS CENTERS...
?
THOSE RATIONS WERE THE VERY CHAINS THAT BOUND YOU TO THE BEETLES, STORY. NOW YOU'RE FREE.
?
FREE...TO STARVE? WHAT ARE YOU TALKING ABOUT?
FOLLOW ME...MY FOOT SOLDIERS.
Don't miss FOOT SOLDIERS, In Spring '96!

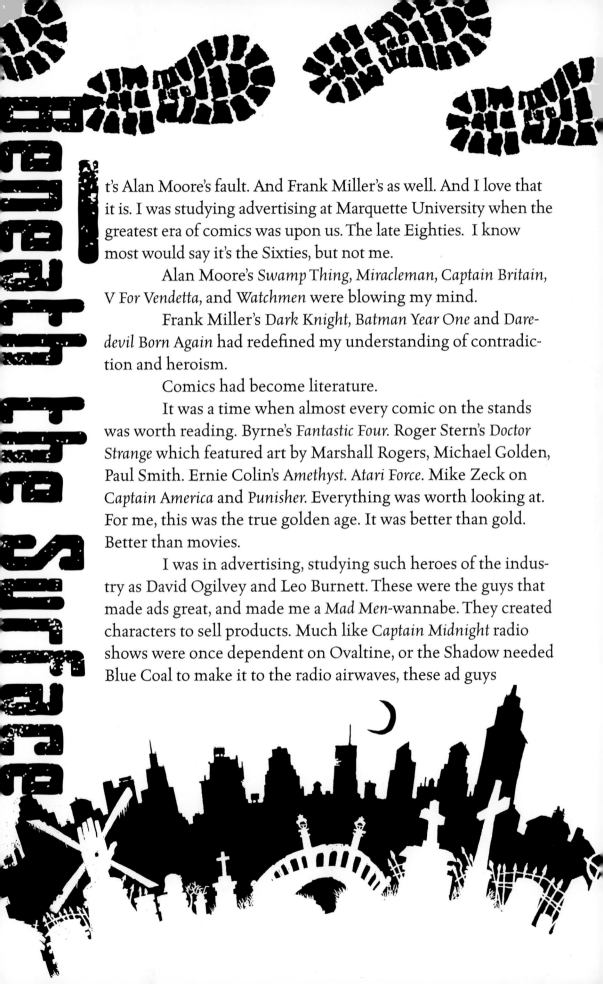

t's Alan Moore's fault. And Frank Miller's as well. And I love that it is. I was studying advertising at Marquette University when the greatest era of comics was upon us. The late Eighties. I know most would say it's the Sixties, but not me.

Alan Moore's *Swamp Thing*, *Miracleman*, *Captain Britain*, *V For Vendetta*, and *Watchmen* were blowing my mind.

Frank Miller's *Dark Knight*, *Batman Year One* and *Daredevil Born Again* had redefined my understanding of contradiction and heroism.

Comics had become literature.

It was a time when almost every comic on the stands was worth reading. Byrne's *Fantastic Four*. Roger Stern's *Doctor Strange* which featured art by Marshall Rogers, Michael Golden, Paul Smith. Ernie Colin's *Amethyst*. *Atari Force*. Mike Zeck on *Captain America* and *Punisher*. Everything was worth looking at. For me, this was the true golden age. It was better than gold. Better than movies.

I was in advertising, studying such heroes of the industry as David Ogilvey and Leo Burnett. These were the guys that made ads great, and made me a *Mad Men*-wannabe. They created characters to sell products. Much like *Captain Midnight* radio shows were once dependent on Ovaltine, or the Shadow needed Blue Coal to make it to the radio airwaves, these ad guys would create a jolly green giant to sell vegetables, or a Mister Whipple to sell paper towels.

And so, for a certain assignment for OdorEaters, I thought of a hero, a super hero who wore giant boots that could stomp out more than just smelly foot odors, but also the competition. His name was Johnny Stomp. He'd jump into the problem, dispatch the bad guys, and then, as people would come around him and cheer for him, they'd pull away because of the smell of his feet. Follow-up ads would have included Johnny's being overwhelmed and dizzied in the midst of battle by the smell of his own feet, or saving the day simply by taking his boots off.

I did the assignment, got some notes from my professor, and went on to the next assignment little realizing that there was far more to Johnny Stomp than a B-minus and the encouragement to come up with something else.

And so Johnny Stomp, like all creative babies, was put to death and buried… until I read Alan Moore's introduction to *The Dark Knight Returns*. It's quite an intro. Not sure I actually read the rest of the book for a while because of how deeply I was affected by Alan's words.

Alan talked about the importance of death to make a hero a legend. That death was the catalyst to legend and a character becoming bigger than merely their exploits. Ironically, I think Alan was telling us all the same thing that Neil Gaiman did in his intro for DKRs – Batman should have died.

The introduction was so amazing. It affected me so deeply, that I immediately coveted it. I wanted it to be my introduction. And it was unfair that it wasn't. I had written a couple scripts that some friends at Capital City Comics had read. *Clockmaker. Alphabet Supes.* I was practicing for something and didn't know what it was yet. But really, it was time to do more.

In the case of this book, though, the question was how to do it? How to make this happen and work? I mean, if the heroes die in the first

issue, and we hardly get to know them, that's not the same as a Robin Hood or a Zorro or a Batman dying. And then I realized the truth. I wasn't telling a story about the heroes who died, I was telling the story of those who came after. They would know nothing about the previous heroes, only a piece here or a bit there. The most important thing to know was that they lived. They did good. And they died.

And so the basic story about these kids robbing from the graves of some lost and forgotten super hero graveyard was born. The title, the names, the powers came to me over a period of time leading up to the early Nineties when my first few advertising jobs ended and I found myself working at Marvel Comics.

But the story itself, like my grave-robbers, was ripped from all those childhood experiences that moved me to nightmare and thrill at an early age. TV, movies, comics, books and more were all the soil from which I stole and re-imagined.

Some people say that good writers borrow and great writers steal. In my case, which still is the case, those who aspire to be great writers also steal. There was a glee and a freedom to grab at pop culture, or tug at it, or find some lost story that when refitted into this universe, it became something more.

I was thinking about movies too, and how this would look on the screen. I didn't like the way I imagined costumes would look on screen. I wanted plain clothes heroes, with hints of greatness about them that only revealed themselves when they went into action.

A couple years after I had figured out the story, I found myself getting to meet artists from everywhere. I had my own character designs, and soon these awesome artists would draw sketches of the characters, and then pin-ups. They helped the imagery form. They helped me see more to these characters.

It was time to put a proposal together. And I did. I even wrote a three page story that Mike Parobeck drew. It was inked twice. Once by the

awesome Steve Pugh, who did not ink over the original pencils, and then again by Teddy Kristiansen. This story, colored by Mike Thomas, plus the sketches from comic industry professionals, plus my breakdown story arcs and etc. went to Dark Horse and they bought it. Outright. On the spot.

Of course it helped a lot that some of the images in the proposal were from Alex Ross, Mike Mignola, Mike Allred, Jason Pearson, John K Snyder III and others.

For all those artists who did a sketch for me, or listened to me blather on about the stories and the set-up, I am so grateful. For my advertising professors, I'm glad these babies didn't stay dead for too long. For the guys at Capital City Comics (first in Milwaukee, then in Madison), thank you for never making me feel like an idiot, or just a customer. You listened. And read scripts. And were the first audience for my actual writing.

And for my friends who supported and listened and laughed (whether it was funny or not), thank you.

On the pages to follow, you'll find both versions of that three-page story that sold the project to Dark Horse. You'll find my sketches, logo designs, and pin-ups and art from both Mike Parobeck (who was originally going to draw the book before his untimely death) and Mike Oeming (who did the book and so made it his own). I will always be grateful for the fact that Mike turned it into an Easter Egg-hunter's dream -- lots of pop culture is buried here. You also experience Alex Ross and John K Snyder III pencils and designs for their covers.

For me, this book made me a lot of friends. And that, actually, is why I'm so in debt to these stories. There are other debts too, of course, but the friendship and relationships that came from working with and talking to such great people make this book it's own little golden age for me.

'Course, for some gold, you have to dig.

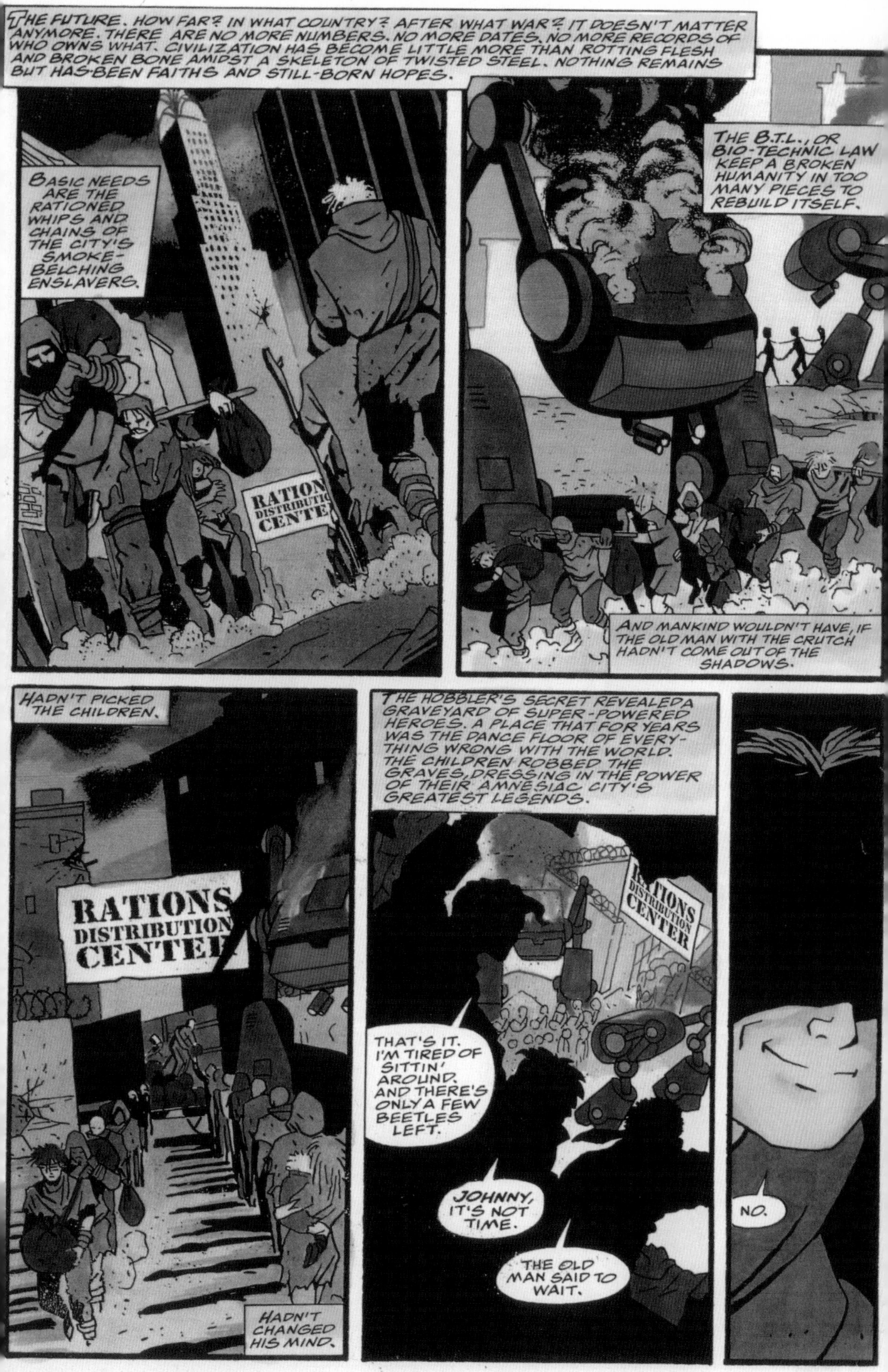
THE FUTURE. HOW FAR? IN WHAT COUNTRY? AFTER WHAT WAR? IT DOESN'T MATTER ANYMORE. THERE ARE NO MORE NUMBERS. NO MORE DATES. NO MORE RECORDS OF WHO OWNS WHAT. CIVILIZATION HAS BECOME LITTLE MORE THAN ROTTING FLESH AND BROKEN BONE AMIDST A SKELETON OF TWISTED STEEL. NOTHING REMAINS BUT HAS-BEEN FAITHS AND STILL-BORN HOPES.
BASIC NEEDS ARE THE RATIONED WHIPS AND CHAINS OF THE CITY'S SMOKE-BELCHING ENSLAVERS.
RATIONS DISTRIBUTIO CENTER
THE B.T.L., OR BIO-TECHNIC LAW KEEP A BROKEN HUMANITY IN TOO MANY PIECES TO REBUILD ITSELF.
AND MANKIND WOULDN'T HAVE, IF THE OLD MAN WITH THE CRUTCH HADN'T COME OUT OF THE SHADOWS.
HADN'T PICKED THE CHILDREN.
RATIONS DISTRIBUTION CENTE
HADN'T CHANGED HIS MIND.
THE HOBBLER'S SECRET REVEALED A GRAVEYARD OF SUPER-POWERED HEROES. A PLACE THAT FOR YEARS WAS THE DANCE FLOOR OF EVERYTHING WRONG WITH THE WORLD. THE CHILDREN ROBBED THE GRAVES, DRESSING IN THE POWER OF THEIR AMNESIAC CITY'S GREATEST LEGENDS.
RATIONS DISTRIBUTION CENTER
THAT'S IT. I'M TIRED OF SITTIN' AROUND, AND THERE'S ONLY A FEW BEETLES LEFT.
JOHNNY, IT'S NOT TIME.
THE OLD MAN SAID TO WAIT.
NO.

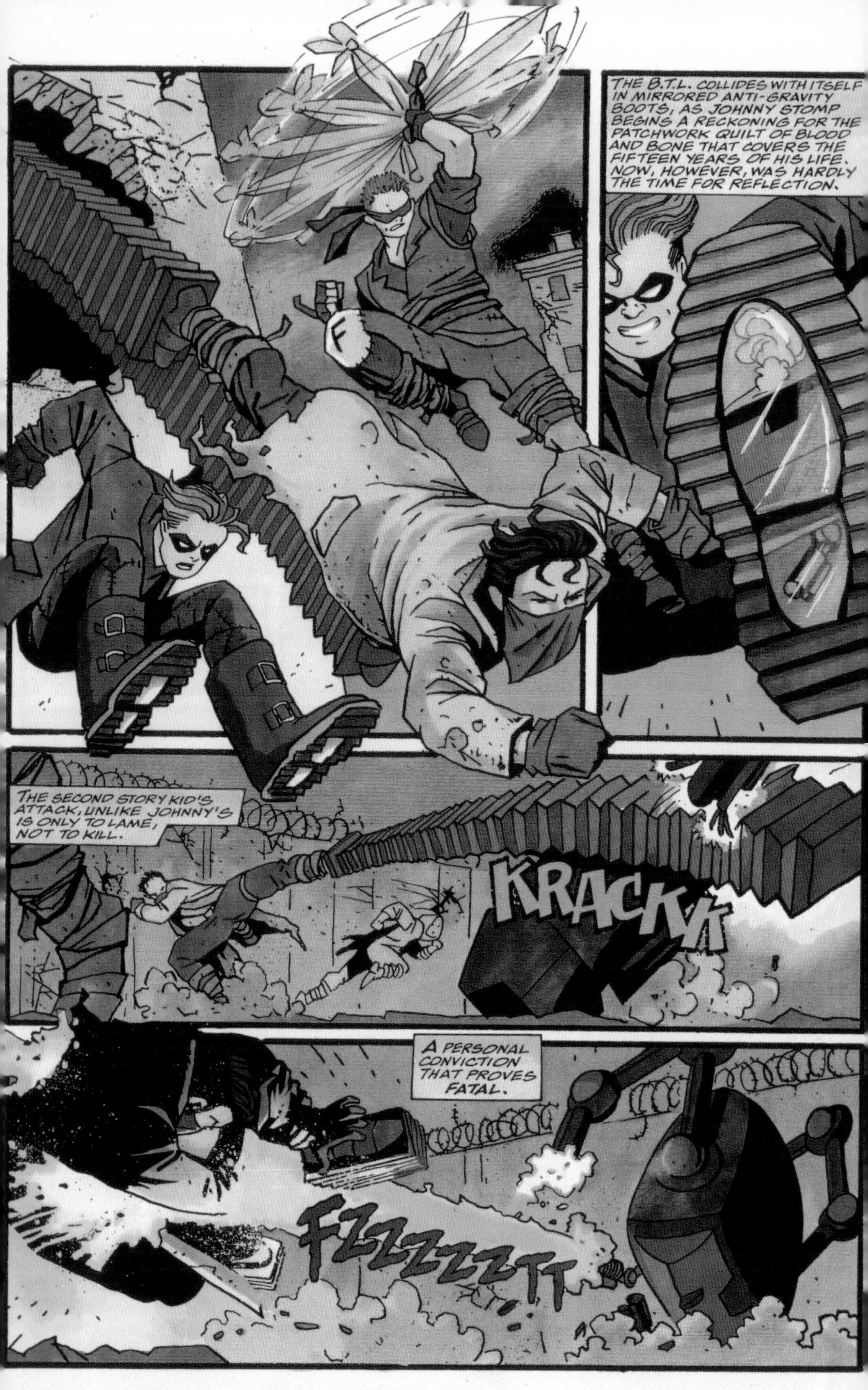
THE B.T.L. COLLIDES WITH ITSELF IN MIRRORED ANTI-GRAVITY BOOTS, AS JOHNNY STOMP BEGINS A RECKONING FOR THE PATCHWORK QUILT OF BLOOD AND BONE THAT COVERS THE FIFTEEN YEARS OF HIS LIFE. NOW, HOWEVER, WAS HARDLY THE TIME FOR REFLECTION.
THE SECOND STORY KID'S ATTACK, UNLIKE JOHNNY'S IS ONLY TO LAME, NOT TO KILL.
KRACKK
A PERSONAL CONVICTION THAT PROVES FATAL.
FZZZZZZTT

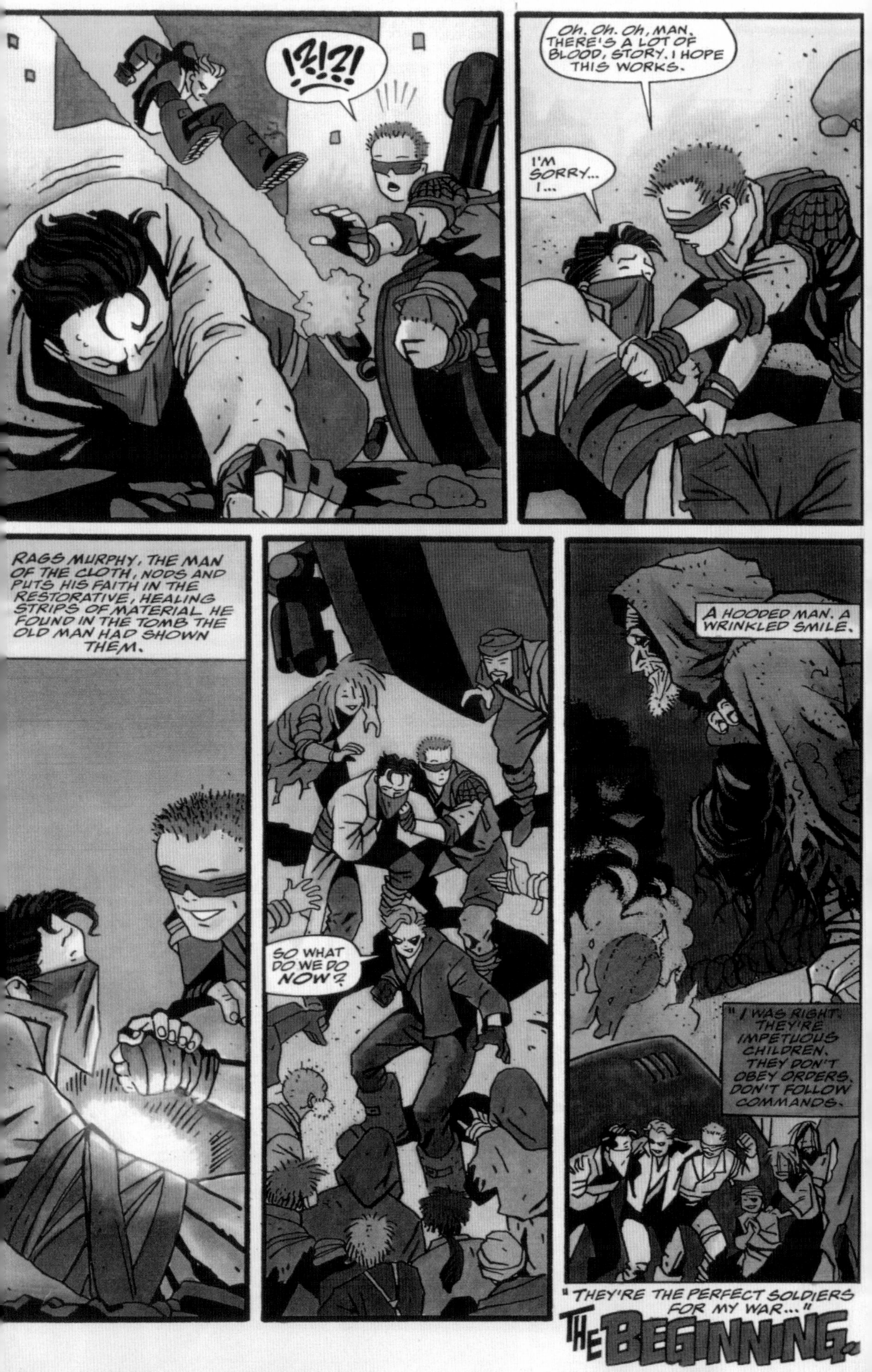
!?!?!
Oh. Oh. Oh, MAN. THERE'S A LOT OF BLOOD, STORY. I HOPE THIS WORKS.
I'M SORRY... I...
RAGS MURPHY, THE MAN OF THE CLOTH, NODS AND PUTS HIS FAITH IN THE RESTORATIVE, HEALING STRIPS OF MATERIAL HE FOUND IN THE TOMB THE OLD MAN HAD SHOWN THEM.
SO WHAT DO WE DO NOW?
A HOODED MAN. A WRINKLED SMILE.
"I WAS RIGHT. THEY'RE IMPETUOUS CHILDREN. THEY DON'T OBEY ORDERS. DON'T FOLLOW COMMANDS.
"THEY'RE THE PERFECT SOLDIERS FOR MY WAR..."
THE BEGINNING..

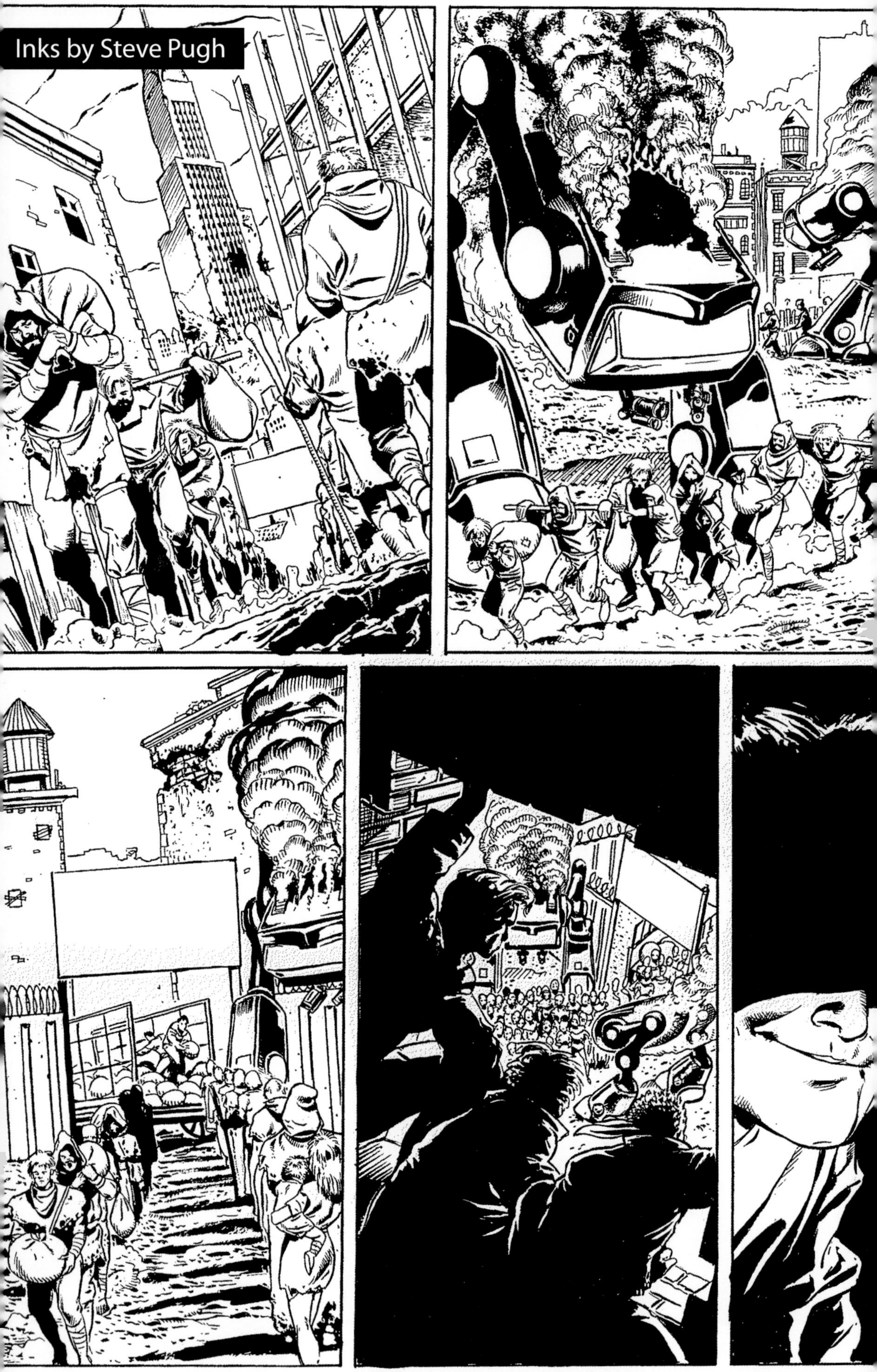
Inks by Steve Pugh

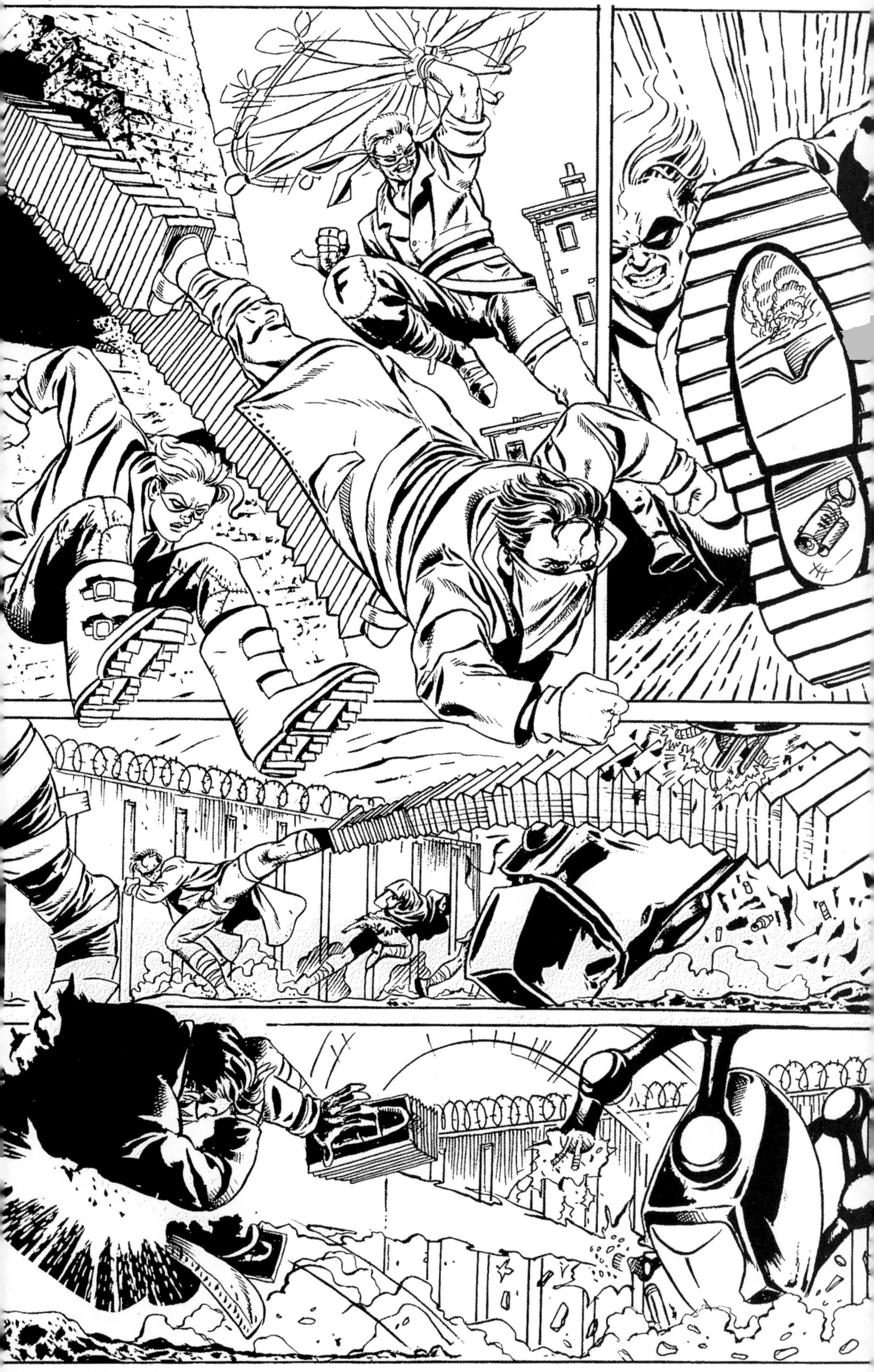

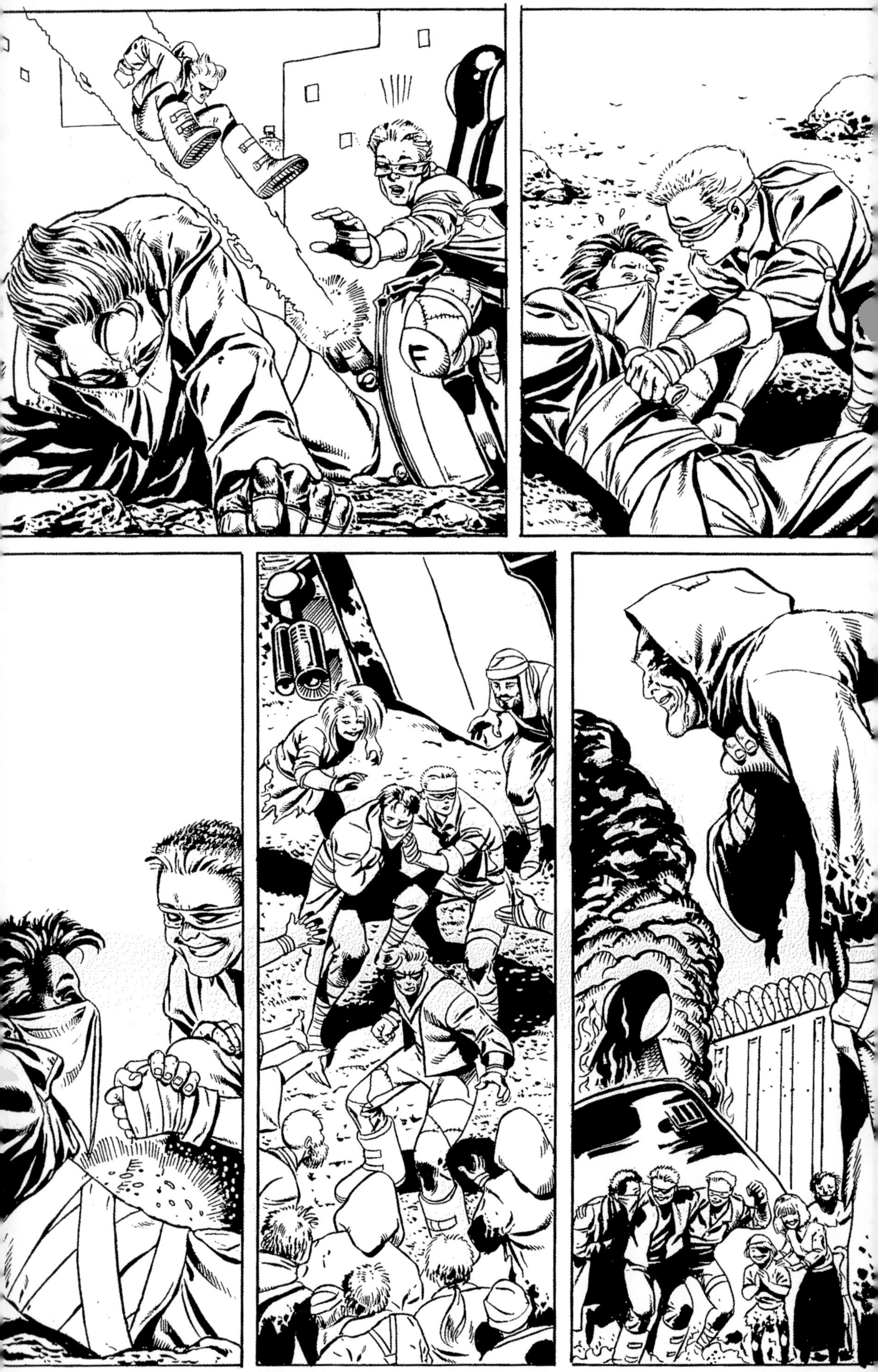

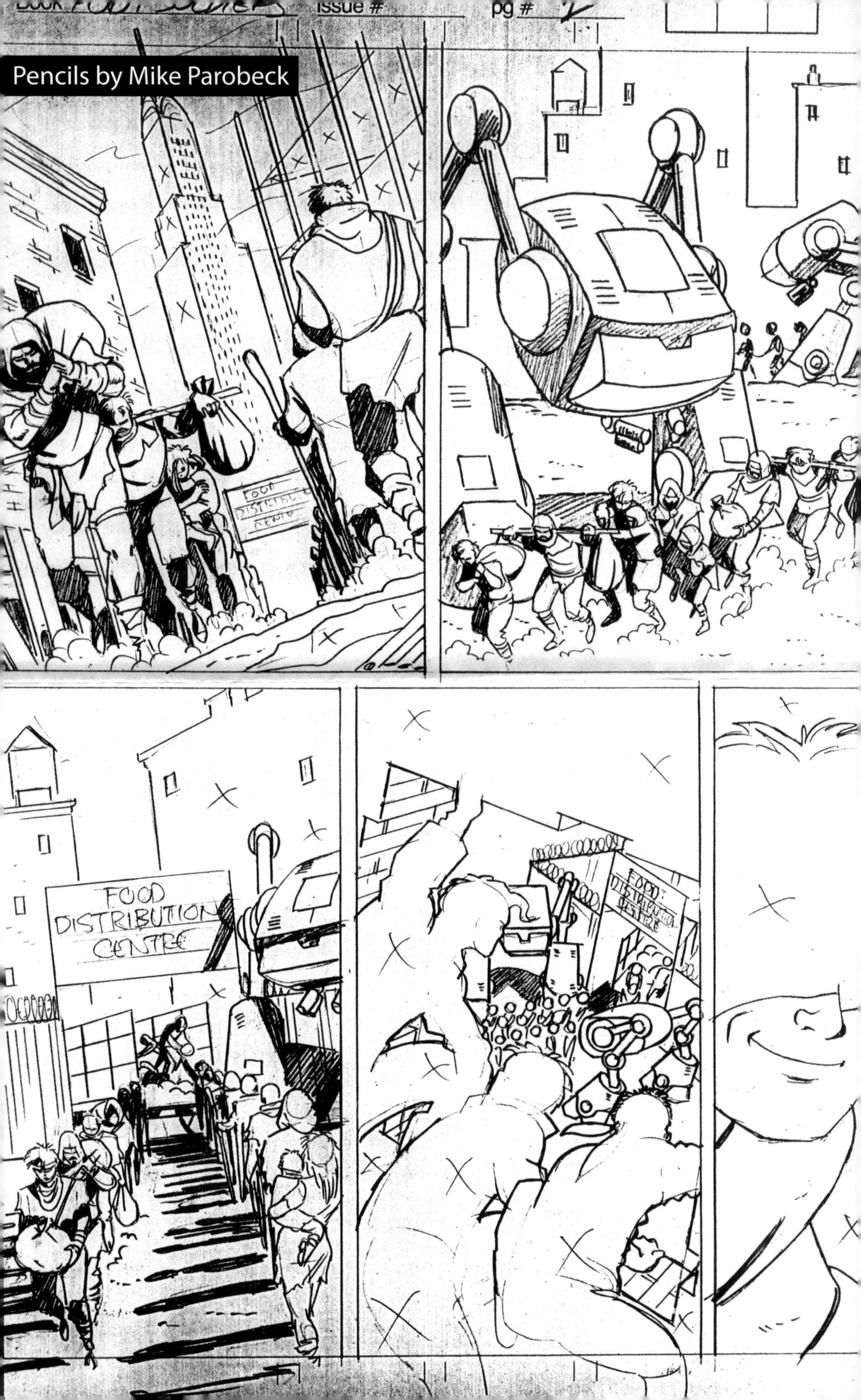
FOOD
DISTRIBUTION
CENTRE

Pencils by Mike Parobeck

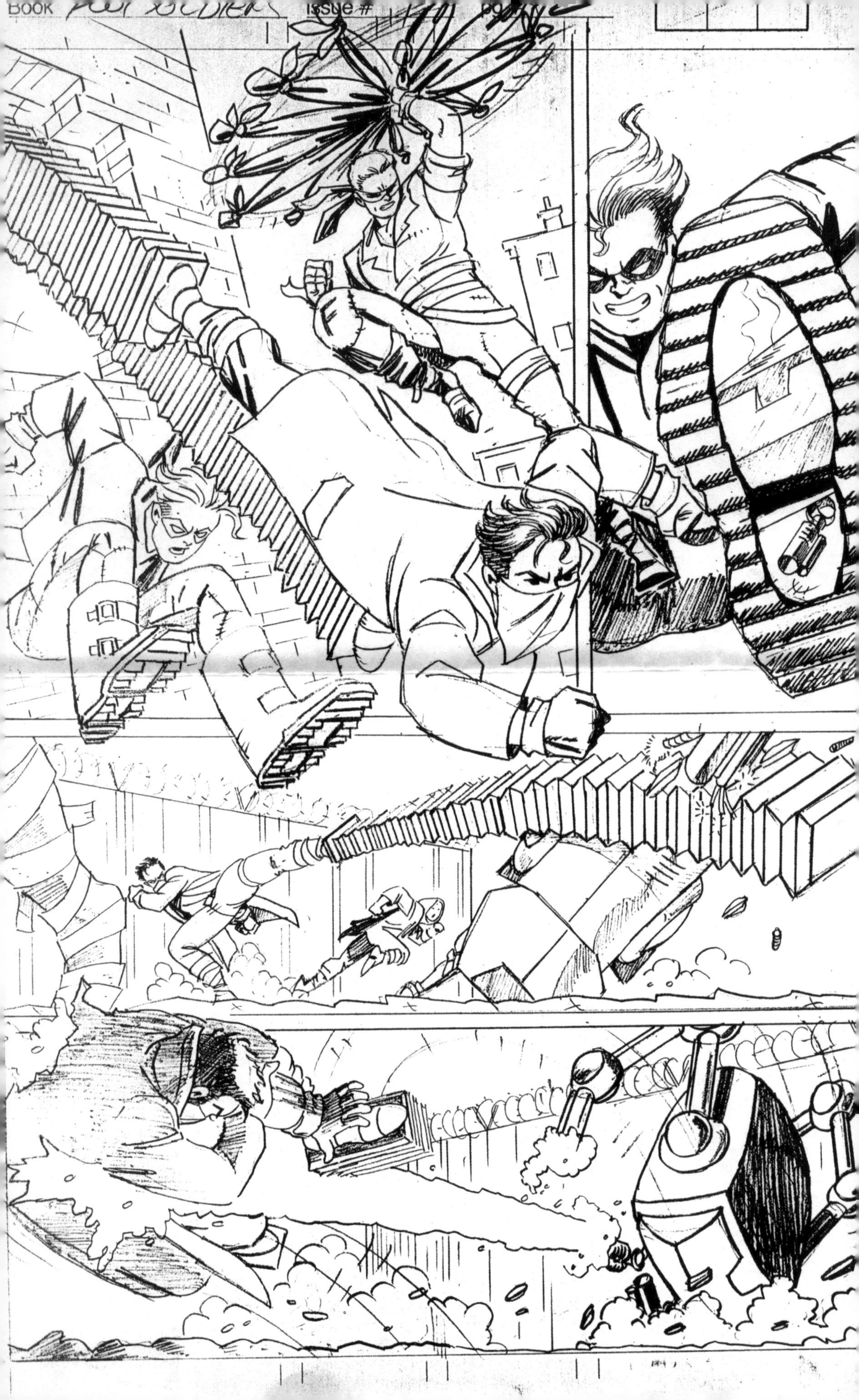

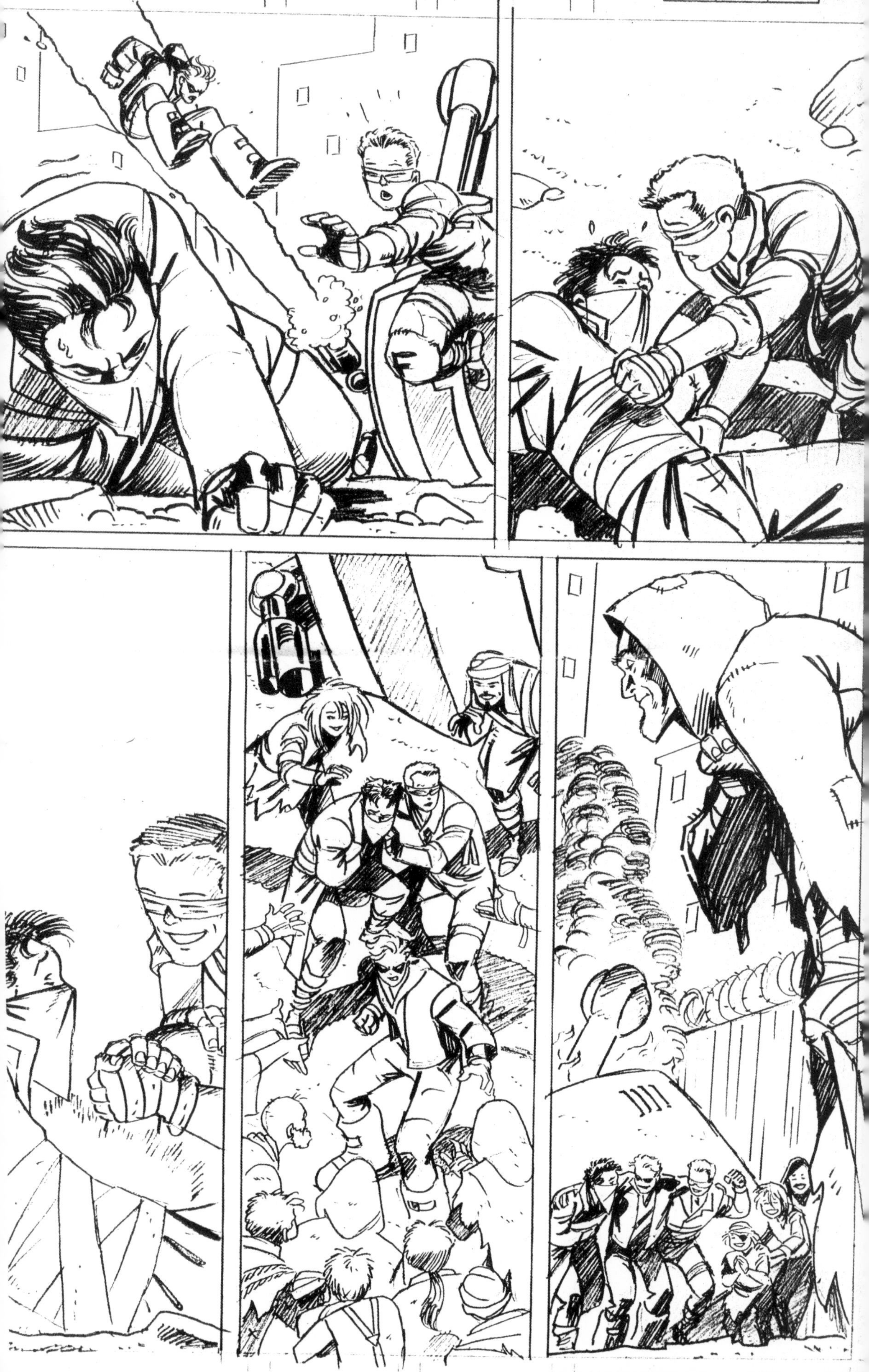

Tracing paper layouts by Mike Parobeck for *Foot Soldiers* Chapter 1

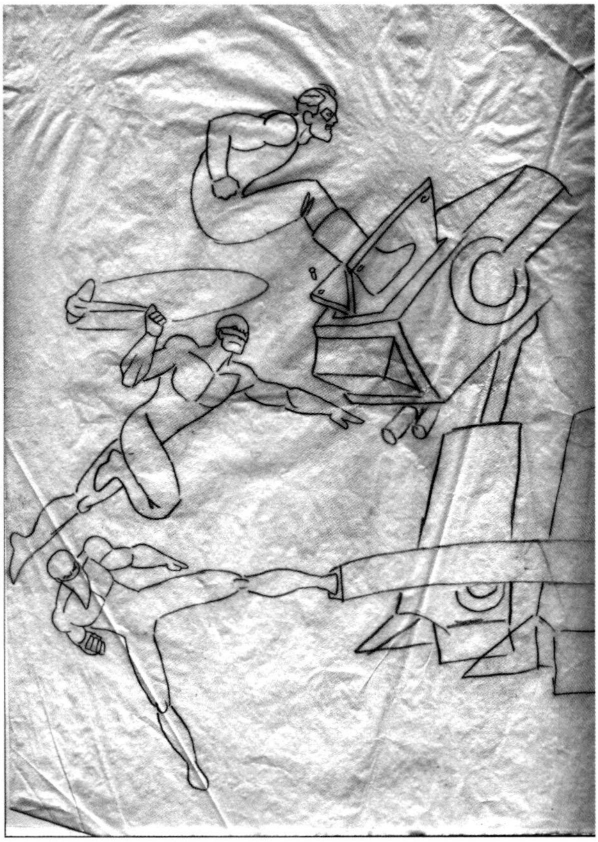

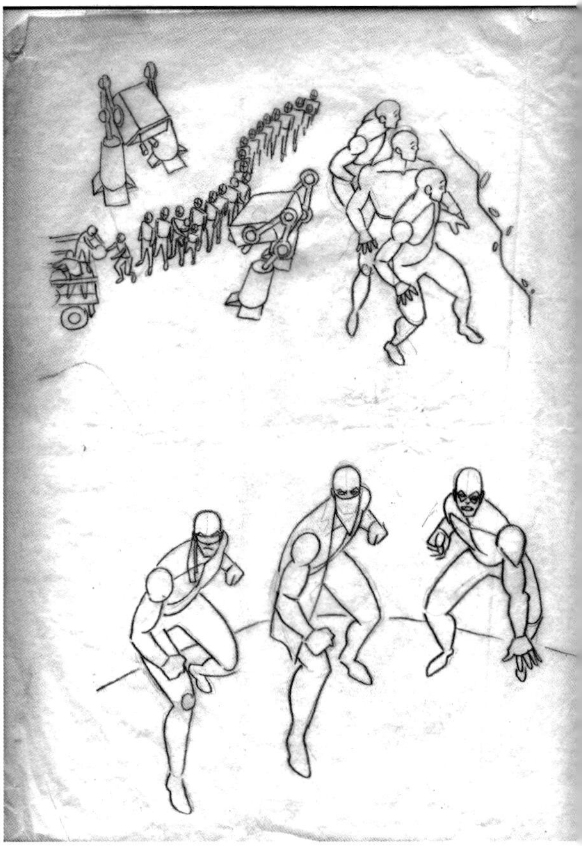

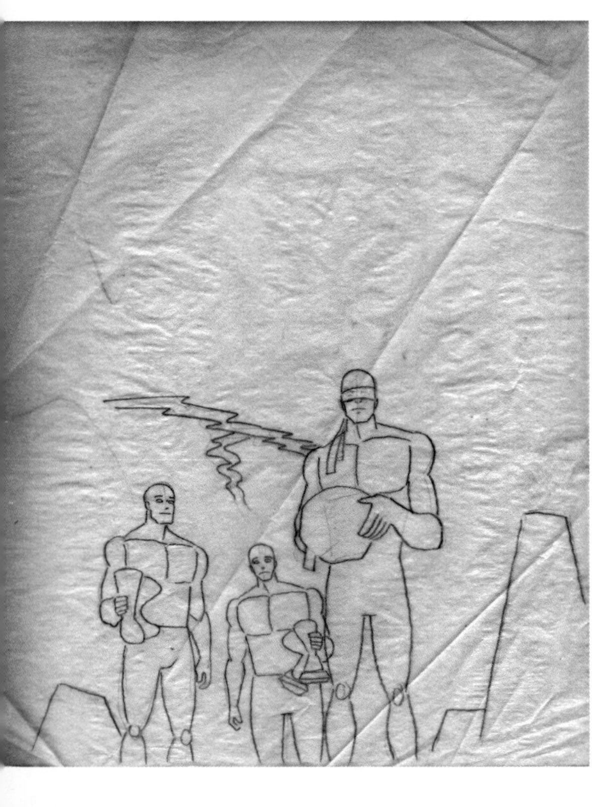

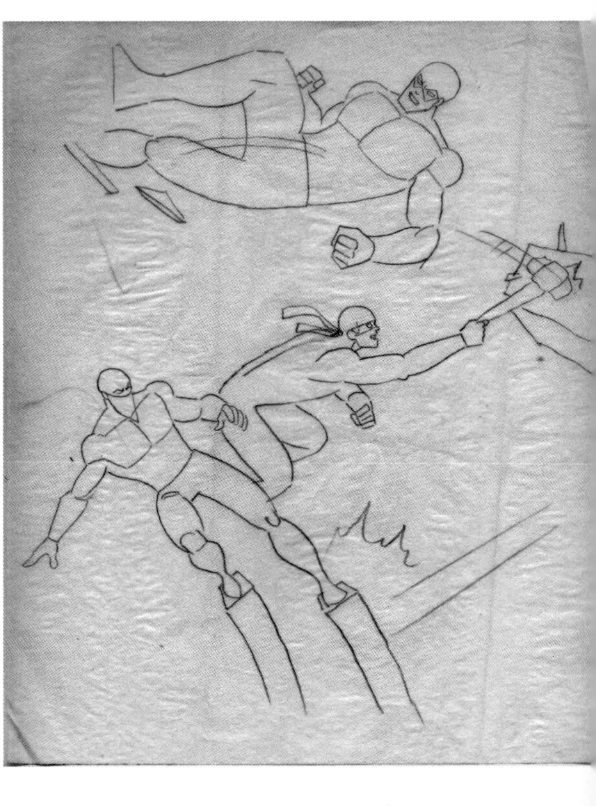

Initial logo designs

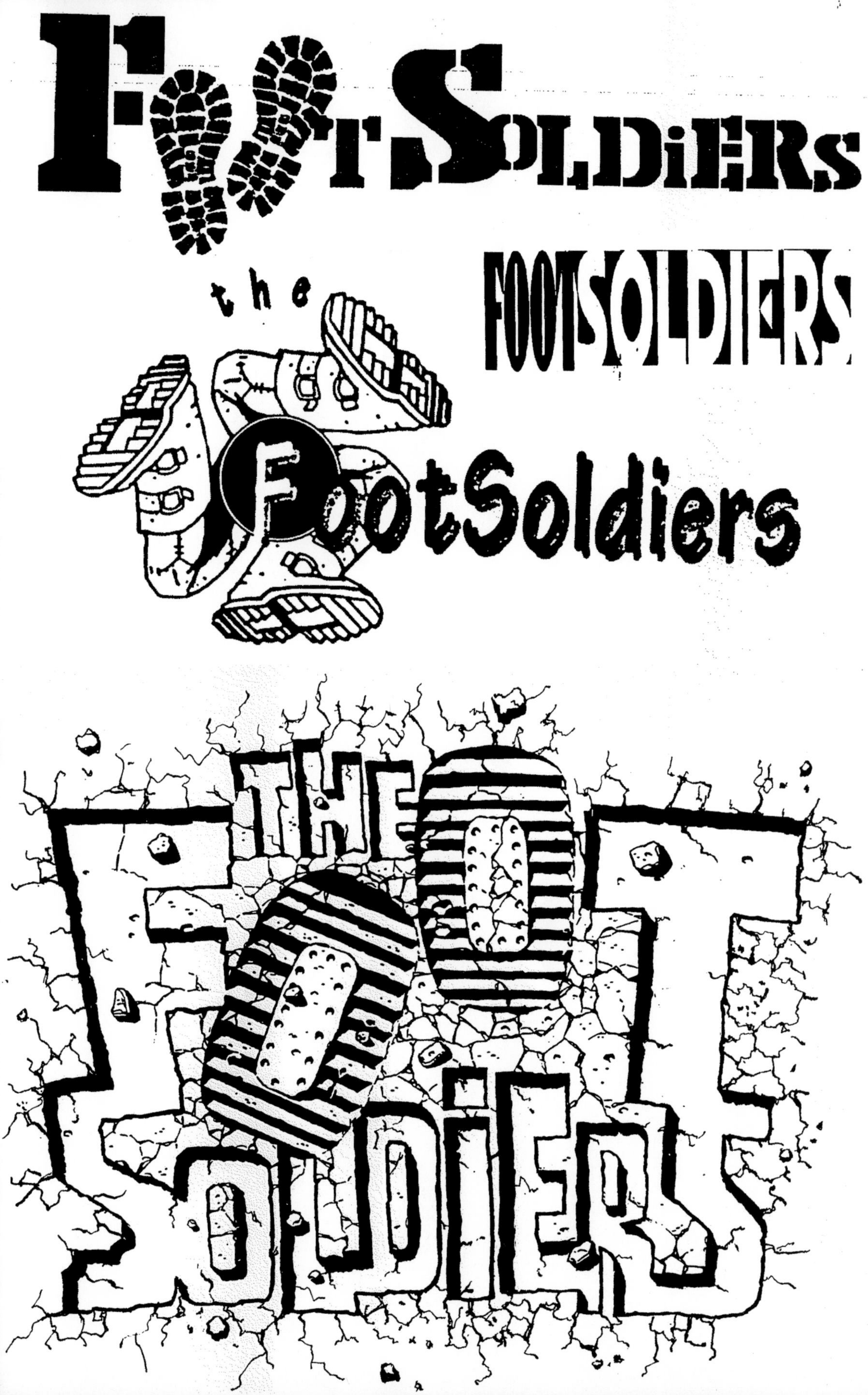
FootSoldiers
FOOTSOLDIERS
the FootSoldiers
THE FOOT SOLDIERS

Michael Avon Oeming pinups, pencils & layouts

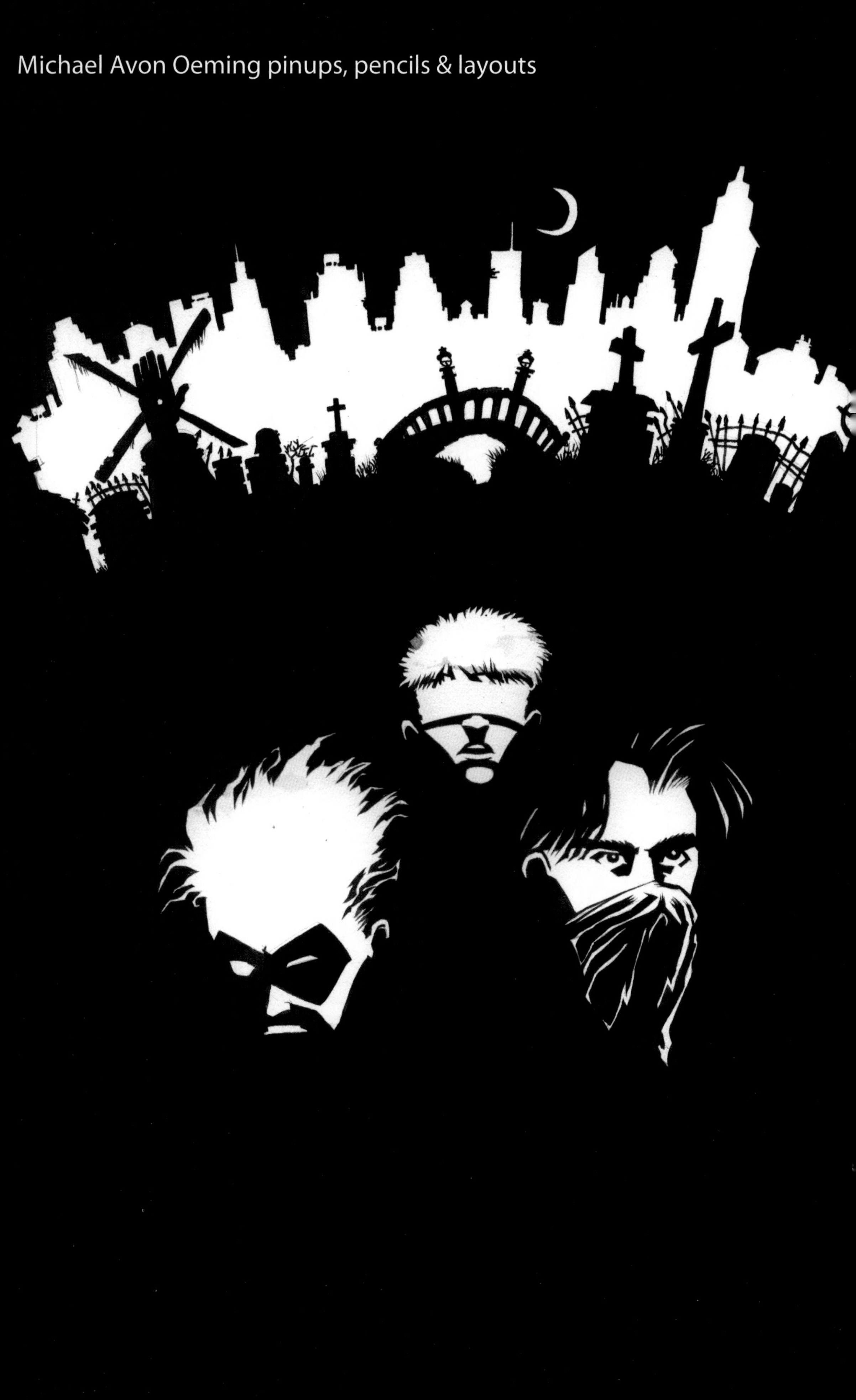

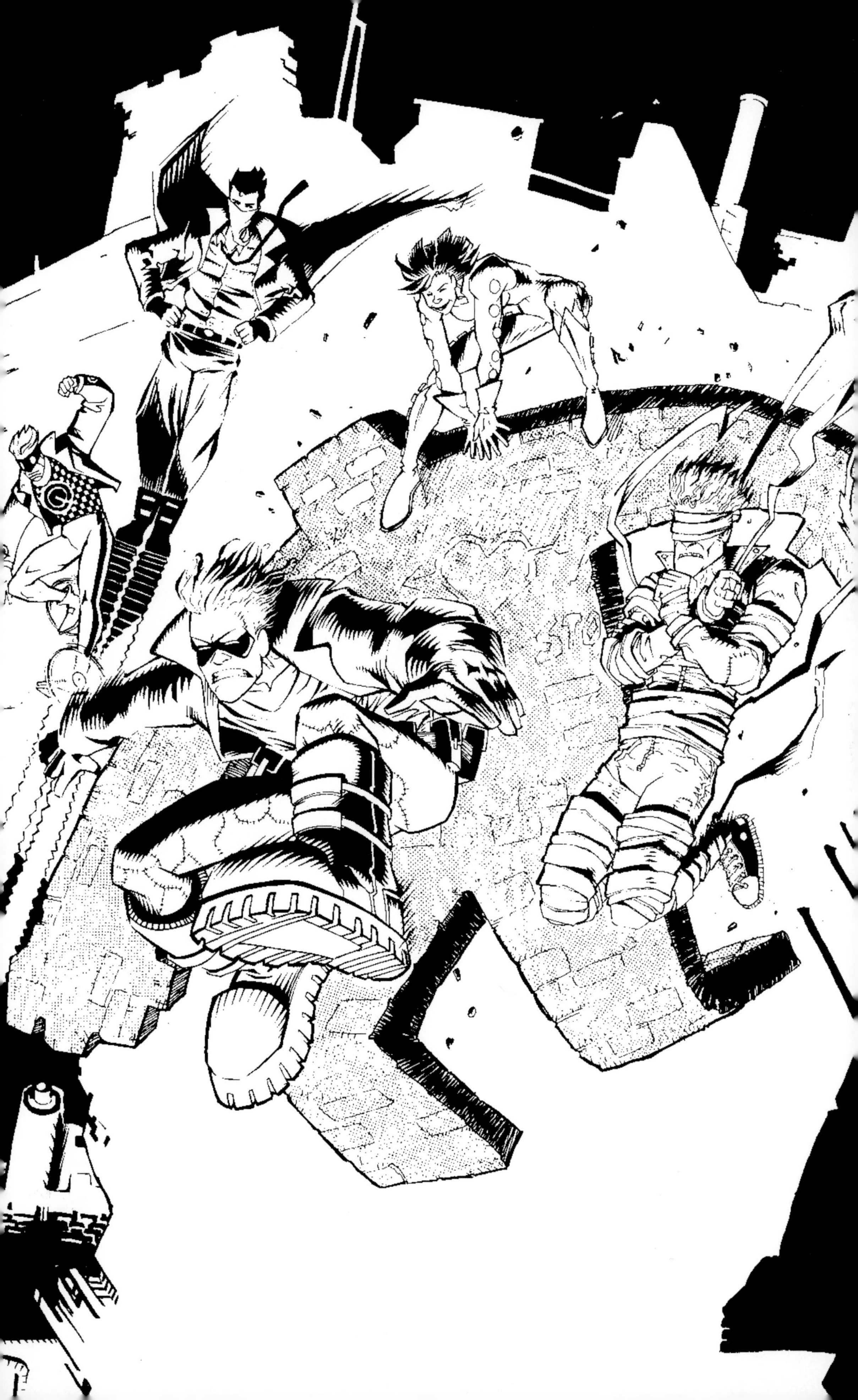

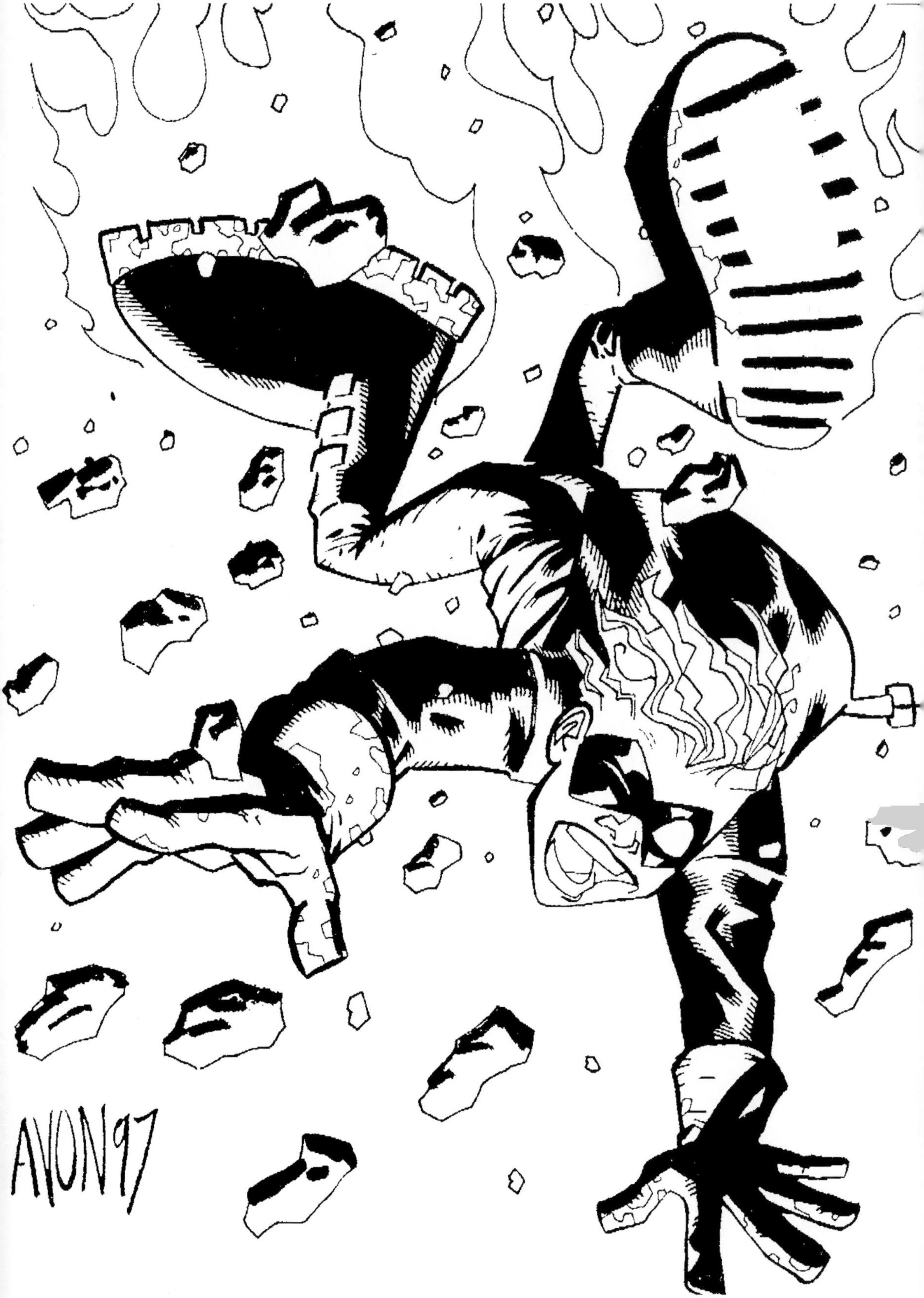
AVON97

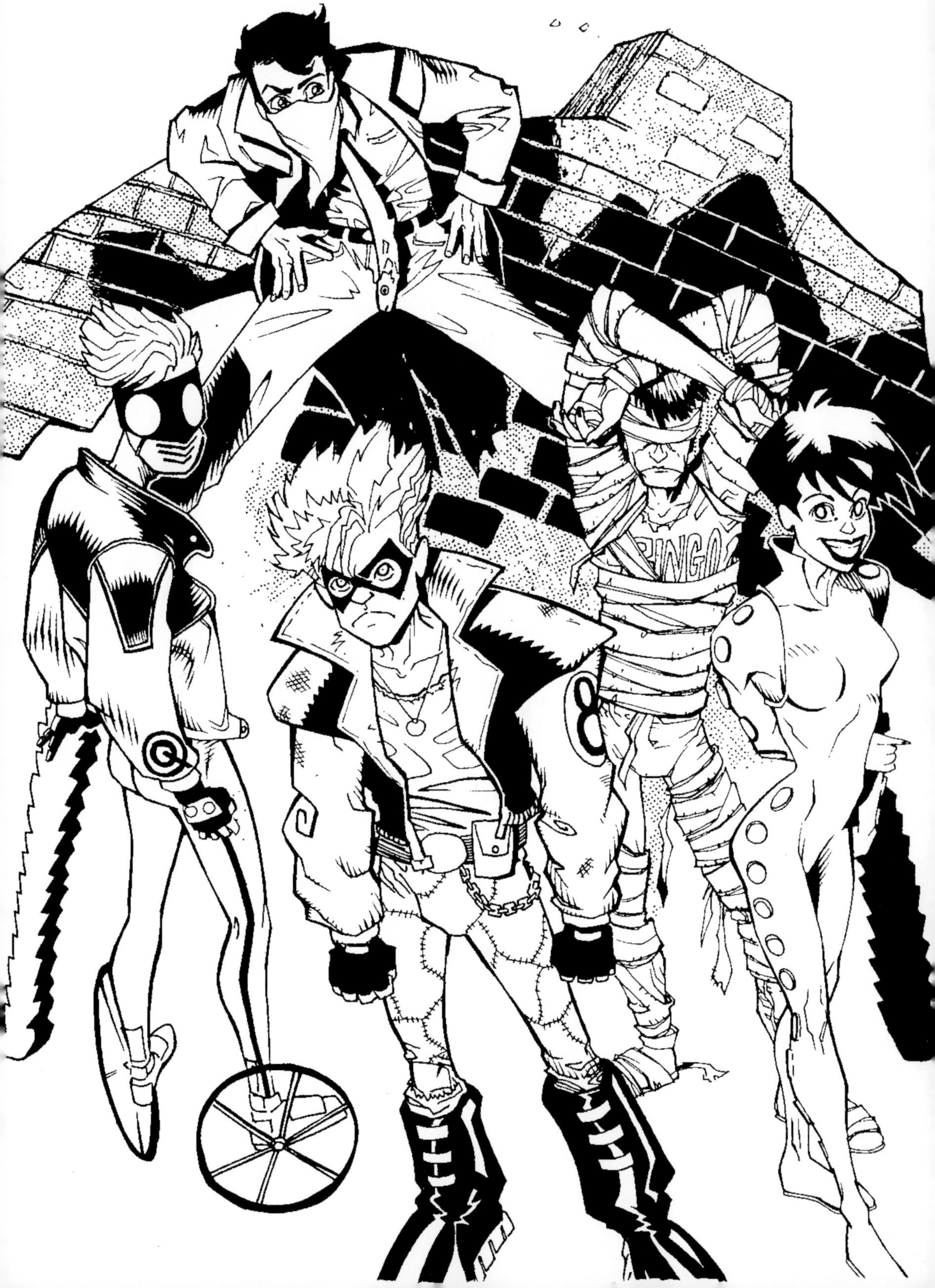

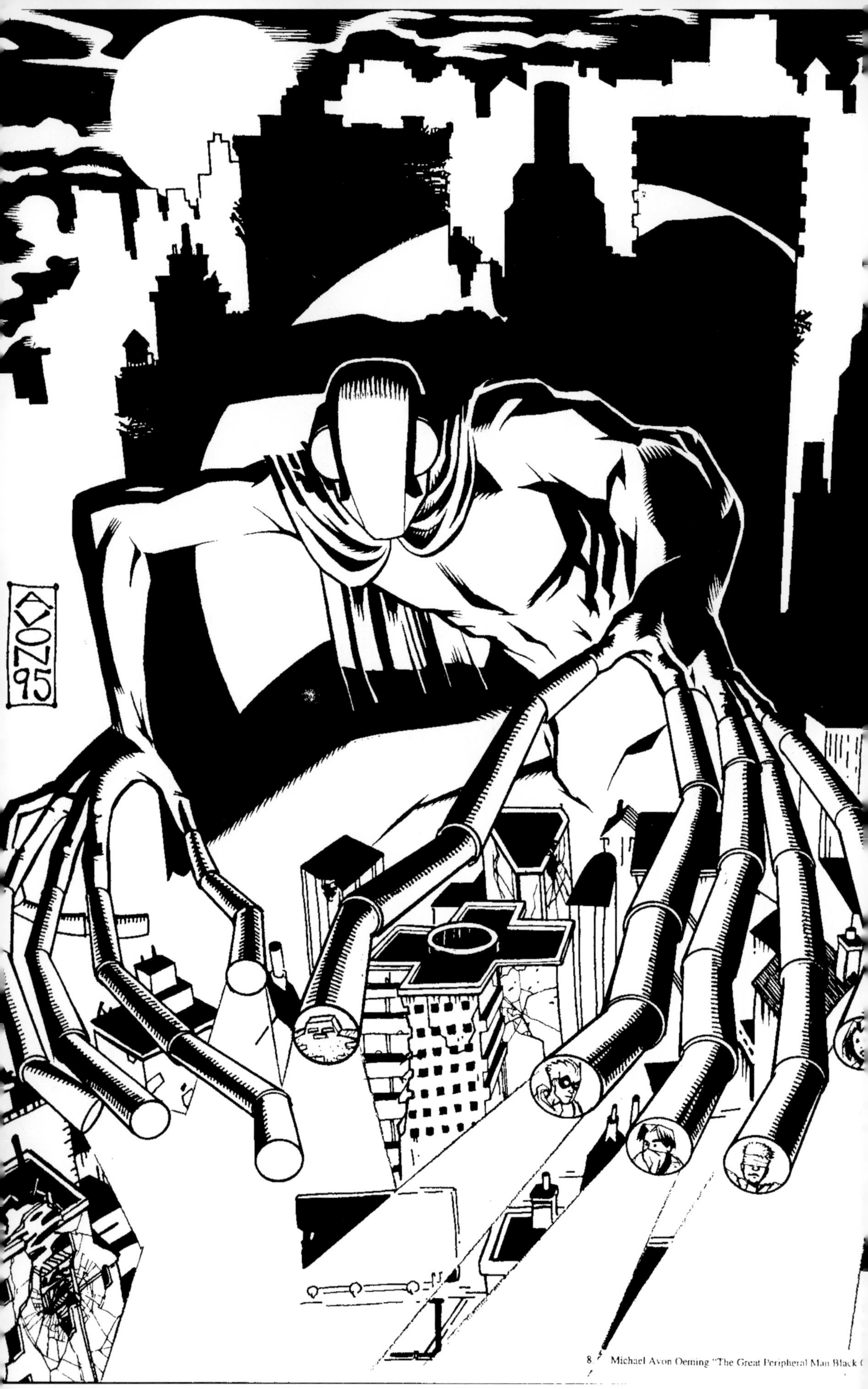

8. Michael Avon Oeming "The Great Peripheral Man Black (

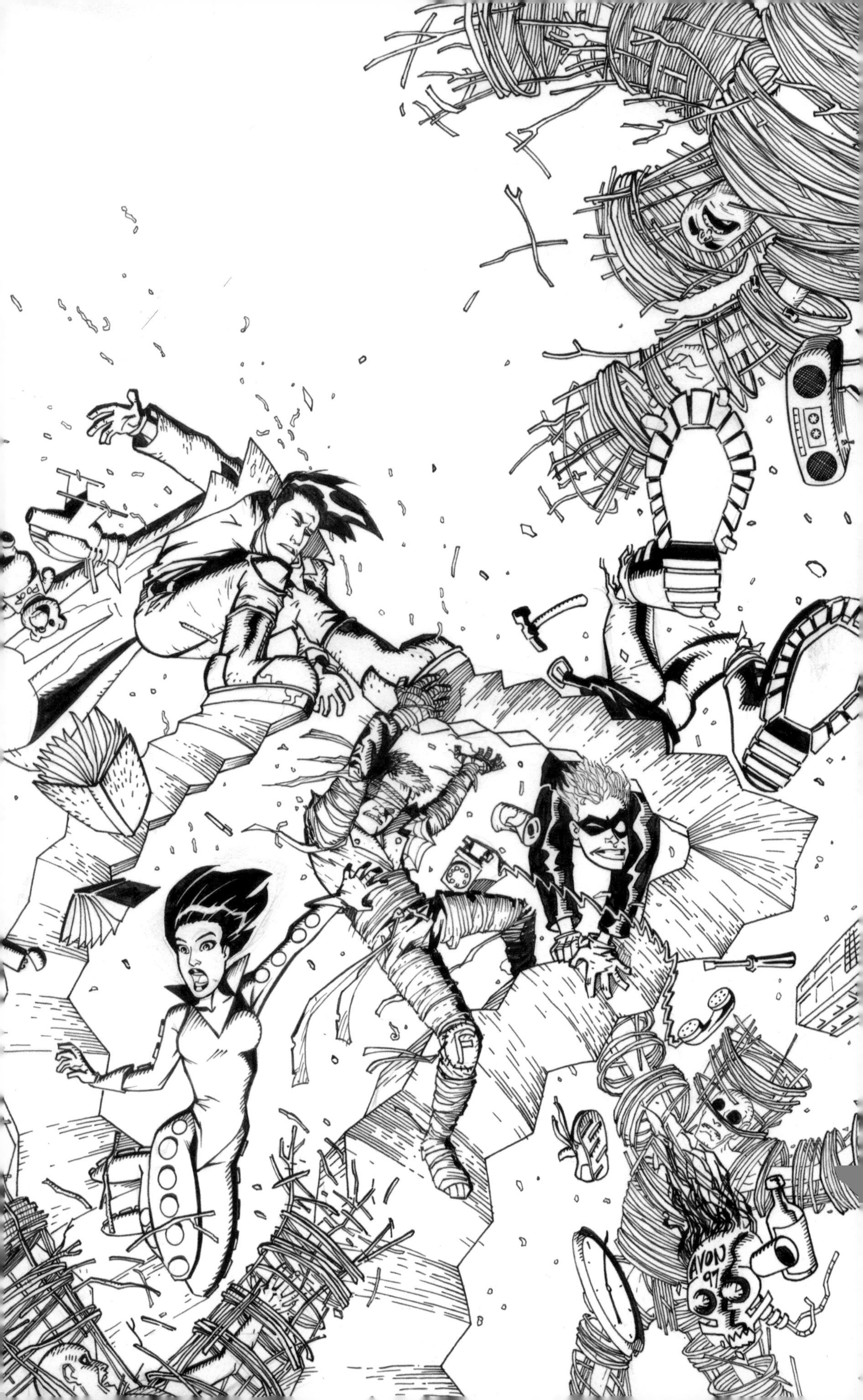
AVON 97

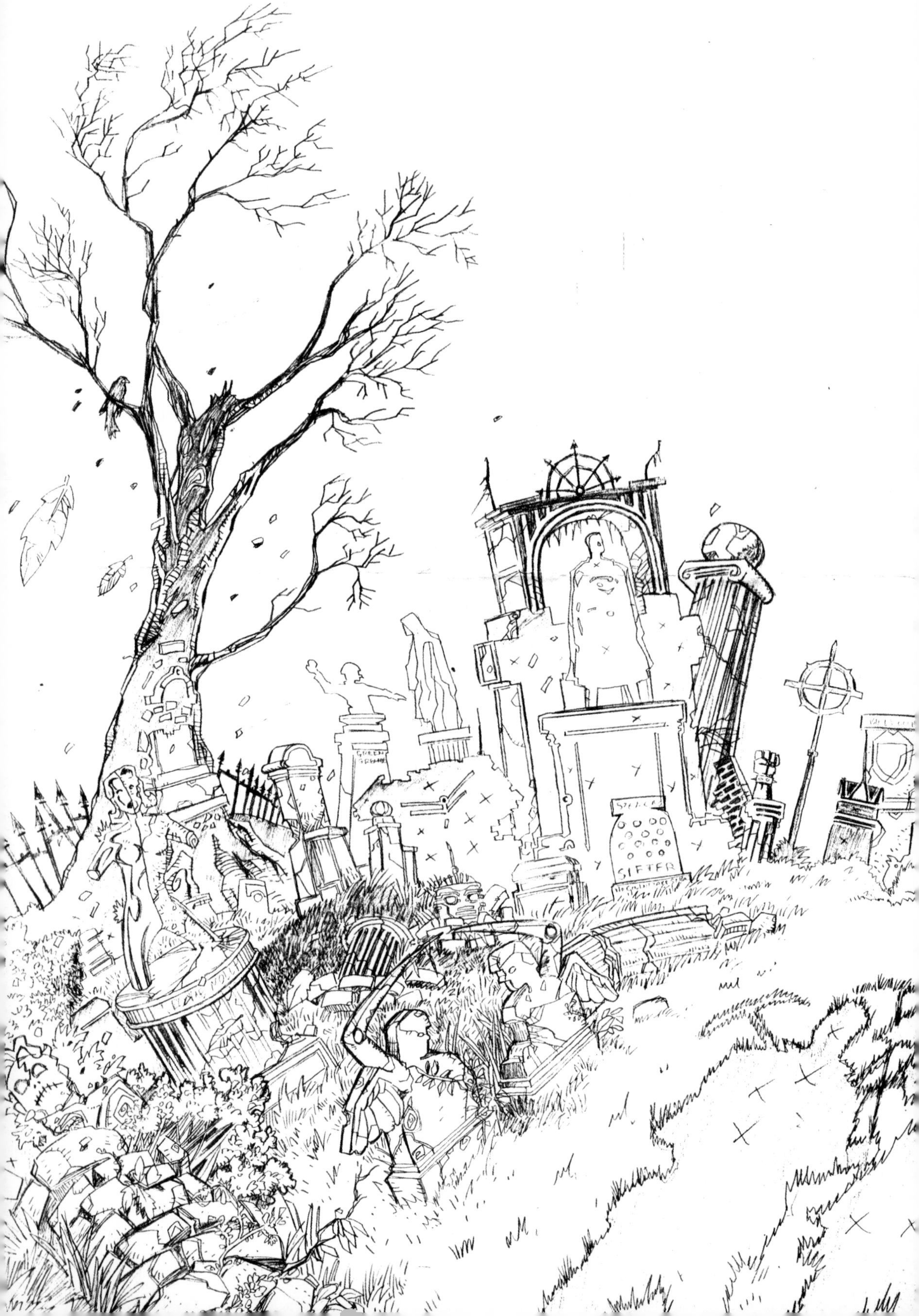
GREEN
SIFTER

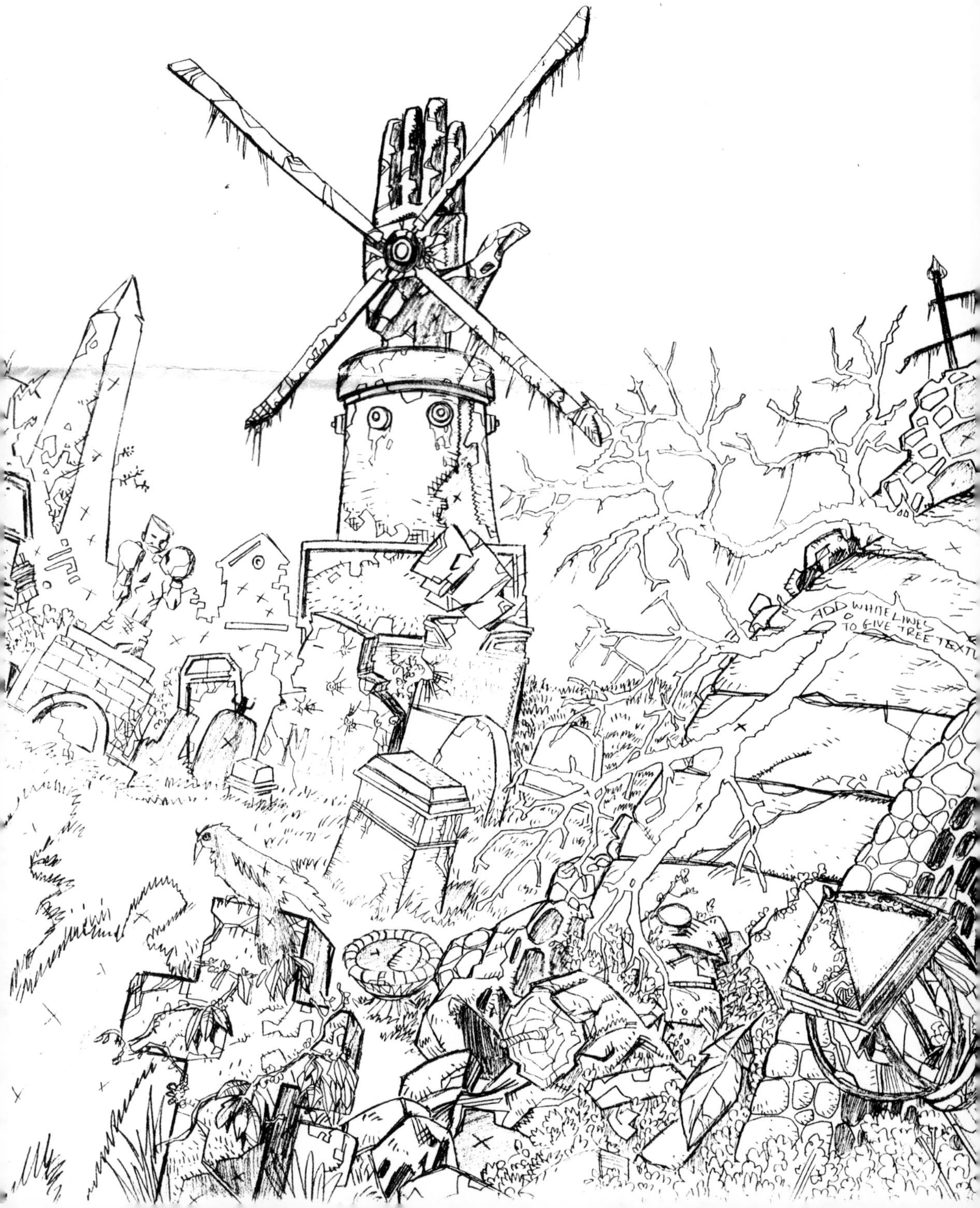
ADD WHITE LINES TO GIVE TREE TEXTU

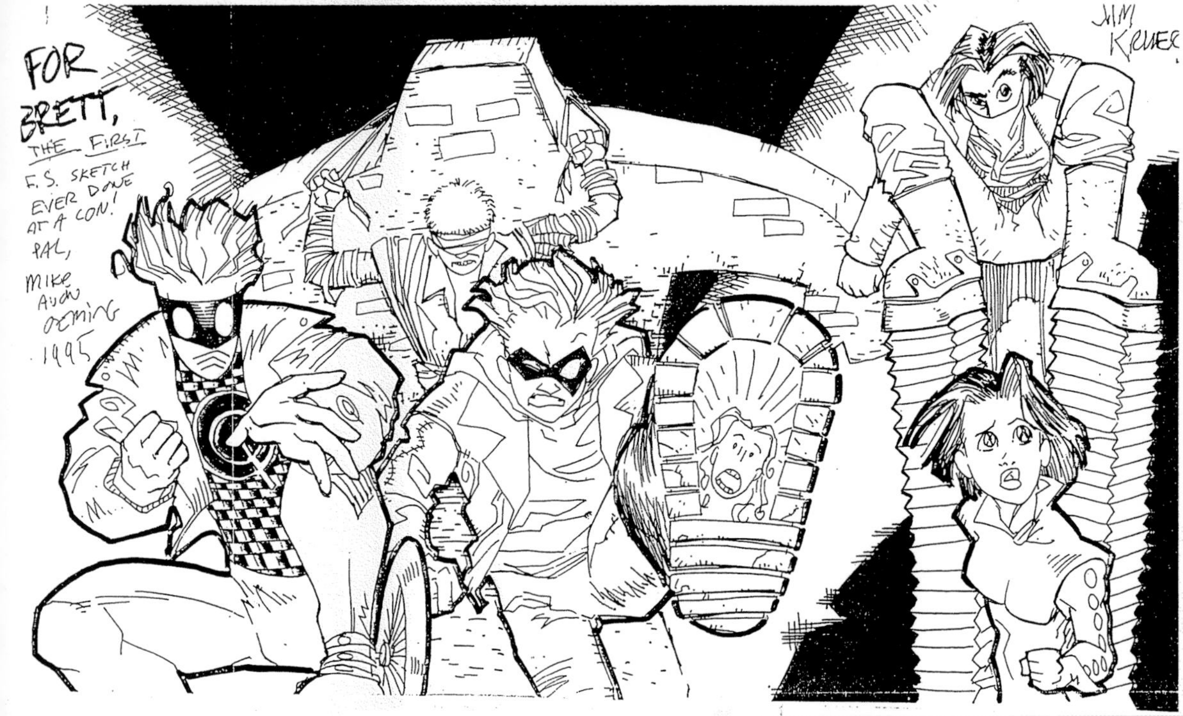
FOR BRETT,
THE FIRST
F. S. SKETCH EVER DONE AT A CON!
PAL,
MIKE AVON OEMING
1995
JIM KRUEG

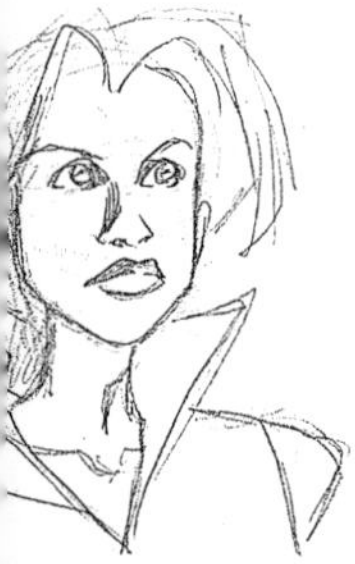

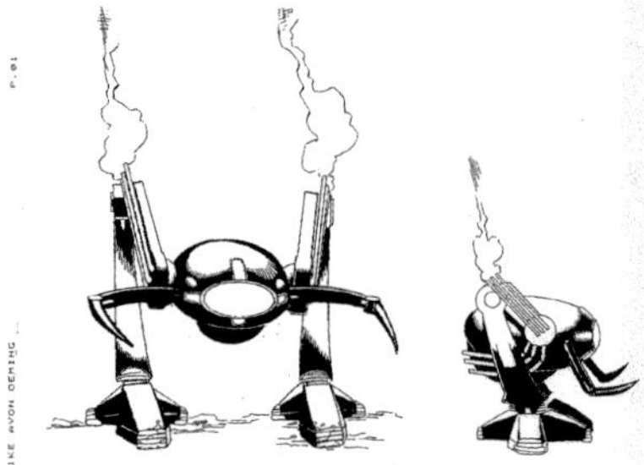
MIKE AVON OEMING

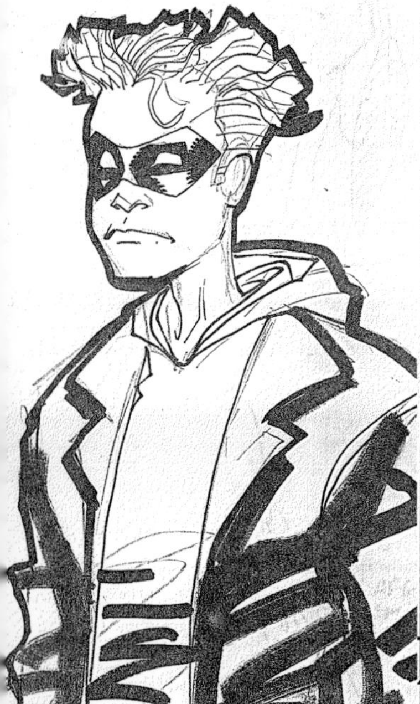

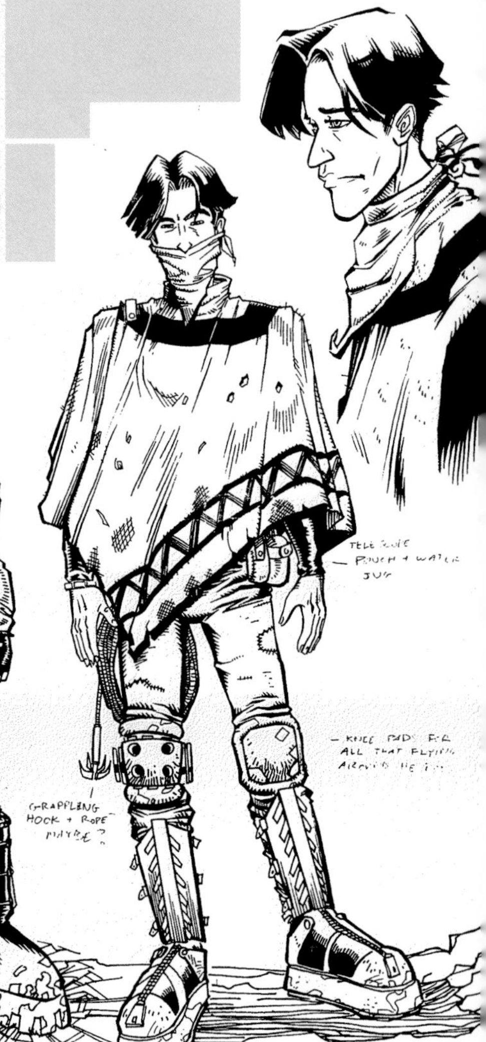
TELESCOPE POUCH + WATER JUG
KNEE BRACES KEEP JONNY FROM SNAPPING OFF AT LEGS FROM HIGH JUMPS?
GRAPPLING HOOK + ROPE MAYBE?
— KNEE PADS FOR ALL THAT FLYING
AVON
TO HIS BELT HE COULD PULL DOWN BUILDINGS + RTL'S IN CONJUNCTION WITH

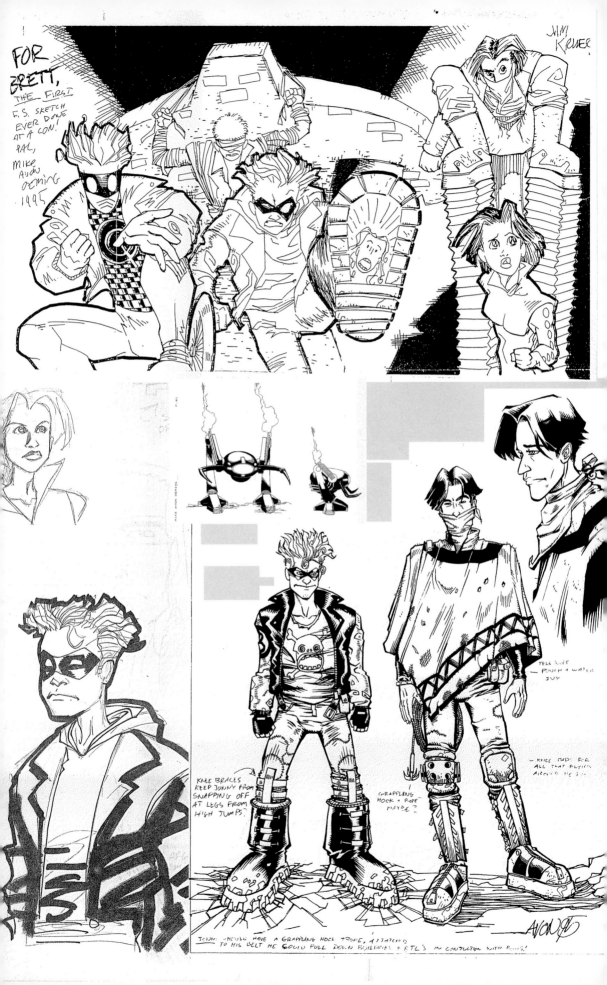

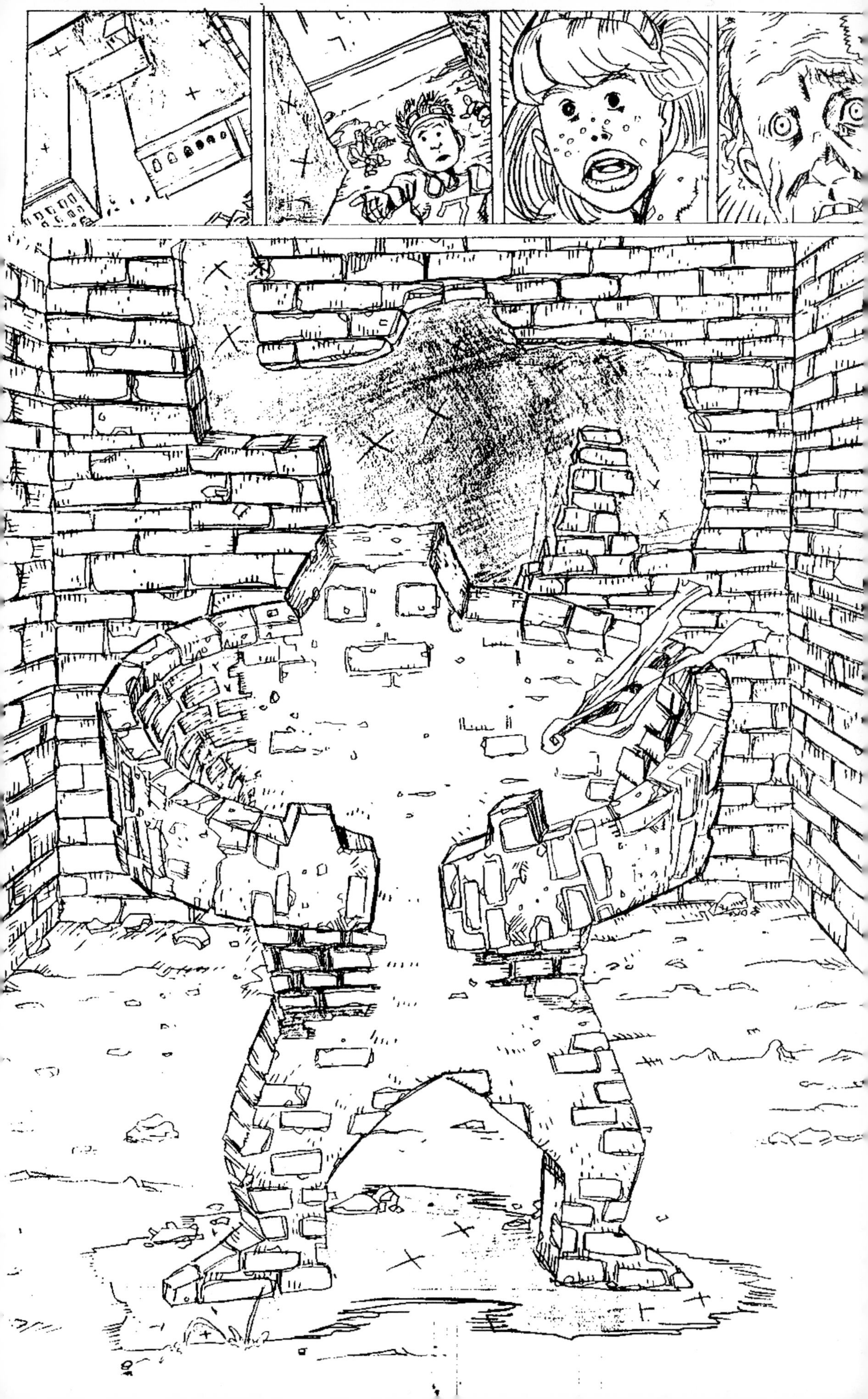

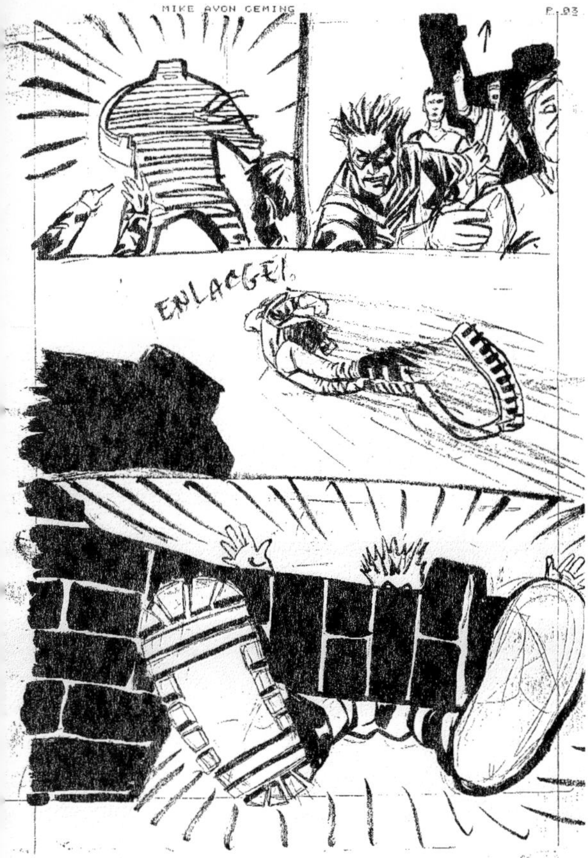
MIKE AVON OEMING
P.03
ENLARGE!

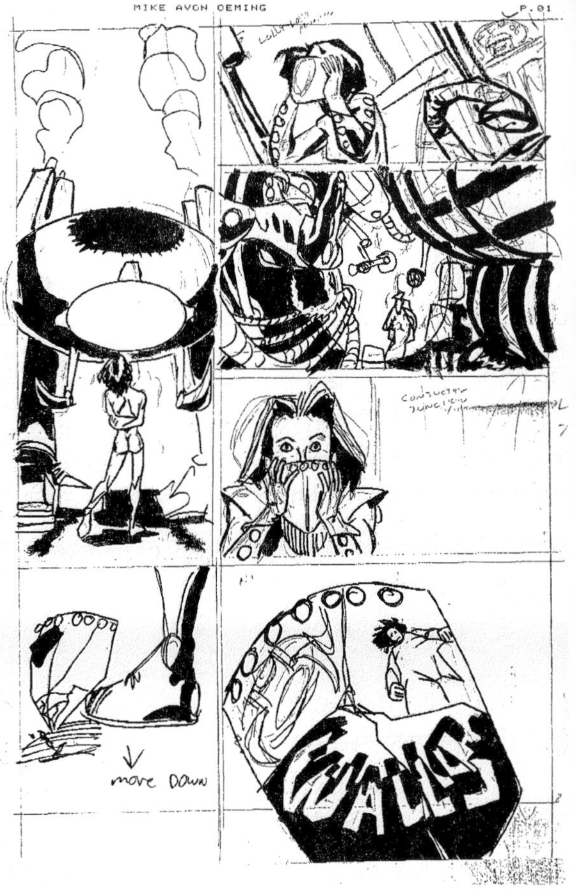
MIKE AVON OEMING
P.01
move DOWN
WALLS

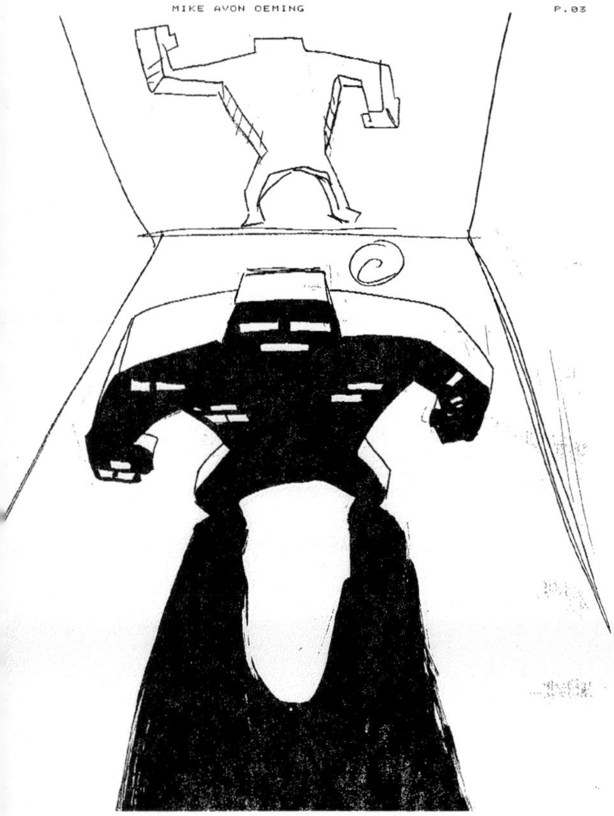
MIKE AVON OEMING
P.03

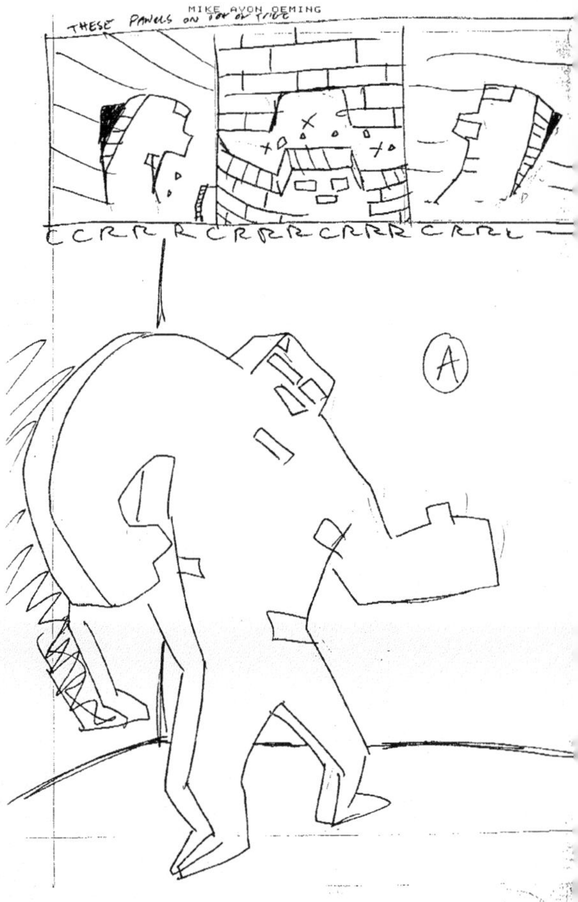
MIKE AVON OEMING
THESE PANELS ON TOP OF TRUE
CCRRR RCRRRCRRRCRRL

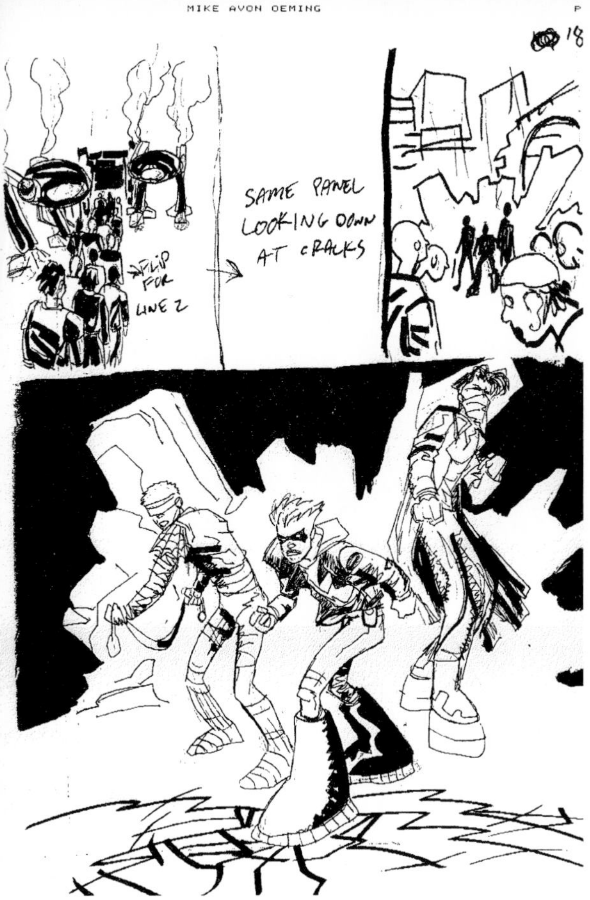
MIKE AVON OEMING
P
18
FLIP FOR LINE 2
SAME PANEL LOOKING DOWN AT CRACKS

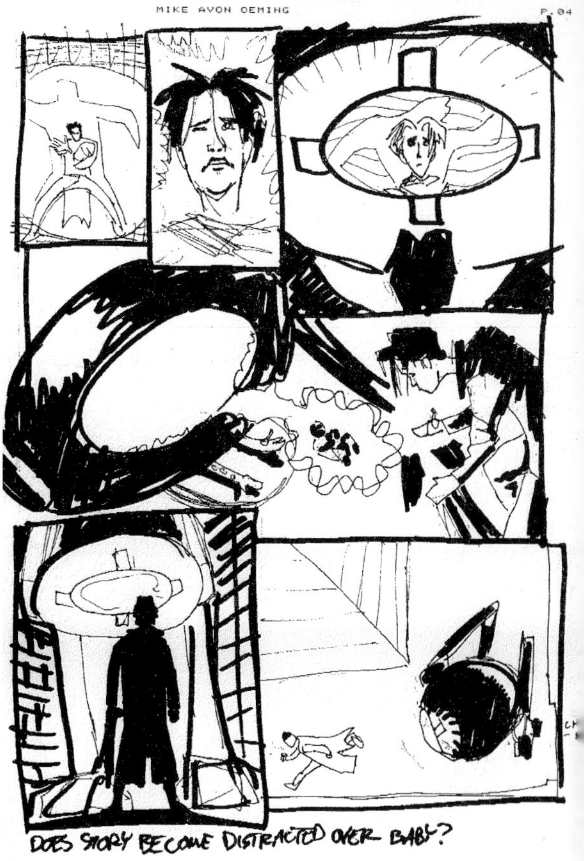
MIKE AVON OEMING
P.04
DOES STORY BECOME DISTRACTED OVER BABY?

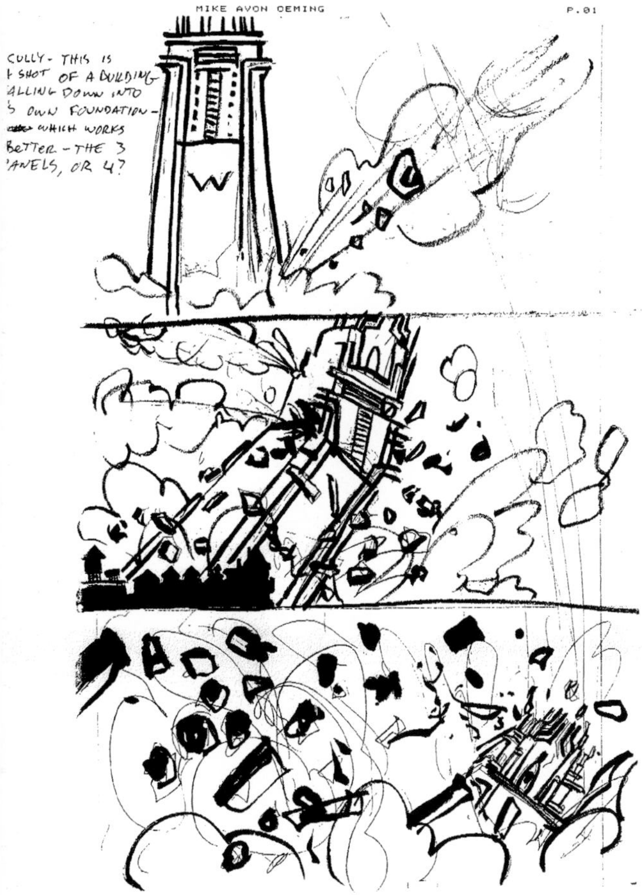
MIKE AVON OEMING
P.01
CULLY- THIS IS
SHOT OF A BUILDING
ALLING DOWN INTO
S OWN FOUNDATION-
WHICH WORKS
BETTER- THE 3
ANELS, OR 4?
W

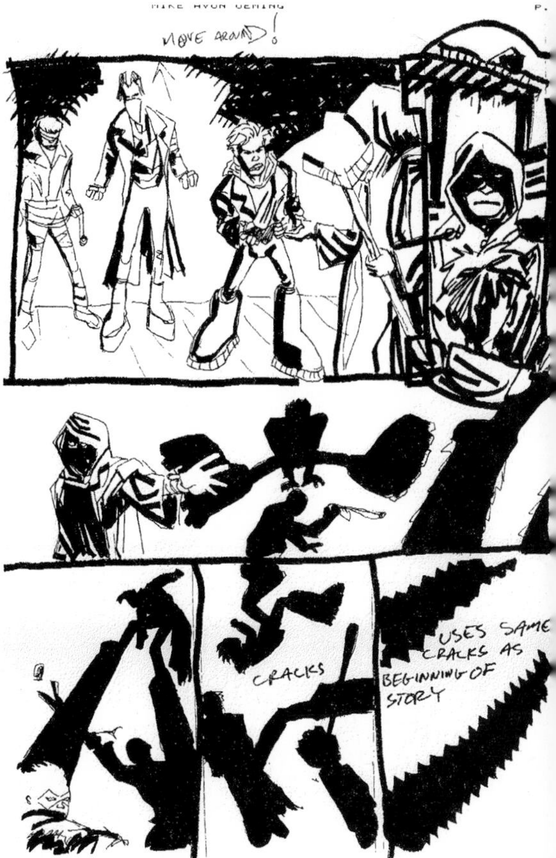
MOVE AROUND!
CRACKS
USES SAME CRACKS AS BEGINNING OF STORY

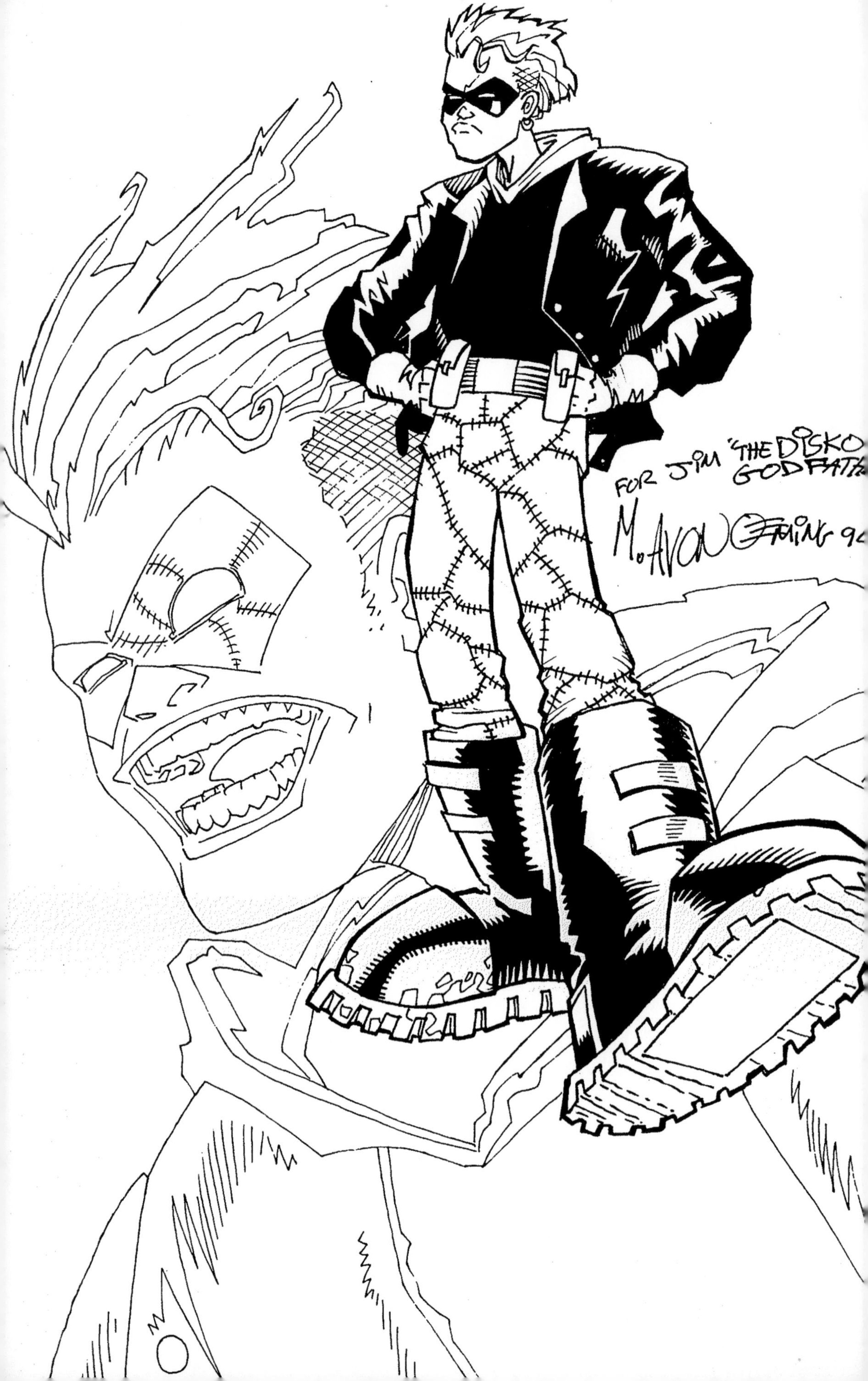
FOR JIM "THE DISKO
GODFATH
M. AVON OEMING 94

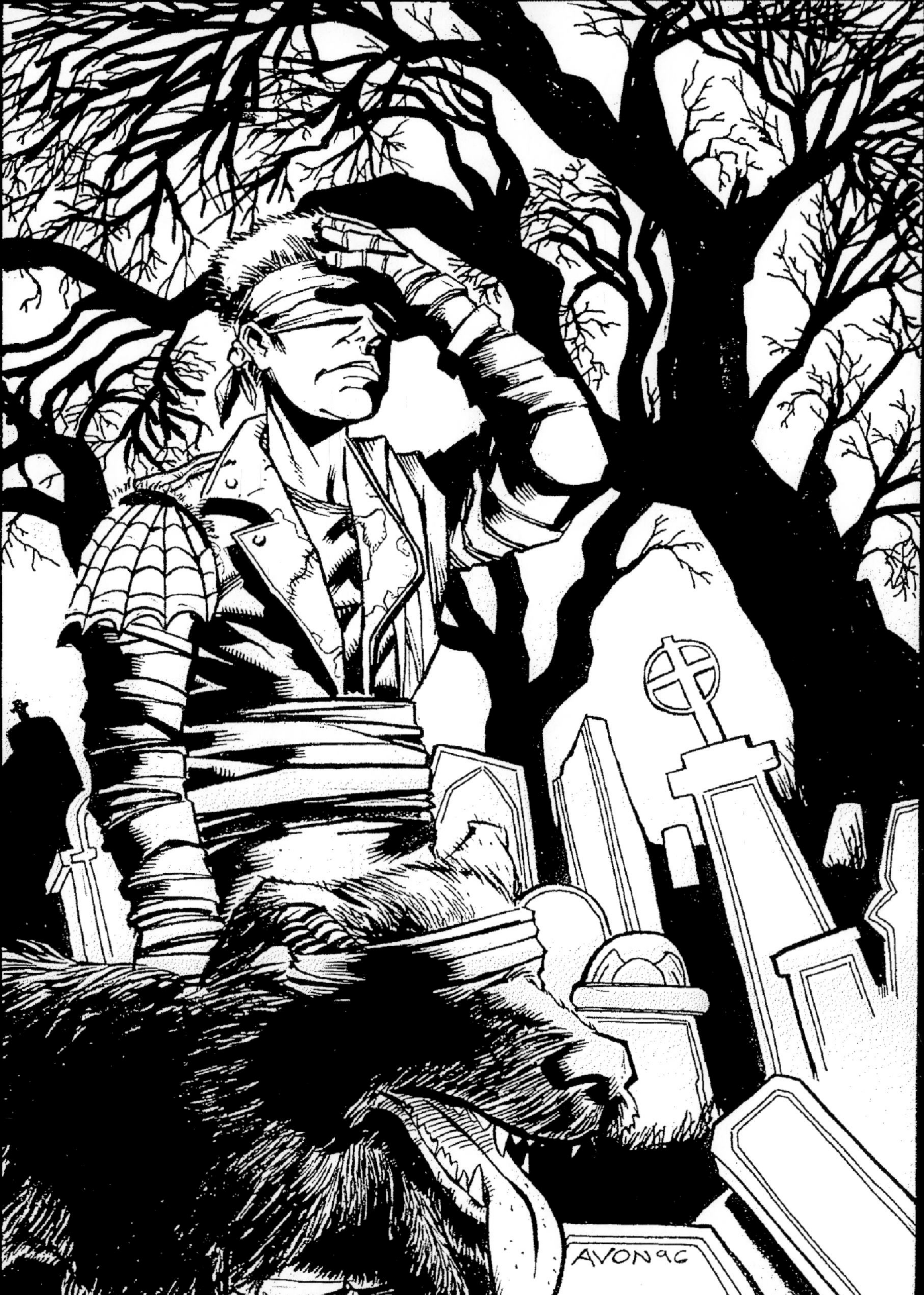
AVON 96

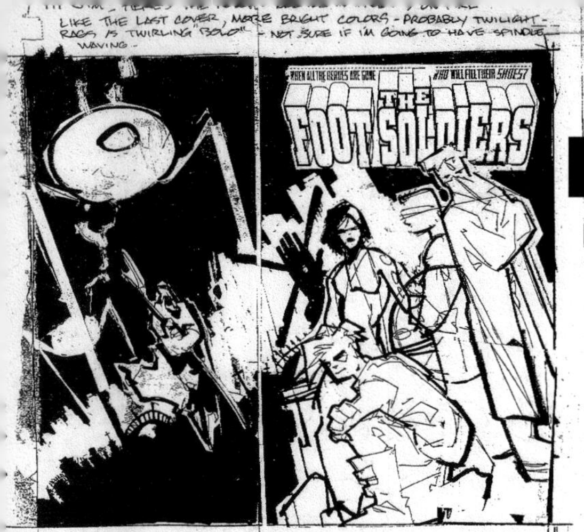
LIKE THE LAST COVER, MORE BRIGHT COLORS - PROBABLY TWILIGHT - RAGS IS TWIRLING "BOLO" - NOT SURE IF I'M GOING TO HAVE SPINDLE WAVING -
WHEN ALL THE HEROES ARE GONE
WHO WILL FILL THEIR SHOES?
THE FOOT SOLDIERS

John K Snyder III cover layout and pencils

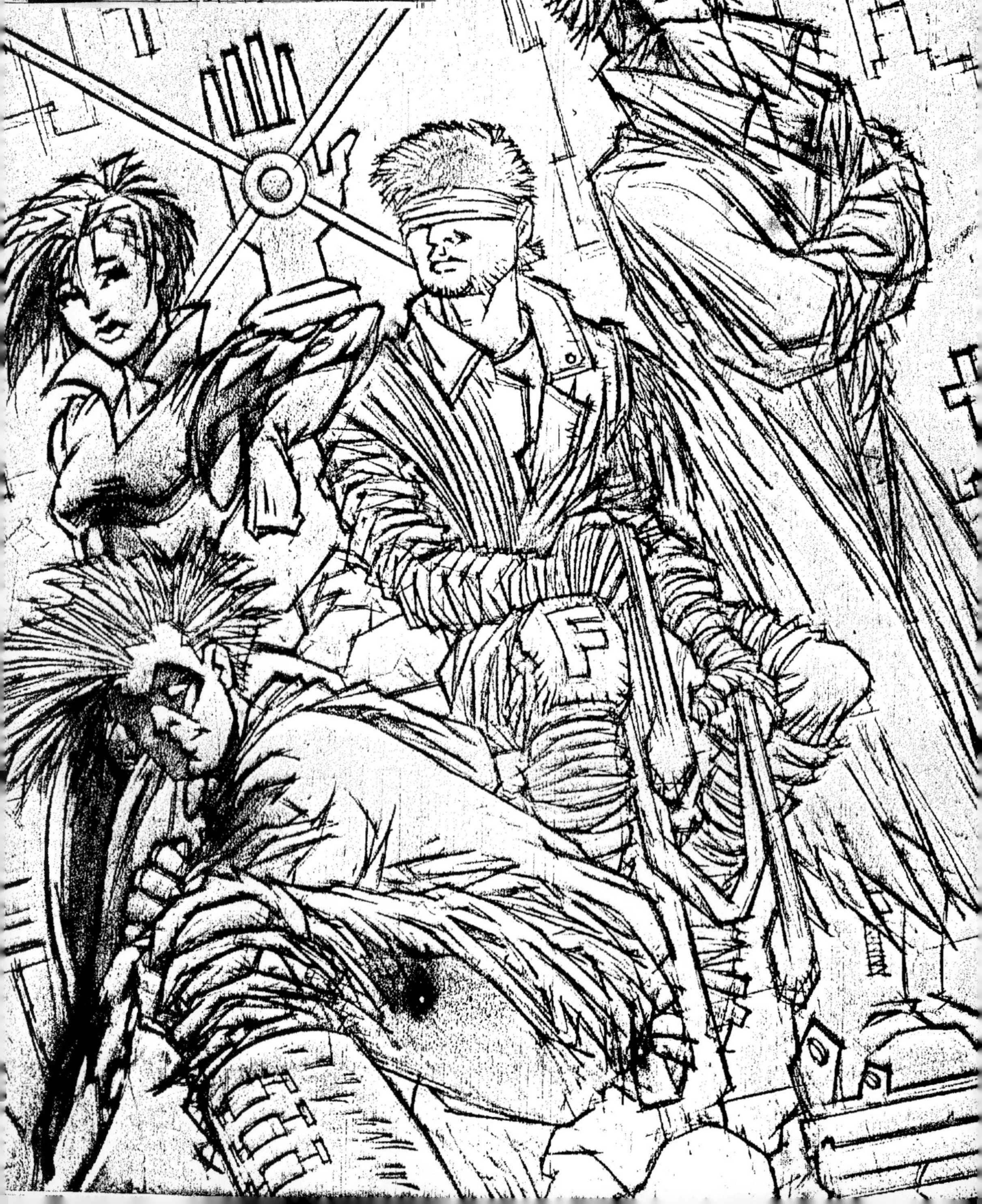

Alex Ross layout & pencils

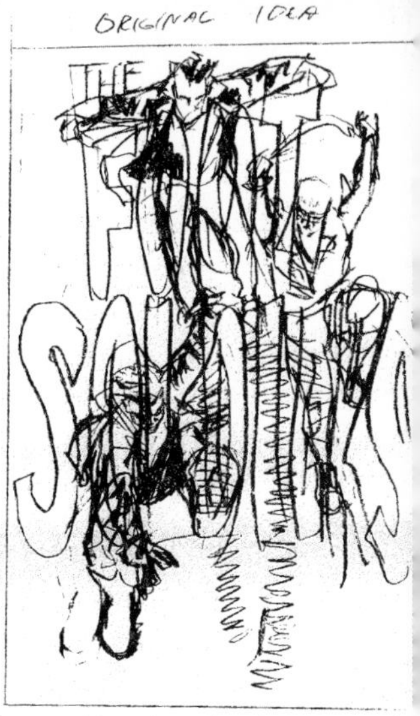
ORIGINAL IDEA

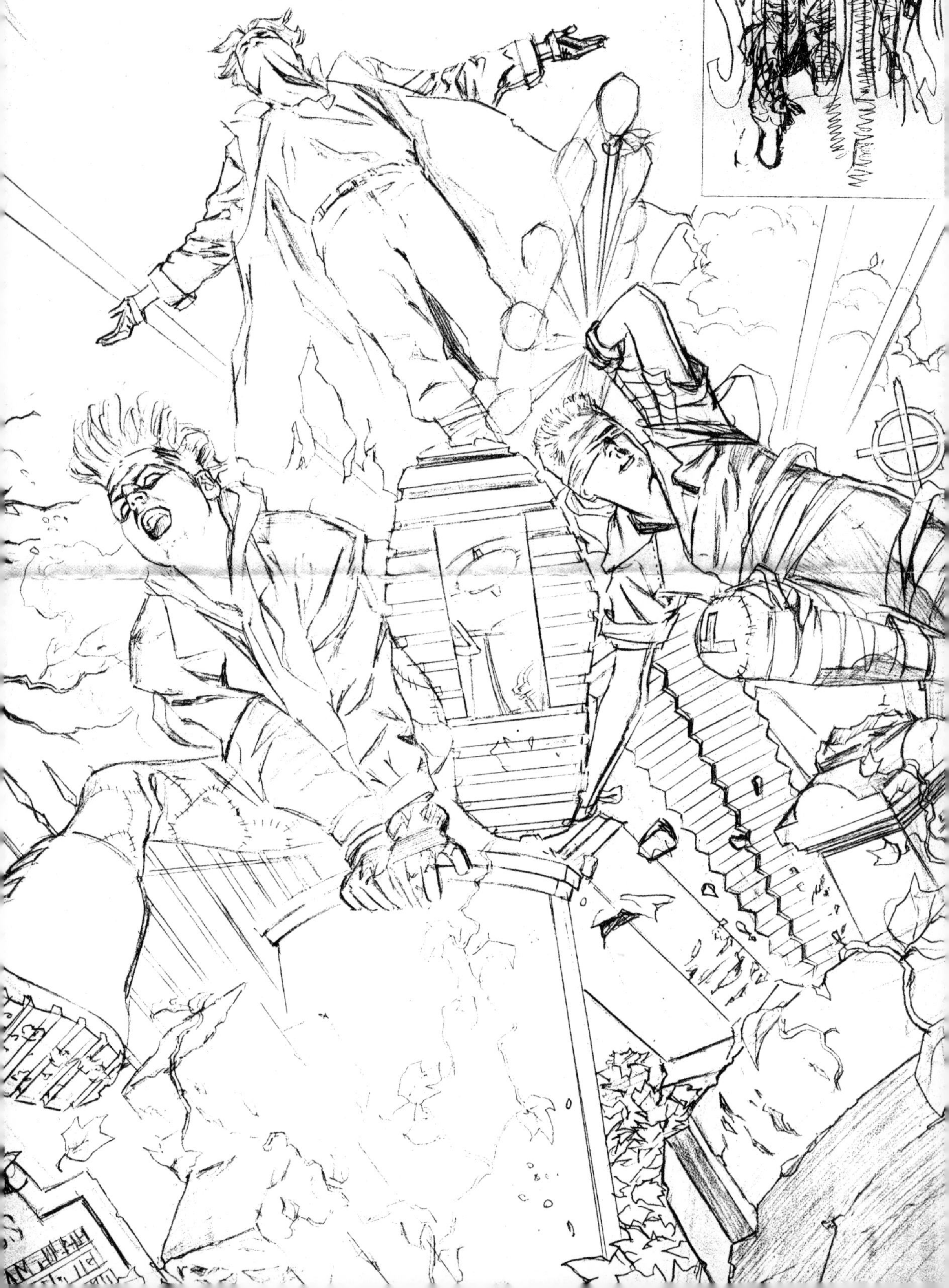

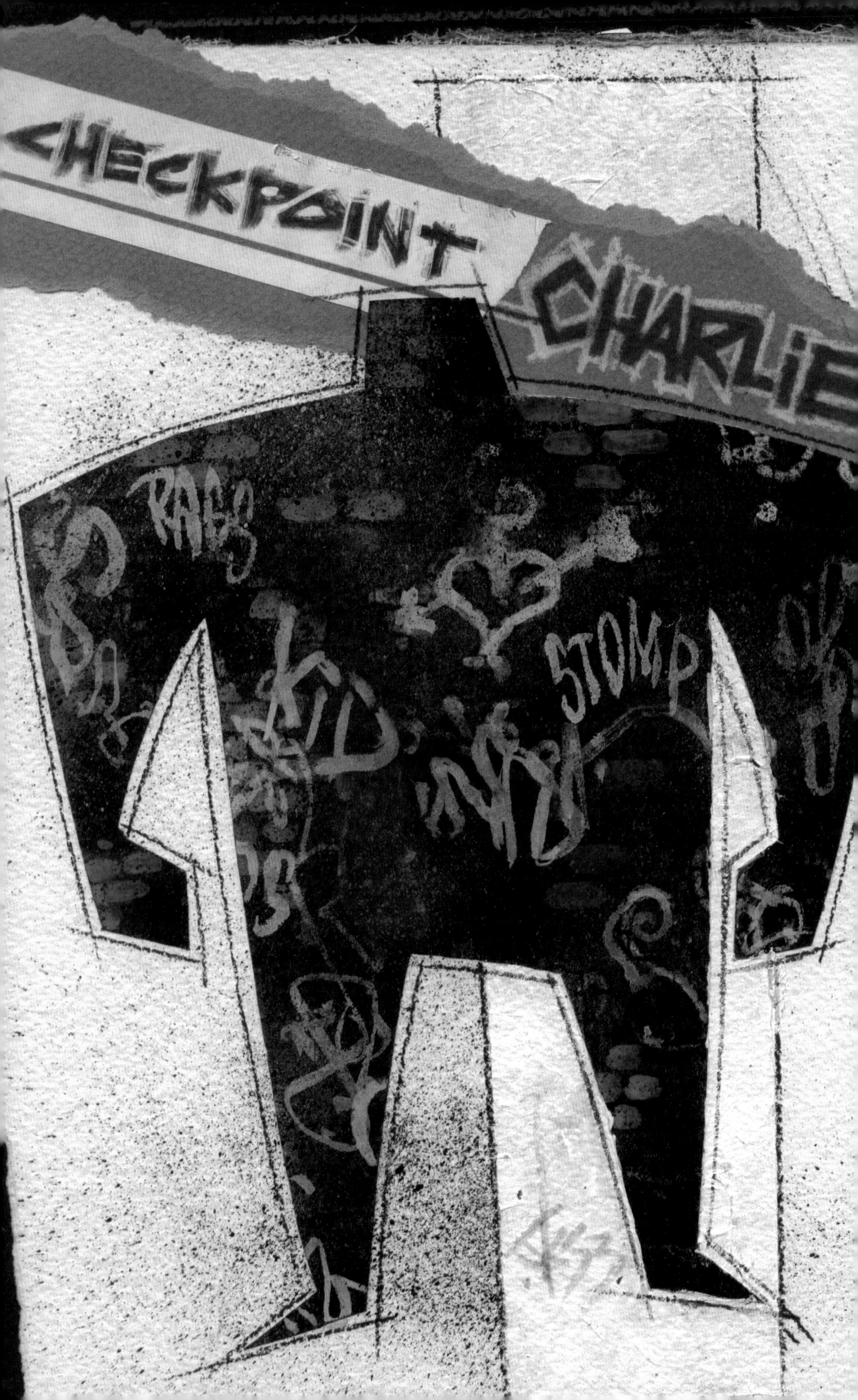
CHECKPOINT
CHARLIE
STOMP